A STUDY OF WAGNER

A STUDY OF
WAGNER

BY

ERNEST NEWMAN

VIENNA HOUSE
New York

This Vienna House edition,
first published in 1974,
is an unabridged republication of
the work originally published by
Bertram Dobell, London, and G. P. Putnam's Sons,
New York, in 1899.

International Standard Book Number: 0-8443-0065-9
Library of Congress Catalog Card Number: 74-75337

Printed in the United States of America

TO

MY WIFE

PREFACE

THE present volume is not intended to add another to the many "Lives" of Wagner, but to make an attempt at estimating the work of his practical achievements on the one hand and of his theoretical speculations on the other. It is hoped that the "Synthetic Table" will not only supply the reader with all the biographical and other details material to the subject, but will present the information in a very easily apprehensible form. The Table will show at a glance the direction of Wagner's musical and speculative activities in any given year, as well as certain contemporaneous events that are of interest in connection with the development of Wagner's mind and of music in general.

It may be necessary to forewarn readers that no account is taken here of sundry writings that do not bear closely on a general study of Wagner's genius. Thus such works as the treatise *On Conducting*, and others dealing with the purely practical side of music, are scarcely, if at all, mentioned, partly for the reason that writings of this kind must be read in their entirety if they are to be of any value to the student; no mere brief exposition of them could serve any useful purpose. Some readers may feel astonished that while I have passed over a portion of Wagner's ablest and most interesting work in this way, I have discussed at fair length many of his treatises that are of far less intrinsic value. The reason is that these latter, though not finally educational or illuminative in themselves, are factors that cannot be overlooked in the attempt at a veracious diagnosis of Wagner; while such writings as the purely musical ones merely illustrate points in his mental structure that are dealt with in other connections. My object has been to study Wagner as a psychological and æsthetic phenomenon; to try to answer the questions "In virtue of what constitution of brain was he so great a musician?" and "How did his peculiarities of mental structure affect his views of the other arts and of life in general?"

I may also put forward an explanation by way of apology for the apparent discursiveness of such chapters as the fifth, and their treatment of many subjects that at first sight may seem foreign to a discussion of Wagner and his work. In the first place, the chapter I have mentioned is intended not only as a criticism of Wagner's theory of poetry, music, and music-drama, but as a contribution to an æsthetic question of very much wider interest than the work of any one musician, a question involving a discussion of many more things than the opera itself. In the second place, I have

thought myself justified in discussing the opinions of a
number of theorists and aestheticians besides Wagner.
One duty of any writer who is conducting an argument
is to anticipate, if he can, whatever objections might be
urged against his thesis, and attempt to meet them in
advance. In the case of an artist like Wagner, on
whom there already exists a huge mass of literature
from every possible standpoint, a new critic, it seems
to me, is in duty bound to take account of the works of
previous labourers in the same field. If he thinks it
well to anticipate arguments that have not yet been
employed against his own theory, it is plainly necessary
for him to deal with these opposing views when they
are actually in print ; otherwise the statement of his
own thesis will look like mere dogmatism.

The edition of Wagner's *Gesammelte Schriften* to
which I refer in the present volume (as G. S.) is the
second German edition, in ten volumes. By the kind-
ness of Mr. W. Ashton Ellis I am enabled to quote
from his translation of Wagner's Prose Works, of which
six volumes have already been issued. Only those who
have had occasion to study Wagner's writings closely
can estimate the debt of all English Wagnerians to Mr.
Ellis for his extremely careful and faithful translations,
the valuable prefaces and editorial information he
supplies, and the magnificent indexes of the volumes.
I have also to express my obligations to Messrs. H.
Grevel & Co. for permission to quote from the English

translations of the *Correspondence of Wagner and Liszt*, and the *Letters to Uhlig, Fischer, and Heine;* and to Messrs. Schott & Co. for permission to make musical quotations from the *Meistersinger* and *Parsifal;* to Messrs. Breitkopf and Härtel for permission to quote from *Tristan;* and to the editors and proprietors of the *Fortnightly Review*, the *University Magazine*, the *Musician*, the *Monthly Musical Record*, and *Music* (Chicago), for permission to reprint such portions of the book as first saw the light in those periodicals.

E. N.

CONTENTS

SYNTHETIC TABLE

OF

WAGNER'S LIFE AND WORKS AND SYNCHRONOUS EVENTS

Year.	Life.	Musical Works.	Prose and Poetical Works.	Synchronous Events.
1813	22nd May. Born at Leipzig.	...	...	Rossini's *Tancredi*
1818	...	...	...	Spohr's *Faust*.
1821	...	...	...	Weber's *Der Freischütz*.
1823	...	...	...	Weber's *Euryanthe*. Schubert's *Rosamunde*.
1824	...	...	...	Beethoven's 9*th* Symphony.
1826	...	...	...	Weber's *Oberon*. Death of Weber.
1827	...	...	...	Death of Beethoven.
1828	...	...	...	Death of Schubert. Marschner's *Der Vampyr*.
1829	...	...	...	Auber's *Masaniello* Rossini's *William Tell*.
1830	...	Overture in B flat (performed at Leipzig under H. Dorn).	...	Berlioz' *Symphonie Fantastique*. Auber's *Fra Diavolo*.
1831	...	Sonata in B flat. Polonaise in D, à 4 mains (both published by Breitkopf and Härtel, 1832). Fantasia in F sharp minor (never published). Overture to Raupach's *König Enzio* (never published). Concert Overture in D minor (never published). Concert Overture in C, with fugue (never published).	...	Meyerbeer's *Robert the Devil*. Bellini's *La Sonnambula*. Hérold's *Zampa*.

Synthetic Table

Year.	Life.	Musical Works.	Prose and Poetical Works.	Synchronous Events.
1832	...	Symphony in C major (performed 10th Jan. 1833). Part of the music to *Die Hochzeit.* Compositions for Goethe's Faust.	...	Bellini's *Norma.*
1833	At Würzburg.	*The Fairies* (not performed during his lifetime. First performance at Munich, 29th June 1888).	...	Marschner's *Hans Heiling.* Brahms born.
1834	At Magdeburg.	2nd Symphony in E major (unfinished).	...	Donizetti's *Lucrezia Borgia.* First number of the *Neue Zeitschrift für Musik* published.
1835	...	*Columbus* Overture (never published).	...	Halévy's *La Juive.* Donizetti's *Lucia di Lammermoor.*
1836	Marries Minna Planer.	*The Novice of Palermo.* " Rule Britannia " Overture (never published). " Polonia " Overture (never published).	...	Meyerbeer's *Les Huguenots.*
1837	At Königsberg and Riga.	...	...	...
1838	Sketches *Rienzi.*	"Der Tannenbaum."	...	Berlioz' *Benvenuto Cellini.*
1839	Completes first two Acts of *Rienzi.* At Paris.	*A Faust-Overture* (finished February 1840; rehearsed by Habeneck at Paris, but not performed). *Songs :*— Sleep, my Baby. Mignonne. Attente. The Two Grenadiers.	...	...
1840	Finishes *Rienzi.*	...	...	Schumann's *Myrthen, Frauenliebe,* and *Dichterliebe.* Donizetti's *Favorita.*

Year.	Life.	Musical Works.	Prose and Poetical Works.	Synchronous Events.
1840–1	...	...	A German Musician in Paris: Essays and Stories:— 1. A Pilgrimage to Beethoven. 2. An End in Paris. 3. A Happy Evening. 4. Music in Germany. 5. The Virtuoso and the Artist. 6. The Artist and Publicity. 7. Rossini's *Stabat Mater*. On the Overture. *Der Freischütz* in Paris. Account of a new Parisian Opera, Halévy's *Queen of Cyprus*.	...
1841	Engaged on the *Flying Dutchman*.	...	...	...
1842	At Dresden.	20th Oct. First performance of *Rienzi* at Dresden.	Autobiographical Sketch.	Death of Cherubini.
1843	Completes poem of *Tannhäuser*.	2nd Jan. First performance of the *Flying Dutchman* at Dresden. *The Love-Feast of the Apostles*.	...	Schumann's *Paradise and the Peri*. Franz' first set of Songs.
1844	...	Funeral Music *At Weber's Grave*. *Greeting of the Faithful*.	Account of the bringing - home of Weber's remains from London to Dresden. Speech at Weber's grave.	Verdi's *Ernani*.
1845	Sketches poem of *Lohengrin*.	19th Oct. First performance of *Tannhäuser* at Dresden under Wagner.	...	...
1846	Produces the 9th Symphony at Dresden. Sept. 1846 to Mar. 1847. Writes 3rd Act of *Lohengrin*.	...	Account of the performance of Beethoven's 9th Symphony in 1846.	Mendelssohn's *Elijah*. Berlioz' *Faust*.

Year.	Life.	Musical Works.	Prose and Poetical Works.	Synchronous Events.
1847	May to June. Writes 1st Act of *Lohengrin*. June to August. Writes 2nd Act of *Lohengrin*.	...	...	Death of Mendelssohn.
1848	Writes poem of *Siegfried's Death*.	...	The Wibelungen: World - history from the Saga (not published till 1850). The Nibelungen-myth as sketch of a drama. Siegfried's Death. Speech at the 300th Anniversary of the foundation of the Royal Musical Chapel in Dresden. Jesus von Nazareth.	Schumann's *Faust*. Schumann's *Manfred*.
1849	Flees from Dresden to Weimar, and thence to Zürich. Later to Paris. Returns to Zürich.	...	A Project for the Organisation of a German National Theatre for the Kingdom of Saxony. Art and Revolution.	Meyerbeer's *Le Prophète*. Death of Chopin.
1850	...	28th Aug. First performance of *Lohengrin* at Weimar under Liszt.	The Art-Work of the Future. Wieland the Smith, sketched as a drama. Art and Climate. Judaism and Music (article in the *Neue Zeitschrift*).	Schumann's *Genoveva*.
1851	Writes poem of *Young Siegfried*.	...	Opera and Drama. A Communication to my Friends. On the Goethe-Foundation : A Letter to Franz Liszt. A Theatre in Zürich.	Schopenhauer's *Parerga und Paralipomena*. Verdi's *Rigoletto*. Death of Spontini.
1852	Writes poems of *Valkyrie* and *Rheingold*. Recasts *Young Siegfried* and *Siegfried's Death*.	...	On Musical Criticism. Recollections of Spontini. Explanatory Programmes :— 1. Beethoven's Eroica Symphony. 2. Overture to *Coriolanus*.	...

Year.	Life.	Musical Works.	Prose and Poetical Works.	Synchronous Events.
1852	...	...	On the Performing of *Tannhäuser*.	...
1853	Working at the *Rheingold*.	Album Sonata in E flat major.	Remarks on Performing the *Flying Dutchman*. Explanatory Programmes:— 3. Overture to *Flying Dutchman*. 4. Overture to *Tannhäuser*. 5. Prelude to *Lohengrin*.	Verdi's *Il Trovatore*.
1854	January. Finishes *Rheingold*. May. Finishes the scoring. June. Begins music of the *Valkyrie*.	...	Gluck's Overture to *Iphigenia in Aulis*: A Letter to the Editor of the *Neue Zeitschrift für Musik*.	Hanslick's *Vom Musikalisch-Schönen*.
1855	In London and Zürich. Working at the *Valkyrie*.	*A Faust Overture* (second version).	...	...
1856	April. Finishes scoring of the *Valkyrie*. Working at *Siegfried*.	...	...	Death of Schumann.
1857	Finishes 1st and part of 2nd Act of *Siegfried*. March. Receives request for an opera for Rio de Janeiro.	...	On Franz Liszt's Symphonic Poems.	...
1857–8	Engaged on *Tristan*.	*Five songs*:— 1. The Angel. 2. Be Still. 3. In the Hothouse. 4. Grief. 5. Dreams.	...	...
1858	In Paris and Switzerland	...	...	Cornelius' *Barbier von Bagdad*.
1859	August. Finishes *Tristan*.	...	Homage to Spohr and Fischer.	Gounod's *Faust*.
1860	At Brussels and Paris.	Albumblatt in A flat major.	Letter to Hector Berlioz.	...
1861	13th March. The *Tannhäuser* fiasco at Paris. Writes *Meistersinger* poem.	...	Account of the Production of *Tannhäuser* in Paris. "Zukunftsmusik."	...
1862	Commences composition of *Meistersinger*.	...	...	...

Year.	Life.	Musical Works.	Prose and Poetical Works.	Synchronous Events.
1863	At St. Petersburg, Moscow, and Mariafeld.	...	The Vienna Court-Opera-House. Nibelungen Poem.	...
1864	King Ludwig sends for him. Wagner at Munich.	*Huldigungsmarsch.*	Poem : To the Kingly Friend. State and Religion (not printed for public circulation till 1873).	Death of Meyerbeer.
1865	Dec. In Switzerland.	10th June. First performance of *Tristan* at Munich under Von Bülow.	What is German? (not published till 1878). Report to his Majesty King Ludwig II. of Bavaria upon a German Music-School to be founded in Munich.	...
1866	Death of Minna.	...	...	...
1867	Finishes *Meistersinger.*	...	Critiques:— 1. W. H. Riehl. 2. Ferdinand Hiller. German Art and German Policy (reprinted in 1868).	Gounod's *Romeo and Juliet.*
1868	...	21st June. First performance of *Meistersinger* at Munich under Von Bülow.	Second Edition of Opera and Drama. Recollections of Ludwig Schnorr of Carolsfeld. Critiques:— 3. Recollections of Rossini.	Death of Rossini. Brahms' *German Requiem.* Boito's *Mefistofele.*
1869	Finishes *Siegfried.* Begins *Götterdämmerung.* Siegfried Wagner born.	22nd Sept. First performance of *Rheingold* at Munich under Wüllner.	Critiques:— 4. Edward Devrient. 5. Appendix to Judaism in Music, accompanying book-form edition. On Conducting.	Death of Berlioz.
1870	25th Aug. Marries Cosima von Bülow. Finishes 1st and 2nd Acts of *Götterdämmerung.*	26th June. First performance of *Valkyrie* at Munich under Wüllner. Siegfried Idyll.	3 Poems:— Rheingold (1868). On the completion of *Siegfried* (1869). 25th Aug. 1870. Beethoven.	...

Year.	Life.	Musical Works.	Prose and Poetical Works.	Synchronous Events.
1871	June. Heckel forms first Wagner Society at Mannheim. Finishes scoring *Siegfried*.	Kaisermarsch.	Poem : — To the German Army before Paris. A Capitulation (not published until 1873.) Recollections of Auber. On the Destiny of Opera. Letter to an Italian Friend on the Production of *Lohengrin* at Bologna.	Death of Auber. Verdi's *Aïda*.
1872	22nd May. Beethoven - Festival at Bayreuth. Foundation-stone of new theatre laid. Finishes 3rd Act of *Götterdämmerung*.	...	Actors and singers. To the Burgomaster of Bologna. To Friedrich Nietzsche. On the name "Music-Drama." Letter to an Actor. Epilogue to the *Ring*.	...
1873	Completes republication of nine volumes of works.	...	A glance at the German Operatic Stage of to-day. The rendering of Beethoven's 9th Symphony. Prologue to a reading of the *Götterdämmerung* before a select audience at Berlin. Bayreuth :— Final Report, &c. The Festival Playhouse at Bayreuth.	...
1874	Nov. Finishes scoring of *Götterdämmerung*.	...	On Spohr's *Jessonda*.	Death of Peter Cornelius.
1875	...	Albumblatt in E flat major.	...	Bizet's *Carmen*. Rubenstein's *Demon*.

Year.	Life.	Musical Works.	Prose and Poetical Works.	Synchronous Events.
1876	...	Aug. 13–17. First performance of the *Ring* at Bayreuth, under Richter. Grand Festival March.	...	Brahms' 1st Symphony.
1877	Feb. *Parsifal* poem finished. Score begun in autumn. In London.	...	Poem of *Parsifal* published.	Saint-Saëns· *Samson and Dalila.* Massenet's *Le Roi de Lahore.*
1878	"Bayreuther Blätter" founded.	...	What is German? Modern. Public and Popularity. The Public in Time and Space. Retrospect of the Stage - Festivals of 1876.	...
1879	...	...	Shall we hope? Open Letter to Herr E. von Weber. On Poetry and Composition. On Operatic Poetry and Composition. On the Application of Music to the Drama.	...
1880	In Italy.	...	Religion and Art. "What boots this knowledge?"	...
1881	...	...	"Know Thyself." Introduction to a work of Count Gobineau. Hero-dom and Christendom.	...
1882	Jan. Finishes *Parsifal.*	26th July. First performance of *Parsifal* at Bayreuth under Levi.	*Parsifal* at Bayreuth. On the production of a youthful Symphony.	...
1883	13th Feb. Dies at Venice.	...	On the Human-Womanly (posthumous fragment). Letter to H. von Stein.	Saint-Saëns' *Henry the Eighth.* Dvořák's *Stabat Mater.*

The posthumous publications are not included in the above list. They will be found in the *Entwürfe, Gedanken, Fragmente,* and the *Nachgelassene Schriften und Dichtungen.* The *Jesus von Nazareth* is also published separately from the *Gesammelte Schriften.*

A STUDY OF WAGNER

CHAPTER I

A PSYCHOLOGICAL PRELIMINARY

IT is usual for a Frenchman to begin a book on
Wagner by exhorting his countrymen to forget and
forgive the stupid squib in which the composer, in
1871,[1] insulted the French nation in its hour of humili-
ation and distress. We in England are happily under
no such constraint. Nevertheless it may be profitable
to commence a study of Wagner, as our neighbours do,
with an historical retrospect—a retrospect, however,
not of the follies of the master and an apology for them,
but of the follies of those who most cordially and most
sincerely detested his music ; and, if our magnanimity
will run so far, with even an apology for these. Any
attempt at scientific criticism must take account of the
clash of human opinion about the great theories of life
and art. It is not sufficient for us to be content with
the victory, after half a century of struggle, of one or
other of these rival theories ; there remains the task of
investigating the causes of the former conflict, of discovering why many musicians and many æstheticians
of high ability have failed to get from Wagner's music
the pleasure which so many others have derived from
it ; and the further task, it may be, of absolving the
majority of these opponents from the charge of malevo-

[1] *A Capitulation* was written in 1870–71, though not published till 1873.

lence or wilful bad faith—of seeing them also, in fact, with the comprehensive and impartial eye of science.

With this object in view it is really worth any one's while, even in the year 1898, to look up some of the contemporary criticisms upon the works that have now a larger vogue than any other operatic music. We are all so used to the phenomenon of a great innovator being misunderstood in his own day, that we have even begun to philosophise quite cheerily upon it—our moralists bestowing posthumous consolation upon the sufferer, to the effect that he would not have been so contemned in his lifetime had he not been so great and original a genius. Music, again, has the questionable distinction of having provided more martyrs than any of the other arts, it being equalled in this respect only by the sciences that touch upon questions of religion and morals. Even with a knowledge, however, of the freaks of musical criticism in the past and present, a man may well lift his hands in astonishment as he reads some of the contemporary judgments passed on Wagner's work.[1] Almost from first to last, the recognised musical critics of Europe denied Wagner's possession of either melodic, harmonic, orchestral, or dramatic gift, and prophesied his speedy extinction. Schlüter, Fétis, Hanslick, Hullah, Macfarren, Chorley, Hauptmann, Gumprecht, Kossmaly, Scudo, Gustav Engel, Otto Jahn, Joseph Bennett— these are the names of only a few of the better known men who have unconsciously enriched the humorous literature of music by their criticisms of Wagner. They were nothing if not comprehensive in their denunciations. The *Tannhäuser* overture was " only a common-place display of noise and extravagance," the pilgrims' chorus being " a poor choral, badly harmonised " ; the opera as a whole was distinguished by " an entire absence

---

[1] The reader will find an interesting collection of them in Mr. Finck's *Wagner and his Works*, and in M. Georges Servières' *Richard Wagner jugé en France.*

of musical construction and coherence " ; *Lohengrin* was described, with true Teutonic grace and lucidity, as "a frosty, sense-and-soul-congealing tone-whining," while the prelude consisted of "strange sounds, curious harmonies without any coherence, and leading to no definite idea"—there being, indeed, "from beginning to end, not a dozen bars of melody " ; the *Meistersinger* overture was an "ugly rioting of dissonances" ; the score was "a boneless tone-mollusc," and the effect simply "horrible caterwauling" ; the *Ring* was "formless," "wearisome," and "painful," and the composer "the most remarkable charlatan who has ever appeared in art " ; *Parsifal* was "an endless desert of discouraging psalmodic recitatives," the music, indeed, reminding one weary gentleman of "piano-tuning with impediments," and another of the howls of a dog undergoing vivisection.

It has to be borne in mind that these prodigies were performed not by the irresponsible gentlemen who "do" the musical criticism for the daily newspapers, but by critics and historians of European reputation.

The explanation of the bovine opposition of men like these to Wagner's music seems to be this—that being, as they all were, musical theorists and pedants of the old school, hidebound in tradition, steeped in conventional formulas, Wagner's music was a product it was impossible for them to assimilate, by virtue of the fact, not that it was formless, but that its form was something entirely new, something for which the peculiar musical training of the critics had given them no intellectual or emotional preparation. And in this connection, stress may be laid upon the point that the very composers whom the critics held up to Wagner as examples of how music with form ought to be written, were in their own day subjected to the same misunderstanding and the same objurgation. One German critic condemned Beethoven's third symphony, and exhorted him to return to the lucid symmetry of

the first, which was in the style of Mozart. To us the
Eroica symphony is simplicity itself ; but to that critic
it was evidently "formless," because its form and its
ideas were somewhat more complex than anything he
had been accustomed to. At a later time, Dionys Weber,
the celebrated musical theorist, in the same way admired
Beethoven's earlier symphonies, but, in a conversation
with Wagner, frankly pronounced the ninth to be pure
nonsense.[1] And when one remembers how many un-
kind things used to be said about the brutality of
Wagner's orchestration, and how the critics used to
hold up to him as an example his predecessor Gluck,
it is refreshing to discover that Gluck's own contemporaries blamed him also for the noisiness of his orchestration. One might almost be listening to a modern
critic of Wagner when one hears Grétry saying that
"Gluck's music is fine, but it has the great fault of
being frequently too loud for human voices " ;[2] or when
we hear Marmontel calling attention to Gluck's excessive use of the brass, and the strain he puts upon the
singers.[3] Once more, when we meet with critics who
find Wagner lacking in melody, and his harmony
confused and obscure, it is pleasant to find the same
things being said more than a century ago of musicians
who then happened to be a little in advance of their
times. Gluck, said one French critic of that day,
"attempts to compensate for his lack of melody by his
profound knowledge of harmony, and the effects which
can be drawn from it."[4] Marmontel said he feared for
the musical stage when the charms of melody were
being banished from it ;[5] and long even before that

---

[1] Wagner, G. S. viii. 365.

[2] See Eugène de Bricqueville, L'Opéra de l'Avenir dans le Passé, p. 37.

[3] " Personne n'a fait bruire les trompes, ronfler les cordes et mugir les voix
comme lui."—Essai sur les révolutions de la musique, Œuvres, x. 416, ed. 1819.

[4] See Bricqueville, op. cit. p. 41.

[5] "L'Opéra sera-t-il privé des charmes de la mélodie ?"—Œuvres, x. 402,
ed. 1819.

time the abbé Desfontaines had accused Rameau of
"sacrificing the pleasures of the ear to vain harmonic
speculations." [1]

But it is the extreme of pleasure to find that Mozart,
the very Mozart who is always held up as a pattern
of musical form and of pure musical delight, was in
his own time and for many years after misunderstood
almost as much as Wagner himself. It is recorded that
upon one occasion, when Mozart had returned to his
publisher in Florence the proofs of some quartettes,
they were sent back to him with certain chords marked,
and an inquiry whether he had not omitted to correct these mistakes. The "mistakes" in question were
simply novel and original harmonic combinations ; and
the story throws an instructive light on some modern
criticisms of Wagner as a harmonist. Even so late as
1801 the finest orchestra in France declared, after ten
rehearsals, that a symphony of Mozart was quite beyond
its power, and far more complex than any music it had
previously met with.[2]

These instances might be multiplied almost indefinitely, but enough have been given to show the real
significance of the fact that so many critics found fault
with Wagner for being formless and obscure, and to
show that the very music which was always contrasted
with Wagner's as the perfection of form, was in its own
day declared to be formless in comparison with the
simpler music to which the theorists of that day had
grown accustomed. But the true psychological state
of the case may best be seen by taking one of the ablest
and sincerest anti-Wagnerians we can find ; and we
may select for this purpose the late Edmund Gurney,
a man of all-round culture, of good philosophical training, fine æsthetic feelings, and practised logical powers,

[1] Bricqueville, *op. cit.* p. 41.
[2] *Journal des Débats*, 1801 ; quoted in Hippeau, *Berlioz et son Temps*,
p. 11.

who has done a great work on the psychology of music, and who is not known in England as much as he deserves to be. In examining Gurney's criticism of Wagner we have the satisfaction of knowing that we are dealing with an antagonist of the utmost honesty of purpose, perfectly accustomed to introspective analysis, and quite above any conscious form of prejudice.

"Professing to cast off Beethoven's shackles," he writes, "*i.e.* the conditions of key and time by which alone successions of sound can be made organic, [Wagner] 'throws himself fearlessly into the sea of music'; and sinking, finds himself naturally in the variegated home of invertebrate strains, things with no shape to be squeezed out of, no rhythmic ribs to be broken, tossed hither and thither, as hard to grasp as jelly-fish, as nerveless as strings of seaweed." [1] Of *Tristan* he asks, "Is not the cloying quality at least as distinctive as the exciting, the sense of strain and mannerism at least equal to that of achievement? To the melody, even at its finest, there clings a faint flavour of disease, something over-ripe in its lusciousness and febrile in its passion. And this effect is strangely cumulative. Steadily through the whole evening one feels a growing sense of being imprisoned in the fragrance of a musical hot-house, across which the memory of some great motive of Handel's or Beethoven's sweeps like a whiff from breezy pine-woods by the sea. Or take a more compact instance, where, even if there lurk a certain strain of coarseness, there is certainly no hint of disease, the familiar overture to *Tannhäuser*—a piece of such superb popular qualities that, had music done nothing greater, she might well hold up her head among the arts. Only—when one thinks of the *Leonora?*" [2]

Here the explanation of Gurney's state of mind is comparatively easy, and throws a light at the same time upon much similar Wagner-criticism. Gurney obviously harked back to the *Leonora* overture because the symphonic form in which it is written assists the comprehension of it, and saves the hearer a certain amount

[1] "Wagner and Wagnerism," in *Tertium Quid*, ii. 19.
[2] *Ibid.*, ii. 25, 26.

of mental effort by giving him ready-made, as it were, the forms under which he is to subsume his emotions. The overture to *Tannhäuser*, being more of the nature of a summary of a number of dramatic scenes, puts a strain upon the intelligence of the hearer who comes to it with expectations of symphonic development, because the emotion is not made to run upon conventionalised external lines; and the complaint as to the formless nature of much of Wagner's music is at bottom nothing more than the protest of sluggish or jaded minds against music that demands some active mental co-operation from the hearer. Thus Gurney's gibe that Wagner, being incapable of the concentration necessary to bind his music organically together like Beethoven's, preferred the easier course of letting it flow on in a formless, inorganic stream,[1] is seen upon analysis to turn against Gurney himself. Once the emotional sequence of the music is grasped, whole acts from the Wagnerian operas are as coherent and continuous as a symphony; and along with the sensuous pleasure of the music itself there may go an intellectual or formal pleasure derived from the consciousness that we have the key to the sequence— the very form of pleasure which Gurney and his kind found in Beethoven and Mozart, and the lack of which in Wagner made his music incoherent to them. Thus while the score of *Tristan* is hopelessly obscure to many people, Von Bülow, who, when he was reducing the

---

[1] *Tertium Quid*, ii. 17, 18, and elsewhere throughout the essay. It must be borne in mind, of course, that I do not allege the dramatic form of Wagner to be *per se* harder to comprehend than the symphonic form, say, of a Beethoven symphony. To appreciate a symphony thoroughly, a musical education is of course necessary. But my point is that to men who have had this education, the purely musical pleasure of the symphony is materially, though unconsciously, assisted by their knowledge of the form in which the music is put together; and that being accustomed to receive this assistance from certain forms, the absence of them, and the constantly disappointed anticipation of them, would make even the purely musical sensation unorderly, and would perhaps cause the discontent to outbalance the pleasure. Hence men like Fétis and Hanslick and Gurney would call the prelude to *Parsifal* chaotic and formless.

orchestral score for the pianoforte, had ample occasion to observe the inner organic connection of the work, wrote to a friend in 1858 :—

"What I know so far of this work is simply superb, remarkably poetic, much finer in details than *Lohengrin*, and everywhere new, bold, original. *At the same time a thematic elaboration as lucid as it is logical, such as no opera heretofore has shown.*"[1]

Well may Mr. Finck say that this

"hits the nail on the head. Here, for the first time, was a musical score to which the test could be applied, concerning which an English critic of literature has said : 'It is the perfection of good English that page should cohere with page in such a manner that only here and there can a few paragraphs be removed without doing injustice to them.' That the German critics of thirty years ago should have, almost unanimously, pronounced this score 'formless,' is one of those extraordinary phenomena which will serve for the amazement and delectation of future generations. It was called 'formless' because it did not follow the slovenly custom of making a simple mosaic of independent and unconnected arias, duos, choruses, and ballets, and calling it an opera ! The gigantic intellects of these critics could not comprehend the simple fact that a work of art, like an animal, to be 'organically' formed, must be *united in all its parts*, and not, like the old-fashioned opera, a string of unconnected parts."[2]

It is to be feared that the brilliant, alert, and cultured Gurney was in this respect as much the victim of unconsidered formulas and catchwords as any of the English or French or German pedants. The point which Von Bülow was acute enough to see so far back as 1860—that there may be an emotional continuity and coherence in music different from that obtained by the use of the set symphonic forms—is the point which even Gurney, the psychologist of music, has

[1] *See* Finck, "Wagner and his Works," ii. 147.
[2] *Ibid.*, ii. 148, 149.

missed. Let any one, after reading the pages in which Gurney rails incessantly at Wagner for his formlessness, his chaos, his inferiority to Beethoven in the power to grasp all the threads of an emotion, and to make everything work harmoniously towards the final artistic purpose, set beside these pages the well-considered reflections of Von Bülow.

" It is not possible," he wrote, " to compose with more perfect organic unity of form than Wagner has done in the *Faust-Overture*. Place any 'classical' overture with an 'Introduction' by its side, and see if Wagner's tone-poem does not throw it into the shade formally." And once more, " The new musical forms of Wagner escaped notice for the reason that they were new, and, as it were, too colossal. We allude here not so much to the finished art of the second finale of *Tannhäuser* . . . as rather, for example, to the first act of *Lohengrin*. Is not that a dramatic symphony cast in one mould, perfect in form? The poet here imposed upon the composer the necessity of erecting a tonal structure, to which, *in regard to broadness of development and immensity of climax, no prototype existed.* If you will conscientiously study this part in its main features, you will be unable to deny that Wagner has created here, specifically in regard to *form*, something absolutely new, an artistic whole, built up without any leaning on predecessors." [1]

And Saint-Saëns could write, after hearing the whole of the *Ring*, that "from the elevation of the last act of the *Götterdämmerung* the entire work seems, in its almost supernatural grandeur, like the chain of the Alps seen from the summit of Mont Blanc." [2]

It is significant, again, that Gurney found the march in *Tannhäuser* worthy of commendation,[3] while having nothing particular to say in praise of such superb passages as the chorus at the end of the 2nd

---

[1] *Ueber Richard Wagner's Faust-Overture ;* quoted in Finck, i. 416–418.

[2] *Harmonie et Mélodie,* p. 94.

[3] " The haunting delight of the march in *Tannhäuser*."—*Tertium Quid,* ii. 26.

Act, or the story of Tannhäuser's pilgrimage. On the other hand, many Wagnerians of the present day would go as many miles to hear these passages as they would go miles *not* to hear the somewhat commonplace march, the beauties of which are of rather too obvious an order. In the same way, while anti-Wagnerians complain that the *Valkyrie* is on the whole lacking in melody, and fasten upon the love-duet as a kind of oasis in the desert, a fervent and thorough-going Wagnerian like Mr. Finck finds the regular rhythmical flow of the opening passage of the duet too much in the un-dramatic style of the older opera—finds it, in fact, somewhat obvious and commonplace.[1] The psychological upshot of it all is, that a man may pronounce Wagner to be chaotic, or formless, or obscure, or restless, either for the reason that he is comparatively new to the music, or for the reason that his mind is constructed on too simple lines to allow him to assimilate the complex beauty of the work—the first explanation holding good in some cases, the second in others. The trouble is that few have the common sense to revise their first impressions, or to see that the confusion

---

[1] The passage in question is that in $\frac{9}{8}$ time—"Winterstürme wichen dem Wonnemond." "There are also weak spots in the score," says Mr. Finck. "The weakest of these is the famous love-song of Siegmund in the scene just referred to. The poetic lines are beautiful, but the melody is trivial and shallow. I confess to a positive dislike for this brief love-song, which seems to me a cheap tune, as unworthy of Wagner's genius as the *Lohengrin* Wedding March. Its chopped-up, four-bar rhythm contrasts painfully with the flowing, continuous, uncadenced melody of the rest of the score."— *Wagner and his Works*, ii. 337. We may not altogether agree with Mr. Finck in this wholesale condemnation of the love-song, but it illustrates, at least, the growing complexity of our sense of rhythm, and casts a side-light on the mental processes of some of the older critics who could only assimilate the more obvious rhythms of Wagner's work. As Mr. Finck puts it, in his lively Transatlantic manner, "At Bayreuth it was amusing to note how some of the critical babes, who had been crying for their toys (Paul Lindau was positively pathetic : 'I beg you, I beg you, dear little birds, for a tune'), rejoiced at Siegmund's love-song, because *that* was something they could whistle, give to the organ-grinders, and work up in the next carnival quadrille."

into which the music throws them may possibly be
their own fault and not Wagner's; and fewer still have
the candour to admit in later years that their first
impressions were wrong. It is not every critic who
has the self-detachment of M. Gabriel Monod, who,
writing in a Paris paper in 1876 his impressions of the
first Bayreuth festival, said that—

"*A priori*, the Wagnerian system has always seemed to me
false; the poems, when I have read them, have given me only
moderate pleasure; at the performances, in spite of some long
and wearisome scenes, I have always been deeply moved, and
have carried away ineffaceable impressions with me; whence I
concluded *that it was my a priori reasonings that were false,
and that probably I have taken for the absolute limits of musical
art what were only the conventional forms in which it has till now
been imprisoned.*" [1]

And fewer critics still have the honesty to admit,
like M. Ernest Reyer, that their first judgment of a
work was hasty and erroneous. M. Reyer, during his
tour in Germany in 1864, heard Edouard Lassen play
two acts of *Tristan* upon the piano, and has left us an
amusing account of the perplexity into which he was
thrown by the interminable "recitatives" of the work.
"In the distance and all around me I could perceive
nothing but horizons of sand; the heat became over-
powering, and there was no oasis in which to rest, nor
the least trickle of water to quench our thirst." While
expressing his willingness to give the *Ring* a fair hearing
when he has the opportunity, he adds that his admiration of Wagner stops short at *Lohengrin*, many, to his
knowledge, not having even got so far as that. [2] Twenty
years after, however, when M. Lamoureux gave the
first act of *Tristan* at one of his concerts in Paris, M.
Reyer discovered that the work, though complicated,

---

[1] Quoted in Georges Servières, *Richard Wagner jugé en France*, p. 202.
[2] *Notes de Musique*, pp. 81, 85.

"is of real beauty"; and he remarks, "What a meta-
morphosis has been effected in my musical faculties in
twenty years!"[1] This is indeed the proper attitude of
criticism; and one could wish that Berlioz had been
able to follow the good example of M. Reyer. In
1860, Berlioz, in criticising some Wagner-concerts in
Paris, was capable of writing thus of the prelude to
Tristan :—

> "I have read and re-read this strange page; I have listened
> to it with the deepest attention and a lively desire to discover
> the sense of it; well, I must confess that I have not as yet the
> slightest idea of what the composer has been aiming at."[2]

The tens of thousands of auditors who now delight
in that profound and moving prelude can only read
such a passage as this with the conviction that if Berlioz
could go so far astray in his judgment of an alien art,
it is not surprising that smaller men should utterly fail
to comprehend it.

The novelty of Wagner's forms and methods of procedure is in fact sufficient to account for the inability of
many musicians to assimilate his music. Thus Spohr
wrote of the *Flying Dutchman* that it gave him "*unheard-
of trouble with its immense difficulties*";[3] the *Dutchman*,
which to us is simplicity itself! Robert Franz wondered
how the singers could remember the music of *Lohengrin*.
Schumann, after a presumably hurried glance at the
score of *Tannhäuser*, laid it down that the music was
"not a straw better than that of *Rienzi*, but rather
weaker, more artificial"; but a few weeks later he was
compelled to admit that the opera "contains profound
and original ideas, and is *a hundred times better* than his

---

[1] Article in the *Débats*, 22 Mars 1884; quoted in Servières, *Richard
Wagner jugé en France*, pp. 267, 268.
[2] Article in the *Débats*, 9 Février 1860; reprinted in *A travers chants*,
p. 311.
[3] Finck, i. 139.

previous operas, though some of the music is trivial."
In the same way the octogenarian Spohr, after remarking
that though *Tannhäuser* " contains much that is new
and beautiful," it has also " several ugly attacks on
one's ears," adds afterwards that " a good deal that I
disliked at first I have got accustomed to on repeated
hearing ; only the absence of definite rhythms and the
frequent lack of rounded periods continue to disturb
me." And to come down to our own times, Mr. W. S.
Rockstro, who once declared that Senta's ballad in the
Holländer would survive all Wagner's operas, lived to
recognise in *Tristan* a drama that affects a modern
mind as the *Antigone* may have affected the Greeks.
The lesson is plain, that the accusation of formlessness
means, in nine cases out of ten, nothing more than the
critic's inability to view the work in its entirety ; while
in the tenth case the hearer declares a later Wagnerian
opera chaotic simply because his own nerves are not
strong enough to bear the complex music, his own
mental processes not rapid enough to keep pace with
it. It is the old question again of the evolution of the
artistic palate. The selections from Wagner now heard
most frequently on the concert-platform, the overtures
to the *Dutchman, Tannhäuser, Lohengrin,* the *Meistersinger,*
and *Parsifal,* the introduction and closing scene of
Tristan, the Good Friday music from *Parsifal,* the
Trauermarsch from the *Götterdämmerung,* the introductions
to the third acts of *Lohengrin* and the *Meistersinger*—
these, which are now the source of the highest pleasure to tens of thousands of hearers, were at one time
disliked and ridiculed by almost every theoretician of
repute. On points like these the average intelligence
has grown clearer and less prejudiced, less formalistic.
And on the further points of the operas as a whole,
a candid hearer goes through something of the same
process as M. Reyer went through in relation to *Tristan ;*
and he learns to see that whole acts of Wagner's music

are as shapely, as coherent, as organic, as intellectual, as a movement of Beethoven. One is finally compelled to say of most of the critics of the past either that they were extremely stupid pedants, or that if any of them were intelligent, their faculties of feeling and judgment had been so atrophied by being allowed to function in only one direction, that they were even less capable of treating a new art fairly than were the untutored public, who, if they had no rules to guide them, had also none to mislead them. Hence the truth of Wagner's saying that the general public were more capable of appreciating him than were the theorists, and that while poets admired his music, musicians allowed that he could write poetry.[1] It is for us to avoid, if we can, the errors of the past. We must not, as M. Monod says, fall into the error of regarding *a* form of art as the only form ; nor need we repeat the general error of laying it to a composer's charge that our nerves are not so fine and our brain not so complex as his ; just as we need not imitate Mr. Clement Scott in calling Ibsen a monster of immorality because Ibsen's ideas on morals are somewhat more advanced than those of Mr. Scott. It is the eternal problem of criticism over again—the problem of how to get rid of the personal or contemporary equation. And whatever difficulties may lie in the way of the final solution of that problem, there can be no doubt that such wildly temperamental criticism as, for example, Nietzsche's, and such obviously formalistic criticism as Hanslick's, exhibit it in its most primitive and most easily recognisable form. It is not by such criticisms as these that Wagner is to be set aside ; the great master of all the chords of human passion, the musician who for so many of

---

[1] Most of the pioneer work for Wagner was, indeed, done in each country by non-musical men. In France, for example, along with the names of Edmund Roche and A. de Gasperini, there are those of Gérard de Nerval, Théophile Gautier, Baudelaire, and Catulle Mendès.

us sums up all the anguish, the pathos, the delight of life, is not to be discredited by the application of a few alien formulas, or by the mere snapping of a bundle of overwrought nerves. The errors of so many critics in the past will make us careful in the application of our own standards ; and if, in the course of the present volume, objections will have to be urged against parts of Wagner's music, it is hoped that they are urged from a consistently rational standpoint, and are not merely the revolt of an outraged formula or the physiological reaction of a jaded nervous system. The final object of criticism is, of course, the appeal to others to see things as we see them ; and such an appeal can only be effectively based upon premises that will be disputed by none, and arguments that must be valid for all. The service done by the otherwise wasted efforts of so many anti-Wagnerian critics, is that they teach us to avoid the more primitive sources of error which were fatal to them ; and, it may be, their blunders will prepare us for an attitude of completer tolerance towards the next great development of music when it comes. Our men of genius have surely something better to do than waste the most precious years of their lives in conflict with pedants who will be forgotten almost as soon as the grave closes over them. Wagner might have enriched the world with three more masterpieces, had not so much of his time and energy been frittered away in the bare effort to stand up against stupidity and malevolence. The many square leagues of arid Wagner-literature that have come down to us hardly compensate us for the fact that one of the most highly organised brains in modern Europe passed away before there had been full time to find expression for all the beauty that lay within it.

CHAPTER II

RIENZI AND THE FLYING DUTCHMAN

EVERY musical reader is by this time well acquainted with the story of Wagner's early years, and the strange excursions he made into many fields before he found his proper habitation. His brain was a medley of poetical and musical intuitions, and he was quite unable to make up his mind at that time whether to be a greater poet than Shakespeare or a greater musician than Beethoven. His poetical attempts, however, were quite juvenile in character ; and after a little hesitation he drifted naturally into music as his proper medium of expression. The various instrumental compositions which he turned out before he had reached his twentieth year were merely signs that he had for the moment missed his vocation ; while the two abortive attempts at opera-writing—*The Fairies* and *The Novice of Palermo*—were indications that he was coming to clearer self-consciousness, and to recognise that nature intended him for a dramatic, not a symphonic composer. *Rienzi* was of service to him, not only because it gave him this perception of where his own strength lay, but because it helped him to cast the slough of the current opera-formulas of the time. Not much, indeed, can be said for *Rienzi* at this time of day. The " poem," no doubt, deserves Meyerbeer's commendation, for it really stands above nine-tenths of the libretti of its epoch ; and though the music is young-man's music, it had all the qualities that could commend it to an operatic audience of 1842, which is precisely what makes it a weariness of the flesh to us, who have been educated by Wagner's later practice. There is very little in it of that anticipation of the future Wagner that makes the *Dutchman* so interesting to us in spite of its many faults. *Rienzi* is earnest in intention, but it is necessarily imitative of the operatic works of its own epoch ; Wagner had not yet had the opportunity to profit by the new spirit that was being breathed into musical Europe. Instrumental music seemed to have died in 1827 with Beethoven, noble and sincere operatic music with Weber in 1826 ; and not only in France, Italy, and England, but in Germany itself, Italian opera was master of the field. Marschner brought out his *Vampyr* in 1828, and *Hans Heiling* in 1833, striving, in his way, to follow in the footsteps of Weber ; but the vast majority of the works between 1828 and 1838 were Italian in form and spirit—some better than others, but all vitiated in some degree by the stupid conventions of the *genre*. *William Tell, Fra Diavolo, Robert the Devil, Zampa, La Sonnambula, Norma, Lucrezia Borgia, Lucia di Lammermoor, The Huguenots*—these were the typical works of the fourth decade of the century. The new spirit, however, was already spreading its wings for flight.

The year 1838, that saw Wagner meditating *Rienzi,* saw also Berlioz's *Benvenuto Cellini;* and the completion of *Rienzi* in 1840 was synchronous with the publication of Schumann's beautiful songs, *Myrthen, Frauenliebe,* and *Dichterliebe.* In the same year Donizetti produced *La Favorita;* and there seems something almost ironic in the appearance of that belated ghost of the Italian opera in the rosy dawn of modern music. 1842 saw the death of Cherubini, the last link between the genuine eighteenth century and the nineteenth ; and the musical history of the next few years may be written round Schumann, Chopin, Mendelssohn, Berlioz, and Verdi— the latter composer just entering at that time upon his second manner, as shown in *Ernani* and *Rigoletto.* So that between 1838 and 1840, when Wagner was

B

engaged on *Rienzi*, the old *régime* was defunct and the new *régime* only in its cradle.   The young Wagner had then to discover a new musical and dramatic faith for himself ; and if *Rienzi* exhibits almost all the conventions of the opera of the period, and is besides frequently futile in its attempts at truly dramatic expression, we can plead in extenuation of Wagner's crime that no one at that epoch and at his age could have done more than he.   The genuine Wagner, feeling his way towards unhampered self-expression, really only begins for us with the *Dutchman* in 1843—the year, by the way, of Schumann's *Paradise and the Peri,* one of the works that in its own way was significant of the new possibilities that lay before dramatic music.

We shall more than once have to remark, in the course of the present study, the intimate connection between Wagner's dramatic works and the circumstances of his life.   That connection is plainly evident in *The Flying Dutchman.*   Just as *The Ring of the Nibelung* is the embodiment of certain of Wagner's revolutionary opinions on society and its moral and economic codes, so the *Dutchman* is expressive of his own history as a weary wanderer in the years from 1839 to 1841.   He also, like the mythical sailor, had been driven from place to place, had been tortured by unappeased longings, and had longed for redemption from the curse that seemed to be weighing on him.   The misery of his own life made the story of the Flying Dutchman doubly appealing to him.   Conceiving life, as he always did, in terms of deep and strongly marked emotions, the old legend immediately became for him a moral and social symbol, an epitome of half the evil of the world and its cure.   It is very interesting to compare Heine's reading of the story [1] with that of Wagner—to note the sane cynicism of the one, that declines to take the old legend too seriously, and passes over the sentimentality

[1] In his *Memoirs of Herr von Schnabelewopski.*

of the conclusion with a smile, and the serious Teutonic immersion of all the other's faculties in the ethical lessons of the story, his intense preoccupation with the moral aspects of Senta and the Dutchman, and his firm belief that in the conclusion of the opera he has told us something good and profitable for our souls to know. Here for the first time we light upon one of the most curious of Wagner's hallucinations—the idea that the musical stage can be the dispenser of profound philosophy, and that his own reading of the cosmos was a matter of universal interest. The seriousness with which he regarded the theatre as an ethical centre was of course only an old Teutonic failing, dating from at least three-quarters of a century before he began his work ;[1] while his own views on ethics were at all times too vaguely sentimental for them ever to be worth regarding as serious contributions to the subject. The *Dutchman* shows him at the beginning of his really Wagnerian career. It is the first work in which a moral problem is distinctly posed, the main characters being merely embodiments of the problem, and the conclusion designed to clinch the three-act argument like a Q.E.D.

It goes without saying, of course, that in point of construction the *Dutchman* is the weakest of all Wagner's works.[2] His artistic vision is not clear enough ; or— to express the same thing in another way—he sees his characters and his problem clearly enough, but has not yet the craftsmanship necessary to handle his material in such a way as to make it clear and convincing to others. There has always been a hopeless confusion in the minds of critics as to whether Senta has or has not plighted her love to Erik ; and it is quite evident that

[1] See Carlyle's remarks on the German view of the theatre in his *Life of Schiller*, Part II.; also Goethe's *Dichtung und Wahrheit*, Book III.

[2] *Rienzi* does not count as a " Wagnerian " work. It is a German-Italian opera.

the reading of her character and the interpretation of her motives in the last Act must be dependent upon how we answer this question. Uncertainty, again, exists as to *why* the Dutchman, in the 3rd Act, is setting sail without Senta; while Erik is altogether too vague for psychological analysis, and Daland is an operatic father pure and simple. For my own part, too, I have never been able to understand how it is that while Senta, immediately on seeing the Dutchman, recognises him to be the original of the portrait in the house, the resemblance never seems to have struck her father—even though the Dutchman has told him at their first meeting of his unhappy doom, and of his desire to meet the woman who will love him. And finally, I have always thought I should like to know what becomes of the crew of the Dutchman's ship when Senta springs into the sea, and the ship sinks with all hands. According to Wagner's stage-directions, " In the glow of the rising sun, above the wreck of the ship are seen the glorified forms of Senta and the Dutchman, held in each other's embrace, rising heavenwards out of the sea." *They*, of course, are "redeemed"; but what of the poor devils who have gone to the bottom of the ocean? Is there no "redemption by woman's love" for any one under the rank of captain, or are the men, by being drowned and done for once for all, freed from the uncertainty that attends the heavenward journey of " the glorified forms of Senta and the Dutchman "?

Wagner, of course, was far too serious to trouble himself about these minor points. When you have a big business of redemption in hand you must not stick at trifles, and Wagner was very much in earnest about his own peculiar views of ethics. We shall see, when we come to discuss his later works, that in almost all of them he tried to put forward an ethical problem, the solution of which lies in somebody or other being "redeemed," which brought upon Wagner the famous gibe of his quondam admirer Nietzsche. It is in the *Dutchman* that Wagner the æsthetic moralist first comes to clear consciousness of himself, and it is typical of his mental constitution and its shortcomings that he should take so seriously the salvation of the Dutchman by the love of Senta—a thoroughly sentimental and somewhat Teutonic manner of looking at life, that appears again, in a modified form, at the conclusion of the *Ring of the Nibelung*. His view of women was, indeed, always sentimental in the extreme. In *A Communication to my Friends*, after relating how he came to be fascinated by the story of the Flying Dutchman, he remarks that the mariner, "like Ahasuerus, . . . yearns for his sufferings to be ended by death ; the Dutchman, however, may gain this redemption, denied to the undying Jew, at the hands of—*a woman*, who, of very love, shall sacrifice herself for him. The yearning for death thus spurs him on to seek this woman ; but she is no longer the home-tending Penelope of Ulysses, as courted in the days of old, but the quintessence of womankind ; and yet the still unmanifest, the longed-for, the dreamt-of, the infinitely womanly woman—let me out with it in one word : *The Woman of the Future*." [1] That manner of sentimentalising over woman has now become somewhat antiquated. It is the Young Men's Mutual Improvement Society view of woman and the world, and we must decline to grow quite so perfervid over it as Wagner and his disciples have been wont to do. It will be argued, in the course of the following pages, that even if Wagner had been a man of clear and searching outlook upon life, the musical drama is by its very nature the least suitable medium for the display of profound philosophy. Here we need only note the first element in the diagnosis of Wagner's character—his intense seriousness, his burning desire to illustrate

[1] G. S. iv. 266 ; Ellis, i. 308.

ethical and humanist problems in his work, and his inability to rise very far out of the rut of ordinary sentimentalism. His perpetual obsession by the ideas of redemption and salvation gives in itself a hint that he failed to see life objectively and clearly; the facile solution of the problem of his first real work by the easy old sentimentalist view that woman "expresses her inmost nature" by sacrificing herself for man, is an indication of the misty cloudland in which his own intellectual life was being spent.

There are, it is said, certain severe Wagnerians who decline to listen to anything of the master's earlier than *Lohengrin,* and extend even to that work only a bare tolerance—the real Wagner commencing, for them, with the *Ring.* Without committing ourselves quite so deeply as that, it must be admitted that the *Dutchman* sounds very queerly at times to the full-fledged Wagnerian. There is, of course, a noticeable advance on *Rienzi* in point of the poetical construction. The characters are few, and an attempt is made to treat them as subjects of a musical instead of a poetical drama,—or, as Wagner himself would put it, to make the action internal instead of external.

"From here," he writes, "begins my career as *poet,* and my farewell to the mere concocter of opera-texts. And yet I took no sudden leap. In no wise was I influenced by reflection; for reflection comes only from the mental combination of existing models: whereas I nowhere found the specimens which might have served as beacons on my road. My course was new; it was bidden me by my inner mood, and forced upon me by the pressing need to impart this mood to others. In order to en-franchise myself from within outwards, *i.e.* to address myself to the understanding of like-feeling men, I was driven to strike out for myself, as artist, a path as yet not pointed me by any outward experience."[1]

He was really feeling his way along the line that

[1] G. S. iv. 266; Ellis, i. 308, 309.

ultimately brought him to the way of writing the "books" of his operas in the style most suited for music. The culmination was reached in *Tristan*, the almost impeccable model of a dramatic poem intended for a musical setting. It was in the *Dutchman* that Wagner first perceived dimly those necessary rules of artistic procedure that he was destined to work out so painfully and so conscientiously in the years to come. He himself has told us that he really conceived the *Dutchman* as a dramatic ballad, and thought at first of having it performed in a single continuous act. That in itself showed that his musical imagination was beginning to take the lead in his artistic conceptions; he was realising that such work as he was most fitted to do was on a different plane of thought from that of the spoken drama, and that therefore the dramatic unity and homogeneity of his works must come from the art of music rather than from that of poetry. There was, of course, to be not merely a bracing up of the opera-poem, but a total rupture with the conventional manner of libretto-writing. The poem was no longer to be a mere *pot-pourri* of disconnected materials, but a real dramatic action set forth in simple, direct, and—as far as might be—artistic language. But though Wagner is to a certain extent justified in calling this reform a re-entry of the *poet* into his proper place in opera—in the sense that he put a coherent and organic substance where only disconnected fragments had been before—he misled both himself and the disciples who have based their æsthetics on him, when he phrased it that by his reform the musician's wings were clipped and greater liberty given to the poet. The question will be fully treated in a later chapter; here we need only anticipate the discussion so far as to say that by making the action "internal," as he expressed it, he was really limiting the range of psychological treatment of the drama to just that point where nothing should be said that was inconsistent with musical treatment. He was indeed casting aside the framework of the old opera-libretto; but his own poem, no matter how coherent and organic he might make it, was from first to last a poem whose sole *raison d'être* was that it was to be set to music.

The *Dutchman* was necessarily only a tentative effort. Much as Wagner might desire to remould the form and the substance of the opera in accordance with the spirit of music, his artistic powers were not yet equal to the task. He was compelled to follow on the lines of the older opera in his frequent repetitions of the words of the text; while, although it is true that he tried to avoid the conventional division of the opera into aria, recitative, and *ensemble*, his own work at times seems to fall too readily into these unconnected forms. As for the music itself, the most irritating feature in it is probably the rhythmical monotony of the more declamatory portions. Ten years later, when he was revising the orchestral score of the work, he himself called Uhlig's attention to this point. "It is striking," he writes, "to see how embarrassed I then was by musical declamation; and the operatic style of singing (for instance ♩.. ♪ ♩.. ♪) still weighed heavily on my imagination." [1] Even in the more lyrical portions the melodic rhythm is painfully uniform in character, owing to the long succession of bars in common time, with a strongly accented note at the beginning of each, as for example:—

Schon sah' am U - fer ich mein Haus,

Sen - ta, mein Kind, glaubt' ich schon zu um - arm - en.

---

[1] Letter 59 to Uhlig; Eng. trans. p. 212.

In many places, again, the music is *obbligato* recitative
pure and simple, with all the shortcomings of that
unfortunate *genre*—unimpressive stretches of unmusical
declamation, broken at times by conventional orchestral figures that may mean anything or nothing.   One
has only to compare with this method of padding the
spaces between the lyrical moments of the opera the
living flood that surges through almost all the body
of the later works, to realise how enormously Wagner
grew in consciousness of his own artistic aims, and
in his power to embody them in organically coherent
sound.   What makes the *Dutchman* so interesting to the
student is the comparison of its musical structure with
that of the true Wagnerian works of later years, showing as it does the positively abnormal rate at which
Wagner's artistic sense must have developed since his
thirtieth year—an age, be it remembered, at which the
musician's brain is generally complete in all its essential
characteristics.   Beethoven, of course, developed with
each year of his life ; but even he shows nothing comparable to the growth of Wagner.   There is no such
difference between the works of 1800—when Beethoven
was in his thirtieth year—and those of 1827, when he
died, as there is between *Rienzi* in 1840 and the *Götterdämmerung* in 1870.   In his musical conceptions, as in
everything else, Wagner lived at a rate quite abnormal
when compared with that of other men ; and whatever
may have been the case with his theoretical work, his
music shows a steady and continual development from
his earliest to his latest years.

It was only to be expected that the *Dutchman*, written
as it was when Wagner had no more than the vaguest
intentions of what the musical drama ought to be,
should be merely experimental both on the musical and
the poetical sides.   The barest passages in the text are
necessarily set to the crudest melodic declamation ; for
Wagner had not yet learnt the art of dealing with the

non-lyrical portions of the drama. In later years he recognised that since these portions are necessary to the evolution of the action, they must be made *musical* in spite of their own non-musical quality; and he accordingly sank them into a merely subordinate place, letting the orchestra carry on the stream of music, and the words merely float upon its surface. A passage like this from the *Dutchman*—

Be still! I think I see the Cap-tain there.

is neither music nor an apology for music. It is simply a bald sentence, whose baldness is none the less apparent because the words are sung instead of spoken. In later years, Wagner, if he was compelled to have passages of this kind in his text, generally managed to lift them by the musical resources of the orchestra out of their dreadfully commonplace associations.

Nor is there much more than a glimpse of the later Wagner revealed in the more lyrical portions of the music of the *Dutchman*. He was undoubtedly a skilled contrapuntist at this time; yet he must have soon realised that the contrapuntal methods of instrumental music were foreign to the needs of the drama. This also was one of the matters in which he developed greatly in after years. Compare, for example, his evident difficulty in combining a voice part with an orchestral motive—as in the passage "*Welch holder Klang im nächtigen Gewühl!*" in the 2nd Act—with his later manner as shown in *Tristan*, the *Meistersinger*, or the *Ring*. There not only are the motives as plastic as clay in the hands of the potter, but the voice is in most cases organically one with them—different in form, but still part of the same living structure. Here it is obtrusively evident that the motive has been placed in the orchestra first, and the vocal part plastered un-

skilfully and mechanically upon it. In speaking of the
music of the *Dutchman* we have, of course, to remember
that though it stands out more than honourably among
the operatic works of its own day, the enormous advance
denoted by Wagner's later practice has made his earlier
work seem more primitive than it otherwise would.
This needs to be borne in mind when, in the light of
our knowledge of the maturer Wagner, we examine the
musical texture of the *Dutchman*. Even the musical
motives of that work are not conceived in the manner
of the later dramas. Wagner's imagination seems to
have spent itself in the mere conception of a motive,
and is afterwards unable to shape it in accordance with
dramatic needs; the tissue through which he merges it
into the next motive or into the body of the work
is frequently not vital, not inevitable enough. It is
musikmacherei pure and simple—the kind of unimaginative note-spinning that he afterwards in his prose
writings deprecated in so many other composers. The
first part of the introduction to the 3rd Act, for
example, is built up of two earlier themes, joined by a
patchwork of quite unmeaning notes, Wagner being
unable, as in his later works, to make the orchestral
prelude a psychologically coherent picture of the coming
dramatic action. At this time, indeed, he was only an
operatic half-breed, showing about an equal number
of traces of the old opera and the new music-drama.
Consistency such as he subsequently attained in his use
of the new musical forms could only come from a consistent musical-dramatic mood, in which every phrase
was born of and shaped by a definite dramatic conception ; and this rare control of new musical form could
only come after long effort. As it is, the *Dutchman* is
full of a kind of music that really has no place in the
true music-drama. More especially in the accompani-
ments at times are there figures that simply lie like
useless embroidery about the vocal phrases, not helping

their expression in any way, and appealing only to what Wagner afterwards called the "absolute music" sense.[1] He was not yet the consistently *dramatic* musician he subsequently became. His inner vision was not yet clear enough to conceive all the components of the vocal and orchestral music as integral parts of the one living body, each existing only in and for the others.

We notice the transitional state of his art, again, in the timidity he shows in relation to rhythm and tonality. It has already been remarked that the rhythm is irritatingly monotonous at times; and this arises partly from the fact that we feel its absolute regularity to be a contradiction of the dramatic purpose and a frustration of the dramatic effect. In the same way, his generally conventional handling of tonality seems hopelessly out of place in dramatic work. Later on he saw with singular clearness that absolute music, unsupported as it is by any verbal expression, and bound, therefore, by purely musical laws of psychology, is necessarily far more strictly conditioned in its formal structure than dramatic music, which appeals to a somewhat different faculty, and whose deviations from the line of music *per se* are justified and made intelligible by the words or the action. An extremely remote modulation, for example, may be highly expressive in dramatic and quite incomprehensible in absolute music.[2] And not only is this boldness of musical form justified, but it is positively demanded, by the drama. A statuesque formality of structure, associated as it generally is with music derived from mental moods that are not stimulated by concrete things, is felt to be incongruous with the more vivid and more rapidly changing emotions that accompany a dramatic action. An excellent

---

[1] See, for example, in Daland's air in the 2nd Act, the passage beginning ' *Sagt, hab' ich sie zu viel gepriesen ?* "

[2] See, on this point, Chapter ix. of the present volume.

illustration of this may be had in the music that accompanies Senta's words in the 2nd Act—

"Feel'st thou the grief, the profound woe, with which he looks on me? Ah! that which robbed him for ever of peace cuts through my own heart!"

where the set regularity of the vocal phrase seems to contradict the perturbed sense of the words. In the duet between Daland and the Dutchman, again, just after the latter has asked the Norwegian captain if he has a daughter, the depressing obviousness of the modulation is quite fatal to any dramatic effect. In later years, Wagner's tonality changed in obedience to every psychological change in the words, as a landscape takes on a new shade of colour with each hour of the day. His formalism and timidity in this respect in the *Dutchman* were due, as already noted, to the failure of his artistic vision, his inability to conceive character and action in terms of dramatic instead of absolute music. Consistently with this feature of his mind at that time, the most impressive portions of the *Dutchman* are, on the whole, the purely lyrical ones. In the great duet in the 2nd Act, for example, where he has simply the passion of the moment to express in beautiful sound, the music has a vigour, a certainty, a coherence, that are absent from the other parts. He once explained some of Mozart's dramatic failures by saying that even he could only write beautiful dramatic music when inspired by really dramatic words and situations. In his own *Dutchman* epoch it was evident that his muse thrilled only to the stimulus of the more purely lyrical parts of the drama ; in his later works he shows us how his vast imagination took within its grasp the whole complex dramatic action from first to last, conceived it all in terms of music, and made the non-lyrical as well as the lyrical moments essential parts of the one vital form.

CHAPTER III

TANNHÄUSER AND *LOHENGRIN*

I

AFTER the completion of the *Dutchman*, Wagner, in his search for a new dramatic subject, was for a time divided between the claims of *Tannhäuser* and those of a story dealing with Manfred, the son of Friedrich II. of the Hohenstaufens.[1] He saw very clearly, however, that the latter subject would have led him back to the old Grand-Opera style, with the regular five acts and all the usual conventionalities ; while the *Tannhäuser* story was far more suitable to the musical drama as he was then beginning to conceive it. Once more the circumstances of his own life made him see in his new opera a kind of philosophical summary of one phase of modern life. The improvement in his worldly lot after taking up his residence in Dresden had come to seem merely ironic and delusory to him. Fame and fortune indeed awaited him, but could only be attained by a denial of the new faith that was coming to life in his brain. To write in the current opera-style was becoming more and more abhorrent to him ; while to develop his own new artistic intuitions to their true consummation was to court inevitable ridicule and misunderstanding. He was already beginning to find materials for the sermon he was afterwards never tired of preaching, on the insufficiency of modern life to satisfy the aspirations of the artist. Thus the

---

[1] The plot of the contemplated drama is given in the *Communication to my Friends*.

story of *Tannhäuser* was to him no mere literary subject, to be taken up and written about for the simple artistic pleasure of writing, but a direct personal expression of everything that lay nearest his heart at the time—an autobiographical revelation of his own secret sorrow and despair. He has told us how he worked at the opera "in a state of burning exaltation"; how towards the end of his labours he dreaded lest he should die before they could be concluded. As the years went on, and he became ever more conscious of the great gulf fixed between himself and the artistic world, the increasing sadness of his thoughts brought with it a more passionate yearning for the ideal conditions in which alone, it seemed, his art could live. The sense of his loneliness in the world after the production of *Tannhäuser* sickened him with "the frivolous present." Like his own hero, fleeing in revolt and disgust from the crude sensuality of life, he was impelled towards the solitary mountain-peaks, where the purer and serener air brought vigour again to his wasted senses. But the mood in which he looked down from those heights was not one of merely philosophical detachment from earth and its surging life, but one of fresh yearning for association with all that was best and purest on earth. This symbolises itself in the form of that "Ever-Womanly" to which he was always driven for strength and consolation—the woman who had redeemed the Flying Dutchman, and had "showed to Tannhäuser the way that led from the hot passion of the Venusberg to heaven." She now took shape as Elsa, while Wagner himself is evident in the conception of Lohengrin. He has left us his own analysis of the characters of the new opera. Lohengrin seeks "the woman who would not call for explanations or defence, but who should *love* him with an unconditioned love." He cannot help carrying about with him the evidences of his high origin; but he desires to cloak these, as far as may be, so that he may win Elsa's love for his own sake. He desires, as Wagner says, to be loved, not to be worshipped; and the tragedy of the drama arises from his ultimate recognition that Elsa cannot give him trustful, unquestioning love, but can only *worship* him, and desire to know the secret of his divinity.

No one, surely, will allege that this is either a profound conception of life and love, or a particularly promising subject for a drama. Hence it is in the highest degree significant that Wagner should have attributed to it the importance he did; and it has not been sufficiently recognised how here, as elsewhere, he was merely expressing himself where he thought he was expressing the universe. Here, for the first time, we get something like the key to the real Wagner. It will be argued, in the course of the subsequent chapters, that he was of an intensely impressionable artistic temperament, but of only minor intellectual powers. His own mental and emotional life was so opulent and so vivid that he saw nothing clearly beyond its borders; his own personal desires, his own personal struggles, became in his mind epitomes of the desires and the struggles of the whole modern world. No estimate of Wagner, it seems to me, can be complete that does not recognise this; it is of the first importance in a diagnosis of the man as he really was. It is possible for a great artist to dramatise his personal experiences; but the peculiarity of Wagner's mind was this tendency to see profound mystic significances in stories that are quite commonplace to other people. He had, that is, the true mystic's constitution. Though no man ever talked more of the necessity of the art-work appealing to our objective, *physical* senses, it is quite evident that to the objective aspects of most of his dramas, as other men see them, he was utterly blind.[1] He treated the

---

[1] See Chapter vi.

story simply as the material in which to embody an abstract thought. Hence the necessity of looking beyond the external features of each of his dramas to the circumstances of his own life at the time he was writing it. In the epoch from which *Tannhäuser* and *Lohengrin* date, the peculiar cast of his thought may be traced to two main elements. In the first place he was beginning to experience those reactions from the sensuous that are inevitable in a nature like his, wherein the very intensity of the physical life at one moment brings with it, in the next, a loathing of the world of sense and an aspiration towards the mystical and the ideal. We can see this current very plainly in *Tannhäuser* and *Lohengrin*, the latter play being only the logical outcome of that mood of disgust with the sensuous life that first found expression in *Tannhäuser*.[1] This current, however, was crossed and complicated by another. Wagner's general reaction against the world was assisted by the sense of his isolation among artists, and the sad conviction, after witnessing the reception of *Tannhäuser*, that although many were impressed by the work, they were not impressed precisely in the way he desired. Like Lohengrin, he was worshipped but not understood.

[1] Wagner protested against the critics reading into *Tannhäuser* " a specifically Christian and impotently pietistic drift " (*A Communication to my Friends; G. S.* iv. 279; Ellis, i. 323). He may have been right in this respect; but there can be no doubt that the *Tannhäuser* and *Lohengrin* epoch was one of physiological reaction against sensuality. I may point out, too, that Wagner is the most unreliable of guides as to the moods that prompted his works. Having no habits of calm, objective thought, his interpretation of the philosophy of his plays varied with the particular philosophical phase in which he happened to be living at the moment. In the present case, we see him denying strenuously the pessimism that had been read into *Tannhäuser*; this was in the optimistic years. Later on, when he was convinced that pessimism was the only true reading of the world, he discovered that the *Dutchman, Tannhäuser*, and *Lohengrin* were pessimistic in essence. (See his letter to Roeckel of 23rd August 1856; and, on the general point, M. Lichtenberger's *Wagner, Poète et Penseur*, pp. 109–116.)

C

"Not wounded vanity," he says, describing his sensations after the production of *Tannhäuser*, "but the shock of an utter disillusionment, chilled my very marrow. It became clear to me that my *Tannhäuser* had appealed to a handful of intimate friends alone, and not to the heart of a public to whom, nevertheless, I had instinctively turned in the production of this my work."

It was in this mood that he turned to the figure of Lohengrin, as the supreme embodiment of this tragedy of his own life; and the next step, as usual with him, was to regard the drama as the expression of the tragedy of universal life. Hence he was doomed to further misunderstanding, further disillusionment. Men who had not the autobiographical key to the play, who saw it merely from the outside and judged it by the standards they would apply to any other drama, were bound to exhibit only a languid interest in Lohengrin and Elsa and their "problem." The characters are not always real; they do not strike us as being figures of flesh and blood; while the conception of the man who comes from supernal heights, loves a maiden, and then leaves her because she asks him his name, seemed a mere aberration of dramatic psychology.[1] Wagner, of course, never looked at the matter in this way; for him the story only existed as the means whereby to preach a philosophy that was then all-important to him.

"The character and situation of this Lohengrin," he wrote, "I now recognise, with clearest sureness, as *the type of the only absolute tragedy*, in fine, of *the tragic element of modern life*; and

---

[1] Wagner sees in this story of the love of the godlike man and the earthly maiden another form of the old myth of Zeus and Semele, and, of course, fathers his own sentimental philosophy upon "the Folk" who created the myth. As a matter of fact, the Lohengrin story had its birth in the savage superstition that regards the name as part of the being of a man. A savage will not tell his name to a stranger because he thinks the possession of the name will give the stranger power for evil over him. (See Andrew Lang, *Custom and Myth*, p. 74; Clodd, *Myths and Dreams*, pp. 104, 105; Hartland, *Science of Fairy Tales*, p. 309.) Mr. Hartland gives a number of savage myths that illustrate the power of this taboo upon the primitive mind.

that of just as great significance for the Present, as was the *Antigone*, though in another relation, for the life of the Hellenic state."

This is the beginning of the real Wagner—the Wagner who elevated all his own personal desires into desires for the whole world ; who thought his own tragedy the type of "the *only* absolute tragedy." It was inevitable that a man like this should be misunderstood. If he could not see the world as it lay before the eyes of other men, it was natural that they should be unable to find the key to his peculiar psychology. And as, in the later case of the *Ring*, criticism of his drama from any other standpoint than his own made absolutely no impression on him, so now he quite failed to see *why* other men could not regard *Lohengrin* as he did.

"It seemed then to me," he wrote in *A Communication to my Friends*, "and still it seems, most hard to comprehend how the deep tragedy of this subject and this character should have stayed unfelt ; and how the story should have been so misunderstood that Lohengrin was looked on as a cold, forbidding figure, more prone to rouse dislike than sympathy. This reproach was first made to me by an intimate friend, whose knowledge and whose intellectual gifts I highly prize."

The criticism passed upon the play by this friend was, we may assume, simply that of every plain man who knows nothing of the mystic meanings Wagner read into it, and who judges Lohengrin as he sees him. But the strain of self-centred idealism in Wagner that made him attach so much importance to his own dramatic "problems," made him at the same time impervious to criticism from minds of a different type.

"In this case, however," he continues, "I reaped an experience which has since been verified by repetition, namely, that upon the first direct acquaintance with my poem the impression produced is thoroughly affecting, and that this reproach only enters when the impression of the art-work itself has faded, and given place to cold, reflective criticism. Thus this reproach was not an instinctive act of the immediate-feeling heart, but a purposed act of mediate reflection. In this occurrence I therefore found the tragedy of Lohengrin's character and situation confirmed, as one deep-rooted in our modern life; it was reproduced upon the art-work and its author, just in the same way as it had borne down upon the hero of the poem." [1]

That is an easy way of disposing of criticism; and one might be tempted to characterise it in rather cynical language, were it not that Wagner's abnormality of constitution is so palpable as almost to disarm criticism. One sees at a glance that such a mind as this was congenitally unfit for sane thinking; that however it might develop on the musical side, in all that concerned purely intellectual matters it was doomed to arrested development, fated to eke out its existence with a few innate preconceptions that took the place of independently obtained ideas, and that no reasoning, no criticism could ever eradicate from the brain. Such was Wagner as his after life showed him to be. On the intellectual side he scarcely grew at all; as he neared his seventieth year he was retailing practically the same primitive fallacies that occupied him in his thirtieth. He lived a mental life that was wholly self-centred; and he grew not by assimilation of other matter, not by the enriching of his own mental substance with the best thoughts of other men, but simply by unfolding, by expansion of what he was at the moment of his birth. He laid stress, with perfect justice, upon the fact that his musical-dramatic system was not the product of reflection, of calculation, but of intuition. That is precisely what gave it its strength. He built up his drama as seemed best to his purely artistic sense, untrammelled by any thoughts of abstract theory. In the same way, he poured forth page after

[1] *A Communication to my Friends*, G. S. iv. 296, 297; i. 342.

page of prose-work, also the product of intuition rather
than of reflection—the mere strenuous self-expression
of a man to whom self-expression is an imperative need.
But on the musical side of his brain he was a heaven-
born genius, while in matters of pure thought his
intelligence was no more than ordinary. He had only
to obey his musical intuitions to put together the most
wonderful dramatic music that ever has or ever will be
seen ; his brain ran spontaneously to the conception of
dramatic character in terms of music, and when once
he had come to maturity, almost everything he did was
right by the grace of God. But there was no such
saving grace in his intellectual work. He was framed
to take his own peculiar view of things, a view no
external influences could ever alter. No man was ever
born so wise that the rude impact of other men's
opinions against his own was not good for him ; and a
mind of Wagner's type, that is quite incapable of pro-
fiting by criticism, that brushes it aside with the remark
that his critic had only to abjure reason and surrender
himself to " feeling," and he would immediately see eye
to eye with Wagner, is not one that can contribute
much of value to the thought of the world. His intellectual life necessarily lost in breadth what it gained in
intensity ; it evolved only the most ordinary and primitive conceptions, yet took them with a seriousness that
is almost inexplicable to us. Read, for example, his
own analysis of Lohengrin and Elsa.

" Elsa is the Unconscious, the Undeliberate, into which Lohengrin's conscious, deliberate being yearns to be redeemed ; but
this yearning, again, is itself the unconscious, undeliberate necessity in Lohengrin, whereby he feels himself akin to Elsa's being.
Through the capability of this 'unconscious consciousness,' such
as I myself now felt alike with Lohengrin, the nature of woman
also . . . came to ever clearer understanding in my inner mind.
. . . This woman, who with clear foreknowledge rushes on her
doom, for sake of Love's imperative behest—who, amid the

ecstasy of adoration, wills yet to lose her all, if so be she cannot all-embrace her loved one; this woman, who in her contact with this Lohengrin, of all men, must founder, and in doing so must shipwreck her beloved too; this woman, who can love but thus and not otherwise, who, by the very outburst of her jealousy, wakes first from out the thrill of worship into the full reality of Love, and by her wreck reveals its essence to him who had not fathomed it as yet; this glorious woman, before whom Lohengrin must vanish, for reason that his own specific nature could not understand her—I had found her *now:* and the random shaft that I had shot towards the treasure dreamt but hitherto unknown, was my own Lohengrin, whom now I must give up as lost; to track more certainly the footsteps of that *true Womanhood*, which should one day bring to me and all the world redemption, after manhood's egoism, even in its noblest form, had shivered into self-crushed dust before her—Elsa, the woman—woman hitherto un-understood by me, and understood at last—that most positive expression of the purest instinct of the senses—made me a revolutionary at one blow.   She was the Spirit of the Folk, for whose redeeming hand I too, as artist-man, was longing." [1]

Well, who, in the name of heaven, takes Lohengrin and Elsa quite so seriously as that ?   It would be pretty tall talk even over the two greatest dramatic conceptions that brain of man had ever given birth to ; but over a pair of operatic puppets it strikes the quiet reader as being precisely what it is—a mere outburst of raw artistic hysteria.   No one disputes for a moment that *Wagner* saw all this in his opera; but it is quite certain that no one else can, unassisted, see it there, and that in this, as in later cases, not one of his partisans would have drawn Wagner's own philosophy from the drama itself, without the clues given in the prose-works.   In any case, the philosophy of *Lohengrin*, even as analysed by Wagner himself, is of no importance and of no more than average interest.   All this

[1] G. S. iv. 301, 302; Ellis, i. 346, 347.

hysterical rhapsodising about Woman, and Love, and
the Spirit of the Folk, and Redemption by Womanhood,
may have seemed to Wagner the wisdom of all the
ages, but it is terribly thin and innutritious to others.
He was abnormal in his needs and in his manner of
satisfying those needs, and one finally sweeps aside his
semi-philosophical lucubrations as we do those of all
other mystics, because their plane of thought is too
remote from ours for us to have any interests in
common. We admit, of course, that original genius
is gifted with intuitions that are denied to ordinary
mortals. But we draw a line of distinction — not,
perhaps, a very clear line, but sufficient for all ordinary
purposes—between originality and abnormality; and
unless a man's thought bears some rational relation to
that of mankind in general, we class him not among
the soaring thinkers, but among the victims of congenital aberration. Wagner's panegyrists have been in
error in taking his nebulous intuitions for profound
thoughts, and in seeing supernal wisdom in the psychological scheme of such an opera as *Lohengrin;* they
have only done so, in fact, because they hold, like
Wagner himself, the crudest of views on the drama.
A great drama is a study of complex human character
under the stress of complex circumstance ; not a mere
posing of personified abstractions like Elsa and Lohengrin and Ortrud.[1] It is not sufficient, as the Wagnerians

---

[1] "The ensuing duet [between Frederick and Ortrud, in the 2nd Act]
is," writes Dr. Hueffer, "musically founded on a new motive, intended to
represent the evil principle of heathenish hatred and revenge, as opposed to
the heavenly purity of the ' Graal-motive.' For Ortrud now discloses herself
as the representative of old Friesian paganism, who by her falsehood and
witchcraft has led her husband to the accusation of the innocent Christian maiden" (*Richard Wagner*, pp. 31, 32). At the risk of offending my
Wagnerian friends, I am impelled to say that to oppose personified abstractions in this manner is not to write a drama ; and none but those whose
dramatic sense is in the most primitive stage of culture could fail to perceive
this. Even a Wagnerian like Dr. Hueffer has to admit that "the introduction in a by-the-way manner of the two great religious principles appears
not particularly happy, and it cannot be denied that the character of Ortrud,

think, to merely state a philosophical or social problem in dramatic form; the production only becomes a drama when we feel that some artistic purpose has been served by choosing this particular mode of presentation in preference to all others. Shelley pointed out that "nothing can be equally well expressed in prose that is not tedious and supererogatory in verse"; and it is necessary to urge against merely partisan admiration of the *Lohengrin* style of drama, that the dramatic form is only an irritating encumbrance upon the philosophical problem if it is incapable of justifying its own existence. Wagner may intend Lohengrin or Elsa to personify anything he likes; but unless we can become interested in his Lohengrin and Elsa as vitalised presentations of human character, we can take no interest in the philosophical abstractions they are supposed to personify. And to the question whether Wagner *has* made his characters sufficiently human in themselves to warrant our bothering about their esoteric significance, the answer must surely be in the negative. Lohengrin is *not* profoundly interesting to sane men and women; Elsa is interesting so long as we can trace her psychology along human and not quasi-philosophical lines; while Ortrud and Telramund are for the most part mere figures of melodrama. The case of Ortrud, indeed, may well be used as an illustration of Wagner's failure to realise his philosophical intentions because he cannot make his character humanly interesting.

"Ortrud," he wrote to Liszt, "is a woman who does not know love. . . . Politics are her essence. The political *man* is repulsive; the political *woman* is horrible, and it is this horror I had to represent. There is a kind of love in this woman, the

---

though grand in its dramatic conception, has slightly suffered through this unnecessary complication of motives." Other people feel that Lohengrin and Elsa are also, in a great degree, abstractions rather than human characters. The stage of dramatic conception represented by *Lohengrin* is really very primitive.

love of the past, of dead generations, the terribly insane love of
ancestral pride, which finds its expression in the hatred of everything living, actually existing." [1]

I appeal to the Wagnerians to say whether this is not
simply the self-delusion of the sincere but uncritical
artist; whether they really see in the melodramatic
Ortrud the type of the woman the foundation of whose
being is politics. The plain truth is that she does not
strike us in the first place as dramatically real, and that
therefore we remain deaf and blind to the philosophical
lessons she is supposed to inculcate. In the same way,
we say of the opera as a whole that since the characters
are not real, the beautiful moral lesson which Wagner
had in view simply bores us. It may or may not be
true that, as M. Kufferath says, the fundamental idea
of the Lohengrin and similar legends is that happiness
can live "only as long as illusion lives; that desire
alone sees beauty in things; that all curiosity is vain
and deceptive; that the ideal—our most absolute need—
falls into dust under the finger that touches it." [2]   All
this, I repeat, may or may not be true; but if Wagner
has no more to say to us than this, he might have said
it in the same form and in the same number of lines
as M. Kufferath. The very essence of the numerous
old legends—Indian, Greek, Mediæval—in which this
theme is set forth, is that the story is made interesting
in the telling; we read it not for philosophical fortifica-
tion but for æsthetic pleasure. In the case of Wagner's
drama, the characters themselves are so unconvincingly
drawn that we either take no artistic interest in them
as human beings, or else the didactic purpose shows
so clearly through the quasi-dramatic form that we
resent its intrusion upon our artistic mood—as when
Ortrud shrieks about the gods of paganism. Altogether,

---

[1] *Letters to Liszt*, 30th January 1852, Eng. trans. i. 192, 193.
[2] Maurice Kufferath, *Le Théâtre de Richard Wagner: Lohengrin*, p. 67.

the study of *Lohengrin* makes us certain of two points of importance in any study of Wagner : (1) that he saw in his operatic characters a whole world of abstract and didactic significances that no one else would have seen there had he left no prose works behind him ; and (2) that this unconsciousness that he was presenting only personified abstractions instead of dramatic characters indicates a serious flaw in his artistic nature.

II

On the artistic side, *Tannhäuser* and *Lohengrin* are interesting not only for their great musical beauty but as stages in what I have called Wagner's progress to self-consciousness.　Taking *Tristan and Isolde* as the most perfect specimen both of Wagner's musical dramas and our nearest approach to what a musical drama ought to be, it is readily seen how far Wagner is in *Tannhäuser* and *Lohengrin* from this standard, and on the other hand how great is the advance from *Rienzi* and the *Dutchman*.　There is still much superfluous matter that merely lengthens the dramatic action without elucidating or intensifying it—choruses, for example, being inserted with an eye rather to purely musical effect than to the conduct of the drama ; the leading characters are not yet as *musical* in conception as they should be—that is, their mental world is frequently incongruous with musical expression, and tends to obscurity under the limitations this mode of expression imposes on it ; and Wagner is not yet able to construct a musical as distinct from a poetical drama—that is, he is compelled to piece together his story with long passages that are quite unfitted for any sort of musical treatment.　The writing of *Tannhäuser* and *Lohengrin* must have been an invaluable lesson to him in the art of text-construction, for he could not fail to be impressed with the fact that though it is easy to set notes to anything, music only springs spontaneously from words whose content is not quite incongruous with musical expression.[1]   We smile when we read that the old Meistersingers, when they set music to a scriptural text, included in their setting such exordiums as " the twenty-ninth chapter of Genesis records," or, " Moses, the eleventh, reports." [2]   But if Wagner will write, as he does in *Tannhäuser,* such words as "When I look around upon this noble assembly, what a fine spectacle causes my heart to glow !   So many heroes, brave and wise ! . . ."[3] or again, as in *Lohengrin,* " One day Elsa took the boy out for a pleasant walk in the wood, but returned without him ; in simulated anguish she asked for news of him, pretending that she had accidentally strayed from him . . ."[4] and will try to set these words to music, he commits an absurdity almost as great as that of the serious German singers of old.   To revert to the distinction already made above, we cannot write music, but only notes, to passages of this kind.   Look, as an illustration, at Wagner's setting of the last-quoted words :—

Lust - wandelnd führte   El - sa den Knaben einst zum

---

[1] I must refer the reader to Chapter v. for a fuller discussion of this question.

[2] See Mr. Krehbiel's charming article in his *Studies in the Wagnerian Drama.*

[3] Vocal Score (Novello's edition), p. 128.   [4] *Ibid.,* p. 8.

Wald, doch oh-ne ihn kehrte sie zurück; mit falscher Sorge

frug sie nach dem Bruder, da sie von unge-fähr von ihm ver-

irrt, bald seine Spur, so sprach sie, nicht mehr fand.

This is not music; one could get as good an effect by putting a number of crotchets, quavers, and semi-quavers in a pepper-box, and shaking them out promiscuously over a stave. The essence of a musical phrase is that there is some reason for the notes going

this way rather than that—we feel an intellectual in-
evitableness in the sequence ; but there is no *raison
d'être* for the notes Wagner has written here.   A thousand men could sit down and throw notes upon the
paper in a thousand different ways, each having as
much—or as little—real reference to the words as the
notes of Wagner.   The truth is, that words of this kind,
since they contain nothing of the nature of music, ask
for no musical setting, and have no place in musical
drama ; just as " The words of this anthem are taken
from the tenth and eleventh verses of the third chapter
of St. Paul's Epistle to the Romans," has no place
in the music of the anthem itself.   It is unfortunate
for the operatic writer that this should be so ; for he is
reduced to the dilemma of having to put unemotional
passages into his opera in order to tell a connected
story, and yet is constrained to seek for these passages
an emotional form of expression.   Wagner himself has
said that the unique form of music being melody, music
and melody are inseparable—it being impossible, indeed, to conceive the one without the other ; and that,
consequently, if a piece of music is without melody,
it means that the musician has been unable to create
a vital form to match the sentiment—he simply writes
quasi-musical phrases that leave the ear indifferent.[1]
That may serve as a precise characterisation of this
and similar passages in *Tannhäuser* and *Lohengrin*.
Wagner's failure, of course, is due not to any deficiency
of musical power, but to the restrictions imposed upon
his musical imagination by the unimaginative quality
of the words.   Purely instrumental music exists in and
by and for itself, being under no constraint of compli-
ance with any mental picture outside itself ; while vocal
music is, broadly speaking, intended to present the
verbal sense in another and more intensive form ; its
function is to *rethink* the speech-utterance in music.

[1] See the " *Zukunftsmusik.* "

It is evident that this is impossible where the words, having no emotional content—being, in fact, a purely intellectual utterance—are incapable of having their meaning expressed in any other but verbal terms. All dramatic recitative is a compromise between the musician's impulse to sheer musical expression for its own sake and his desire to follow the lead of the poet ; and while sheer musical expression is—on a less emotional plane than that of pure music—out of the question in connection with merely *banal* words, there is also nothing in the words to stimulate the composer to even a modified exercise of the musical imagination. The average opera-composer skipped blandly over this difficulty ; he candidly confessed that he only desired you to listen to him as a musician in his arias and concerted pieces, and that the recitatives were inserted between these merely because a story *had* to be told somehow or other. For Wagner the solution of the main problem of opera was not so easy. To the end of his days he cannot be said to have fully recognised that musical drama cannot be homogeneous throughout, precisely because of this necessary intrusion of merely ordinary matter upon the lyrical excitement of the higher moments of the drama ; though he strove more and more to exclude from his operas whatever was not in some degree congruous with the spirit of music, and once, in *Tristan*, achieved a libretto that is still our nearest approach to the ideal drama for music.

In a sense, then, his partisans are right in saying that the progressive excellence of his work was due to his growth as the poet, not the musician, of his material —though, as we shall see later, his improvement as a poet was really only a by-product of his improvement as a musician, in that the increasing clearness of his musical conceptions, and his desire to realise them in drama, led him intuitively to put only such matter into his poems as would lend itself to musical treat-

ment.   Upon the purely musical side his art was,
of course, developing by leaps and bounds.   The
great faculty necessary to the dramatic musician—
that of transmuting the verbal sense spontaneously into
an equivalent musical speech—which no musician has
ever possessed in like degree, was now coming to full
maturity in Wagner.   One has only to look at the
recitative with which Tannhäuser opens the opera in
order to realise this ; there is nothing in the *Dutchman*
to place beside this and a score of similar passages
for their combination of musical beauty and dramatic
significance.   Wherever the musician has a free hand,
indeed, Wagner can now compel what shapes he likes
of beauty ; they rise as obediently to his call as spirits
to the incantations of a magician.   He is beginning
to *think* his characters in music ; he is learning how to
conceive them plastically, and to symbolise them in
suggestive phrases.   In this respect the advance from
the *Dutchman* even to *Tannhäuser* is very obvious.   The
Dutchman himself is statuesquely portrayed ; one believes in his existence more even than in that of Senta ;
but the other characters of the opera do not really live.
In *Tannhäuser*, not only are the spiritual forces of the
drama—such as the pilgrim-music—conceived with
a positiveness to which there is no parallel in the
earlier work, but the characters themselves are made
to stand out plastic and concrete and individual by
the peculiar definiteness of the music that is given to
them.   Characters like Venus and Ortrud are rather
abstractions than human beings, yet even they have
a certain musical distinctness of form ; while such
characters as Tannhäuser, Elizabeth, Wolfram,[1] the
Landgrave, Lohengrin, Elsa, and the King are musically differentiated with the utmost clearness.   This is

---

[1] Although Wolfram is really only a minor character in *Tannhäuser*, his
nobility of nature is clearly defined immediately upon his entrance ; see the
vocal score, p. 59.

an effect achieved as much by Wagner's orchestration as by any other musical factor. In *Tannhäuser* he had shown how a skilful change of orchestral colouring could induce a profound imaginative sympathy with the changes of the dramatic picture—as in the 3rd Act, where the tones of the wood-wind, becoming ever more ethereal, more virginal, towards the end of Elizabeth's prayer, gradually merge into the deeper colour of tuba and trombone as the more sombre grief of Wolfram comes to the forefront of the action. In *Lohengrin* this clarity of perception of the pictorial and suggestive power of the orchestra leads to the most wonderful results. No one can ever forget those exquisite harmonies in the violins that set before us the ethereal nature of Lohengrin as no words and no painting could do ; or the maidenly suggestiveness of the wood-wind that accompanies the entry of Elsa, and her dreamy song upon the balcony; or the solemn, heroic chords of brass in the accompaniment to the King's prayer. In all that concerns the musical representation of character, *Lohengrin* is almost as much in advance of *Tannhäuser* as *Tannhäuser* is in advance of the *Dutchman;* and it is only the still greater development shown in Wagner's later works that hinders us from appreciating *Lohengrin* at its proper value. Had Wagner died in 1850, *Lohengrin* would now appear to us as a most astonishing achievement in musical characterisation.

As a dramatic musician, of course, he had not yet attained his full development. The monotonous regularity of rhythm we noticed in the *Dutchman* appears now and again in *Tannhäuser* and *Lohengrin;* and besides the difficulty, already pointed out, of finding interesting music for uninteresting words, Wagner is seen to be face to face with the eternal problem of the compromise between the lyrist and the dramatist. In the *Dutchman,* as I have said, we are sometimes disturbed by the

incongruity between the regular sequences of tonality
in a musical phrase and the shifting colour of the
dramatic emotion which it is intended to portray.   In
Lohengrin we find Wagner, in his anxiety to be dramatic
rather than "absolute-musical," sometimes falling into
the opposite error, wilfully disturbing the natural cadence
of a phrase in order, as it were, to clinch an argument,
and giving us a strange sense of being thrown violently
from the musical into another world.[1]   Wagner had in
fact developed, as was only to be expected, far more
rapidly as a lyrist than as a dramatist.   While there is
nothing in *Rienzi*, for example, one-tenth as beautiful
as the lyric music of *Tannhäuser* or *Lohengrin*, much of
the dramatic music of the two later works is hardly
above the level of that of *Rienzi*.   Failing to conceive
the less emotional passages of his poem as definitely as
the more emotional ones, he is forced into mere unmusical declamation, or into purely conventional figures of
melody and harmony.   Hence those frequent upward
runs in the violins, terminating in a chord of the seventh
or the ninth—a device that fails ultimately to make
any impression whatever upon us ; hence also the
numerous attempts to get a strenuous dramatic effect
by a mere succession of diminished sevenths and their
inversions.   These are evident signs of an inability to
rethink the poem in music, to find a true and spontaneous musical equivalent for the words or the situation.
We see the same difficulty, on a larger scale, in such
scenes as the first of the 2nd Act of *Lohengrin*.   The
seasoned Wagnerian does not altogether agree with
the non-Wagnerian verdict that this is the dullest music
in the opera ; on the contrary, it shows in some respects,

[1] See, for example, the passage in which Lohengrin tells the King of his
determination to abandon the proposed campaign (vocal score, p. 235).   The
conclusion of the phrase leads us to expect a modulation into the key of A ;
but instead of descending from E to A, the last note rises unexpectedly to F,
with the tonic harmony of that note.

particularly in that of dramatic orchestration, Wagner on his way to the later marvellous triumphs of expression. But there can be no dispute that to a certain extent the popular judgment is right; a great deal of the scene between Frederick and Ortrud is not music, but rhetoric that just falls short of being music. Even here, however, the advance on all the earlier works is again obvious. However Wagner may fail at times in the vocal portions, the orchestra has become more potent, more significant than it had ever been before; the expressive phrase that writhes in and out among the general texture of this scene is so dramatically illuminative of the passions of the protagonists that we are often unconscious of the defects of the vocal phrases. Plainly, so far as Wagner fails in *Tannhäuser* and *Lohengrin* it is not so much because of any shortcomings as a musician, but because he had unknowingly set himself the stupendous task of uniting music with the base and the ugly. It is noticeable that while, as I have said, he puts notes into the mouths of Frederick and Ortrud that are really not music at all, the music of the Herald is always a delight to hear—although the Herald is not in any way a dramatic figure, and Frederick and Ortrud are, at least in intention, strenuously dramatic. The reason is that these are characters fitted more for poetical than for musical treatment. A poet can show us all the vileness of a character, its baseness and its villainy, while the verbal medium in which he works, being apprehended less in its sensuous than its intellectual qualities, cannot lead to any sense of incongruity between what is conveyed and the manner of conveying it. With music the case is different. It is a truism to say that music must be beautiful in order to be music; and a difficulty immediately rises when an attempt is made to link it with unbeautiful things. If it is sensuously pleasing, the mind cannot realise the ugliness of the character with whom it is supposed to be

associated ;[1] while if the ugliness of the character be
stressed so much as to make the tonal phrases un-
pleasing, the mind takes no interest either in the actor
or his utterance. There is only one escape from the
difficulty, as Wagner partly realised in later years.
Vocal music can hardly be descriptive ; for a singer
who produces sounds that are not beautiful in themselves will not be listened to. The dramatic composer,
then, must make use of the *orchestra* to suggest all those
things that are strictly non-beautiful in themselves, but
yet are necessary to his drama. Wagner may write
page upon page of recitative in *Lohengrin*, accompanied
simply by a *tremolo* in the strings, without either giving
us musical pleasure or portraying a dramatic character.
But he has only to suggest ugliness in his orchestra,
without attempting to make the ugliness beautiful in
the singer's phrases, and he has achieved his purpose.
One realises the brute strength of Hunding, or Alberich's
sunless hate of life, far more vividly by the orchestral
colouring associated with them, than would be possible
from any amount of pseudo-descriptive recitative. This,
then, is the direction in which the dramatic composer
ought to work, if he wishes to represent the unbeautiful
and non-lyrical in the medium of the most beautiful
and most lyrical of all the arts. Even in *Lohengrin*,
Wagner has partly become conscious of this truth ; the
tortuous theme that winds its way through the first
scene of the 2nd Act is really more expressive than the
bulk of the music actually put into the mouths of
Frederick and Ortrud.[2]

The point to which Wagner has attained in *Tannhäuser* and *Lohengrin*, then, may be defined as one at

---

[1] See the remarks on Verdi's *Otello* in Chapter v.

[2] The psychological difference between a purely symbolical or suggestive
theme like this, and a vocal theme that must appeal to quite a different musical
sense, may be seen from p. 218 of the score, where the phrase that has been
so expressive in the bassoons becomes curiously inexpressive and uninteresting
when sung by Elsa.

which his lyrical faculties have developed beyond the dramatic, the failures in the purely dramatic portions of these works being due partly to inexperience, partly to a bad constitution of the poem. For the rest, we see the later Wagner most clearly in the prelude to *Lohengrin*. There for the first time he writes a purely orchestral piece that is not a *pot-pourri*, like the overtures to the *Dutchman* and *Tannhäuser*, of the main themes of the opera, but an attempt to represent in sound the whole psychology and philosophy of a drama. Thus the prelude to *Lohengrin* stands much nearer to his later preludes than do those to *Tannhäuser* and the *Dutchman*, where the construction is more formal, the sequence less logical, the total picture less homogeneous. Liszt has pointed out that, although the *Tannhäuser* overture is built up of themes drawn from the opera, it is really something distinct from the opera itself, comprehensible and admirable to those who know nothing of the drama ; whereas the prelude to *Lohengrin* cannot be properly understood except as the formula into which the whole subsequent drama is compressed.[1]

[1] Liszt, *Lohengrin et Tannhäuser de Richard Wagner* (1851), pp. 47, 48.

CHAPTER IV

ART AND LIFE

LOHENGRIN, though not performed until 1850, was completed in the summer of 1847. From that year until 1853, when he commenced the *Rheingold*, Wagner entirely ceased from musical composition, and devoted himself to thinking out the principles of art and life and drama which were implicit in the best of his creative work up to *Lohengrin*, and more consciously incorporated in the later works. It is at this period that his literary activity may really be said to commence, for with the exception of the *Autobiographical Sketch*, written in 1842, the sketches and articles already published by him were hardly of more than passing interest.[1] During the early years of his exile Wagner not only thought out several subjects for dramatic treatment, but published a goodly number of treatises dealing with his own ideals of poetry and music and the drama, and the relations of art and politics in modern times. A reference to the Synthetic Table at the commencement of this volume will show that the most important of these writings all fall within a period of about three years—*Art and Revolution* appearing in 1849, *The Art-Work of the Future*, *Art and Climate*, and *Judaism in Music* in 1850, *Opera and Drama* and *A Communication to my Friends* in 1851.[2] *Opera and*

---

[1] An exception may perhaps be made in favour of *A Pilgrimage to Beethoven*, which contains some characteristic Wagnerisms on music and the drama.

[2] He writes to Liszt (Dec. 14, 1851) that "the three operatic poems, with a Communication to my Friends, will appear at the end of this month." On Jan. 1, 1852, he tells Uhlig, "Yesterday I received the book."

Drama will be considered subsequently ; here it will be well to discuss simply the general tenor of Wagner's opinions upon life and art and politics.

One must do him the justice, at the outset, to say that with politics in the ordinary sense of the word Wagner concerned himself but little. The fact that in 1849 he had to flee from Dresden, a warrant being issued for his arrest, and the fact that he is known to have taken *some* part in the revolution, have given colour to the theory that he really aimed at political revolution for its own sake ; and his speech at the *Vaterlandsverein* has been looked upon as the expression of a practical communism in social life, and a practical desire for a republic rather than a monarchy in Saxony. Hence when he came, in later years, to acclaim the young Ludwig of Bavaria as the possible Messiah of German culture, and to expatiate at great length on the necessity of the Kingship,[1] he was regarded as having been guilty of at any rate a little apostasy. Without having the slightest sympathy with his later idealist and sentimentalist views on the function of the monarchy, one must do him the justice to say that the charge of renegadism is quite ill-founded. There is nothing in the *Vaterlandsverein* speech [2] to bear out the imputation of communistic or republican ideas ; and as to Wagner's political theories as a whole, one need have no hesitation in accepting his own statement that he meddled with politics not for their own sake, but simply as a means of bringing about the artistic conditions which, he thought, were essential for civilisation, but which could not be attained under the existing *régime*.[3] As he himself wrote in 1872 :—

---

[1] See *State and Religion* (1864).

[2] It is given in the fourth volume of Mr. Ellis's translation of the prose works. It is plain, too, from the speech, that Wagner was only half a republican.

[3] " . . . It was just this earnestness " [of his artistic aims] " that once constrained me to enter realms apparently so distant as State and Religion.

"I believed in the Revolution, and in its unrestrainable necessity, with certainly no greater immoderation than Carlyle: only I also felt that I was called to point out to it the way of rescue. Far though it was from my intent to define the new, which should grow from the ruins of a sham-filled world, as a fresh *political* ordering: I felt the rather animated to draw the outlines of the *Art - Work* which should rise from the ruins of a sham-bred *Art*."[1]

All that we know of Wagner, indeed, is quite incongruous with the assumption that he ever cared seriously for politics for its own sake, or that during the stormy days of 1848 and 1849 he was actuated by any other desire than that of placing art upon a surer footing. That he was in an exceedingly febrile condition at the time is plainly apparent from the glowing fervour and mad idealism of the views he propounds, as well as from the ill-ordered enthusiasm of the writing.[2]

The object of *Art and Revolution* is to discover the relations between art and the modern state. The

What there I sought was really never aught beyond my art—that art which I took so earnestly, that I asked for it a basis and a sanction in Life, in State, and lastly in Religion. That these I could not find in modern life, impelled me to search out the cause in my own fashion ; I had to try to make plain to myself the tendence of the State, in order to account for the disdain with which I found my earnest art-ideal regarded everywhere in public life. But it certainly was characteristic of my inquiry, that it never led me down into the arena of *politics* proper ; that is to say, the politics of the day remained as entirely untouched by me, as, despite the commotion of those times, they never truly touched myself. That this or that form of government, the jurisdiction of this or that party, this or that alteration in the mechanism of our State affairs, could furnish my art-ideal with any veritable furtherance, I never fancied. . . ." *State and Religion*, in G. S. viii. 3, 4 ; Ellis, iv. 5, 6. On the whole question see Praeger, *Wagner as I knew him*, and Mr. Ellis's *1849 : A Vindication*,

[1] *Introduction to Art and Revolution*, G. S. iii. 2 ; Ellis, i. 24.

[2] He himself, when writing the Introduction to the third and fourth volumes of the Prose Works, in 1872, acknowledged "the fervid enthusiasm which pervaded my style, and gave to my remarks more of a poetic than a scientific character," and the "impassioned tangle of ideas" that came from his imperfect assimilation of the philosophy of Feuerbach.

Greek drama, Wagner thinks, was so great because it was the expression of the whole community at its best and noblest, the expression of a free people untainted by egoism. When the Athenian State declined, Tragedy fell along with it, the community being now rent into innumerable warring units; and the two thousand years between the Athenians and us belong not to Art but to Philosophy. In the Roman world, the only bond of union was the universal slavery and misery under which the community lived. From a condition such as this no art could come, for art is "pleasure in itself, in existence, in community"; whereas the Roman system bred only disgust and weariness of life. The product of it was Christianity, which is neither art itself, nor capable of evoking art. Whereas the free Greek lived openly, in full enjoyment of himself and of the world, the Christian retired into his cloister, and, despising the world of sense, could receive no artistic impulse therefrom. There was in Christian Europe, in fact, a feud between the "instinct of life" and the "force of conscience," which was fatal to art. The Renaissance only came when the Church openly showed herself in her real light as a mere temporal power; and even the Renaissance had root in the art of Greece. In the days of Louis XIV., worldly dominion took art under its own protection; in our own day art is sold, body and soul, to another master—Commerce. The true essence of our art is Industry; "its ethical aim, the gaining of gold; its æsthetic purpose, the entertainment of those whose time hangs heavily on their hands." The modern stage does indeed reflect our modern life, as the Greek stage mirrored the life of Athens; but the world represented in *our* art is one of hollowness and corruption. The Drama is no longer the supreme picture of man's essential life. Its impotence is shown in the fact of its division into two contrasted orders, the spoken play and the opera ; a division whereby the drama is prevented from rising to its true height of passion, and the opera becomes a mere mechanical mixture of a number of scenic, vocal, and instrumental effects, without any informing dramatic aim. Thus on the one hand we have the shallow audience, fatigued with its day's ignoble labour, coming to the theatre solely for an evening's relaxation ; on the other hand, the artist willing to sell himself and his art for gold and fame. The Greek tragedy was the expression of the deepest and noblest consciousness of the people ; our deepest and noblest consciousness finds expression, not in the stage, but in denunciation of it. What to the Greek was art, has to us become mere handicraft. The Greek, however, was enabled to live so free and elevated a life by reason of his manual labour being done for him by slaves ; and we can see now that " Beauty and Strength, as attributes of public life, can then alone prove lasting blessings, when they are the common gifts of all mankind." Unfortunately, the last two thousand years have seen not the slave raised to the level of the free man, but the free man dragged down to the level of the slave. Gold is the only means by which a man can now become relatively free ; and after gold all strive, even the artist.

Among the Greeks, art lived in the public conscience ; among us it lives only in the private conscience. Thus Greek art, being the expression of the communal conscience, was in its essence conservative ; our art, being opposed in spirit to the main forces of the community, is of necessity revolutionary. Only revolution can reunite the dissevered arts that sprang from the disintegration of the Greek drama ; only revolution can give us the real art-work of the modern world. We must be born again as free men. Culture has destroyed civilisation, and must in her turn be overthrown by Nature ; this will constitute Revolution. In the free world of mankind, the ignoble cares of life being less dominant than now, the best energies of men will be revealed as pure artistic impulse. Mankind will no longer find all its strength wasted in the mere effort to maintain life ; industry will be so developed that only a relatively small amount will assure comfortable existence, thus leaving men more leisure and more desire for artistic work. The culture of physical beauty will raise the pulse of joy in life, until ultimately the healthy activities of men will make each of them, in some field or other, an artist—all individual artistic impulses, however, being focussed in the one great art-work, the Drama. Every art, in fact, suffers from the present reign of industrialism—the Drama most of all ; and the prime requisite for its salvation is the freeing of the Theatre from the curse of mere commercial speculation. It must be conducted on none but artistic lines, and for none but artistic purposes, the public having the right of free admission.

Art and Revolution was published in the autumn of 1849. On 16th September Wagner writes to Uhlig :—

"Wigand is already publishing a pamphlet of mine, *Art and Revolution*. . . . Get this little work as soon as it appears : it will be only a precursor—as soon as I get to work again I shall follow it up by one of greater detail, *The Art-Work of the Future ;* to which, afterwards a third, *The Artists of the Future*, will form the conclusion. . . . It is most essential that I should accomplish this work and send it into the world before going on with my immediate artistic productions. I must come myself, and those who are interested in my artistic being must come with me, to a clear understanding ; else shall we forever grope about in hateful twilight, which is worse than absolute darkness in which one sees nothing and only religiously clutches hold of the old-accustomed balustrade." [1]

He felt, in fact, the need of some clarification of his

[1] Letter 2 to Uhlig, Eng. trans. p. 7.

ideas before proceeding to further creative work ; as he himself goes on to say in the letter just quoted from— " If I accomplish this to my satisfaction, I shall then set to work at the music of my *Siegfried;* for that is what I yearn after, with all my soul's sincerity." But there was a further reason for his giving utterance to himself in prose at this time. His flight to Switzerland had brought before him in the most pressing manner the problem of daily maintenance. He could expect very little remuneration from his operas, and was, in fact, to a large extent dependent during the whole of his exile upon the support of noble-minded and generous friends. We may accept his own assurance, made more than once in after years, that he cared nothing for wealth except as a means to the furthering of art ; and that he wanted nothing more than a bare competence, something that would preserve him from the necessity of wasting his finest energies in fruitless and ignoble toil, and leave him free to give the world the best that was in him. There may be a touch of weakness and of egoism in the wish ; for other men than he have had to work as best they could for truth and beauty, carrying withal burdens infinitely heavier and more grievous than his—and have wrought with noble patience and dignity and without complaint. But human nature is a complex thing, and if we are to call Wagner's lamentation egoistic, we must do so in a spirit of sympathy rather than of censure, recognising him to be the peculiar organism he was. No man ever took his art more seriously ; few have made such sacrifices for their ideal ; and if we are compelled to see some slight touch of weakness in his constant reliance upon the pecuniary support of others, the magnitude of the cause for which he was fighting preserves the weakness from any taint of the ignoble.[1] Without passing, as it is so easy to do, exaggerated

---

[1] See the last chapter of the present volume.

moral censure upon him, we may be content to look objectively at the phenomenon of this egoism in its relation to his art and his theories. From the rough outline already given of *Art and Revolution*, it can readily be seen how insistent Wagner was upon the importance of art to social well-being. In this at all events he was perfectly sincere; but the pressure of pecuniary need upon himself, at a time when his feverish brain was filled with thoughts and visions of new things to be done in music, was undoubtedly at the bottom of his thesis that the artist was out of touch with the modern world, and that art ought to be the most important factor in the lives of men. The leap from the purely individual case to the universal proposition was of course unconscious, instinctive; but, as we have already seen in connection with *Tannhäuser* and *Lohengrin*, a quite Wagnerian procedure. In this same letter to Uhlig, dated 16th September 1849, he writes :—

"You see, dear friend, it is such trifles as conventional fame-seeking and anxiety for daily bread which threaten to exert—and in a decisive manner—their august modern sovereignty over the true, free sphere of man's art. But can there be a choice here? Certainly not, not even if persons like you begin to be prudent and practical. I will be happy, and a man can only be that if he is free; but that man only is free who is what he can and therefore must be. Whoever, therefore, satisfies the inner necessity of his being, is free; because he feels himself at one with himself, because everything which he does answers to his nature, to his true needs. Whoever follows a necessity, not from within but from without, is subject to compulsion; he is not free, but an unfortunate slave. The free man laughs at oppression from without, if only inner necessity be not sacrificed to it. . . . I don't care what happens to me, if only I become what, according to my nature, I ought to become. So shall I be right, even if no idler take notice of me. *Apropos!* If you know any persons who would give me as much per year as would satisfy my wants, in exchange for all that I may do during my life, in the way of writing poetry and music, please give them my address.   Without this help I can do nothing."

It was the unconscious egoism that ran all through Wagner's work that made him assume that because *he* wished to be supported by other men in order that he might write as he desired, therefore all the world should join in placing art and the artist on the topmost pinnacle, and in reshaping society to this end.

No sooner had he completed *Art and Revolution*, however, than he seems to have felt the necessity of giving further and ampler expression to his views. Almost before the pamphlet is published he writes to Uhlig that he has been "seized with a furious desire to produce a new literary composition, *The Art-Work of the Future*"; and later on he writes that "this will be my last literary work"—a promise which he lamentably failed to keep.   Feeling that *Art and Revolution* had not made his position quite clear enough, he designs *The Art-Work of the Future* to show in detail what in the former work had only been broadly sketched out.

"The genetic origin of our mutilated modern art from collective Grecian art," he says in one of his letters, "could only be made clear by showing in a precise manner the important moment when this art passed from direct representation into indirect representation; from Tragedy into the so-called plastic art. . . . But if I wish to show that plastic art, being artificial—only an art abstracted from true art—must cease entirely in the future, if to this plastic art—painting and sculpture—claiming nowadays to be principal art, I deny a life in the future,[1] you will

---

[1] Mr. Houston Stewart Chamberlain, whose intimate knowledge of all Wagner's works is beyond question, strangely remarks in one place that "it is not true, as has been asserted again and again by malicious and ignorant people, that Wagner denied the right of any art to exist singly" (*Richard Wagner*, pp. 201-202).   If the words quoted above do not mean this, it is difficult to say what they do mean; and if his remarks on instrumental music are not quite so definite, they express the same point of view (see Letter 55

allow that this should not and could not be done with two strokes of the pen." [1]

This, then, is the thesis of *The Art-Work of the Future*. It begins with some not very illuminative remarks on Man having sprung from Nature, and Nature first coming to consciousness in Man. [2] As Man stands to Nature, says Wagner, so stands Art to Man.

"Man will never be that which he can and should be, until his life is a true mirror of Nature, a conscious following of the only real necessity, the *inner natural necessity*, and is no longer held in subjugation to an *outer* artificial counterfeit—which is thus no necessary, but an *arbitrary* power. Then first will Man

---

to Uhlig, Eng. trans. p. 190). In his treatise *On Musical Criticism*, again, he distinctly says that "we have nothing in the least to do with our music of *to-day*, excepting in that we wage war to the death against it as an absolute separate art" (G. S. v. 61 ; Ellis, iii. 69). The instances which Mr. Chamberlain cites to the contrary are quite futile, and do not apply in any way. The 14th letter to Uhlig, I may say in passing, does not quite bear the interpretation Mr. Chamberlain tries to put upon it. And he simply stultifies himself when he remarks that so far from Wagner denying the right of each art to exist separately, he maintained that "in the drama, illuminated by music, the people will find itself and every art ennobled and beautified. True, none of the single arts will appear alone in the drama ; here the rays of different colour and refrangibility are united again to the original, pure white light of the sun. But from this source of all true inspiration each single art will draw fresh strength and undying life." I confess my inability to see any distinction between saying that the separate arts can find true life only in their union in the drama, and denying the right of any single art to exist separately. When Wagner, for example, talks of "the release of plastic art taking place when the stone is resolved into the flesh and blood of men, when the rigid monument of the past becomes the moving life of the present, and the soul of the sculptor passes into the body of the dancer," and of plastic art being "changed from stone into the flesh and blood of men," one can only say that he takes from it everything that makes it plastic art. His argument, indeed, if one really must use plain language, is perilously like arrant nonsense—in the capacity for which, at times, he has been surpassed only by some of his fanatical disciples.

[1] Letter 6 to Uhlig, Eng. trans. pp. 25, 26.

[2] Wagner is, unfortunately, given to a form of empty verbiage that one has to recognise as typically Teutonic. Such aphorisms as "All that subsists, depends on the conditions by which it subsists" are not very remarkable for either lucidity or force.

become a living man; whereas till now he carries on a mere existence, dictated by the maxims of this or that Religion, Nationality, or State. In like manner will Art not be the thing she can and should be, until she is or can be the true, conscious image and exponent of the real Man, and of man's genuine nature-bidden life; until she therefore need no longer borrow the conditions of her being from the errors, perversities, and unnatural distortions of our modern life."

The vital force which alone acts from necessity, and from which alone redeeming art can come, is the Folk —the Folk being defined as "the epitome of all those men *who feel a common and collective want.*" The enemies of the Folk feel only an artificial need, the satisfaction of which is *Luxury.*

All life and all thought depend in the first and last instance on physical perception. Abstract thought, that tries to shape the world from itself, and Fashion, which is mere arbitrary need, are the ruling elements of the modern world, and are altogether antagonistic to art, which must spring from actual life. The artist's thought "can only gain redemption in a physically-present art-work." His ideal is unattainable under existing conditions; the great united art-work, employing each separate art as a means to the great end—"the unconditioned, absolute portrayal of perfected human nature"—can be the product only of the united Manhood of the Future. Hellenic art was so great because it came from the activity of the whole race working in community; we in our turn must make our art the expression of universal human nature.

The outer man expresses himself to the eye, the inner man to the ear. When he comes to the limit of his utterance by external movement and gesture, there comes to his aid the expression of *vocal tone,* which springs directly from the emotion within the breast.

Speech, again, comes to the aid of vocal tone, making clear and definite and unmistakable what was formerly vague and general.

"*Speech* is the condensation of the element of Voice, and the Word is the crystallised measure of tone. In Speech, feeling conveys itself by ear to feeling, but to that likewise to be condensed and crystallised feeling to which it seeks to bring itself in sure and unmistakable understanding.[1] It is thus the organ of that special feeling which reasons with itself and yearns for others' understanding—the Intellect. For the more vague and general feeling the immediate attributes of Tone sufficed."

As the understanding and its needs have developed, the language of the understanding has grown until it no longer makes any use of the emotional elements afforded it by Tone. It is only in moments of deep feeling, when the particular fades away and man stands face to face with the universal, that he is impelled to seek once more the assistance of Tone and Movement —"borrowing from the emotional man the physical tones of feeling, from the corporeal man the physical gestures of the body." Wishing to express the whole man, he must make use of the organs of expression of the whole man, not relying upon either the understanding singly, or the emotions, or physical gesture. Thus the transition is made from the particular to the universal, from the unit to humanity, from the art-variety to *Art*. Each sense having its limits, the art that springs from each sense must also be limited; thus only Art—the harmonious co-operation of all the senses and all the faculties in the one art-work—is really *free*, the mere single art, or art-variety, being bound by the limitations of the particular sense to which it appeals. Dance, Tone, and Poetry—each of

[1] "In ihr theilt sich das Gefühl durch das Gehör an das Gefühl mit, aber an das ebenfalls zu verdichtende, zu gefestigende Gefühl, dem es sich zum sicheren, unfehlbaren Verständnisse bringen will."

these can express but a fraction of man and nature; only from their union in the art-work comes the expression of the universal instead of the individual.

The failure of the single art-variety may be seen from the history and from the analytic psychology of each art. *Dance* only becomes art when mere spasmodic gesture is controlled by rhythm; but rhythm is the essence of the art of *Tone*. "This other branch of art into which Dance yearns instinctively to pass, therein to find again and know her own true nature, is the art of Tone; which, in its turn, receives the solid scaffold of its vertebration from Dance's rhythm." Tone, again, finds its highest range of definition in speech; and so the one emotion, expressible first by physical movement, passes over from this into Tone, and from this again into Poetry. It is in the Drama that this union of the means of expression takes place—Dance there becoming refined to its noblest form, Mimicry.

"What Speech endeavours to convey, the whole wide range of feelings and emotions, ideas and thoughts, which mount from softest tenderness to indomitable energy, and finally proclaim themselves as naked Will—all this becomes an unconditionally intelligible, unquestioned truth through Mimic Art alone; nay, Speech itself cannot become a true and quite convincing physical utterance without the immediate aid of Mimicry. From this, the Drama's pinnacle, Dance broadens gradually down again to her original domain : where Speech now only hints and pictures ; where Tone, as Rhythm's soul, restricts herself to homage of her sister ; and where the beauty of the body and its movements alone can give direct and needful utterance to an all-dominating, all-rejoicing feeling."

The history of absolute music has been the history of its endeavour to achieve redemption by the power of the Word ; this it attained in Beethoven's Ninth Symphony. On the other hand, Poetry, having broken loose from its union with Dance and Tone, has become

E

mere *literary* Poetry, making no appeal to the actual eye in a stage setting. The Opera of the past was no real union of the arts, but simply an egoistic and constrained association—Dance, Tone, and Word merely stipulating each for its own part in the performance. Only in the dramatic art-work of the future can the three humanistic arts meet in reciprocal self-assertion and surrender—the arts of architecture, sculpture, and painting further co-operating in their own way. But this art-work can only be an *associate* work, called forth by an associate demand. The true Artist of the Future must be the Folk.

Such, in rough outline, are the theories put forward in *Art and Revolution* and *The Art-Work of the Future*. So far as these two works deal with the nature and possibilities of music, poetry, and the drama, the discussion of them may best be postponed until this subject is dealt with *à propos* of *Opera and Drama*.[1] Here it is only necessary to point out such characteristics of the two works now under consideration, as throw light on the peculiarities of Wagner's psychology. That his schemes for a state of society in which art shall hold the foremost place, and be the joint work of associated artists, are wholly visionary, need hardly be insisted upon. He himself seems to have recognised this, though he curiously failed to see the effect of such an admission upon other of his theories. Nothing could more clearly prove Wagner's fundamental incompetence to deal with any but purely musical questions, than the blithe self-confidence with which he undertakes not only to settle some of the most obscure problems of the past, but to shape afresh the vast and complex body of our modern civilisation. A disposition to deal in this jaunty way with huge, vexed problems

[1] See Chapter v.

comes only from inability to appreciate the difficulty of them; and, as might be expected, Wagner's treatment of them is hopelessly *à priori* from start to finish. He cannot write the history of the development of Greek civilisation and art in any other way than as a series of "moments" designed to support his assumptions and preconceptions. He seems to know nothing of the actual causes that led to so wonderful an efflorescence as was seen in the art and philosophy and drama of Athens in her prime; nothing of the vast, obscure forces that made against art in the Dark Ages; and even in his own day he cannot see how deeply rooted are all the evils against which he contends, and how impossible it is to eradicate them by the mere rhetoric of sentiment. It is characteristic of a mind of his order never to look facts squarely in the face, never to try to explain, to feel the need of explaining, any phenomenon in terms of the forces that have brought it into being. A few pseudo-generalisations, a few bogus formulas, an outburst of rhetoric, and all is done. One may sympathise with the artist fighting against the imbecility, the ignorance, the brutishness, the apathy of the world towards all that is beautiful and noble; but social diseases of this kind are no more to be cured by vaporous rhetoric than the epidemics of the Dark Ages were to be cured by the tolling of church-bells. The revolt against the evil is something, but it is merely the beginning of the long fight. One who is not steeped in prepossessions, in absurd rhetorical formulas, recognises that the problems of social regeneration are too vast to be solved by anything but infinite patience and steadfast will and tireless thought. To adopt Wagner's plan of cursing the present, and sketching crude Utopias for the future on the lines of a hopeless misunderstanding of the past, is only to add to the evil of the situation, only to make still deeper and more despairing our sense of the insolubility of prob-

lems so vast as those we are now confronted with.
Above all, to hold up to our admiration the Athenians
of one brief period, and to sigh for a future community
in which art shall be to us what it once was to them,
is only to show one's failure to realise the difficulty of
our problem.   The artistic life of a small town, with a
few thousand people, living upon slave-labour, devoting
a great deal of their time to questions of art and
politics and philosophy, can never be reproduced in
our modern Europe, with its teeming millions strug-
gling for a bare subsistence, and its art mainly dependent upon the patronage of the wealthy.   To say
that all this should *not* be is as useless as it is inexpensive ; and Wagner's fulmination against the dependence
of modern art on the luxury of the rich is empty and
futile.   It is not for the prophets who wander about
shrieking in the mist to change the constitution of
things ; and he who imagines mere vain rhetoric to be
any contribution towards the solution of a huge problem does little more than show his own incompetence.

Hence Wagner's polemic misses the mark, as it
always does.   And not only is he grievously unilluminative on the side of practical sociology, but he is, if
anything, even less a counsel of perfection on the side
of art.   Leaving for a future chapter the consideration
of the main question as to the nature and limits of the
musical drama, it is sufficient to point out here a fact
which will frequently have to be insisted on at a later
stage—that Wagner was almost insusceptible to pleasure from any art but music, and that he was quite
ignorant of everything that made the other arts what
they are.   To me it is the surest sign of the paralysis
with which he seems to have smitten the critical
faculties of his admirers, that his perfectly grotesque
reading of poetry, painting, sculpture, and architecture
should so long have been received in solemn silence
and adoration.   Wagner, as I hope to show in detail,

was a musician and nothing but a musician ; and he
unconsciously looked at every art from that standpoint.
His doctrine of the union of all the arts in the musical-
dramatic art-work was not in any sense a reasoned one.
His disciples have, one and all, been assiduous in pointing out that he did not first think out a scheme of
music-drama, and then proceed to work upon its lines.
They are right ; Wagner's theoretical writings were
indeed, as they insist, but the bringing into the light of
day of principles of procedure that were already implicit in his artistic nature.   But they do not see that
on these terms his æsthetic doctrine is already shorn of
half its value.   It immediately sinks into its proper
place as the work not of a cool and impartial thinker,
guarding against prepossessions, checking himself at
every turn by an appeal to history and to fact, always
on the watch for the snare of the personal equation—
but of a musician born with a certain peculiar mental
constitution, filled through and through with certain
emotions that inevitably led to certain methods of procedure, blindly laying it down that the scheme that was
imperative for him was imperative for all the world.[1]
Nothing stands out more clearly from his prose
works than the fact that he was before everything else
a musician, though his mind was of a slightly more
concrete nature than that of most musicians, and his

[1] Mr. George Bernard Shaw has pointed out, in his *Quintessence of
Ibsenism*, that both Wagner and Ibsen were guided by their artistic intuitions to results they could not have attained to at that time by reason.
That is quite true, and one recognises the value of Wagner's intuitions in
his musical and dramatic practice.   He makes an error, however, in stepping
out of this purely imaginative world into the world of facts and realities.
The very fact that Wagner chooses an argumentative instead of an artistic
mode of expression shows that he is appealing to the reason of men ; and it
is because our reason is outraged by his arguments that we reject them.   No
one denies that Wagner's prose works are merely the expression of the intuitions that made him so great an artist.   The difficulty is that these intuitions, though they led him to the most suitable medium of expression for his
peculiar genius, have no objective truth for us, whose ideas and sensations are
different in essence from his.

inspiration came from less abstract sources than generally set the musical intelligence to work. Even a glance
at some of the leading motives of his music will suffice
to show that the musical current was generally confined
within the banks of a concrete idea. This, indeed, is
one of his chief glories ; it is precisely what makes
him inimitable, unapproachable, distinct from all other
writers for the musical stage. The man who could
imagine, for example, that wonderful Hunding motive
in the *Valkyrie*, with its expressive scoring for the tubas,
must have had a brain unique among musicians—a
brain that imaged to itself the whole essence of the
nature of a character, but saw it in terms of sound
instead of in terms of form and colour. This faculty,
and all that grew out of it, is what lifts Wagner above
all other dramatic composers. But it is still a *musical*
faculty ; in the admission that he had this unique power
of conceiving a character musically, just as a painter
would conceive it pictorially, there is involved the
further admission that such a faculty would make him
insensitive to all other modes of conceiving life. Proof
will, in the course of the present volume, be forthcom-
ing that Wagner was not only primarily a musician,
but a musician of a most peculiar constitution. Granted
that fact, one can readily see how, looking at the world
through such a glass, everything must have been sub-
dued to its colour. From the psychological fact that
he could conceive human character most completely in
terms of music, there necessarily followed the further
fact that he was blind to all other modes of its conception. For him the primitive emotional play of speech
and gesture upon the musical stage, helped out as it
was by the enormously suggestive power of his own
art, was sufficient to express all he knew or wished to
know of life, sufficient to give him every artistic emotion
of which he was capable. Hence his contempt for the
æsthetic emotions afforded to other men by other arts.

To say that sculpture must pass over into the person of the actor—thus being "redeemed" from stone into living flesh ; that when man learns to portray himself vitally upon the musical stage, painting will begin to disappear ; that architecture can have no nobler func- tion than that of designing theatres for the "purely- human" drama ; and that the landscape-painter, instead of painting small canvases for the private house, can employ his powers to the finest purpose by painting scenes for the theatre ; all this is to exhibit the most ludicrous ignorance of what these arts can do, and of the undying elements in human nature to which they appeal. The man who could write thus must have been lacking in most of the artistic nerves with which other men are equipped. No doubt it is to this, to the concentration of all the gigantic nervous energy of his frame upon the one order of impressions and the one faculty of utterance, that we owe the grandeur and the beauty of his work. None the less have we to protest against the foolish attempts of his uncritical admirers to make out these æsthetic perversities to be the flower of æsthetic wisdom. If Wagner was only partially right in his view of the union of poetry, music, and dance in the Greek drama, he was altogether wrong in his account of the development of the single arts, and hopelessly blind to the beauties of each of them as they exist for the modern man.[1] To tell us that we will get them all in the united art-work of the future is the merest trifling. On the face of his own argument it is evident that what we will get, even in the most favoured cases — those of poetry and music—is a limitation of the full power of each

[1] Liszt thought Wagner was "equally sensible to the charms of all the arts" (*Lohengrin et Tannhäuser*, p. 38). The error of this will be shown in greater detail in the next chapter. On the Wagnerian fallacy that his or any other "Art-work" can compensate us for the loss of the individual arts, or is in any way a combination of all the arts just at the point where each feels its own powers failing, see Chapters viii. and ix.

art in favour of the other. Owing to the peculiarly
dominating nature of music, this may not mean a very
great deprivation upon that side; but the lover of poetry
can at the best get only the husks of the art. And
to tell the devotees of sculpture and painting, the
men whose nerves thrill with delight at a thousand
subtle delicacies of effect that can be had only from
these arts—to tell *them* that they must be content with
theatrical scene-painting and the gestures of a singer,
is really too grotesque for serious criticism. Finally,
as for the notion that the world will ever again unite in
its appreciation of the one art, after the fashion of the
Athenians listening on certain days to their drama, one
wonders how any man, even in the pre-evolutionary
days, could be so ignorant of the great forces that are
incessantly making for differentiation in art as in everything else. The notion that fifty million people can
ever be brought back to the social and artistic conditions
that once held good for a few thousand Athenians, is
too much dignified even by the compassionate epithet
of a dream. Some small sense of the reality of things
may reasonably be demanded even of a musician.

One is forced to conclude, from a perusal of the
prose works and letters of this epoch, that Wagner was,
on the whole, unfortunate in his friends. Devotion
they certainly gave him ; but what he needed even
more than this was the uncompromising criticism of
some one of entirely different opinions. This alone
could have opened his eyes to the absurdity of some
of his theses. Such opposition as he had from enemies
served only to confirm him in his most illogical theories ;
for he regarded absolute sympathy with his work and
his ideals as the indispensable prerequisite of a critic.
But one friend whose sympathy he could rely on, who
would have opposed him strenuously from first to last,
making him revise every impression, scrutinise every
assumption, and test each link in the chain of his argu-

ment, would have been able to do him incalculable
service. Such a friend he never seems to have met.
Neither Liszt nor Uhlig appears to have been able to
withstand the torrential fallacies of his writings; and
Roeckel, who seems to have been a man of stronger
and more independent mind, less inclined to bow the
submissive knee to the dictator, probably lacked some
vibration of sympathy, some charm of manner, in
his intercourse with Wagner. It is perhaps in this
way that we can account for the fact that though
Roeckel was a much abler man than either Liszt or
Uhlig, and had known Wagner intimately before
either of them, he never seems to have had much
influence upon the composer's thought. Mr. Chamberlain, in his preface to the English edition of the
Letters to August Roeckel, somewhat strangely puts it
that "Uhlig's cleverness showed itself in nothing more
than in the sagacity with which he gauged the immense
superiority of Wagner's mind over his own" (pp. 15, 16).
From Roeckel, on the other hand, "Wagner looked
for contradiction and discussion . . . nor was he disappointed. Moreover, in the hard school of adversity,
during the dreary years of imprisonment, Roeckel's
mind seems to have acquired a considerable inflexibility,
not to say stubbornness. Wagner pushed on boldly;
once he had admitted the premises, he followed them
out to their ultimate conclusions. Roeckel refused to
follow him" (p. 17). It was no doubt a quality of
Wagner's peculiar brain that he was indocile to intellectual opposition; certainly all that Roeckel's criticism
did was to call forth justificatory expositions of some
of the composer's theories. In no case do the theories
themselves seem to have undergone any modification.[1]

[1] He seems, indeed, only to have sought the society of people who agreed
with him. "In Berlin," he writes in the *Communication to my Friends*, "where
for the rest I was entirely unknown, I received from two persons—a gentleman
and a lady, previously total strangers to me, whom the impressions produced

It was certainly unfortunate that a mind so prone to confident assumption and paralogism as Wagner's should have had no regular fire of criticism from friends at once sympathetic and intelligent. The ordinary critics of the German press made, of course, no effect whatever on him. They did indeed call forth replies from him, but never succeeded in inducing him to modify his opinions. He sighs that he is constantly misunderstood—which as a rule means nothing more than that the critic does not agree with his peculiar views on life and art.

" Only a true artist," he wrote on one occasion to Uhlig, after the publication of *The Art-Work of the Future*—"and he must be a man as well as artist, can understand the matter under discussion ; but no other, not even if he have the best will thereto. Who, for instance, amid our artificial-egoistic handicraft copyings, can possibly grasp the natural attitude of plastic art to direct, pure, human art ? I entirely set aside what a statue-sculptor, or a history-painter, would say to this ;[1] but that even a writer on the æsthetics of art, in other respects well-disposed—who is not working for his daily bread, like the one in the *Deutsche Monatsschrift*—should display such absolute want of thought; that on this subject he should fall into such nonsensical babbling about art as he has done, that is sad. Well, I read the notice of my

---

by the *Flying Dutchman* had made my instant friends—the first definite expression of satisfaction at the new path which I had struck out, and the first exhortation to continue thereon. From that time forward I lost more and more the so-called ' Public ' from my view : the judgment of definite individual human beings usurped, for me, the place of the never to be accurately gauged opinion of the mass, which hitherto—without my own full consciousness—had floated before me in vague outlines, as the object to which I should address myself as poet. The *understanding* of my aim became each day more clearly the chief thing to be striven for, and, to ensure myself this understanding, involuntarily I turned no longer to the stranger *Mass*, but to the individual persons whose moods and ways of thought were familiar to me" (G. S. iv. 282, 283: Ellis, i. 326, 327). Plainly, he wanted friends who would simply see eye to eye with him in all his theories—about the worst kind of friend any artist or literary man could have.

[1] He would, of course, have objected to a sculptor "setting aside" *his* nonsensical views on their respected arts.

last work. Then I went home with K.,[1] read clearly to him and to myself the section relating to the arts of sculpture and of painting; and, although thoroughly disposed to question (*sic*), we both found the turning-point of all human history and art so clearly expressed, and intentionally developed at length, with special emphasis in the section dealing with sculpture, that we were compelled to decide that these critics—who had not even noticed this *important argument*, but only seemed to assume that I, through ignorance, and because I wished to say something about these other kinds of art, had fallen into vagueness and uncertainty —that these critics had misunderstood the whole book, since they looked upon the chief point, insisted on with energy—the downfall of the egoistic-*monumental* in favour of the communistic-*present* with all *its* movements—only as a secondary aberration. At such moments one's hands fall, and one becomes convinced that all talking and writing on the matter is vain and unprofitable." [2]

'Twas ever thus. It never seems to have occurred to Wagner that men could differ from him and still be right; opposition was simply "misunderstanding." [3] One critic in the *Deutsche Allgemeine Zeitung* of 15th January 1850 took exception to Wagner's attempt to employ the ancient Hellenes as social and artistic examples for modern Europe, since the climatic conditions were so different.

"Whence," he wrote, "beneath our northern skies, shall we derive that rapt intoxication of the sense of beauty, which even upon the Ionic horizon did not loom so pure as we are wont to conceive when we sum up the æsthetic life of olden times in the principle of Hellenism? . . . These wailings are fantastic, unfruitful, and can be answered by no kind of Revolution, excepting by that of the whole earth-rind, and a new cycle of the world." [4]

---

[1] *i.e.* Karl Ritter, one of his Zurich friends, son of the Madame Julie Ritter who so generously helped the composer from 1851 to 1856.

[2] Letter 14 to Uhlig; Eng. trans. pp. 50, 51.

[3] See the remarks already made on his attitude to the critics of *Lohengrin*, and (in Chapter vi. of the present volume) his method of meeting Roeckel's criticism of the *Ring*.

[4] Quoted by Mr. Ellis, in the preface to *Art and Climate* (*Prose Works*, i. 250).

Beyond laying down the very obvious dictum that it is
not climatic conditions alone that make great art, and
that it was not in the hot climates of Asia and Africa,
but "on the naked, sea-plashed rocks of Hellas, upon
the stony soil and beneath the scanty shadows of the
olive-trees of Attica," that the cradle of civilisation was
laid—beyond this, Wagner's verbose reply does not
throw much fresh light on the question. He does
nothing more than repeat the fallacies that seemed
fundamental to him—as when he makes his favourite
distinction between Nature and Civilisation :—

"The first thing that strikes us, in glancing at the evolution
of our modern nations, is this : that it has not only most condition-
ally been governed by the influence of *nature*, but quite unconditionally by the confounding and distorting operation of an alien
Civilisation ; that, as a matter of fact, our Culture and Civilisation
have not sprung upwards from the nether soil of Nature, but
have been poured down upon us from above, from the Heaven
of the priests and the *Corpus Juris* of Justinian."

" . . . our whole art is good for nothing because it has had
no origin in our actual being, nor in any harmonic supplementing
of the 'climatic' Nature which surrounds us."

"No, the glory of [our present degeneration] belongs to our
clergy-ridden *Pandect-civilisation*, with all its fine results ; among
which, beside our Industry, our worthless heart-and-soul-con-
founding *art* fills out its seat of honour. For the whole *posse*
must be set down to this Civilisation, in its entire variance with
our nature, and not to any Nature-born *necessity*. Wherefore,
not from that Civilisation, but from the future true and generic
Culture, which shall bear a right relation to our climatic Nature,
will one day also bloom that art-work which is now denied both
breath and air to breathe in, and as to whose peculiar properties
we shall never be able to form a notion until we *Men*, the creators
of that art-work, can conceive ourselves as developed to a rational
concord *with this Nature*."

All this is the merest juvenility. The notions that
"civilisation" is the antithesis of "nature," and that

"national" development ought to take place without fertilisation from other nations, are the crudest blunders of the amateur sociologist [1]—almost too gross to be worth arguing against at this time of day. Even Wagner himself, further on, partly sees that modern life and art are not to be parcelled out into a number of self-existent products.

"But to men," he writes, "who know themselves united in one all-capable species, the natural character of this or that particular climate can no longer set up cramping bounds: to them, as a species at one with itself, the total like-united Nature of this Earth alone can form a confine."

Quite so ; but he does no more than hit upon this point in opposition to the objections of his critic in the *Deutsche Allgemeine Zeitung*. He fails to see the correlative fact that as civilisation develops, "nationalism" in art, in politics, in social life, becomes a factor of diminishing importance ; and that the essence of civilisation is the stimulation of one "national mind" by another. Had he been able to perceive this, we might have been spared a great deal of the absurd heroics, both from himself and from some of his followers, which at a later time were sounded on the topic of the virtues of the "German mind" and the "German nature."

[1] It is of clumsy paralogisms of this kind that Mr. Benjamin Kidd's *Social Evolution* is made up.

CHAPTER V

WAGNER'S THEORY OF MUSIC, POETRY, AND MUSIC-DRAMA

I

THIS is probably the most convenient point for entering upon the discussion of Wagner's theoretical ideas upon poetry and music and their combination in music-drama. Towards the end of 1849, during his exile in Switzerland, he seems to have conceived the idea of putting into connected exposition his reflections upon the arts. Various schemes and titles seem to have suggested themselves to him, and finally in a letter to Uhlig, dated 9th October 1850, we read :—

"My would-be article on opera is becoming rather a voluminous piece of writing, and will perhaps be not much less in size than the *Kunstwerk der Zukunft*. I have decided to offer this writing under the title *Das Wesen der Oper* to J. J. Weber. . . . I have only finished the first half; unfortunately I am now quite hindered from continuing the work." [1]

Two months later he writes again to Uhlig :—

"You would not believe what trouble I give myself with this object, to call forth full understanding from all those who only half understand; yes, even to make myself intelligible to my enemies who do not or will not understand me; and lastly, I rejoice merely because I am always myself coming to a better understanding. My book, which now is to be called *Oper und Drama*, is not yet ready; it will be at least twice as big as the *Kunstwerk der Zukunft*. I have still the whole of December to devote to the conclusion, and then certainly the whole of

[1] Letter 17 to Uhlig; Eng. trans. p. 74.

January for copying and revising. In advance I can only give you
the outline. (1) Exposition of the nature of the opera up to our
time, with the conclusion, 'Music is a reproductive organism'
(Beethoven has used it, as it were, to give birth to melody)—
'therefore a female one.' (2) Exposition of the nature of the
drama from Shakespeare up to the present day; conclusion—'the
poetical sense is a procreative organism, and the poetical purpose
the fertilising seed which only comes with the ardour of love, and
is the stimulus to the fructification of the female organism which
must beget the seed received in love.' (3) (Here *only* I begin.)
'Exposition of the act of reproducing the poetical purpose by
means of perfected tone-speech.' . . . I will still add a diagram;
I am not so sure whether I shall put it into my book."[1]

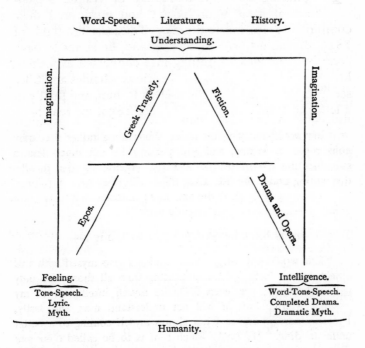

The book was completed about January 1851.

As Wagner mentions in his letter to Uhlig, *Oper*

---

[1] Letter 19 to Uhlig; Eng. trans. pp. 84, 85.

und Drama is divided into three parts—" Opera and the Nature of Music," " The Play and the Nature of Dramatic Poetry," and " Poetry and Music in the Drama of the Future " ; and as it is a tolerably safe surmise that few even of the musical admirers of the musician have read the book, and few of those who have read it have quite understood it, it may be as well to give a short summary of its long argument in a style somewhat less Teutonic than Wagner's own.

1. Until the present time, men have indeed felt that the opera was a monument of the corruption of artistic taste, but criticism has not fully fathomed the matter ; and it therefore becomes the task of the creative artist to practise criticism, in order at once to " crush error and root up criticism." The writer of an article on modern opera in Brockhaus' *Gegenwart* has pointed out the defects of this form of art, showing its artificialities and conventions ; but when he comes to the practical problem, " How is all this to be remedied ? " he can only regret that Mendelssohn's too early death " should have hindered the solution of the riddle." But this is still proceeding on the wrong track. Had Mendelssohn any musical gift which Mozart, for example, did not possess ? Could anything, from the standpoint of music, be more perfect than each individual number of *Don Giovanni?* Plainly the critic cannot wish for better music than this. It is evident, then, that what he wants in opera is the power and force of *drama*. But he is blind enough still to expect this from the *musician;* that is, wanting a house built for him, he applies not to the architect but to the upholsterer. And by the very failure of the critic's effort to solve the problem in this way, there is driven home the conclusion that *this way* the problem is really insoluble. Yet the true solution, so far from being difficult of

attainment, simply stares one in the face; and the formula for it is that—

"The error in the art-genre of Opera consists herein:—*that a Means of Expression (Music) has been made the end, while the End of Expression (the Drama) has been made a means.*"

The truth of this formula can be attested by an appeal to the history of the opera. It arose not from the folk-plays of the Middle Ages, in which there were the rudiments of a natural co-operation of music and drama, but at the luxurious courts of Italy, where the aristocrats engaged singers to entertain them with *arias,* that is, with "folk-tunes stripped of their naïveté and truth," embroidered on a story whose only *raison d'être* was the occasional advent of these arias. Music, in fact, was the all-in-all of opera, as is clearly shown by the old-time domination of the singer; while all the poet had to do was to stand as little as possible in the way of the musician. The great merit of Metastasio, according to the standard of the practice of his own day, was that he almost effaced his own art in favour of music—"never gave the musician the slightest harass, never advanced an unwonted claim from the purely dramatic standpoint." Nor has the situation changed, in its main features, down even to the present day. It still is held to be necessary for the poet to shape his material according to the necessities of the musician from first to last. The whole aim of the opera is simply *music,* the dramatic story being only utilised to serve music as a means for its own display. The anomaly has finally become so fundamental a part of men's lives that they no longer realise that it *is* an anomaly; and accordingly they still have hopes of erecting the genuine drama on the basis of absolute music—that is, of achieving the impossible. The object of *Opera and Drama* is to prove that great artistic results can follow from the collaboration of music with

F

dramatic poetry, while from the unnatural position which music bears towards opera in our present system nothing but sterility can result.

Let us, then, in the first place, consider "Opera and the Nature of Music."

Music has been betrayed into a position where she has lost sight of her own limitations; although in herself she is simply an "organ of expression," she has fallen into "the error of desiring to plainly outline the thing to be expressed." The musical basis of the opera was the *aria*, that is, the folk-song deprived of its own original words, and adapted at once to the vanity of the singer and the luxurious tastes of the world of rank. Aria and dance-tune, with an admixture of recitative, made up an opera, into the musical domain of which the poet was only allowed to enter in order to supply a little narrative cohesion. The significance of the so-called reformation of Gluck has been greatly exaggerated. All he did was to curtail the arrogant pretensions of the singer, while leaving the texture and plan of opera untouched. His was a revolt of the composer fighting merely for his own hand, not for the ends of *drama;* and every means by which he increased the power of music in opera was necessarily a further shackle on the limbs of the poet. Méhul, Cherubini, and Spontini in their turn broadened the old musical forms of opera, and made the musical expression more consonant with that of the words, but did nothing for opera *except* from the standpoint of music. The poet may have had to provide a slightly better and firmer groundwork for the musician, but it was to the musician, and to him alone, that he still owed his existence in opera. People failed to see that the source of regenerative power could be nowhere but in the drama; and the trouble was that music tried by itself to perform the functions of drama, to be a "content" instead of mere "expression."

Mozart, again, was so entirely a musician that his

work throws the clearest light on the relations of musician and poet; and we find him unable to write at his best where the poem was flat and meaningless. He could not write music for *Tito* like that of *Don Giovanni*, or for *Cosi fan tutte* like that of *Figaro*. He, the most absolute of all musicians, would long ago have solved the operatic problem had he met the proper poet. This poet he was never fortunate enough to meet; all his "poets" did was to give him a medley of arias, duets, and *ensembles* to set to music. But the flood of beauty and expression which Mozart poured into opera was too great for that narrow bed; the stream overflowed into wider and freer channels, until it became a mighty sea in the symphonies of Beethoven.

The aria was a degeneration of the folk-song, in which poetry and music had been spontaneously one. The operatic aria was the *music* of the folk-song, arbitrarily wrested from the words, and made to serve the indolent pleasure of the man of luxury. In course of time people forgot that a word-stave should by rights go with the melody. It was Rossini who took this artificial flower, drenched it with manufactured perfume, and gave it the semblance of life. Rossini saw that the life-blood of ordinary opera was melody—"naked, ear-tickling, absolute-melodic melody." Spontini erred in imagining the "dramatic tendency" to be the essence of opera; the real essence, as Rossini showed, and as the future history of opera proves, was simply absolute melody.

Earnest composers, however, while by no means negating the claims of melody, held that Rossini's melody was cheap and superficial, and endeavoured to derive it more directly from the fountains of expression of the Folk. This was the course taken by Weber, who gave opera-aria the deep and genuine feeling of the folk-song; though the flower, thus torn from its native meadow, could not thrive in the *salons* of modern luxury and artificiality. And Weber, no less than Rossini, made his melody the main factor of opera, though of course it was far worthier and more honest than the melody of the Italian composer. Weber repressed and controlled the poet of *Der Freischütz* as much as Rossini did the poet of *Tancredi*. And Weber's failure proves afresh the assertion that instead of the drama being taken up into the being of music, *music must be taken up into the drama*.

Weber's success in harking back to the Folk was envied by the composers of other nationalities, and a number of operas were produced which tried to proceed on similar lines—such as *Masaniello* and *William Tell*. The Folk, in fact, was exploited, but its real inspiration could not, from the very nature of the case, be embodied in opera. In the epic and the drama the Folk celebrated the deeds of the Hero, and in true drama the action and the character are recognised as *necessary;* but under the influence of the modern State, dramatic characters lose their personality and become mere masks. This was particularly the case in opera, where the folk-song has degenerated into the aria, and the Folk itself has become the Mass, the Chorus. "Historic" opera became the fashion, and even Religion was dragged upon the stage, as in the operas of Meyerbeer. But the outlandishness thus imported into opera in its turn led to worse and worse degeneration ; and the "historic" mania became "hysteric" mania— in other words, Neo-romanticism.

Up to this time, every influence that had shaped the course of opera had come from the domain of absolute music alone. After Rossini, operatic melody was varied by the introduction of instrumental melody. People had not perceived that instrumental music was also unfruitful, by reason of its not expressing the purely-human in the form of definite, individual feelings.

"That the expression of an altogether definite, a clearly-understandable individual Content, was in truth impossible in this language that had only fitted itself for conveying the general character of an emotion—*this* could not be laid bare, before the arrival of that instrumental composer with whom the longing to speak out such a content first became the consuming impulse of all his artistic fashioning."

It was the function of Beethoven to show what music can do if it confines itself to its true sphere, that of *expression*. In his later works, Beethoven, having his mind filled with a definite content, burst the bounds of many of the old absolute forms, and stammered through tentative new ones. Future symphonists followed him from this point, without seeing *what* it was in Beethoven that made him act in this way; they consequently mis-applied his forms, copying the externals only. Hence the vogue of programme-music, of which the great re-presentative was Berlioz. Then there came an influx of the wealth of instrumental music (developed inde-pendently of vocal music) into operatic melody. This is modern *characteristique*, of which Meyerbeer, the cos-mopolitan Jew, is the great example, and which differs from that of Gluck and Mozart in that the poet is infinitely more degraded, and absolute melody more exalted. This held good even in Paris, where the poet had always hitherto had *some* rights; but now Meyer-beer forced Scribe, his librettist, to run wherever he chose to drive him. The secret of his music is "Effect." Yet even Meyerbeer wrote fine music where he allowed the poet to guide him—as in parts of the great love-scene in the fourth act of *Les Huguenots*.

To sum up, then, Music has tried *to be the drama*, and the attempt has ended in impotence. The only salvation for it lies in sensible co-operation with the poet. This may be seen by a glance at the nature of our present music. The most perfect expression of the inner being of music is melody; it is to harmony and rhythm what the external side of the organism is to the internal. Now the Folk's melodies were a revelation of the nature of things. Christianity, however, with its anxiety to lay bare the soul, found itself face to face not with life but death; and the Folksong, the indivorcible union of poetry and music, almost died out. In the ages of human mechanism the longing of things was to produce the real man, which man "was really none other than Melody, *i.e.* the moment of most definite, most convincing utterance of [Music's] actual, living organism." The struggle of Beethoven's great works is the struggle of mechanism to become a man, an organism, uttering itself in melody. Thus while other composers merely took melody, ready-made, from the mouth of the Folk, and applied it to their own purposes, Beethoven's melody was the spontaneous effort of Music's inner organism to find expression. But it was only in the verbal outburst of the Ninth Symphony that Beethoven brings melody to true life; music was sterile until fertilised by the poet. The error had always been that operatic melody, coming as it did from the Folksong, ran on certain rhythmical and structural lines, out of which the musician could not stray; so that melody had no chance to be born spontaneously out of poetry, for the poet had simply to adapt his words to the invariable musical scaffolding. "*Every musical organism is by its nature a womanly;* it is merely a *bearing,* and not a *begetting* factor; the begetting force lies clean *outside it,* and without fecundation by this force it positively cannot bear." In the Choral Symphony Beethoven had to call in the poet to fertilise absolute music; and the folly of the latter is seen in its attempts not only to bear but also to beget. "*Music is a woman,*" whose nature is to surrender in love. Who now is to be the Man to whom this surrender is to be made? Let us look at *the Poet.*

2. When Lessing tries to mark out the boundaries of poetry and painting in the *Laocöon*, he has in his eye descriptive, literary poetry, not "the *dramatic Art-work* directly brought before the senses by physical performance." Now the literary poem is an artificial art, appealing to the imagination instead of to the senses. All the egoistically severed arts, indeed, appeal only to the force of imagination. They "*merely suggest;* an *actual representation* would to them be possible only could they parley with the universality of man's artis tic receptivity, could they address his entire sentient (*sinnlichen*) organism, and not his force of imagination; for the true Art-work can only be engendered by an advance from imagination into actuality, *i.e.* physicality (*sinnlichkeit*)." There should be no *arts*, there should be *one veritable Art.* It is an error to look upon Drama as merely a *branch of literature;* although it is true that our drama is no more true Drama than a single musical instrument is an orchestra.

The modern drama has a twofold origin — in Romance, and in the Greek drama; the flower of the former being Shakespeare—of the latter, Racine. Our dramatic literature hovers undecidedly between these two extremes. The romance was not the portrayal of the complete man; this only became possible in drama, which actualised life, presented it visibly to the senses. Shakespeare "condensed the narrative romance into the drama"—made it, that is, suitable for stage representation. The great characteristic of his art was that human actions did not come before us merely in descriptive poetry, but by the actors addressing themselves directly to the actual eye; and the poet had to narrow down the diversity of the old Folk-stage to suit the scenic and other demands of the theatre. The action and the characters had to be made more definite, more individual, more circumstantial, in order to give the spectators the impression of an artistic whole. The appeal, in short, was no longer to Phantasy but to Sense, the only domain left to phantasy being *the imagining the scene itself*—for the stage-craft of those days fell short of actually *representing* reality. This mixture of phantasy and sense in the drama was the source of endless future confusion in dramatic art; the giving-up to phantasy of the representation of the scene left an open door in drama through which romance and history might pass in and out at pleasure.

In the French drama, outward unity of scene determined the whole structure of the play, diminishing the part played by action, and increasing the function of "mere delivery of speeches." For the same reason, the French dramatists could not choose for representation the romance, with its bewildering multiplicity of incident; they had to fall back on the already condensed plots which they found in Greek mythology. Instead of dealing with his own people's life, then, as Shakespeare had tried to do, the French tragedian merely imitated the finished Greek drama. This unnatural, artificial world was reproduced in French opera, and most saliently in the French opera of Gluck.

"Opera was thus the premature bloom on an unripe fruit grown from an unnatural, artificial soil. With what the Italian and French Drama *began*, to wit the outer form, to that must the newer drama first attain by organic evolution from within, upon the path of Shakespeare's Drama; then first will ripen, also, the natural fruit of Musical Drama."

German dramatic art found itself between the Shakespearian play on the one side and the scenic Southern opera on the other—between the appeal to hearing, aided slightly by phantasy in the representation of the scene, and the appeal to the eye alone. There were two final courses open: either, as Tieck suggested, to act Shakespeare with no more scenery than was employed in Shakespeare's own theatre, or to represent each change of scene in the plays—that is, employ the gigantic apparatus of scenic opera. The result to the modern poet was perplexity and disillusion. The play was neither literature—as it was when men merely read it, allowing their phantasy to represent the scene— nor actual, visualised drama. Hence he either wrote plays simply to be read, not to be acted, or, if he wrote for the stage, he employed the reflective type of drama, whose modern origin we have traced to the pseudo-antique drama, constructed according to Aristotle's rules of unity. These results and tendencies are exhibited in Goethe and Schiller. Goethe, after various experiments, found expression in *Faust*, which makes no pretence of stage-representation, and which is therefore really neither romance nor drama. *Faust* is "the watershed between the mediæval *romance* . . . and the real *dramatic matter* of the future." Schiller was always perplexed by the contradiction between history and drama. The whole dilemma is this. On the one side are romance and history, with all their multiplicity of character and action ; on the other is the ideal dramatic form, pre-senting a simple, definite action, and real, moving characters, visibly to the eye ; and a compromise has to be effected between these two. The plain truth is " that we have no Drama, and can have no Drama ; that our Literary-drama is every whit as far removed from the genuine Drama, as the pianoforte from the symphonic song of human voices ; that in the Modern Drama we can arrive at the production of poetry only by the most elaborate devices of literary mechanism, just as on the pianoforte we only arrive at the produc-tion of music through the most complicated devices of technical mechanism—in either case, however, a soul-less poetry, a toneless music." With *this* drama true music can have nothing to do.

Man, conceiving the external world, is impelled to reproduce his conceptions in art, in a mode that shall be intelligible to others. This has only been thoroughly done once—in the expression of the Greek world-view in the Greek Drama. The material of this drama was the myth—the Folk's mode of condensation of the pheno-mena of life—" the poem of a life-view in common." The Christian myth was concerned with death where the Greek had been concerned with life. It could therefore be painted or described, but not *represented* in drama. The Germanic myth was like the Greek, in its essence a religious intuition, a life-view in common ; but Christianity laid hold of it and dispersed it into fragments of fable and legend—the Romance of the Middle Ages. What the artist had to do was to find *Man* under all this *débris*. Now whereas the drama selects an action from a mass of actions, and limits the surroundings to just so much as will illuminate and justify this action, the romance has to enter circumstan-tially and at great length into the surrounding circum-stances, in order to make the action and the character artistically convincing. The drama goes from within outwards, the romance from without inwards ; the drama lays bare the organism of mankind, the romance shows us merely the mechanism of history ; the art-procedure in drama is organic, in romance merely mechanical ; the drama gives us the man, the romance the citizen ; the drama exhibits the fulness of human nature, the romance the penury of the State. In the evolution that has gone on since the Middle Ages, Burgher-society has come uppermost ; but it offers nothing to romance but unloveliness. Everything in life is being disintegrated past the capacity of art to reunite it ; the poet's art has turned to politics, and until we have no more politics the poet cannot come to light again. As Napoleon said, the rôle of Fate in the ancient world is filled in the modern by politics ; and this is what we shall have to comprehend before we can discover the true content and form of drama.

Now the myth is true for all time, and its content forever inexhaustible. Understanding it well, we see in it "an intelligible picture of the whole history of mankind, from the beginnings of society to the inevitable downfall of the State." The political State lives on the vices of society ; salvation and art are only to be found in the free, purely-human individual. The essence of the State is *caprice*, of the free individual, *necessity*. It is then essential for us to annul the State and create afresh the free individual. The poet who tried to portray this individual found that he was face to face with him *only as he had been shaped by the State ;* he could not then portray him, but only imagine him ; could only represent him to thought, not to feeling. Our drama, in consequence, has been forced to make its appeal to the *understanding*, instead of the *feeling*. Out of the mass of man's modern surroundings the poet has to reconstruct the individual, and present him to feeling, to sense, instead of to understanding. But this the poet cannot do ; he can only address the understanding, and that through the organ of understanding, "abstract and conditioned word-speech." "The return from understanding to feeling will be the march of the drama of the future, in so far as we shall advance from the *thought-out* individuality to the genuine one." By the annihilation of the State, society will realise its purely-human essence, and determine the free individual. And it is only in the most perfect art-work, the drama, that the poet's insight into life can find complete expression, because this drama will address not the understanding, but the feeling, through the senses. It will present the poet's view of life physically to the eye ; it will be a true *emotionalising of the intellect*. It must present things to us in such a manner that we cannot help realising their necessity. This can only be done by avoiding the by-paths of the intellect, and by appealing directly to the feeling. The *action*, then, must be so chosen as to make this appeal instinctively. Now an historic action, or one "which can only be vindicated from the standpoint of the State," is only representable to the understanding, not to the feeling; that is, by its very multiplicity and lack of warmth it cannot be seized definitely and quickly by the senses, but needs the combining function of thought. The true dramatic "action" must be seen at once to be the essential centre of the periphery of circumstance. Man and nature, as cognised by the understanding, are split up into fragments; it is the *feeling* that grasps the organic unity of things; and it is from this point *outwards* that the true drama must work. In other words, it must be generated from the *myth*.

Up to a certain point the intellect can work in the selection of material, and express itself through its own organ, word-speech; but for the full *realisation* of the action and the motives to the feeling, the organ of feeling—tone-speech—has to be called in. "Tone-speech is the beginning and end of word-speech; as the feeling is beginning and end of the understanding, as mythos is beginning and end of history, the lyric beginning and end of poetry." The lyric "holds within itself each germ of the intrinsic art of poetry, which necessarily can but end with speaking out the vindication of the lyric; and this work of vindication is precisely the highest human art-work, the *Entire Drama*."

The primal organ of utterance of the inner man is tone-speech, the fundamental nature of which may be seen by removing the consonants from our word-speech. The latter came by the addition of prefixes and suffixes to the open sound, as distinguishing and delimiting signs of objects. In this way speech-roots were formed from the primal melody of tone-speech. In alliteration, or *stabreim*, speech, by combining these roots according to similarity and kinship, "made plain to the feeling both the impression of the object and its answering expression, in equal measure, through an increased strengthening of that expression," ; showed, that is, the unity in multiplicity of the object. By *stabreim* in poetry the similarity of sound to the ear brings a collective image to the feeling. The *stabreim* and the word-verse were fundamentally conditioned by that melody which, is the expression of primal human feeling, because the breathing-conditions of man's organism determined the duration and segmentation of the utterance. When poetry developed along the line of the understanding instead of that of the feeling, word-speech became dissociated from its sister, tone-speech ; and having lost the instinctive sense of this bond, tried to find "another bond of union with the melodic breathing-snatches." This was done in the *end-rhyme*, which was the sign of forgetfulness of the natural bond of tone-speech and word-speech in the *stabreim*. This line of degeneration ended in "the grey morass of prose" ; and the separation from the feeling was complete. We go now upon convention instead of upon conviction. We cannot properly express our emotions in this language, for in it we can only speak to the understanding, not to the feeling ; which is why the feeling "has sought a refuge from absolute intellectual-speech by fleeing to absolute tone-speech—our music of to-day."

The poet, then, cannot realise his aim in modern speech, because he cannot speak directly to the feeling. Yet he must not simply work out his drama on the lines of the understanding, and then try to add expression to it by means of music. *This was the error of opera.* The emotional expression itself must *also* be governed by the poetical aim. "*A tone-speech to be struck-into from the outset* is therefore the organ of expression proper for the poet who would make himself intelligible by turning from the understanding to the feeling, and who for that purpose has to take his stand upon a soil on which alone he can have any commerce with feeling." We must go back, in fact, to the *ur-melodic* faculty, to which is given the expression of the purely-human ; the drama must utter itself in a form that shall be the marriage of understanding and feeling, of word-speech and tone-speech.

3. Until now the poet has tried in two ways to attune the organ of the understanding—word-speech—to an emotional expression which would find its way to the feeling ; through *rhythm* and through *melody*. It was a mistake to try to import the rhythms of Greek verse into modern poetry, for these rhythms were conditioned by the gestures of the dance, and the dislocation of the speaking-accents was atoned for by melody. Our modern languages not being adapted to this ruling into longs and shorts, Greek prosody is impossible for us. Our iambic verse, for example, hobbles along mechanically, "doing grievous violence to the live accent of speech for the sake of this monotonous rhythm." "Longs" become "shorts" and "shorts" become "longs," simply to get the requisite number of feet into the line. On the other hand, where, as among the Romanic peoples, this kind of rhythm is not in vogue, the *end-rhyme* has been imported into poetry, and has become indispensable. The whole line is built up with reference to this end-rhyme, as the up-stroke to the down-stroke. The result is that the attention of the ear is only momentarily won, and the poet does not reach the *feeling*, for all he does is to make understanding speak to understanding.

We have seen that word-speech and melody have gone along divergent lines of development, and now neither can be properly applied to the other. Even where, as in Gluck's music, the composer tries to find a bond of union in the speaking-accent of the word-speech, his selection of this mere rhetorical accent leads to a disintegration of the rest of the line *as poetry ;*

it becomes dissolved into prose, and the melody itself becomes merely musical prose. The usual course is for the melody to do what it likes with the verse; to dislocate its rhythm, ignore its accents, and drown its end-rhyme, according to its own pleasure. The poet ought really to " so employ the speaking accent as the only measure-giving ' moment' for his verse, that in its symmetrical return it should establish a wholesome rhythmos, as necessary to the verse itself as to the melody." Instead of this, we find on the one hand that many of Goethe's verses are declared too beautiful to be set to music, while on the other hand Mendelssohn writes *Songs without Words*.

We shall have to deal with speech as we dealt with action and the content of the drama. Just as we took away from the action all that was extraneous and accidental; just as we took away from the content all that savoured of the State or of history, in order to reach simply the purely-human; so we must " cut away from the verbal expression all that springs from . . . these disfigurements of the purely-human and feeling-bidden," so that only the purely-human core shall remain. Thus we shall arrive " at the natural basis of rhythm, in the spoken verse, as displayed in the *liftings and lowerings* of the accent," which in turn can only find full expression when intensified into musical rhythm. The strong and weak accents must correspond to the " good " and "bad " halves of the musical bar. We must reach back through the understanding and its organ to " the sensuous substance of our *roots of speech*"; we must breathe the breath of life into the defunct organism of speech. This breath is music. The roots of words were brought into being by the Folk's primal emotional stress; the essence of these roots is the open sound, which finds fullest sensuous uplifting in music; while the function of the consonants is to determine the general expression to a particular one. The *stabreim* indicates to the feeling the unity of sensation underlying the roots—shows their emotional kinship. It appeals, as it were, to the " eye " of hearing, while the vowel is addressed to the " ear " of hearing. And as a man only reveals himself fully to us by addressing both eye and ear, so " the message-bearer of the inner man cannot completely convince our hearing, until it addresses itself with equal persuasiveness to both ' eye and ear ' of this hearing. But this happens only through *word-tone-speech*, and poet and musician have hitherto addressed but half the man apiece : the poet turned towards this hearing's eye alone, the musician only to its ear." The musician will take the vowel-sounds of the poet, and display their fundamental kinship by giving them their full emotional value by means of musical tone. Here then the word-poet ends, and the tone-poet begins. The melody of the musician is " the redemption of the poet's endlessly - conditioned thought into a deep - felt consciousness of emotion's highest freedom." This was the melody that rose from Beethoven's Ninth Symphony to the light of day.

When Beethoven wrote the simple melody with which he accompanies the *"Freude, schöner Götterfunken,"* he was writing as an absolute musician. This melody " did not arise *from out* the poem of Schiller but rather was invented outside the word-verse and merely spread above it." But in the " *Seid umschlungen Millionen,"* and the *"Ahnest du den Schöpfer, Welt?"* he obeys the dictates of the poetic aim, and the broadening of the key-kinship leads the feeling back to the purely-human.

The kinship of feeling which the poet can only approximately express by the *stabreim*, the musician can bring to full expression by key-modulation. Take, for example, the line *"Liebe giebt Lust zum Leben."* The one emotion being expressed throughout, the musician would keep in one key. When setting " *Die Liebe bringt Lust und Leid,"* however, the change of feeling at the

end of the line would be expressed by a modulation ;
while if this line were followed by "*Doch in ihr Weh
auch webt sie Wonnen,*" at the *webt* a modulation would
be effected back into the original key.   It is from this
poetico-musical "*period*" that the true art-work, the
perfected drama, must take its rise.

Melody is the horizontal surface of harmony ; and
in harmony "the ear . . . obtains an entire fulfilling
—and thus a satisfying—of its sensory faculty, and
thereafter it can devote itself with the necessary com-
posure to [an appreciation of] the melody's apt emotional expression."   But harmony in absolute music
has existed solely for and in itself ; whereas the melody
ought to be conditioned by the speaking-verse, and the
concurrent harmony be used for making this obvious to
the feeling.

In the drama of the future there must be no characters whose only function is to swell the harmonic
volume of sound ; there must only be such characters
as are essential *in themselves* to the plot.   The chorus,
then, "as hitherto employed in opera, . . . will have to
be banished from our drama."   Neither the chorus nor
the main characters "are to be used by the poet as a
symphonic body of musical tones for bringing to light
the harmonic stipulations of the melody."   The musician,
however, possesses an organ which can make plain the
harmony and characterise the melody in a far superior
way to that of the vocal-mass.   This organ is the orchestra, which is an immense aid in the realisation of the
poetic aim.   Until now the error has consisted in writing *absolute* melody in opera—melody, that is, which
was conditioned by the orchestra itself, not by the
word-verse, and which was therefore only "vocal"
melody in the sense that it was given to the voice.   It
ought really to come from "an announcement of the
purely emotional content of the verse, through a dissolution of the vowel into the musical tone " ; the verse

G

melody in this way becoming the mediator and bond of union between word-speech and tone-speech, the offspring of the marriage of poetry and music.

The great value of the orchestra is its power of uttering the *unspeakable*, *i.e.* that which is unutterable through the organ of the understanding. It may do this in three ways—by its organic alliance with *Gesture*, by bringing up the *remembrance* of an emotion, when the singer is not giving voice to it, and by giving a *foreboding* of moods as yet unspoken.

All the constituents of the drama have now been enumerated. It only remains to consider how they are to be knit together into a single form corresponding to the single substance. Just as the poet obtained his action by compressing all the motives into an easily comprehended content, so, for the realisation of this action, must he proceed with the composition on the same principles. The expression, like the action, must be free from the accidental, the contingent, the superfluous.

We approach the drama in a mood of expectancy, that is ministered to by the orchestra in its quality of a producer of foreboding—although this preliminary utterance of the orchestra must by no means be interpreted to mean the ordinary overture. This expectancy is afterwards satisfied by the word-speech of the performer, lifted into the higher emotional sphere of tone-speech. The unity of content in the drama must be made evident in a unity of artistic expression ; that is, the expression "must convey to the feeling a wide-reaching aim of the poetic understanding." Wherever the word-speech approaches the language of ordinary life—the organ of the understanding—the orchestra must keep the expression still on the higher plane, by means of its faculty of conveying foreboding or remembrance. Yet it must assume this function not through the mere caprice of the musician, but in obedience only to the poet's aim. Unity of content and unity of expression must go hand in hand. These melodic moments of the orchestra will take their rise only from *the weightiest motives of the drama*, which are the pillars of the edifice. In this way a binding principle of musical form may be obtained which springs directly from the poetic aim, and far surpasses the arbitrary, *merely musical* form of the old opera, which was loose, uncentralised, and inorganic.

Finally let us ask, " Has the poet to *restrict* himself in presence of the musician, and the musician in presence of the poet ? " The answer is that they ought not to restrict each other, but raise each other to higher potency, in order thus to generate the true drama. If both the poet's aim and the musician's expression are visible, the necessary inspiration of each by each has not been effected. We must not be reminded of either aim or expression, " but the content must instinctively engross us as a human action vindicated 'necessarily' before our feeling." In every moment of the musician's expression the poetic aim must be contained ; and this poetic aim must always find complete realisation in the musician's expression. Whereas Voltaire said, "When a thing is too silly to be said, one sings it," we now may say, "What is not worth being sung is not worth the poet's pains of telling."

There is no need to assume that poet and musician must necessarily be one person. Only in the present egoistic relations of these two—who are types of the egoism of the modern State—does it seem necessary for one man to become the unit of creation.

Three nations—the Italians, French, and Germans —have contributed to the evolution of opera ; but the German language alone " still hangs directly and conspicuously together with its roots," and hence is alone adapted for the new art-work. But the practice of singing operas with German words merely translated from the French or Italian, and therefore not coinciding in meaning and accent with the music, has mis-educated and demoralised German singers. In *our* drama, the melody is always conditioned by the word-verse, and singers must learn to render it intelligently, bringing out not merely the melody but the *verbal sense* of the melody. And gesture must be employed with intelligent understanding, in order to make the orchestral moments of foreboding and remembrance[1] in their turn intelligible. But the primary condition for this new drama is a new public, that shall look at it seriously, as at an organism; that wants an artwork and not a mere evening's distraction. We are less fortunate than the older artists, whose audience, whatever its social faults may have been, had at least delicacy and high breeding; whereas we are ruled by the vulgar and ignorant Philistine, the characteristic product of our commercial civilisation. Yet even under the *débris* of modern life the artist can see the primal source of things, can reach to the *human being*, to whom the future belongs.

II

Now it seems necessary at the outset to point out one main fallacy in Wagner's treatise, which seems to have been overlooked by most of his admirers, but which is fatal to a good half of his argument. The dictum on which he bases the first part of his book is that "The error in the Art-genre of opera lies herein, *that a means of expression (Music) has been made the end, while the end of expression (the Drama) has been made a means.*" And he proceeds to lay down the, in the main, indisputable fact, that in the opera of the past the poet existed solely for the musician.

"Has this relation of the poet to the musician," he continues, "altered in the slightest even to the present day? . . . The

---

[1] That is, in modern phrase, the "leading-motives."

chief characteristic of the situation . . . is to-day what it was a hundred and fifty years ago; that the poet must receive his inspiration from the musician, that he shall listen to the whims of music, accommodate himself to the disposition of the musician, choose his material according to the latter's taste, mould his characters by the different kinds of voices expedient for merely musical combinations, provide dramatic bases for certain set musical forms, in which the musician may wander as he chooses —in short, that in his subordination to the musician he shall construct his drama with a single eye to the specifically musical intentions of the composer. . . . The aim of opera has thus ever been, and still is to-day, confined to music. Merely so as to afford music with a colourable pretext for her own *excursions* (*Ausbreitung*) is the purpose of Drama *dragged on*—naturally, not to curtail the ends of music, but rather to serve her simply as a *means*." [1]

In his polemic against the place of undue importance which music usually took in the opera, Wagner is of course right. Even in the eighteenth century sensible men were revolted at the imbecility of the stories of operas, the weakness of the libretti, and the extraordinary liberties which composers and singers allowed themselves. But the recognition of this is by no means equivalent to accepting Wagner's great formula, that "a means of expression (music) has been made the end, while the end of expression (the drama) has been made a means." The whole fallacy lies in the use of the word "drama," *which does not and cannot mean, in relation to music, what it always has meant in relation to poetry;* that is, the word drama has always meant a spoken play, involving certain intellectual processes, and designed to produce a certain psychological effect,[2] whereas in any combination of words and music

[1] G. S. iii. 232, 233; Ellis, ii. 19.

[2] We need not pause to consider how much in the Greek drama was spoken, and how much sung, or what was the precise relation of the musical mood to the poetical. We are not living in ancient Greece but in modern Europe, and as Wagner's use of the word "music" implies not ancient but modern music, so when he speaks of drama it is to the drama of modern Europe that he must be held to refer.

there is a change from the spoken drama both in the character of the words employed, the extent to which they can appeal to us, and the æsthetic nature of the final effect. It is evident at once, in a word, that if Wagner is going to use the term *drama* as equivalent to *musical drama*, so much of his argument as depends upon this confusion of terms is flawed at the very foundations.

Palpable as this fallacy seems to be, however, I cannot recall the name of a single Wagnerian who has noticed it. All have followed him uncritically in accepting his formula,[1] and arguing upon it, as Wagner himself has done, by means of thoroughly false analogies. Thus one French admirer writes—

"We shall see in the course of this study that Wagner's reform bears not on the musical side but on the whole economy of the opera. . . . By intuition he has re-established the lyrical drama on a rational basis by making the poet dominant there, just as the architect is dominant in the erection of a house. And herein he was perfectly logical, since the poet, like the architect, ought to control and resume in himself all those who concur in putting the material into shape."[2]

Surely it is evident that on the face of the case the proper analogy to an architect planning the form of a house is the poet planning the scheme of a drama, or the musician planning the scheme of a symphony; and that in a combination of two arts like poetry and music, equally powerful in their respective spheres, it is folly to speak of the poet as being "dominant." Wagner and his disciples have, in fact, in their revolt against the domination of the musician, fallen into precisely the opposite error.[3] A musical drama in which, as M.

[1] See, for example, besides the names and works cited in the text, Edmond Hippeau, *Parsifal et l'Opéra Wagnérien*, p. 25.

[2] J. G. Freson, *L'Esthétique de Richard Wagner*, i. 12, 13.

[3] Theoretically, that is, for I hope to show that Wagner's practice does not always conform to his theory. Further, as will appear later on, the critics

Freson has it, the poet should be master, or in which, according to Wagner, the drama should be the end, would be as inartistic a monstrosity as the older opera in which the musician was dominant (in the worst sense), and music an end instead of a means.

An abler critic than M. Freson, indeed, has fallen into the same error. M. Georges Noufflard, in his exceedingly thoughtful study of Berlioz, has pointed out with great clearness the difference between the art of the *ancien régime* and modern art—the former having "its distinctive character in the search for an interesting form that should be ornamental in itself," the latter tending to substitute for a form agreeable in itself, but more or less conventional, the forms of things themselves; the difference being clearly marked, for example, in the transition from the symphony and oratorio of Haydn to the opera of Wagner and his more intellectual contemporaries. The period of transition, he remarks,

"Is necessarily longer and more laborious in music than in any other art, for besides the difficulties of a general order which all have to contend with, music has to meet certain difficulties which are peculiar to it. I have already said that music is an ornamental art like architecture. Its expression, so superior to any other in intensity, has not sufficient clearness to be able to command its own forms. The different parts of a composition would not hold together if they were not united by the bond afforded by the balancing of tonalities and the symmetrical repetition of the figures. Thus, then, in order to constitute an artistic unity with its own resources, music is obliged to dispose itself in an ornamental fashion. Singular art! By its inner nature it is an expression more lively and more subtle than speech; by the forms in which it has to clothe itself in order to exist, it is only an ornamental art like arabesque—nothing more. It resembles

who think they are expounding Wagner's ideas in passages like that quoted above from M. Freson, are really mistaking the psychological significance of some of his theories.

the human soul, which seems to be made for a more immaterial life than that permitted it by the body in which it is imprisoned, but without which it cannot live. To free itself from it, our soul must find in another world the conditions of a new life. In the same way, in order that music may rid itself of its architectural envelope and abandon itself entirely to the need of expression with which it is possessed, it is indispensable that it should seek in another world the organs necessary to a new existence; it must incarnate itself in poetry, which, being alone capable of determining its expression, becomes its necessary form as soon as, in order to obey the sentiment entirely, music ceases to have a form of its own." [1]

Most of this, of course, no one will dispute. But M. Noufflard, under the influence of the Wagnerian theory, goes on to argue that when two arts are associated, it suffices if *one* of them has a definite form.

"Music paints the sentiments and speech defines them. The first place must then be given to music or to poetry, according as the sentiment in itself or the circumstances which direct it are of the greater importance. That is to say, lyric poetry ought to be dominated by music, while dramatic music ought to be dominated by poetry." [2]

I venture to suggest that only the influence of the Wagnerian fallacy could have led M. Noufflard into such a fallacy as this. Is there, in the first place, any such division between drama and lyric as he appears to allege? Do not, that is to say, many lyrics that have been set to music partake of the dramatic form and expression, and are there not in any musical drama many passages that can only be called lyrical? What is the distinction? Where does lyrism, in relation to music, end, and drama begin? What are the signs by which we can distinguish one from another? M. Noufflard has, in fact, fallen into the trap of Wagner. He

[1] Noufflard, *Hector Berlioz et le Mouvement de l'Art contemporain*, pp. 14, 15.   [2] *Ibid.*, p. 17.

has used the words poetry and drama without noticing that these terms do not and cannot mean, in relation to music, precisely what they mean in their ordinary connotation. That this is so is evident from the contradiction in which M. Noufflard is landed only a page further on. He has laid it down, like Wagner, that in the drama music should be controlled and directed, and its form determined, by poetry. Yet he goes on to say that—

"It is necessary that the dramatic action should be motived and constantly determined; the first place then ought here to belong to the words. *Doubtless the poet ought to penetrate himself with the sentiment of the music sufficiently to write nothing that is not congruous with the intervention of music; but finally, as Gluck has said* (without, as a matter of fact, always putting it into practice), *it is for poetry to trace the outline which the musician has only to colour.*" [1]

Self-contradiction surely could not further go. How in the name of consistency can poetry be said to dominate music in opera, to determine the form which music must assume, if its own form has to be modified in order to suit the music; and if the poet thus draws his outline to suit the colour of the musician, how can it be argued that all the musician has to do is to colour the outline afforded by the poet? The reference to Gluck is doubly vain. Gluck, as I have attempted elsewhere to show in detail, laid such stress upon the function of poetry simply because he belonged to an age when poetry was relatively more developed than dramatic music; [2] and further, nothing could be more contradictory than Gluck's theory and practice, except, perhaps, the theory and practice of Wagner. Even Gluck's theory was not consistent with itself. In the

---

[1] Noufflard, *Hector Berlioz et le Mouvement de l'Art contemporain*, pp. 17, 18.

[2] See *Gluck and the Opera*, Part II. Chapters iii. and iv.

preface to *Alceste* he laid down the oft-quoted dictum that " I sought to reduce music to its true function, that of supporting the poetry, in order to strengthen the expression of the sentiments and the interest of the situations, without interrupting the action or disfiguring it with superfluous ornament. I imagined that the music should be to the poetry just what the vivacity of colour and the happy combination of light and shade are to a correct and well-composed design, serving to animate the figures without altering their contours." Here music is undeniably made the servitor of poetry ; yet in his letter to the *Journal de Paris* (12th October 1777) he argued that the two arts should stand on a footing of equality, that all the parts "should strive after one end— expression—and the agreement between the words and the song should be such that neither the poem should seem to be made for the music nor the music for the poem." [1] It is useless to argue that these two statements are not contradictory. Gluck's opinions varied from time to time, and the relations of poetry and music presented themselves to him now under one form, now under another. But it is most significant to note how Gluck himself illustrates the contention that for Wagner and his disciples to speak of the drama controlling the music is quite erroneous, in face of the fact that, as we have seen even M. Noufflard admitting, the drama has to be modified in accordance with the demands of the musician. Any one who will read Gluck's letter to Guillard, the author of the libretto of *Iphigenia in Tauris*, concerning the construction of that opera, will see the rigorous way in which he dictates his own terms, and makes farcical his own contention that all the musician had to do was to paint the outline afforded him by the poet. The key to the apparent paradox is given in the concluding lines of the letter : " I explain myself rather confusedly, *for my head is*

[1] See *Gluck and the Opera*, Part II. Chapters iii. and iv. p. 172.

excited with the music." [1] This once for all disposes of
the theory that Gluck or any other dramatic composer
simply waited for the poet's "lead"; and proves that,
so far from music being merely the handmaid of
poetry, the musical imagination, equally with the
poetical, is capable of conceiving a dramatic situation
under its own forms and in its own colour—that there
is, in fact, what an able French writer has recently
designated *la pensée musicale.* [2]

[1] It may be noted, in passing, that even among those who accept Wagner's
statement of his own theory there is considerable variation of opinion with
regard to the relation of the theory and practice of Gluck to the theory and
practice of Wagner. In *Opera and Drama*, Wagner remarked that "the so
famous revolution of Gluck, which has come to the ears of many ignoramuses
as a complete reversal of the views previously current as to Opera's essence,
in truth merely consisted of this: that the musical composer revolted against
the wilfulness of the singer" (G. S. iii. 237; Ellis, ii. 26). This, and all
that follows, is extremely unfair to Gluck, as will be seen from the present
chapter. It is curious to note, however, that while many ardent Wagnerians
follow Wagner upon this point, others hold Gluck to have been a real precursor of Wagner. Mr. Dannreuther, for example, echoes the opinions of
Wagner upon Gluck (*Richard Wagner: his Tendencies and Theories*, pp.
26–28); while A. de Gasperini, one of the earliest of Wagner's French
adherents, regards the modern master as the logical outcome of the older
composer. "The true master of Wagner, his direct ancestor, is Gluck. It
is easy to demonstrate this; easy to show, in the works of the old German
master or in the fragments of his letters, the germ of *all* the ideas which
Wagner at a later date put forward and developed with such power. Wagner
. . . has never been just to Gluck." Gasperini proceeds to prove the injustice of limiting Gluck's reform to a mere revolt against the tyranny of the
singers, and to show, point by point, the absolute similarity of the theories
of the two German composers (*La nouvelle Allemagne musicale: Richard
Wagner;* [1866], pp. 118–120). See also Edouard Schuré, *Le Drame musical,*
i. 258–273; and Eugène de Bricqueville, *L'Opéra de l'Avenir dans le Passé,*
pp. 64–82. A. B. Marx long ago referred to Gluck as the reformer of the
drama in opera, recognising at the same time that "in the German opera, the
purely dramatic element has never been able to attain full ascendancy; the
musical element, or the expression of individual sensations, has always been
predominant" (*The Music of the 19th Century* [Eng. trans.; 1855], p. 60.)
But Marx gave the true reasons for this, pointing out how the form of the
musical drama had been determined both by the peculiarity of music and the
social conditions of the last century. Liszt, again, writing in 1850, declared
that "Wagner would certainly have written the preface to *Alceste*, had Gluck
not already done so" (*Lohengrin et Tannhäuser de R. Wagner*, p. 103).

[2] See Jules Combarieu, *Les Rapports de la Musique et de la Poésie,
considerées au point de vue de l'expression.*

The confusion that has been introduced into musical æsthetic by Wagner's uncritical use of his terms may be further illustrated by a letter which the late Dr. Hueffer addressed to the *Daily News*, in reply to some strictures upon the Wagnerian theory :—

" I claimed for Wagner," he wrote, "the honour or dishonour (whichever it may be) of having urged theoretically, and shown by his creative productions, the necessity of a poetical basis of music. The meaning of the word 'poetical' in such combination differs essentially from the sense in which the word is generally used, and this *nuance*, perhaps not sufficiently explained by me, has, I think, given rise to some misapprehension in your article. By 'poetical' I mean only the original passionate impulse, which every artist must feel, and which he tries to embody in his work, be it by means of articulate words, sounds, or colours. In this sense every artist must be first a poet ; and without such a fundamental conception, poetry proper will degenerate into mere rhyming, painting into the worst kind of meaningless *genre*, and music into a shallow display of sound, or *Musikmacherei* as the Germans appropriately call it. Of this original impulse music had lost hold for a long time, chiefly owing to the destructive influence of the Italian operatic stage of the last century. Even in great composers like Mozart or Haydn, the poetical idea was encumbered by the strict forms of absolute music. My meaning is, to be quite explicit, that they would conceive a melody, perhaps full of sentiment, and certainly full of beauty of sound, and develop it exclusively with a view to displaying such beauties. It was Beethoven who first distinctly felt, and Wagner who first expressed in words, the necessity of a previous 'poetical' impulse to which the forms of music proper would have to yield. The unimpaired vitality of pure instrumental music, on these grounds, is of course obvious, it being altogether a secondary consideration whether the 'poetical basis' be expressed in words or not. Much less is the possibility of poetry as a separate art denied by the above theory. Still it is equally true that where a thorough blending of words and music is effected, and most of all in the drama, the very essence of which is passionate impulse, the common effort of both arts will be of a higher kind than is ever attainable by either in its individual sphere. Both have to resign some of their peculiarities, but both gain new strength and beauty in their supreme surrender. They are not, to adopt the equestrian simile of your contributor, 'two riders on the same horse, where one or the other must ride behind,' but rather like two noble steeds drawing with double force and swiftness the fiery chariot of divine pathos." [1]

The question as to whether poetry and music in combination can or cannot exist on the terms of amicable equality indicated by Dr. Hueffer will be discussed later in the present chapter. Here it is sufficient to note that it is an error to employ the term "poetical" as signifying the fundamental impulse of all art, and that nothing but confusion can result from employing it in such a manner. Used as Dr. Hueffer uses it, it simply means that a composer must take his art seriously, earnestly, and intelligently ; and from this standpoint there is no real justification for saying that the pre-Beethovenian composers did not look at their art in this way. Conventions there must be in every art ; that is, certain artificial modes of procedure must be adopted, their artificiality being lost sight of in the superior æsthetic pleasure that is given by their employment. In this sense there are as many conventions in poetry and painting as there are in "absolute music." Princes of Denmark, for example, do not usually carry on their conversations in blank verse ; and if Shakespeare's Hamlet does so it is because the departure from plain external truth in this respect is more than compensated for by the artistic delight which blank verse gives us. In this respect all the arts except architecture stand upon the same footing ; and "absolute music," with its strict forms, was simply doing what every other art does—seeking the best means within its power of obtaining the maximum of expression, and employing certain necessary conventions to that end. All that one can complain of is the employment of these

[1] Hueffer, *Richard Wagner and the Music of the Future*, pp. 105, 106.

conventions where they are no longer required, with the result that instead of increasing the artistic pleasure they diminish it by their incongruity. The object of the symphonic conventions was to make absolute music self-supporting and self-sufficing in the absence of words. As soon as words were combined with the music, the necessity for most of these conventions disappeared, and their continuance was felt as an anomaly and an element of detraction from the total æsthetic pleasure. This was all that was involved in the transition from absolute music to poetic music ; and to phrase it that it was necessary for the musician to have a " poetical basis " for his music is to obscure the whole æsthetic problem. There is bound to be fallacy all along by the use of the term " poetry " when something else than poetry, something *less* than poetry always means for us, is implied. If, as Dr. Hueffer admits, when poetry and music combine, each has to surrender some of its peculiarities, where is the justice of using the term " poetry " as if its meaning were unchanged ; and where is the justice of designating their union " drama," when the word in this sense cannot possibly mean what drama has always meant for us ?

The bearing of all this upon Wagner's dictum— "that a Means of expression (Music) has been made the end, while the End of expression (the Drama) has been made a means "—is, it is hoped, quite evident. The point I am urging is that the drama is *not* the end of expression in a combination of music and poetry, for the reasons that (1) everything which goes to make a drama is so modified by the introduction of music that the term, with its former connotations, is no longer applicable, and (2) the use of music has introduced quite a new factor, a new and very important element of æsthetic pleasure of a quite different kind, which cannot be looked upon as subordinate to the " poetical idea." This second point will be enlarged upon at a further stage of the argument; meanwhile we may follow up the first point to its logical conclusions. I have contended that Wagner's use of the terms "poetry" and "drama" is quite misleading. His complaint is that—

"Music, which, as an art of *expression*, can in its utmost wealth of such expression be nothing more than *true*, has conformably therewith to concern itself alone with *what* it should express: in opera this is unmistakably the Feeling of the characters conversing on the stage, and a music which fulfils this task with the most convincing effect is all that it ever can be. A music, however, which would fain be more than this, which should not connect itself with any object to be expressed, but desire to fill its place, *i.e.* to be alike that object: such a music is no longer any kind of music, but a fantastic, hybrid emanation from Poetry and Music, which in truth can only materialise itself as caricature. With all its perverse efforts, Music, the in any way effective music, has actually remained naught other than Expression. But from those efforts to make it in itself a Content—and that, forsooth, the Content of a Drama—has issued That which we have to recognise as the consequential downfall of Opera, and therewith as an open demonstration of the radical un-nature of that genre of Art." [1]

Here, it seems to me, Wagner makes the mistake of supposing that music is *merely* an art of "expression"; that is, that music cannot of itself be satisfying, cannot do more than "illustrate" or strengthen a poetical idea. This will perhaps be more clearly seen from one of the opening sentences of *Opera and Drama*, in which he says that—

"Music was therefore destined to credit herself with possibilities which, in very truth, were doomed to stay for her *im*possibilities; herself a sheer organ of expression, she must rush into the error of desiring to plainly outline the thing to be expressed; she must venture on the boastful attempt to issue orders and

---

[1] G. S. iii. 243, 244; Ellis, ii. 33, 34.

speak out aims *there*, where in truth she can only have to subordinate herself to an aim *her* essence cannot ever formulate (*fassen*), but to whose realising she gives, by this her subordination, its only true enablement."[1]

Here the origin of his confusion is plainly evident. He cannot mean[2] that music *per se* is incapable of "plainly outlining the thing to be expressed"; for in the symphony the "thing to be expressed," though not susceptible of statement in words, is "expressed" with quite sufficient decision and clearness and completeness to satisfy the organs to which it is addressed. To argue upon this point would be superfluous; for no one would go the length of maintaining that the utterance of a piece of symphonic music left in the mind a craving for a "poetical basis," or left a sense that the web of sound was merely the "expression" of some other "thing to be expressed."[3] Wagner, and the partisans who have unthinkingly adopted his æsthetics, have missed the psychological fact that the delight we take in absolute music is a thing *sui generis*, the satisfaction of a certain set of faculties, not to be discredited by individual attempts to discover a poetical basis.[4] What he is really thinking of when he complains that music has tried to do what it is essentially incapable of doing, is the imposition of the forms of absolute music upon the opera; and this he confuses with *music* encroaching upon the

[1] G. S. iii. 234; Ellis, ii. 23.

[2] Perhaps it would be more accurate to say that the majority of musicians would not contend for this. I hope to show in the sequel that Wagner's mind was in many ways unique, and that, probably from reasons of cerebral construction, he could not look at music apart from poetry in the way other men do.

[3] No one, that is, but Wagner. See the previous note, and a passage in Letter 5 to Uhlig—"Our cursed writing of *abstract poetry and music* is the very devil to get on with" (Eng. trans., p. 23). The use of the condemnatory phrase "*abstract* music" shows that music apart from words had little meaning, little satisfaction for Wagner—that it did not impress him as it impresses most men.

[4] Compare the remarks in his *Beethoven* (G. S. ix. 103; Ellis, v. 103).

field of poetry.[1] Thus in discussing the development from Gluck he writes :—

"The traditional divisions of the Aria, though still substantially preserved, were given a wider play of motive; modulations and connecting phrases (*Uebergänge und Verbindungsglieder*) were themselves drawn into the sphere of expression; the Recitative joined on to the Aria more smoothly and less waywardly, and, as a necessary mode of expression, it stepped into that Aria itself. Another notable expansion was given to the Aria, in that— obediently to the dramatic need—more than *one* person now shared in its delivery, and thus the essential Monody of earlier opera was beneficially lost. Pieces such as Duets and Terzets were indeed known long before; but the fact of two or three people singing in one piece had not made the slightest essential difference in the character of the Aria : this had remained exactly the same in melodic plan and insistence on the tonality once started (*Behauptung des einmal angeschlagenen thematischen Tones*) —which bore no reference to any individual expression, but solely to a general, specifically-musical mood—and not a jot of it was really altered, no matter whether delivered as a monologue or duet, excepting at the utmost quite materialistic details, namely, in that its musical phrases were either sung alternately by different voices, or in concert through the sheer harmonic device of combining two, three, or more voices at once. . . . The essential musical substance of this Ensemble was still, indeed, composed of Aria, Recitative, and Dance-tune. . . ."[2]

Now music, in order to be music at all, *has* to employ certain devices like any other art ; and, as has already been pointed out, the most that one can object to is the employment of these devices where they have ceased to be necessary, and where, consequently, instead of adding to the æsthetic pleasure they diminish it by their incongruity. Thus in a purely instrumental piece of music, certain forms of repetition and certain key-sequences assist the mind to grasp the music as a coherent whole; but these same forms may be quite

[1] See again G. S. ix. 111, 112; Ellis, v. 112.
[2] G. S. iii. 239; Ellis, ii. 29.

superfluous in a piece of vocal music, where the thought receives sufficient support and sufficient coherence from the words ; and the employment of the symphonic devices is here felt as the imposition of altogether alien conditions.[1] And if Wagner admits, as he does, that composers were trying to make their expression more dramatic, to make the sentiment of the music conform more closely to the sentiment of the words, all he really has to complain of is that the *forms* of absolute music were imported into opera, where of course they were quite superfluous. But this is a very different thing from saying that music, "herself a sheer organ of expression," had rushed "into the error of desiring to plainly outline the thing to be expressed." It had done nothing of the sort. It had always, in the hands of serious musicians, tried to move in emotional concord with the verse ;[2] its only error consisted in the mistaken notion that musical forms which were so efficacious in the absence of words would be equally efficacious when words were present.

Let us see how Wagner's argument develops. Speaking of the reform carried out by Gluck, and the consequent greater warmth of expression which was being put into the aria, he writes :—

"In the situation of the *Poet* towards the Composer not one jot was altered ; rather had the Composer grown more dictatorial,

---

[1] Conversely, a style of music such as recitative, that is not really self-existent, whose only *raison d'être* is its association with words, is quite out of place in symphonic music, which must be justified to the ear by its own meaning, and by that alone. See, for example, the curious sonata of Beethoven, Op. 31, No. 2, with the strange descent, near the close of the first movement, into recitative. Music like this is out of place in a sonata, just as the sonata-form is out of place in dramatic music.

[2] M. Schuré, Mr. Dannreuther, and others have regarded all operatic forms between the Greek drama and Wagner as merely bastard products. A scientific corrective has been administered by M. Henri Coutagne in *Les drames musicaux de Richard Wagner* (pp. 52–55), where the essentially evolutionary nature of the Wagnerian drama is shown, as well as its utilisation of materials "much nearer to hand than Æschylus or Sophocles."

since, with his declared consciousness of a higher mission—made good against the virtuoso Singer—he set to work with more deliberate zeal at the arrangement of the opera's framework. To the Poet it never occurred to meddle with these arrangements; he could not so much as dream of Music, to which the Opera had owed its origin, in any other form than those narrow, close-ruled forms he found set down before him—as binding even upon the Musician himself. To tamper with these forms by advancing claims of dramatic necessity, to such an extent that they should cease to be intrinsic shackles on the free development of dramatic truth, would have seemed to him unthinkable; since it was precisely in these forms alone—inviolable even by the musician—that he could conceive of Music's essence. Wherefore, once engaged in the penning of an opera-text, he must needs pay even more painful heed than the musician himself to the observance of those forms; at utmost leave it to that musician, in his own familiar field, to carry out enlargements and developments, in which he could lend a helping hand but never take the initiative. Thus the Poet, who looked up to the Composer with a certain holy awe, rather confirmed the latter's dictatorship in Opera, than set up rival claims thereto; for he was witness to the earnest zeal the musician brought to his task." [1]

Here it is quite evident that what Wagner is driving at is the *à priori* imposition of the forms of absolute music upon the opera, and the old-established convention by which the librettist had to fall in with this particular structure. But if Wagner had been careful to employ the historical instead of the metaphysical method, he would have seen that this was not a case of "music" trying to usurp the functions of "poetry," but simply an inevitable development from the pre-existing social and musical conditions. There was in the first place the growing delight of the composers in the resources of their art, and the first tentative reaching-out to completeness and beauty of form; in the second place, the mainly unintelligent character of the audiences before which opera was produced, some

[1] G. S. iii. 238; Ellis, ii. 28.

of these audiences having little notion of dramatic con-
gruity, and, indeed, hardly desiring it when they could
get from the music alone a sensuous and easily-won
pleasure which of itself was perfectly satisfying; and in
the third place, the static conditions of musical art in
the eighteenth century, under which convention ruled
supreme much longer than it could do in our own day.
Taking into consideration all that we know of the development of opera during the first two hundred years
of its existence, it is not difficult to see how it came to
be such a mass of convention; and Wagner's complaint
against it is, as I have pointed out, at bottom simply a
complaint against the employment of certain musical
forms in circumstances where they were no longer required, and where their presence was in consequence
felt as an anomaly.

This may be seen more clearly from a further passage of *Opera and Drama*, and a comparison of it with
some of his own methods of procedure.

"Now how did this Poet bear himself towards Spontini and
his colleagues? With all the maturing of Opera's musical Form,
with all the development of its innate powers of Expression, the
position of the Poet had not altered in the slightest. He still
remained the platform-dresser for the altogether independent
experiments of the Composer. . . . Thus, in the wake of the
Composer, the Poet certainly won an access of importance; but
only in exact degree as the Musician mounted upwards in advance, and bade him merely follow. *The strictly musical possibilities, as pointed out by the composer, the poet had to keep in eye as
the only measure for all his orderings and shapings*, nay even for
his choice of Stuff; and thus, for all the fame that *he* began to
reap also, he remained ever but the skilful servant who was so
handy at waiting on the 'dramatic' composer."[1]

Once more the historical method would have saved
Wagner from the confusion into which the *à priori*
method has led him. The plain fact is that it is not

[1] G. S. iii. 241, 242; Ellis, ii. 31, 32.

until lyric and dramatic music have reached a certain
point of development that they are able to deal with
poetry otherwise than by arbitrarily bending it to their
own forms.   As Dr. Hubert Parry puts it—

"A composer who has enough cultivation and refinement of
mind to appreciate great poems, and commensurate mastery of
the arts of choral music and instrumentation, may emphasise the
beauties of a poem and bring out its meaning far more effectually
than any amount of commentary and explanation.   This is emi-
nently a case which illustrates the value of the rich accumulation
of resources of various kinds, and the wide facilities which they
offer to modern composers ; for till comparatively lately the range
of design and the power of composers to wield varieties of means
so as to make the form intelligible was so limited, that unless
poems were constructed purposely to fit into conventional types
of musical form, they could not be effectively set." [1]

With the advance of the modern grasp of form,
certain old artificialities spontaneously tended to disappear from opera, because their incongruity with the
dramatic content was bound to be apparent.   But when
Wagner lays it down that it was wrong for the musician
to decide the construction of the poet's material for
him, his zeal carries him beyond the limits of logic.
He lays himself open to the retort that in any opera, the
"drama," as he would call it, is, consciously or unconsciously, so shaped as to be adapted to the peculiar
nature of music ; and he provokes the further retort
that he himself has modified his drama in this way.   He
frequently writes, for example, verses in a form which
no poet, writing for poetry's sake alone, would employ.
Look, for instance, at a few lines from *Tristan* :—

> "Höre ich nur
> diese Weise,
> die so wunder-
> voll und leise,

---

[1] *The Evolution of the Art of Music*, p. 285.

Wonne klagend
Alles sagend,
mild versöhnend
aus ihm tönend,
auf sich schwingt,
in mich dringt,
hold erhallend
um mich klingt?
Heller schallend,
mich umwallend,
sind es Wellen
sanfter Lüfte?
sind es Wogen
wonniger Düfte?
Wie sie schwellen,
mich umrauschen,
soll ich athmen,
soll ich lauschen?
Soll ich schlürfen,
untertauchen,
süss in Düften
mich verhauchen?
In des Wonnemeeres
wogendem Schwall,
in der Duft-Wellen
tönendem Schall,
in des Welt-Athems
wehendem All—
ertrinken—
versinken—
unbewusst—
höchste Lust!" [1]

Or again—

"O Wonne der Seele!
O süsse, hehrste,
kühnste, schönste,
seligste Lust!

---

[1] G. S. vii. 80, 81.

Ohne Gleiche!
Überreiche!
Überselig!
Ewig! Ewig!
Ungeahnte,
nie gekannte,
überschwänglich
hoch erhab'ne!
Freude-Jauchzen!
Lust-Entzücken!
Himmel-höchstes
Welt-Entrücken!
Mein Tristan!
Mein Isolde!
Tristan!
Isolde!
Mein und dein!
Immer ein!
Ewig, ewig ein![1]

These lines may be, and actually are, admirably adapted for a musical setting,[2] but they are no more poetry than an auctioneer's catalogue is poetry. Wagner has unconsciously done precisely what he blamed the older composers for—he has dragged the poet along at the heels of the musician. *And he has rightly done so;* for, as he ought to have seen, the element of musical pleasure counts for so much in opera that its presence compensates for the absence of poetry in the ordinary

[1] G. S. vii. 36, 37.

[2] On this point see Wagner's *Beethoven*, in G. S. ix. 103, 104, 105, 111, 122; Ellis, v. 104, 105, 112, 122. Note especially p. 104. "Moreover, the experience that a piece of music loses nothing of its character even when the most diverse texts are laid beneath it, shows the relation of Music to *Poetry* to be a sheer illusion: for it transpires that in vocal music it is not the poetic thought one seizes—which in choral singing, in particular, one does not even get intelligibly articulated—but at most the mood that thought aroused in the musician when it moved him to music." In other words, poetry, *as poetry*, makes little effect on us when united with music. All we care for is the generalised emotion of music. But on these terms musical drama can never be "drama" in the proper sense of that word. Everything must be modified to suit the music.

sense ; and he ought further to have seen that to a combination of the arts such as this, into which quite a new element of pleasure has been introduced, it is folly to apply the old term "drama." There can be no question, in any case, that Wagner allowed the musician in him to dominate the poet just as much as did Gluck or any previous composer. The extent of the dominance was the same ; the form of it alone had altered. He could not, in fact, any more than other men shape a musical drama without sacrificing much of the dramatic form and texture to the necessities of the music. As Marx expressed it in the early fifties, in a not unfriendly spirit to the new *genre*—

"Whilst Wagner—and every one labouring in the same sphere —is greatly indebted to them [*i.e.* Spontini, Weber and Meyerbeer], he has not been able to repudiate that ominous heritage which Spontini and Meyerbeer were obliged to accept from the hands of fate, and enlarge to exuberance; we mean that broad and pompous scenic display which originated in the insufficiency of the opera for a rapid progress of the action, and greater richness of the spiritual contents, and which reacts upon both with greatly increased effect."[1]

The justice of these remarks with reference to *Rienzi, The Flying Dutchman, Tannhäuser,* and *Lohengrin*—which were all that were known to Marx at that time— is indubitable ; while one has only to examine the form and structure of all the later opera-poems to see at once that the same principle applies to these. And, as I have already attempted to show, a confused recognition of this fact is implicit in the contradictions of most of those who have accepted Wagner's theory in his own form of statement of it. Mr. Dannreuther, for

---

[1] *The Music of the* 19*th Century* (Eng. trans.), p. 98. See also pp. 94, 95, on the extent to which music hinders dramatic construction. Marx ends (p. 104) by saying that " we must not, however, forget that the opera is, above all, a drama." Here the term "drama" is clearly to be taken with all the modifications already insisted upon.

example, falls into the old fallacy. He begins by laying it down that "the *ideal* so ardently striven after, a genuine musical drama, cannot be attained otherwise than by a radical change in the relative position of its two principal components, poetry and music." [1] Yet he himself afterwards admits, in the completest terms, that Wagner also shapes his poetry in accordance with the needs of the sister art. To argue as Mr. Dannreuther, following Wagner, argues, that the relative positions of poetry and music in the Wagnerian opera are the reverse of those they held in the operas of previous composers, simply because Wagner dispenses with the set *forms* in which the old opera was cast, is, as already pointed out, merely a confusion of the question at issue. Mr. Dannreuther remarks that "the fire and the fascinating charm of Weber's melody made a still greater autocrat of the musician, and Weber thought himself justified in dictating to Helmine von Chezy, who wrote the libretto of *Euryanthe* for him, not only details of expression, but even the dramatic movements of the characters and the motives for their actions." If Mr. Dannreuther had objected to Weber's stipulation for an act composed of so many arias, duets, choruses, and the rest of it, one could have sympathised with his strictures ; but to imply that the composer was wrong in asking that "the dramatic movements of the characters and the motives for their actions" should be determined beforehand by the necessities of musical expansion, is to lose sight of the real question at issue between the claims of poetry and music in opera. Mr. Dannreuther himself gives an account of Wagner's dealings with the myth for operatic purposes, which to the unprejudiced eye seems hardly distinguishable from the procedure of Weber with Frau von Chezy.

[1] *Richard Wagner, his Tendencies and Theories*, p. 41. See also pp. 24, 28, 29, 38.

" The mythical subject-matter," he remarks, "has a plastical unity; it is perfectly simple and easily comprehensible, and it does not stand in need of the numberless small details which a modern playwright is obliged to introduce to make some historical occurrence intelligible.   It is divided into a few important and decisive scenes, in each of which the action arises spontaneously from out of the emotions of the actors ; which emotions, by reason of the small number of such scenes, can be presented in a most complete and exhaustive manner."

(In other words, while the myth cannot give us everything we require in a drama, it can give us everything we require in an opera.   Both psychologically and structurally it lends itself to musical treatment.)

" In planning these scenes according to the distinctive nature of the mythical subject-matter, *it is unnecessary to take any preliminary account of specific musical forms* [1] as the opera has them —*arias, duets, ensemble pieces*, &c.[1]—for *as the myths are in themselves emotional, and as the dramatist moulds them in accordance with and under the influence of the spirit of music,*[2] they resolve themselves, as it were quite spontaneously, into musical diction." [3]

If *this* is not admitting that in the Wagnerian, as in the older opera, the music is the dominating and shaping force, it is difficult to say what the words mean.   To harp on the fact that Wagner discards the old form of aria, duet, and *ensemble*, is, I repeat, quite superfluous. They owed their origin not, as Wagner implies, to purely psychological causes, not to a desire to make music " plainly outline the thing to be expressed," but to definite historical conditions.   In everything that concerns the real *psychological* relations of poetry and music in opera, there is no difference between the older opera and the Wagnerian.   In each the need was instinctively felt to deal with the poetical subject-matter

---

[1] Italics Mr. Dannreuther's.   [2] Italics mine.

[3] Work cited, p. 59.

in such a way as to allow scope for the peculiar qualities of music to display themselves. There is no practical difference between the psychological mood in which we listen to the finest operas of the older school and those of Wagner—apart, of course, from the differences of form and of melodic, harmonic, and orchestral complexity.

"The entire work of art, then, intended by Wagner," continues Mr. Dannreuther, "is *musical* in spirit, and could have been conceived by none but a man of universal artistic instincts, who is at the same time a great modern musician. Its mythical subject-matter, chosen because of its essentially emotional nature; its division into scenes, and the sequence of these; the use of alliterative verse, and its melodious declamation; the use of the orchestra, preparing, supporting, commenting, enforcing, recalling; all its factors are imbued with the spirit of music. Their task is not accomplished if any one side of the subject remains to be supplied by some process of abstract reasoning on the hearer's part. They are to appeal exclusively to our feelings. The sole test of what sort of thing is to be said lies in the expressive power of music."[1]

All which is perfectly true; but on these terms what becomes of the theory that Wagner is restoring the sceptre to the hands of the poet, and of the theory that the object of opera should be the drama? Can anything but the direst æsthetic confusion result from applying the same term "drama" to a spoken play, with all its wealth of character, variety of incident, and subtlety of psychology, and to the musical play, with its paucity of well-defined figures, its simplicity of outline, and its relatively small gamut of psychology?[2]

[1] Work cited, pp. 68, 69.

[2] It can readily be seen that there are many mental states which may be made fascinating studies in the spoken or written drama, but for which no appropriate musical expression can be found. In a similar way, the opera has difficulty in attaching itself to modern life. We can be interested in Tristan singing his passion to King Marke's wife in a garden, but we should only

Wagner's new art-work, be it remembered, was to take the place of the scattered arts, and particularly of the merely literary drama. He forgot that these arts give us something that neither music nor poetry-and-music can ever give us; that they lead us along psychological by-paths which are intensely interesting to us, but along which music has no power to travel. There can be no doubt, as I shall afterwards try to show, that Wagner himself cared very little for the individual arts, and thought that the essence of drama could be adequately expressed by music. But Wagner thought thus simply because he *was* Wagner—simply because nature had made him comparatively insensitive to æsthetic impressions from any other art but music, and had limited, *à priori*, his conception of "drama" to something which had better be called merely "musical drama." He imagined that *his* drama was the expression of "the purely human," and that all that remained for the other arts to express was the reflective, the adventitious, the superfluous. It seems to have been a difficult matter for his worshippers to recognise the very obvious truth, that if Wagner could think nothing "purely human" that was incapable of presentation in musical drama, his conception of what constituted the "purely human" must have been quite peculiar to his own nature—an idiosyncrasy that is interesting as a psychological study, but not something to be made into a canon of æsthetic for other men. He used the term "drama" where he should have used the term "musical drama," simply because from the very nature of his constitution he was

smile at the young stockbroker singing the *Tristan* music to the lawyer's wife in a drawing-room. The incongruity would be too great. For situations of this kind we must have resort to the less emotional and more analytical expression of words. The partisans of Wagner, of course, tell us that the one situation is more fundamentally true, more *universal*, than the other; to which the answer may be made that tens of thousands of cultured minds would take far more dramatic interest in the second situation than in the first. That is, while Ibsen's dramas, for example, are quite unfitted for music, they satisfy artistic needs in us that cannot be satisfied by any musical drama.

incapable of dramatic emotion except as shaped and coloured by music. There can be no sense in for ever echoing, as his disciples have done, his own æsthetic formulas, without making some attempt to discover the peculiar cast of mind that gave birth to them. Not to recognise that Wagner was completely a musician, unable to conceive thought and emotion in terms of anything else but music, and that this inevitably coloured his theories of the drama, is to fall into perpetual fallacy and self-contradiction.[1]

It is impossible, then, in the face of admissions and self-contradictions of this kind, to still maintain that Wagner, in so far as the essence of the opera is concerned, departs from the modes of procedure of his predecessors in that he "makes the poet dominant" in

---

[1] Without burdening the text by further elaboration of this argument, I may call the student's attention to the extraordinary see-saw of Mr. H. S. Chamberlain upon this subject—the inevitable outcome of trying to make Wagner's formulas stand good, without recognising the peculiar senses in which the words of the formulas must be taken. Even from Mr. Chamberlain's wavering exposition, however, there finally emerges the truth that the music determines the poem. "In conception, in the main lines of the dramatic execution, as well as the smallest detail of versification and choice of words, a poem like that of *Tristan* has sprung as truly from music as Aphrodite, the goddess of perfect beauty, has sprung from the waves of the sea" (*Richard Wagner*, p. 243). The remainder of Mr. Chamberlain's chapter, in which he strives to show that in Wagner's earliest works the music was predominant not because Wagner was a musician but because he was a poet, is tiresome sophistry (see, in the present volume, pp. 293–295). M. Schuré, again, practically gives up the case when he admits that what led Wagner to the use of the myth as subject-matter for his dramas, was a subtle perception that the myth lent itself very easily to *musical* treatment (*Le drame musical*, ii. 334). Yet a few lines afterwards M. Schuré tells us that in the Wagnerian drama, so far from the music determining the poetry, the poetry determines the music. "If the music gives the drama its spirit, communicates its power to it, the drama dominates all the musical forms" (ii. 335). Is it not clear, then, from all this self-contradiction, that though Wagner's works may differ from those of his predecessors in that alien forms are not imposed upon the music, none the less are they *operas*—that is, stories modified in form, in contents, in psychology, to render them suitable for combination with music? In this process of modification they necessarily lose many points that make them interesting to the non-musical mind; and the product certainly ought not to be called by the term "drama."

his musical drama.[1]   It is clear that although he discarded the set forms of absolute music which had been imposed upon opera from without, he, as much as any other man—as much as Gluck or Weber—allowed the musician to dictate to the poet what the form and scope and structure of the opera should be.

"While writing the poem," as Dr. Parry truly says, "he probably had a general feeling of what the actual music was going to be, just as a dramatist keeps in his mind a fairly clear idea of the scene and the action of the play he is writing; and as certain general principles of design are quite indispensable in musical works of this kind, he evidently controlled the development of his stories so as to admit of due spreading of groundwork and of variety of mood; and devised situations that admitted of plain and more or less diatonic treatment, and crises which would demand the use of energetic modulation, and so forth."[2]

If all this is not making the poet keep in view "the strictly musical possibilities of the composer," it is difficult to say what is.   Once more, Wagner is doing exactly what he censured the older composers for doing; and he is making it more and more evident that the fault of these composers lay mainly in im-

[1] Mr. Dannreuther, for example, lays it down, in spite of all he has elsewhere said, that "Wagner is a poet first and foremost" (work cited, p. 3).

[2] *The Evolution of the Art of Music*, p. 322.   I am afraid, however, that Dr. Parry was under the Wagnerian influence when he continued: "But in reality this requires less restriction than might be imagined; for *the working and changing of moods in a good poem is almost identical with the working and developing and changing of moods adapted for good music.*   They both spring from the same emotional source, only they are different ways of expressing the ideas.   As poetry and music approach nearer to one another, it becomes more apparent that the sequence of moods which makes a good design in poetry will also make a good design in music."   This is only partially true; and it is still less true that in the Wagnerian opera poetry and music are "only different ways of expressing the same ideas."   Any one can judge for himself whether the bald disjointed prose which I have quoted from *Tristan* is only a different way of expressing the passion of that exquisitely beautiful music.   The plain fact is that not only did Wagner, as Dr. Parry says, plan the whole drama on musical lines, but he wrote the words also in obedience to musical possibilities and demands.

posing upon opera the alien forms of symphonic music, in filling the opera with concerted forms, drawn from non-dramatic, non-vocal quarters.

Thus his fallacy becomes clear. He has blamed music for usurping the speaking, indicative power that really belongs to poetry, whereas he really meant to condemn the practice of constructing operas upon the lines of structure of absolute music. The point may be made still clearer by another quotation from him :—

"That in the Drama itself, however, there lay possibilities which could not be so much as approached within that art-form [*i.e.* opera]—if it were not to fall to pieces—this, perhaps, is *now* quite clear to us, but could by no chance occur to the poet or composer of that epoch. Of all dramatic possibilities, they could only light on such as were realisable in that altogether settled and, of its very essence, hampered Opera-music form. The broad expansion, the lingering on a motive, which the Musician required in order to speak intelligibly in his form—the purely musical accessories he needed as a preliminary to setting his bell a-swinging, so that it might sound out roundly, and especially might sound in a fashion to give fitting expression to a definite character—made it from the first the Poet's duty to confine himself to dramatic sketches of one settled pattern, devoid of colour, and affording ample elbow-room to the musician for his experiments. Mere stereotyped rhetoric phrases were the prime requirement from the poet, for on this side alone could the musician gain room for the expansion that he needed, but which was yet in truth entirely undramatic." [1]

But "the broad expansion, the lingering on a motive," is not a characteristic of the old opera only, *but of music per se.* Wagner himself is full of it, as may be seen by any one who will look at the scene between Eva and Sachs in the 2nd Act of the *Meistersinger*, or the great love-duet in the *Valkyrie,* or the Good Friday music in *Parsifal.* He is, besides, utterly astray when he says that " mere stereotyped rhetoric phrases were the

[1] G. S. iii. 242 ; Ellis, ii. 32.

prime requirement from the poet, for on this side alone could the musician gain room for the expansion that he needed." To write thus is not only to psychologise wrongly but to falsify history. A great part of what was best in the old opera was *not* " mere stereotyped rhetoric phrases " ; the words were in many cases models of simple, direct expression, giving as full play to all the art and passion of the musician as any of Wagner's poems ; and the reason that music needed scope for " broad expansion," for " lingering on a motive," was not because it wanted to develop at the expense of the words, or to usurp the function of poetry, but simply because it *was* music.

" Music," he continues, " which, as an art of *expression*, can in its utmost wealth of such expression be nothing more than *true*, has conformably therewith to concern itself alone with *what* it should express : in Opera this is unmistakably the Feeling of the characters conversing on the stage, and a music which fulfils this task with the most convincing effect is all that it can ever be. A music, however, which would fain be more than this, which should not connect itself with any object to be expressed, but desire to fill its place, *i.e.* to be alike that object : such a music is no longer any kind of music, but a fantastic, hybrid emanation from Poetry and Music, which in truth can only materialise itself as caricature. With all its perverse efforts, Music, the in any way effective music, has actually remained naught other than Expression. But from those efforts to make in itself a content— and that, forsooth, the Content of a Drama—has issued That which we have to recognise as the consequential downfall of Opera, and therewith as an open demonstration of the radical un-nature of that genre of art." [1]

One has only to look at the facts of the case to see that Wagner's *à priori* zeal has led him astray. There never was a time in which vocal music, the mere art of " expression," tried to " fill the place of the object to be expressed." The mass of it was poor stuff, because the

[1] G. S. iii. 243, 244 ; Ellis, ii. 33, 34.

intellectual and social soil on which it grew was poor ; but in its better moments, and in the hands of the best men, it simply aimed at doing what Wagner says it should do—it tried to express " the Feeling of the characters conversing on the stage " with sincerity and naturalness. There is then no ground, even on the lines of his own treatise, for Wagner's condemnation of the older opera. His dictum on the ideal abstract relations of poetry and music may or may not be true, but at all events his condemnation of the old opera for the reason that in it the music tried to do what poetry alone can do, is seen to be purely arbitrary. What he really seems to have had in his mind is the unwarrantable importation of symphonic forms into opera ; for a very slight analysis of his own or any other music will serve to show that music *has* to control poetry in many ways [1] in a combination of the two arts, and that his attack

---

[1] It is curious how Wagner's mere statement of his badly thought-out theories should prevent so many acute readers from noticing their radical contradiction with most of his practice. M. Lichtenberger may serve as an example. After the composition of *Lohengrin*, Wagner turned over in his mind two or three subjects for his next work ; and he finally gave up the scheme of *Frederick Barbarossa*, and adopted that of *Siegfried*, because the mythical nature of the latter subject was more adapted to musical treatment than the historical nature of the former—there being a number of details in a historical play that are essential to the comprehension of its action, but which are unsuited to music. M. Lichtenberger, swayed by the Wagnerian theory, puts it that " He gave up *Barbarossa*, not because he recoiled before a work which would not allow him to display his musical genius, but because he felt that his *dramatic* genius itself could not work freely except in some subject fitted to be set to music " (*Wagner, Poète et Penseur*, p. 258). That seems to me merely sophistry—quite unconscious, of course, but sophistry all the same. To admit as much as M. Lichtenberger has done is to admit that Wagner wanted no subject that could not be treated in music ; that is, he wanted not a dramatic subject, but a musical-dramatic subject—which is a very different thing. M. Lichtenberger goes on, following Wagner, to say that the composer now saw " that the true drama is *necessarily* musical, and therefore historical and political subjects are unsuitable not only for the opera, but in a general manner for the drama itself." That is going too far. No one disputes that a mythical subject is well suited for musical treatment, because the simplicity of its outline concedes everything that the expansive power of music—the dominant factor —requires ; but on the other hand, men are greatly interested in subjects more

I

on the grand opera for the importance which music
assumed there is mainly the outcome of an unconscious
parti pris.

III

Further light on the Wagnerian conception of the
relative possibilities of poetry and music may, however,
be had by looking at the ideas of Berlioz on the same
subject. Berlioz's opinions on the matter varied from
time to time, as more than one of his critics has pointed
out; but even this indecision of idea is interesting. The
theory—or one of the theories[1]—of Gluck, that the
musician was to be the humble servitor of the poet,
merely filling with colour the outlines that were given
to him, was at an early stage of his career criticised by
Berlioz, who not only pointed out many inconsistencies
between Gluck's theory and his practice, but opposed
him very pronouncedly on the question of the relations
of poetry and music.

"Now when he says," writes Berlioz, "that the music of a
lyrical drama has no other function than that of adding to the
poetry just what the colour adds to a design, I believe him to
be fundamentally mistaken. The task of the composer in an
opera, it seems to me, is of quite another importance. His
work contains both design and colour, and, to continue the
comparison of Gluck, the words are the *subject* of the picture,
and little more. *Expression is not the sole aim of dramatic
music; it would be as maladroit as pedantic to disdain the purely
sensuous pleasure which we find in certain effects of melody,
harmony, rhythm, or instrumentation, independently of their connection with the painting of the sentiments and passions of the*

---

complex than primitive myths, and their desires in this direction can only be
satisfied by the poetical drama. Hence it was mere dogmatism on Wagner's
part to lay it down that the musical drama alone expressed the totality of the
" purely-human." Hence also a further proof of his delusion in imagining
that when he wrote operas he was writing " dramas."

[1] See *ante*, p. 106.

drama.[1] And further, even if it were desired to deprive the hearer of this source of delight, and not to permit him to re-animate his attention by turning it away for a moment from its principal object, we would still be able to cite a goodly number of cases where the composer is called upon to sustain alone the interest of the lyrical work.   In the *danses de caractère*, for example, in the pantomime, in the marches, in every piece, in short, in which the instrumental music takes the whole of the work upon itself, and which consequently have no words, what becomes of the importance of the poet?   In these cases the music must necessarily contain both design and colour." [2]

Berlioz seems to me to have struck, in the passage I have italicised above,[3] upon one of the great omissions of the Wagnerian theory—an omission so simple and so obvious that one can only explain Wagner's blindness to it by the peculiar constitution of brain that made him blind to many things that were palpable to every one else.   He made the great mistake of ignoring the enormous part played in opera by the mere sensuous pleasure of the music.   This is an element of such importance in our artistic pleasure that it alters our whole outlook upon the musical stage, and makes it, as I have argued, entirely wrong for Wagner to use the term drama, in connection with opera, as if that word still meant in the new connection what it means in the old.   It was in pursuance of this train of thought that Berlioz further wrote :—

" It has frequently happened that Gluck has allowed himself to be so preoccupied by his search for expression that he has forgotten about melody.   In some of his airs, after the exposition

---

[1] This is a point that Wagner failed to notice. He, like Schopenhauer, tended to lay too much stress on the more abstract qualities of the arts, and to overlook the important part played by the sensuous media in which they work.

[2] *A travers chants*, pp. 155, 156.

[3] M. Noufflard, however, thinks that "tout ceci est absolument réactionnaire" (*Hector Berlioz et le mouvement de l'art contemporain*, p. 36).

of the theme, the vocal portion becomes measured recitative. It is good recitative—I am far from denying that—but it is certain that, on account of the small melodic interest as well as of the style of the vocal part, it seems as if the air were interrupted until the re-entry of the motive. Gluck probably did not recognise that this was a fault; on the contrary, he declares formally that he has sought to avoid too striking a disparity between the recitatives and the airs. . . . It is certain that the application of this rule has diffused over several parts of the work of the great tragic writer a uniform and monotonous tint which is too much for the most robust attention. Music lives only by contrasts, . . . and it is well recognised now that a wisely regulated variety is the very soul of it. . . . To seek to efface the difference which, in an opera, separates the recitative from the melody, is to wish, in spite of reason and experience, to deprive one's self, without any real compensation, of a source of variety which flows from the very nature of this species of composition." [1]

We need not subscribe to the reactionary portion of this manifesto; [2] but we cannot help recognising that Berlioz, in a somewhat haphazard way, has hit upon the truth I have already dwelt upon—that we seek a more sensuous pleasure from opera than from drama,

[1] *Voyage musical*, ii. 271.

[2] It was probably on account of the reactionary element here that Berlioz omitted this particular passage when, in later years, he reprinted his article on Gluck in *A travesr chants*. (See Noufflard, *Hector Berlioz et le mouvement de l'art contemporain*, p. 35, *note*.) Berlioz was afterwards bound to recognise that, in so far as his argument might be looked upon as advocating the retention of the old divisions in opera, he was going quite astray. He was led into this fallacy by the bad phrasing of his first sentences, which, however, are psychologically correct. He really meant that Gluck was sometimes *musically uninteresting*, and therefore lacking in pleasure-giving quality, from his too great anxiety to tie the music down to the level of the words—which is the point brought out in the passage already quoted from *A travers chants*. M. Edmond Hippeau thinks that the un-reprinted passage of 1844 was inserted at that time as a "*plaidoyer* for the extenuating circumstances in favour of the air of Teresa, in *Benvenuto Cellini*, a cavatina full of roulades, and constructed on a triple return of the principal motive—in short, an *aria di bravura* pure and simple. It would have been better to avow that this number was a concession to the cantatrice who took the part." *Berlioz et son temps,* pp. 146, 147.

and that any interruption of this pleasure, as in the descent from coloured melody to plain recitative, is felt as a positive pain to the æsthetic sense. We need not make the case more complex at present by inquiring whether there ought to be any distinction in opera between melody and so-called recitative, or, if so, how far this distinction ought to extend. That will be a subject for discussion later, with especial reference to some of Wagner's own music. Here we have only, for theoretical purposes, once more to recall to ourselves the fundamental æsthetic truth which is being insisted on. It may be shown in a clearer light by a rapid survey of the opera and its critics in pre-Wagnerian days, which will not only bring out the historical causes —as distinguished from the merely pseudo-æsthetic causes dwelt on by Wagner—that led to the decline of opera as a serious art-form, and prove the fundamental similarity of Wagner's notions of reform to those of the critics of the eighteenth century, but will also pave the way for a discussion of the relations of " aria " and " recitative " in Wagner's own work.

One is sometimes tempted to ask whether, under more favourable social and political conditions, there might not have been a continuous development during the eighteenth and nineteenth centuries from the opera as it then was to all that is best in the opera of Wagner. A few careful and thoughtful treatises upon the structure and capacities of the opera have come down to us from the last century, evidently the work of men who, though they felt the power and acknowledged the beauty of this new art-form, were anxious to rid it of its abuses, to develop it upon its best instead of its worst side, and to bring it nearer the dignity and potency of the drama.[1]

---

[1] Mr. Matthew, in his recent volume on *The Literature of Music*, thinks that the Italian literature on the subject is meagre. Anything Mr. Matthew says on the subject of musical literature is of course entitled to respectful consideration ; but it seems to me that the amount of reflection given to the æsthetics

It is hardly a paradox to say that the development of art owes more to the critics than to the artists, in that the fresh play of many-sided criticism is the most vitalising of all artistic forces, stimulating as it does both artist and public to incessant readjustment of view. And considering the amount of criticism that must have been directed upon the opera in the eighteenth century, by satirist, panegyrist, and æsthetician, it seems more than likely that had it been free to develop on its own lines, as other arts have done, it would have reached in the present century a position something like that given to it by Wagner. That the opera has not developed in this manner is due not to the quite *à priori* reasons given by Wagner, but mainly to two causes, which are really the inverse and obverse of the same phenomenon. In England, of course, the opera has been hindered by the forces that have hindered the development of our music as a whole—the enormous hold of Handel and the oratorio upon the musical public (followed by that of Mendelssohn), and the prevailing mediocrity of the ignoble epoch that followed Waterloo, when an uncultured, reactionary, religious middle-class was the main power in the land, loving mediocrity as we now love the abnormal. English opera of any freshness or originality could not well flourish in an atmosphere like this ; while the religious reaction, creating an enormous demand for religious music, called forth a vast number of writers of hymns, anthems, and oratorios—men whose third-rate imitative power would not have gained them a moment's hearing in any other art, but who succeeded in completely bastardising English musical taste. A nation that still has the *Messiah* every Christmas, and waits thirty years

of the opera in the eighteenth century was larger than is usually thought. Not only did the really good books go through several editions, but the standard of criticism in them was really high in comparison with that of our own day ; while they certainly do not rank below the general æsthetic and philosophical literature of their epoch.

to hear *Tristan*, is somewhat too far removed from musical intelligence to give birth to new forms of musical art; and under conditions like these it is not surprising that we have either imitated foreign opera or been content with the more pecuniarily successful of its products.

On the Continent, again, political and social causes have combined with purely psychological causes in bringing about a progressive degeneration of the opera. Music being the most sensuous of all the arts, the simplest and most direct of all in its appeal, must necessarily attract many whose mental constitution and education unfit them for the more intellectual arts; and catering for a public like this has a tendency to seduce the purveyors of the music into providing the most obvious and most easily assimilated form of it. The high ideal—wrong as it was in parts—set before themselves by the early Florentine reformers was too noble and too severe for any but a refined and educated minority. When, under the pecuniary stress of theatre-management, an impresario found himself compelled to appeal to the suffrages of the multitude, the attempt to imitate "the music of the ancient Greeks" had not much chance of survival. What the public wanted was simply pleasing melody, fine singing, and gorgeous decoration. This movement from academic pedantry to lyrical spontaneity would not have been so harmful as it actually was, had not two causes assisted the most dangerous elements of the movement, and thereby rendered the degeneratiou of the opera permanent. In the first place, the Italian language lent itself too readily to anything that composers and singers wished to do with it—the decadence along this line being helped by the further fact that Italy had no great drama, and therefore no theatrical public with traditions of a nature to withstand the onset of operatic sensuousness. In the second place, the rule of Austria, while it ground the country down in innumerable ways, not only filled the theatre with its own officials but left the Italian nobility no other outlet for its energies. Political life being denied to them, men of wealth and leisure, but not possessed of much all-round culture, will inevitably fall back upon music—and the opera for preference—if they take to art at all ; it being at once the most easily assimilated and the least troublesome of the arts. Thus began all the abuses with which we are made familiar by Des Brosses and other letter-writers of the eighteenth century—the stereotyping of all the formulas of the opera, the tyranny of the singers, the opulence of decoration, the apathetic public making the theatre a social meeting-ground, playing chess during the recitatives, suspending the game to listen to an aria, and resuming it when the next recitative began. It was in the days of Italy's degradation that these abuses got so strong a hold upon the opera that a century and a half have scarcely sufficed to throw them off. Meanwhile the contagion spread to other countries. In Germany the low state of culture of the nation as a whole made the princes and nobles an almost entirely separate class, looking abroad rather than at home for culture ; and as France influenced the German upper classes in the courtesies of private and public life, Italy was laid under contribution for the opera. Hence the spectacle of every German court—small or large—with its Italian opera-house, performing scarcely anything but Italian operas, and maintaining almost none but Italian singers and conductors. Honest old Germans like Keiser might growl about the preference shown to the "protzigen Italiener und prahlerischen Franzosen"; but they were powerless against the general stream of things. Thus in Germany, as in Italy, the opera was unfortunate in that all the abuses crept in at a time when the new art-form was only in its infancy—it being thus almost impossible to eradicate them when the organism was full-grown; while in France the same series of phenomena followed, though later in time and, perhaps, less virulent in effect—the French having always a solid opera of their own, which prevented the Italian from taking such firm root in France as it did in England and in Germany. At a later time, when, after the Napoleonic wars, the country was again opened to foreigners, and Paris became the haunt of the pleasure-loving wealthy of all nations, it was necessarily Italian opera that provided the chief amusement. The music was sensuous and the attention demanded not too great, while Italian-opera Italian was a language sufficiently comprehended by these cosmopolitan audiences.[1]

Thus opera has always been unfortunate in that political and social circumstances have combined with its own qualities of beauty and sensuousness to bring about its degeneration.[2] No other art has been so unfortunate. One can see, for example—to take a kindred case—how instrumental music has been saved from a like degeneration by the facts that (1) concerted music was kept up in the first place by enthusiastic amateurs for no other reason than pure love of the art, the public counting for very little; (2) the practice of the German nobles of maintaining an orchestra at their own expense tended to keep up a higher standard of instrumental music than an impresario could have afforded to do—the system of patronage of composers working to some extent in the same direction, relieving the composer, as it did, from the necessity to sell his

---

[1] It has to be noted, in this connection, that Napoleon's own preferences were for Italian music, and that he discouraged any other upon the Parisian stage. See the recently published *New Letters of Napoleon.*

[2] To the causes enumerated above there must be added another. In France, Germany, and England, the practice of singing operas in a foreign tongue necessarily militated against intelligent comprehension on the part of the audience, while at the same time it made composers sink into the carelessness born of security. The aria and concerted forms alone could be properly treated, while the recitative was inevitably neglected.

work in a wider but lower market;[1] (3) instrumental
music thus, at the beginning of the nineteenth century,
when the patronage system broke down, and the public
became the supporter of art, having behind it a tradition
of dignity which opera had never been able to acquire.
That the opera did degenerate, however, cannot be laid
to the charge of its critics. In this respect, indeed, it
was singularly fortunate. Apart from satirists like Mar-
cello—who are always the best friends art or literature could have—the opera was discussed in serious
fashion by the most scholarly and intelligent of men,
aiming, like Gluck and like Wagner, at discovering the
best manner of combining poetry and music, and at
reducing habits of practice to comprehensive theory.
Planelli's *Dell' Opera in Musica* (Naples, 1772), Arteaga's
*Le Rivoluzioni del Teatro Musicale Italiano dalla sua origine
fino al presente* (Bologna, 1783–88, 3 vols.), Algarotti's
Saggio dall' Opera in Musica (Livorno, 1763), and Brown's
Letters upon the Poetry and Music of the Italian Opera
(Edinburgh, 1789)—to take these four books alone—
represent a standard of æsthetic criticism relatively
quite as high, to say the least, as the bulk of musical
criticism in our own day. All of them seem to have
felt the necessity of some reform of the opera. Algarotti's book, it will be remembered, preceded the preface
to Gluck's *Alceste* by about six years—the opera being
produced in 1767, while the score containing the
famous dedicatory epistle, in which Gluck enumerates
the reforms he had aimed at, was published in 1769;
and it is extremely probable that Gluck had seen the

---

[1] Perhaps I may be allowed to note, in passing, that my previous remarks
on the evil effects of patronage in the eighteenth century (in *Gluck and the
Opera*) should be slightly modified. The mistake lies in trying to sum up
any historical factor as "good" or "bad" in itself. While in some quarters
the system of patronage undoubtedly worked for harm, in others it as certainly
wrought for good. See, for example, Grove's *Dictionary of Music*, p. 204;
Wagner's *Beethoven;* G. S. ix. 88, 91; Ellis, v. 88, 91, &c.; Oulibicheff,
Beethoven, pp. 87, 88, 98; and the lives of the old musicians generally.

book and had profited by it.   The points laid down by
Algarotti are worth recalling in connection with Wagner's
work.   They were, in brief, that some check should be
put upon the licenses of the singer and the composer,
and that the libretto should be made more interesting,
"the helm being given again into the hands of the poet,
from whom it has been wrongly taken"; that the overture should be made a real introduction to the opera
and not a mere instrumental symphony having no
psychological connection with the work that followed
it; that greater attention should be given to the recitative, more particularly *obbligato* recitative, in which
the dramatic and descriptive powers of music were at
their height; that by the greater elaboration of *obbligato*
recitative the gulf between the lyrical and the non-lyrical
portions of the opera might be lessened; that dramatic
expression being the object of dramatic music, trills,
roulades, and all similar ornaments, which were introduced merely for vocal effects, were quite superfluous,
and ought, therefore, to be discountenanced; that the
da capo ought not to be abused as it had been by the
majority of Italian composers, the words being only
repeated where they are required by the circumstances
of passion, and where the whole sense of the aria is at
an end; that "the *ritornelli* are too long, and generally
superfluous, it being highly improbable in a passionate
aria, for instance, that the actor should stand with his
arms crossed, waiting for the *ritornello* to come to an
end before he can give his passion play"; that the
orchestration must be made more appropriate to the
dramatic scheme, and that counterpoint for its own
sake, which may be pleasing enough in church music,
is out of place in opera; that the aria should conform
in expression to the sentiment of the words, and not be
bent merely on gratifying the ear; and that there should
be an all-round levelling up in the matter of composition
and performance.

It will be seen at once that these were not only the reforms actually carried out by Gluck, and expounded by him in the dedicatory epistle to *Alceste* and elsewhere, but that they coincide to a great extent with much that Wagner contended for. Planelli's book covers almost the same ground, his practical observations all leading to the same conclusions as those of Gluck and Algarotti.[1] Arteaga, who was a Spanish Jesuit of very wide culture and great ability, not only touches upon the matter of practical reform, but enters, in Wagner's style, into a philosophical discussion of the natures of poetry and music, and the modifications each has to undergo when they combine in opera. " Data la intrinseca unione della poesia colla musica, quai mutazioni debbono risultare da si fatto accopiamento in un tutto drammatico ; " [2] this, he remarks, is the problem of the musical drama. The opera, he has already said, is not a single art, but a combination of poetry, music, decoration and mimetics ; and as the music is always looked upon as the chief part of the drama, the element which gives force and beauty to the poetry, the modifications introduced by music form the special characteristics of the opera.[3] Poetry, he continues, has three main qualities; it can move the passions, it can paint or describe, and it can instruct. Music, on the other hand, while it shares the first two qualities with poetry, has no part in the last. Thus any combination of music and poetry must take the two arts on the sides which are turned towards each other, ignoring the qualities which are found in one but not in both ; emotional and descriptive verse must be joined to emotional and descriptive music. But since the main object of the opera is to stir the emotions, and since music is easily pre-eminent in this respect, it follows

---

[1] See especially, in Planelli's book, pp. 85, 138, 139, 140, 144, 145.
[2] Work mentioned, i. 32.
[3] *Ibid.*, pp. 29, 30.

that this art must have the privilege of determining the
words, and making them conform to its peculiar needs.[1]
From this two main results follow.   In the first place,
the subject of opera must be emotional, not sententious,
reflective, or didactic.   In the second place, the action
of the drama must be greatly simplified, because the
expansive nature of music requires an ampler space to
work in than poetry.   Arteaga illustrates this by comparing the long and eloquent appeal of Merope, in Voltaire's
tragedy, that Polyphontes will restore her son to her,
with the simple brevity of the words Metastasio puts into
the mouth of a mother in similar circumstances :—

> "Rendimi il figlio mio :
> Ahi ! mi si spezza il cor :
> Non son più madre, oh Dio !
> Non ho più figlio." [2]

Here, although the words are so simple, and apparently so bald, the art of the musician can move the
hearer much more deeply than the mere verbal declamation of Voltaire.   The style of a tragedy, he con-
cludes, must then be *drammatico*, the style of a musical
drama *drammatico-lirico*.[3]   And from this he arrives at

---

[1] Work mentioned, pp. 35–40. Note particularly, on pp. 38, 39, and
again on pp. 42, 43, passages on the power of music which anticipate
Wagner's theory of the "purely-human."

[2] *Ibid.*, pp. 40, 41.   The reader will again note the similarity between
Arteaga's theory and Wagner's *Opera and Drama*.   I may remark, in passing,
that any one who feels that Wagner's so-called "poetry" is at times somewhat poor stuff—regarded as poetry—and that what makes us put up with it
is simply the magnificence of his music, may be confirmed in this opinion by
a simple perusal of his sketch of a drama on the subject of *Wieland the Smith.*
Anything more utterly absurd and childish than some of the scenes could not
well be imagined ; yet it is quite certain that had Wagner carried out his intention of setting the drama to music, he would have thrilled us with it as he
does with the *Ring.* See especially the second, third, and fourth scenes of
the last act of *Wieland.*

[3] Compare Rousseau—"It is a deep and important problem to resolve,
how far we can transmute language into song, and music into speech.   On a
true solution of this question depends the whole theory of dramatic music."—
Œuvres, ix. 578.

the further conclusion that not every character that is fitted for the spoken drama is congruous to the scheme of opera. Wagner has enforced the same point with undue prolixity ; and Mr. Ruskin also has told us that "the maiden may sing her lost love, but the miser may not sing his lost money-bags."

From this it will readily be seen that Wagner is doing both the old opera and the old critics an injustice in his analysis of the history and the nature of opera. Both composers and critics were really striving after results similar to those desired by him ; and it had become as clear to their consciousness as it was to his, that the power of music is greater than that of poetry in the sphere where the two arts touch each other, that a musical drama must try to represent no more than a simple, easily apprehensible action, and that it must content itself with the great primary human emotions— what Wagner would call the "purely-human." Only the æstheticians of the eighteenth century saw what Wagner could not see—that the musical drama was only one among other arts. Arteaga's distinction between a poetical tragedy as dramatic, and an opera as *lyric-dramatic*, cuts much more deeply than Wagner's rough-and-ready assumption that the only "true" drama is the musical—an assumption that, when looked at from the point of view of normal æsthetic, is plainly seen to involve the necessary shaping of every factor to suit the needs of music, just as, according to Arteaga's demonstration, was the consecrated practice in his day.

IV

Let us now look at the matter from quite another side, and endeavour to discover the genesis of Wagner's ideas upon poetry and music. It has already been suggested in the foregoing pages that Wagner tended to conceive life in terms of music where other men would

conceive it in terms of speech—this accounting for the
fact that the *musical* drama for him outweighed in importance all other forms of drama and of poetry.   The
other side of the question now calls for consideration.
We shall find that in many respects his mind was *sui
generis,* and that on this account some of his opinions,
though of the utmost interest to the æsthetic psychologist, cannot possibly be elevated into norms of art for
the mass of men.   His artistic conceptions seem to
have been a kind of blend of poetry and music; it
being almost impossible for him to generate his verse
apart from his music, or his music apart from his verse.
"You perhaps cannot imagine it," he once wrote to
Uhlig, "but everything comes quite naturally.   The
musical phrases fit themselves on to the verse and the
periods without any trouble on my part; everything
grows as if wild from the ground."[1]   Many passages
in *Opera and Drama,* indeed, raise the suspicion that
Wagner could not as a rule cognise music apart
from certain poetical associations—that he flooded his
musical impressions of a work with other and more
concrete impressions derived from poetry.   And many
instructive passages in his letters confirm this idea.
Let us look at some of them in relation to Beethoven.
In one of his letters to Uhlig he lays stress upon what
he would call the poetical basis of Beethoven's great
music, and the necessity of comprehending this basis if
we would hear the music as Beethoven meant us to
hear it.

"A subject is here touched upon," he writes, "truly fatal to
our post-Beethoven musical doings: in my opinion, nothing
less than the proof that Beethoven, in his true essentials, is
universally and absolutely *not* understood.   I, at least, cannot
view the matter otherwise, as I myself have become convinced
that *I,* too, have only understood Beethoven since I sought for

---

[1] Letter 30 to Uhlig; Eng. trans. p. 115.

the poetical subject of his tone-utterances, and at last found it: *Coriolan* proves this clearly to me. I maintain that until now people, when they performed the real Beethoven, have only imitated and listened to a language of which they perceived only the outward sound, which indeed they only understood as you perchance understand sonorous Greek verse when you hear it recited; *i.e.* you take pleasure in the sound—now soft, now strong, now muffled, now clear—but you do not perceive the sense which is contained in the verse. Is it otherwise? What now is all our idolatry of Beethoven?—Answer!" [1]

Most significant of all, however, is the letter in which he refers to his own interpretation of the *Coriolan* over-ture—a letter which, long as it is, must be quoted almost entire, as it is perhaps the most important of all the documents that help us to an understanding of Wagner's psychology :—

"The conductor of compositions such as those of Beethoven has seldom hitherto conceived the special nature of his task. He should clearly be the channel for their understanding by the laity; and if, at bottom, this can only be achieved by a com-pletely adequate performance, the question must next be—How is such a performance to be brought about? *The characteristic of the great compositions of Beethoven is that they are actual poems: that in them it is sought to bring a real subject to representation.* The stumbling-block in the way of their comprehension lies in the difficult task of finding with certainty the subject represented. Beethoven was completely possessed by his subject: his most pregnant tone-pictures are indebted almost solely to the in-dividuality of the subject with which he was filled; in conscious-ness of this, it appeared to him superfluous to denote his subject otherwise than in the tone-picture itself. Just as our word-poets address themselves only to other word-poets, so did Beethoven in this unconsciously address himself only to the tone-poets. *Even the absolute musician, that is to say, the ringer of the changes of absolute music, could not understand Beethoven, because this absolute musician looks always for the 'How' and not the 'What.'* The

---

[1] Letter 56 to Uhlig; Eng. trans. pp. 196, 197.

laity, on the other hand, could but be completely confused by these tone-pictures, and at best be only led to pleasure in *that* which served the tone-poet merely as the material means of his expression.

"It is only by absolute musicians that the tone-poems of Beethoven have hitherto been presented to the public; and it is obvious that such a course could only result in misunderstanding. The only province of the absolute musician was the 'How'; and even this he could not see aright if he did not first understand the 'What,' for which the 'How' was only a vehicle. Thus the mutual relationship of the conductor and the orchestra remained one of complete misunderstanding; the conductor laboured only to give voice to musical phrases which he himself did not understand, and had only appropriated to himself, as a reciter learns by heart pleasant-sounding verses according to their sound which are composed in a foreign tongue, and one unknown to him. Naturally it is only the sheer externals that can here be seized; the speaker can never deliver and intone with personal conviction —he must slavishly hold fast to the merest outward accident of sound, in the manner in which he has been taught to repeat the phrase by rote. *Let us conceive for a moment what measure of understanding a poet would meet with if, by the reciter on the one hand, and the hearer on the other, the word-tones only were reproduced and received; as must be the case were the poem presented in a tongue which neither the declaimer (who had only learnt it by ear) nor the hearer understood.* Yet this comparison with the customary performances of Beethoven's works one can only pronounce exaggerated,[1] insomuch as one ascribes to tone-speech, as the more universal, an easier and more immediate comprehensibility than to rational word-speech. But here we find the fallacy to lie in the particular sense in which we use the word 'understanding.' Provided no special poetic subject is expressed in the tone-speech, it may by all means pass as easily understandable; for there can be no question of real understanding. If, however, the expression of the tone-speech is conditioned by a poetical subject, this speech becomes straightway the least comprehensible of all, if the poetical subject be not at the same time defined by some other means of expression than those of absolute music.

---

[1] One can, indeed—though not in the sense intended by Wagner!

K

"The riddle of the poetical subject of a tone-piece by Beethoven is thus only to be solved by a tone-poet; for, as I remarked before, Beethoven involuntarily appealed only to such, to those who were of like feelings, like culture, nay, well-nigh like capability with himself. Such a man alone can interpret these compositions to the understanding of the laity, and above all by clearly defining the subject of the tone-poem, to the executants as well as to the audience, and thus making good an involuntary error in the technique of the tone-poet, who omitted such denotement. If a right understanding be not effected in such a way, every performance of Beethoven's veritable tone-poems, however technically perfect, must, in a measure, remain misunderstood. The most convincing proof of this we may easily win by accurately gauging the attitude of our modern concert-audience towards Beethoven's creations. Were these really understood by the audience, that is to say, consonantly with their poetical subject, how could this same public tolerate a modern concert-programme? How were it possible to set before the hearers of a Beethovenian Symphony at the same time a medley of musical compositions utterly lacking in depth of content? Yet do not our musical conductors and composers themselves, for the same reason, namely, that they have not recognised the poetical basis of these tone-creations, prove by the matter and the manner of what, in spite of Beethoven's warning example, they compose to-day, that they have never rightly understood them?

"Were the confused and erratic instrumental composition-mongering of the day possible, if these people had understood the true essence of Beethoven's tone-poems? This essence of the great works of Beethoven is that they are only in the last place *Music*, but, in the first place, contain a poetic subject. Or shall we be told that this *subject* is only taken from the realm of music? Would this not be as much as to say that the poet takes his subject from speech, the painter his from colour? *The musical conductor who sees in one of Beethoven's tone-works nothing but the music, is exactly like the reciter who should hold only by the language of a poem, or the explainer of a picture who should see in the painting nothing but its colour.* This, however, is the case with our conductors, even in the best instances—for many do not even so much as understand the music—they understand the key, the theme, the distribution of the voices, the instrumentation, and so on, and think that herewith they understand all the contents of a tone-work.

"It is only the non-professional musician who has opened the path to the understanding of Beethoven's works, as involuntarily he longed to know what special thought had influenced the composer in his music. But here men met their first obstacle. Imagination, striving for understanding, laid its hand on all kinds of arbitrary conceits, of romantic scenes and picturesque adventure. The grotesqueness, and for the most part triviality, of such interpretations was soon detected and thrust on one side by minds of finer calibre. As such pictures proved distasteful, folk thought it the best plan to lay aside once for all any kind of explanation. Yet in the impulse that led to such attempts at interpretation there lay a right sound instinct; but it was only possible for one completely intimate with the characteristic traits of the tone-work to designate its subject, in such a manner as it had—even though unconsciously—hovered before the vision of the tone-poet himself. Again, the great difficulty of such interpretations lay in the character of the subject itself, which is only presented to us by the tone-poet in his tone-painting; and only one who had well weighed this difficulty could successfully dare attempt to assist a right understanding in the needful manner. . . . It was, however, in my ' Coriolan Overture' that I was able to arrive at the clearest interpretation of the poetical subject. I may say that he who knows accurately my explanation of this subject, and follows its clue from phrase to phrase, must admit that without this explanation he had never understood this most plastic of all tone-works; unless, indeed, he had from the general title, 'Overture to Coriolan,' felt out for himself the scene just as I did myself. With such an understanding the enjoyment of such a composition is immeasurably enhanced." [1]

These citations will, I think, prove conclusively that Wagner listened to symphonic music in a state of mind different from that of other people; as I have already expressed it, he seemed to flood his purely musical impressions with other impressions derived from more

[1] Letter 55 to Uhlig, Eng. trans. pp. 184–190.

concrete associations. And of this he was evidently quite unconscious—quite unaware, that is, of the fact that his was a thoroughly abnormal case. He does, indeed, make the very naïve confession that he was guided to the comprehension of the poetical basis of the *Coriolan* overture by his previous knowledge of the poetical play;[1] and further, that there was practically no means of knowing, in the case, say, of a Beethoven symphony, which *was* the correct "poetical interpretation," so that if any one chose to have an interpretation of his own, Wagner could only oppose to this his mere dogmatic *dixi*. But he seems never to have realised how entirely abnormal some of his own conceptions of music were, how utterly alien they were to the majority of minds. It is an error for his admirers to follow him along this course. The great lines of art, which have been marked out by the constant toil of all men's minds striving in the same direction, are not to be effaced in a moment by being crossed by a mind that is *sui generis;* and it is much the saner course to recognise frankly that Wagner's brain was in some ways of a constitution so radically different from that of the great majority of men, as to make many of his perceptions of no general value to the æsthetic of music,

---

[1] See also his *Beethoven*, G. S. ix. 108; Ellis, v. 108. In the same way, he was only able to read the "drama" of *Fidelio* into the great *Leonora* overture because the opera itself had already afforded him the key. "This opera-subject," he writes, "embraced so much that was foreign to Music and unassimilable, that in truth the great overture to *Leonora* alone makes really plain to us how Beethoven would have the drama understood. Who can ever hear that thrilling tone-piece without being filled with the conviction that Music includes within itself the most consummate *Drama?* What is the dramatic action of the librettist's opera *Leonora* but an almost repulsive watering of the drama we have lived through in its overture, a kind of tedious commentary by Gervinus on a scene of Shakespeare's?" (*Beethoven;* G. S. ix. 105; Ellis, v. 106). The exaggeration of all this must be evident. No man who does not know the story of *Fidelio* ever saw a "drama" in the overture; to him it is only a fine composition in symphonic form. On the other hand, if we once begin to read "drama" into music in this way, there would be really no symphony whatever in which some one or other might not discover a drama.

though they may be interesting enough to the psychologist. It is as absurd to follow him in some of his theories because we admire his music, as it would be to attempt to see blue yellow because a great poet was colour-blind. It takes very little power of psychological analysis to see, as I have said, that Wagner stood almost alone in the peculiar manner in which he listened to a Beethoven symphony; and that neither the mass of men, nor, we may say, Beethoven himself, ever infused into this music, as they listened to it, conceptions of a " poetical basis."

The psychological state of the case may best be seen by re-examining some of the passages of these two letters. Four times he uses the same simile to describe the ordinary way of cognising a symphony, as compared with his way :—

(a) "I maintain that until now people, when they performed the real Beethoven, have only imitated and listened to a language of which they perceived only the outward sound, which indeed they only understood as you perchance understand sonorous Greek verse when you hear it recited; i.e. you take pleasure in the sound—now soft, now strong, now muffled, now clear— but you do not perceive the sense which is contained in the verse."

(b) "Let us conceive for a moment what measure of understanding a poet would meet with if, by the reciter on the one hand, and the hearer on the other, the word-tones only were reproduced and received; as must be the case were the poem presented in a tongue which neither the declaimer (who had only learnt it by ear) nor the hearer understand."

(c) "The conductor laboured only to give voice to musical phrases which he himself did not understand, and had only appropriated to himself as a reciter learns by heart pleasant-sounding verses according to their sound which are composed in a foreign tongue, and one unknown to him."

(d) "The musical conductor who sees in one of Beethoven's tone-works nothing but the music, is exactly like the reciter who should hold only by the language of the poem."

Nothing could be more utterly wrong than this; nothing could more clearly show how Wagner's abnormal prepossessions blinded him to the most elementary fallacies of his writings. There is not the slightest analogy between the pleasure *any one* gets from music and the pleasure he would get from hearing a poem recited in a language unknown to him. It is one more signal proof of how little Wagner was capable of the true appreciation of poetry *as* poetry, by reason of the abnormality that made him conceive poetry in terms of music, and music in terms of poetry. Who, let us ask, even if he would receive *any* pleasure from hearing Arabic verse read to him without his comprehending it—which I very much doubt—would for a moment rank that pleasure as being similar to the pleasure he receives from even an octave passage played upon a 'cello, or the mere holding of the common chord upon a piano? The fallacy is the old one—due to the verbal blunder of speaking of the "music" of a poet's verse—that the delight in poetry is in any way, except on the side of rhythm, of the same order as the delight in music. As Edmund Gurney puts it, the musical sensation is "the element of measured rhythm or time-regularity in the order of sounds"—which music shares with poetry—plus an element of quite another sort, the order of "sounds in respect of pitch"—which is peculiar to music alone; and "*the product is as different from each of its components as water is different from oxygen and hydrogen.*" [1] It is this product which causes the specifically musical, as distinct from the poetical, delight; and there is not the faintest analogy, as Wagner supposes, between this sensation and that derived from hearing a number of vowels and consonants declaimed in a tongue we do not understand.

We do not, in fact, *hear* a mere sound—in the psychological sense—exactly in the same way as we

[1] Essay on *Poets, Critics, and Class-Lists*, in *Tertium Quid*, ii. 158, 159.

hear a musical sound ; the two sensations are not the same.   For it is important to note that not only is the *meaning* of one note of a melody conditioned by what goes before and after it, but its very *beauty* is conditioned in the same way.   Our pleasure in an exquisite melody is not due to the single notes themselves—for these, sounded separately, or played in another order, would either give us a different pleasure or no particular pleasure at all—but comes from the conceptual whole into which they are bound.   Where is the analogy to this in Wagner's simile?   Our reader of Arabic might transpose the words of the poem as he liked, or he might read it backwards, or he might read mere nonsense-verse, without our being any wiser, without our feeling the intellectual frustration that ensues upon the distortion of a melody ; and such pleasure as we might derive from his reading would come merely from some peculiarity in a sound here and there that momentarily captured our interest, but which would not be linked in intellectual bonds to what went before or after.[1]   Our main appreciation of poetry does not spring from the mere sensation of tone, but from the throng of allied moods and emotions evoked, by association, by the words, which therefore *must* be understood.   In music, on the contrary, the tonal texture *is* pleasing in itself ; and for Wagner to argue as if there were any analogy between the impression made on us by such a poetical reading as I have supposed, and the impression made by even the simplest strain of music, is simply to reduce argument to caricature.   I am well aware that æstheticians of calmer logic than he have unawares given him countenance for part of his simile, by arguing that in certain fine poetry the intellectual or emotional impression is inseparable

---

[1] On this and other points see Gurney's essay already cited, in which he argues that the truly poetical delight has only the very faintest similarity to our delight in music, and that it comes from the "representative" rather than the "presentative" functions of the words.

from the impression of the sound *quâ* sound, and that the latter is able to evoke the former in the mind of a hearer ignorant of the language in which the poem is written. Mr. Theodore Watts, for example, thinks that "Sappho's passion is expressed so completely by the mere sound of her verses that a good recitation of them to a person ignorant of Greek would convey something of that passion to the listener"; and that "Poe's *Ulalume*, properly intoned, would produce something like the same effect upon a listener knowing no word of English as it produces upon us."[1] One has only to test the theory to see how utterly it breaks down. If we are ignorant of Italian, a leading article from an Italian newspaper, arranged in verse-rhythm, will impress us as much as the finest verse of Dante. One of the stumbling-blocks to our appreciation of any foreign poetry is, indeed, this tendency to be impressed by sound purely as sound; for we constantly catch ourselves admiring on these grounds a line which a native will assure us to be perfectly ordinary and un-poetical; while the finest lines create their effect not by mere sound but by the evocation of associations along with each word—an evocation that can only ensue if the word is understood. Shakespeare's fine line "The multitudinous seas incarnadine" would, I think, affect a foreigner ignorant of English no more than "A primrose by the river's brim," or "Let dogs delight to bark and bite."[2]

---

[1] Article on Poetry in *Encyc. Brit.* (9th ed.), p. 260.

[2] As Edmund Gurney says, "I have seen foreigners of literary tastes, but ignorant of English, simply amused by what seemed to them the sing-song of fine English verse properly 'intoned.' I am certain that, if due precautions were taken, ''Twas brillig,' &c., or 'The Jumblies' would impress such persons quite as much as *Ulalume*, and that they could be made to detect some of the passion of Sappho in many a Greek prize-poem, if not in the *Needy Knifegrinder;* in short, that there is no limit to the 'sells' of which they would readily become the victims. . . . Language has got much too far away from its origin in the emotional cry for its symbols to produce by their abstract sound-arrangements any certain emotional colouring; and even the

It is clear, then, that Wagner is altogether wrong in his opinion that any man could listen to even the most unintelligent reading of a symphony, and receive therefrom the same kind of impressions as he would receive by listening to a recitation of poetry in a language unknown to him. There can be no question, however, of the sincerity with which Wagner puts the opinion forward, and consequently of the prime importance of it in the attempt to estimate his psychological structure. He carries his prejudice against what he calls the merely musical interpretation of the symphonies so far as to say that "in a certain most weighty, and perhaps the only right sense, Beethoven has hitherto been only understood by non‑musicians, and by professional musicians not at all."[1] He really imagines, that is, that while non-musicians have listened to Beethoven as I would listen to the reading of a poem of Shelley, the "professional musicians" have listened to the symphonies as I might listen to the *Shah-Nameh* read to me in Persian!

"Mendelssohn's performance of Beethoven's works," he continues, "was always based only upon their purely musical side, and never upon their poetical contents, which he could not grasp at all; otherwise he would himself have brought far other wares to market. For my own part, Mendelssohn's conducting, despite its great technical delicacy, always left me unsatisfied as to the root of the matter; it was always as though he could not trust to letting that be said which Beethoven meant, because he was not at one with himself as to whether anything at all was meant, and if so, what?"[2]

On the surface it might read as if he were merely criticising Mendelssohn's handling of the *tempi*, &c. ;

slight suggestiveness possible to such arrangements can just as easily contradict as conform to the sense—as shown in almost any good parody."—Essay on *The Appreciation of Poetry*, in *Tertium Quid*, ii. 202, *note*.

[1] Letter 55 to Uhlig, Eng. trans. p. 190.
[2] *Ibid.*, pp. 190, 191.

but looked at in conjunction with the other passages of his letter to Uhlig, it is evident that Mendelssohn's reading displeased him because it did not harmonise with his own notion of the "poetical basis" of the music. Later on he exhorted Uhlig to "read in Prutz's *Deutsche Museum* an article *Der Geist in der Musik*, by Otto Gumprecht; . . . among other things you will find in it a heavenly explanation of the A major symphony, in which everything is frenzy, despair, and— God knows what else! There's choice reading for you! It is inconceivable what a fine thing absolute music is!"[1] Well, one can only retort that whatever absurdities may be committed by the Gumprecht method of interpreting symphonic works, they are at least paralleled by the Wagnerian method; and that when Lachner roused his ire by putting the following notice in a concert-programme as an explanation of the *Tannhäuser* overture—" Holy, serene frame of mind! Night draws on — The passions are aroused — The spirit fights against them—Daybreak—Final victory over matter—Prayer—Song of Triumph"[2]—he might, if he had been wise, have recognised the perils that also beset the path of him who undertakes to demonstrate the "poetical basis" of music.

His case, however, admits of further psychological elucidation. "Let us hold fast," he once wrote, "to the principle which I laid down in my letter to Brendel: Ever to raise, strengthen, and develop music, where it is developing itself in the direction of poetical art; and where this is not the case, to point out the mistake, and condemn what is faulty."[3] Clearly, the man who could write thus knew nothing of the æsthetic pleasure given to the average musical hearer by a symphony, and knew still less of poetical pleasure as all

---

[1] Letter 69 to Uhlig, Eng. trans. pp. 243, 244.
[2] Letter 90 to Uhlig, Eng. trans. pp. 299, 300.
[3] Letter 55 to Uhlig, Eng. trans. p. 190.

other men experience it. Poetry to him had always something of the breath of music in it, and so was not poetry as we understand it ; while music to him had something of the peculiar psychological coherence of poetry, and so was not music in our acceptation of the term. Thus in *Opera and Drama*, in discussing the relation of absolute music to opera, and the significance of the work of Beethoven, he begins boldly with the statement that—

"The history of Instrumental-music, from the moment when that longing first evinced itself,[1] is the history of an artistic error ; yet of one that ended, not in the demonstration of an impotence of Music's, like that of the Operatic genre, but with the revelation of a boundless inner power. The error of *Beethoven* was that of Columbus, who merely meant to seek out a new way to the old known land of India, and discovered a new world instead. . . . For us, too, has there been unveiled the exhaustless power of Music, through Beethoven's all-puissant error. Through his undaunted toil, to reach the artistically Necessary within an artistically Impossible, is shown us Music's unhemmed faculty of accomplishing every thinkable task, if only she is content to stay what she really is—an *art of Expression*.

"Beethoven's error, however, alike with the boon of his artistic deed, we could not fully estimate until we were in a position to survey his works in their totality, until he and his works had become for us a rounded whole, and until the artistic labours of his followers—who adopted into their own creations the error of the master, without either the right of ownership or the giant force of that longing of his—had shown us the error in its clearest light. The contemporaries and immediate successors of Beethoven, on the other hand, saw in his separate works, whether in the magical impression of the whole or the peculiar shaping of its details, precisely That alone which, always according to the strength of their receptivity and comprehension, was

---

[1] That is, "the longing for a clear and intelligible portrayal of definite, individual human feeling." The characteristic of Beethoven, he continues, was that he strove to express "an altogether definite, a clearly-understandable individual Content," instead of "the general character of an emotion."

obvious to them at a glance. So long as Beethoven was at unison with the spirit of his musical era, and simply embedded the flower of that spirit in his works: so long could the reflex of his art-production prove nothing but beneficial to his surroundings. But from the time when, in concord with the moving sorrows of his life, there awoke in the artist a longing for distinct expression of specific, characteristically individual emotions—as though to unbosom himself to the intelligent sympathy of his fellow-men—and this longing grew into an ever more compulsive force; from the time when he began to care less and less about merely making music, about expressing himself agreeably, enthrallingly or inspiritingly in general, within that music; and instead thereof, was driven by the Necessity of his inner being to employ his art in bringing to sure and seizable expression a definite Content that absorbed his thought and feeling—thenceforth began the agony of this deep-stirred man and imperatively straying (*nothwendig irrenden*) artist. Upon the curious hearer who did not understand him, simply because the inspired man could not possibly make himself intelligible to such an one, these mighty transports and the half-sorrowful, half-blissful stammerings of a Pythian inspiration, could not but make the impression of a genius stricken with madness.

"In the works of the second half of his artistic life, Beethoven is un-understandable—or rather misunderstandable—mostly just where he desires to express a specific, individual Content in the most intelligible way. He passes over the received, involuntary conventions of the Absolute-musical, *i.e.* its anyway recognisable resemblance—in respect of expression and form—to the dance or song-tune; he chooses instead a form of speech which often seems the mere capricious venting of a whim, and which, loosed from any purely musical cohesion, is only bound together by the bond of a Poetic purpose impossible to render into Music with full poetic plainness. The greater portion of Beethoven's works of this period must be regarded as instinctive efforts (*unwillkürliche Versüche*) to frame a speech to voice his longing; so that they often seem like sketches for a picture, as to whose *subject* indeed the master was at one with himself, but not as to its intelligible grouping."[1]

---

[1] G. S. iii. 277–279; Ellis, ii. 70–72.

Wagner is undoubtedly right in noting the change that came over Beethoven in his later compositions, where the colossus seems to be stammering and moaning in the effort to find expression for his thought ; but there is no warrant for saying that this change was due to Beethoven having, somewhere in the recesses of his brain, a kind of poetical content which was absent from his earlier works. The interesting thing in Wagner's exposition is not the light it throws on Beethoven but the light it throws on Wagner himself. It is evident that his peculiar cerebral constitution made him comparatively insensitive to Beethoven's symphonic music, except in those works where the inspiration seemed, like that of Wagner's own music, to flow from concrete suggestions of life and the world. Wagner, in fact, seems to have been by nature a musical *dramatist* —that is, he conceived character in terms of sound as other men conceive it in terms of line and colour, or of words. The imaginative vision of a character found spontaneous realisation in music in a way that indicated how concrete his musical conceptions must have been, and how different from those of a pure symphonist. On the other hand, we have the same mental constitution revealed, in another way, in his prose works. He laid stress on the superior value of the *musical* drama as an art of life, because he himself conceived all human emotion and action in terms of music ; and he further tended, by virtue of this peculiar structure of his brain, both to despise what other people would call pure musical pleasure, and to read poetical meanings into such instrumental music as impressed him deeply. A brief investigation into the true psychology of the musician would enable us to explain Wagner's antipathy to certain symphonic products, his preference for music that seemed to him to have a poetical content, and his perception of poetical contents in music where other men fail to perceive them. We have seen from his letters that music needed to stimulate this concrete mood in him before he could appreciate it highly.   Now if, as we may suppose, his brain did not run easily along the lines of pure, absolute music, he would experience a difficulty in summing up the conception of a work of this order—of getting at its rationale, as it were—because the intellectual coherence of the work was of a different kind to that which was easiest to his own brain.   He has told us that one of the differences between Beethoven's earlier and later works is that in the latter we have "a form of speech which often seems the mere capricious venting of a whim, and which, *loosed from any purely musical cohesion, is only bound together by the bond of a Poetic purpose* impossible to render into Music with full poetic plainness."   Could there be a better description than the lines I have italicised of the peculiarity of Wagner's own musical psychology?   Compare a funeral march of Beethoven or Chopin, for example, with the *Trauermarsch* in the *Götterdämmerung*, and you will see the fundamental difference between the two orders of imagination that give birth to these so different products.   Wagner has all the time before his mind's eye a more concrete picture than the other composers ; his brain is filled with images of human life and its vicissitudes ; and the cohesion of his work is of quite a different mental order from that of Beethoven or of Chopin, whose inward picture is much vaguer and more diffused. We shall see, when we come to discuss *Tristan* and the *Meistersinger*, how this very quality of Wagner's mind could sometimes betray him into blunders of psychology. Let any one recall the prelude to the *Rheingold*, with its 135 bars of what is practically the chord of E flat, and compare it with a Beethoven symphony, and he will see the force of the remark that there was a vast difference between the musical psychology of the two men.   And just as Wagner's prepossession of certain

philosophic and social concepts made him blind to the
fact that other men did not see life quite as he saw it,
so the bias of his musical constitution tended to make
music built on a different psychological plan from his
simply colourless and inexpressive to him.   He was
able, in Beethoven's later works, to fix on certain
passages where the musician's mind seems to have lost
its externality of manner, and to be pouring forth the
lamentation of bitter personal experience.   Thousands of
people have noticed the same thing, both before and
after Wagner, but they do not explain it in the same
way as he.   In his case the more poignant accents of
Beethoven's latest works evidently acted as a stimulus
to his own brain, setting free the concrete associations
to play upon the musical flood ; and thus conceiving
the music in terms of articulate life, of action, of drama,
he imagined Beethoven to have had before his eye a
definite poetical content that in truth existed nowhere
but in Wagner's own brain.   The later change in
Beethoven's music was simply due to the fact that as
he grew older his experience of life became deeper
and more vitalised, and his art in the same degree
more poignant and forceful.   There is no warrant,
however, for supposing that the emotional moods that
prompted his later utterances were *psychologically* different
from those of his earlier works.   Different in degree
they may have been, but assuredly not different in kind.
Beethoven simply went through the course of development which every great artist experiences, the shadows
of the later days taking the place of the earlier sunlight ; and if he developed more than other musicians,
if his art became more poignant, more moving, more
human than theirs, it was simply because his was the
larger and the finer brain.   There is no reason whatever, short of the necessities of satisfying an *à priori*
theory, for supposing that he began to conceive music
under any more concrete terms than in his earlier

years. And some of us may be inclined to think that much of the strange procedure of some of his latest work — which Wagner imagines to be due to his attempt to achieve in absolute music what absolute music can never achieve—was the temporary aberration of a mind distraught with woe; a lapse from the serenity, the mastery of all his conceptions even in the hour of greatest spiritual anguish, which is the mark of the supreme artist. Some of Beethoven's later passages seem indeed to be at war with the limits of expression of symphonic music. He is not the first artist, nor is music the first art, to find that there is a borderland beyond which emotion ceases to be art, or amenable to the shaping hand of art; but we are not disposed to alter our frontier-lines of æsthetic psychology on that account. Beethoven's case, in fine, is not that of an artist who in his later years reaches out to the modes of utterance of another art, but of one who moves consistently along the lines of his earlier life, only finding in the end the brain so enriched with experience that expression becomes tortured and at times almost inartistic. There is no warrant for Wagner's theory.[1] One might as well say that Shakespeare, in the transition from the period of *Romeo and Juliet* to the period of *Hamlet* and *King Lear,* illustrated the inability of poetic speech to carry on the action of the drama, and revealed the fact that the "basis" of his later and finer works was something other than poetical. Once more let me repeat that while the peculiarities of Wagner's psychology are of profound interest to the æsthetician, it is simply foolish of his disciples to attempt to elevate them into norms for other men. We *do* see wonderful beauty in a mass of music that to Wagner was quite inexpressive;

---

[1] For a sanely critical study of Beethoven's development see Mr. J. F. Runciman's article on *Beethoven and his Ten Symphonies,* in the *New Review,* June and July 1896.

we do *not* see poetical meanings in music where he
says they exist; and by tracing his notions to their
fountain-head in the peculiarities of his mental structure, we are able to understand both the reasons for
his lack of appreciation of certain kinds of music, and
the unequalled power of his own dramatic gift. The
one phenomenon was simply the obverse of the other.
From his earliest manhood the tendency to read
poetical contents into music was observable; in his
early story of *A Pilgrimage to Beethoven* (1840), for
example, he makes poor Beethoven talk a great deal
of *à priori* Wagnerian æsthetic—thus showing that,
years before he had formulated his congenital bias
into a system of coherent thought, his brain ran
spontaneously to the conception of instrumental music
in terms of concrete life and action, instead of to the
conception of it as the embodiment of *une pensée
musicale*.

V

It may be thought that some justification is necessary of the position taken up in the preceding pages,
in order to bear out the statement that Wagner was
abnormal in some of his musical perceptions. It has
been insisted on throughout that he made a fundamental error in asserting the " drama " to be the end
in a combination of poetry and music, and that he
constantly loses sight of the peculiar significance of
poetry apart from music, as of music apart from
poetry. We have seen more particularly in his criticism of the ordinary readings of Beethoven's symphonies how blind he was to much of the delight
music can give us even when not associated with
words. He has not recognised, in fact, that the
musical state of mind can exist without any support
from the verbal, and is thoroughly self-sufficing. It
was part of his theory of art that just as the literary

L

drama was a degeneration from the acted drama, so absolute music was a degenerate branch of that primal art of sound whose origin was the human cry. The fallacy was not peculiar to himself, though in his attempt to make it bear out his theory of the musical drama he has pushed it farther than any one else has done. Briefly the fallacy is the old one that music arose as an imitation or an intensification of the tones of natural speech—a theory upon the truth or error of which a great part of Wagner's æsthetic must stand or fall. In our own day the leading exponent of the theory is Mr. Herbert Spencer, whose essay on *The Origin and Function of Music*[1] has been the starting-point of so much controversy. Mr. Spencer's theory, which may be taken as the representative of all similar theories, is that "variations of voice are the physiological result of variations of feeling"; that in obedience to these variations of feeling, the tones in which they are expressed vary in loudness, in timbre, in pitch, in intervals, and in rapidity; that these peculiarities of excited feeling are just those "which specially distinguish song from ordinary speech"; that song is therefore the extreme of all these alterations of voice, being distinguished from excited speech, as excited speech is distinguished from ordinary speech, by greater or less loudness of tone, greater resonance of timbre, higher or lower pitch, and wider intervals between the tones. Song, then, is simply, according to this theory, hyper-excited speech; and we may infer that it "originally diverged from emotional speech in a gradual, unobtrusive manner."

It would be foreign to the purpose of the present chapter to examine Mr. Spencer's theory in detail. It has to be observed, however, that while non-musicians have been impressed by his theory, æstheticians of really musical constitution have disagreed with it abso-

[1] *Fraser's Magazine*, Oct. 1857; reprinted in vol. ii. of his *Essays*.

lutely. It errs in supposing that because song exhibits
some of the characteristics of speech, the one has
necessarily taken its rise in the other. The resemblance between the external characteristics of speech
and those of song are only what might be expected,
seeing that both are phenomena of sound, and sound
can only vary in the ways indicated by Mr. Spencer.
There is no necessity, however, to assume, merely on
the basis of these resemblances, that song is only an
intensification of speech ; any more than when a man
has a headache and looks pale, we need assume that the
paleness is due to the headache—the truth being that
both headache and paleness are due to some underlying common cause. The mere resemblance of song
and speech in their most external characteristics is not
a proof that one is the outcome of the other, but
simply that they have certain causal phenomena in
common ; while the internal differences between them
are greater than their resemblances. Mr. Spencer himself admits that his theory affords no explanation of
the place of harmony in modern music,[1] while many
musical æstheticians have found it almost as unsatisfactory in respect to the origin of melody. The main
objection to the speech-theory is, briefly, that it leaves
unexplained precisely those elements in music that *make*
it music. Speak in your ordinary manner, for example,
and then in a slightly intensified manner, and the
mental transition is felt to be very slight. Hardly
more noticeable is the transition from excited speech
to ordinary recitative ; the mind feels that it is still in
the same atmosphere, though the breathing is a little
quickened. But sing a song, or play an adagio upon
the piano, and you will realise at once that you have
got upon quite a different plane of psychology. There
is no longer a mere difference of degree, as there was
in the transition from speech to recitative ; there is now

[1] *Essays*, vol. ii. pp. 447, 448.

an absolute difference in kind. As M. Combarieu puts
it, in criticising and extending Mr. Spencer's theory of
the origin of music from speech—

"Mr. Spencer neglects or ignores everything that gives to the
art he is studying its special and unique character; he does not
appear to have realised what a *musical composition* is, what are
the rules it obeys, what is the nature of the charm and the beauty
we find in it. In short, we can bring against him a fundamental
fact, in comparison with which everything else has only a quite
secondary value: that is, the existence of a *musical manner of
thinking* (*une pensée musicale*). The musician thinks with sounds,
as the *littérateur* thinks with words. It is a mysterious privilege,
but indubitable. If, in the vague domain of æsthetics, there is a
solid basis on which we can build, it is this; yet all the empirical
explanations have foundered upon this special faculty which
represents all the originality and perhaps all the psychology of
the musician. . . . Music has two different significations, united
in the one form like the soul and the body, of which the one is
very simple, while the other eludes all verbal analysis: it is at
once a direct imitation of the emotional life and of external
objects, and the language of a *sui generis* mode of thought which
dominates things. . . . Not only do poet and musician not
speak the same language nor obey the same laws, but they do not
think with the same faculty."[1]

The discussion of the psychological origin of music
and the connection of music with speech, has hitherto
been carried on mainly by æstheticians by way of
analysis of musical effects. In our own day, however,
fresh evidence has been brought to bear upon the

---

[1] Jules Combarieu, *Les rapports de la musique et de la poésie, considerées
au point de vue de l'expression;* Préface, pp. xxiii–xxvi. M. Combarieu, who
devotes nearly 180 pages to a very acute examination of the speech-theory,
points out that although Mr. Spencer cannot be gainsaid in the external
facts he adduces, his observations have not gone beyond externalities. On
the question as a whole see Hanslick, *Vom Musikalisch-Schönen;* Gurney,
The Power of Sound, chapters xiv. and xxi.; Saint-Saëns, *Harmonie et
Mélodie,* p. 12; Rousseau, *Essai sur l'origine des langues,* chap. xii., and *Lettre
sur la musique française;* Herder, *Ueber den Ursprung der Sprache;* Du
Bos, *Réflexions critiques sur la poésie et sur la peinture,* vol. i. chap. xlv.

question from physiological quarters; and the theory
that the *pensée musicale* is something quite different from
poetical thought or from ordinary speech, has been
strengthened by the demonstration—or partial demonstration—that music and speech proceed from distinct
cerebral centres. Dr. Stricker, by a series of careful
experiments, has shown (1) that the physical organs
with which speech is concerned are mainly situated in
the tongue, teeth, lips, and palate, while those of song
are in the larynx; and (2) that these distinct groups
of organs are controlled by distinct mental spheres.[1]
Further, it is now not only placed beyond dispute that
the faculty of articulate speech has its distinct cerebral
centre, but it has been localised in the third frontal
convolution of the left hemisphere of the brain; and
Dr. Wallaschek, in a brilliant paper, has striven to
show that there must be another centre that controls
musical thought and speech.[2]   Without going into
Dr. Wallaschek's theory in detail, it may be sufficient
here to note some of his facts and conclusions : (*a*) "the
forming of concepts goes on in a different part of the
brain, and the concepts travel along other channels,
than the expression of the feelings and the merely
automatic processes;"[3] (*b*) children with aphasia (*i.e.*
destruction or disturbance of the faculty of articulate
speech) are yet able to sing;[4] (*c*) patients with aphasia,
who cannot speak connectedly upon ordinary occasions,
can sometimes articulate the words when singing a song
—the words being brought up into consciousness by
association with the melody;[5] (*d*) the third left frontal

[1] See his book, *Du Langage et de la Musique* (Paris, 1885).
[2] *Ueber die Bedeutung der Aphasie für den musikalischen Ausdruck*
(*Vierteljahrsschr : für Mus-Wiss.*, September 1891).
[3] Article cited, p. 57.   [4] *Ibid.*, p. 60.
[5] For example : "One patient, from the beginning of his disease to his
death, could say nothing but *Yes* and *No*. . . . One morning a patient began
to sing 'I dreamt I dwelt in marble halls.' The speechless patient joined in
and sang the first verse with the other, and then the second verse alone,
articulating every word correctly."—*Ibid.*, p. 61.

convolution (which controls articulate speech) is very small in idiots and lower races, who yet are highly susceptible to music ; [1] (e) the faculty of musical memory may be destroyed without disturbing the other mental faculties ; [2] (f) consequently "we express ourselves and hear in quite a different manner when we sing and when we speak." [3]

Now all this throws a light both on the psychology of Wagner and on his theories. It shows in the first place how wrong he was in basing music upon "the primal cry" of early man, and in regarding song as "just speech aroused to highest passion"; [4] and in the second place it shows how abnormal his own mental constitution must have been for him to wish to limit the enjoyment of music to only that music which was suffused with "poetical contents." The specifically "musical manner of thinking," which is the essence both of a symphonic composition and of our appreciation of it, seems hardly to have been known to him. It would be easy enough to prove from his music how fundamental this musical attitude of mind is to our appreciation of music ; but it will be more to our purpose to show from other quarters the immense importance of the element which Wagner's theory neglects—the element of sheer delight in musical sound as musical sound, in musical structure as musical structure, in musical coherence as musical coherence.

The very fact of the long domination of Italian

[1] Article cited, p. 53, note: "Many idiots, who are scarcely capable of other impressions, are extraordinarily susceptible to music, and can remember a song which they have once heard."

[2] "A peasant, who as the result of a heavy blow on the head lay unconscious for three days, found, when he came to himself, that he had forgotten all the music he ever knew, though he had lost nothing else."—*Ibid.*, p. 64 (quoted from Carpenter, *Mental Physiology*, 4th edit. p. 443).

[3] *Ibid.*, p. 65.

[4] G. S. v. 72 ; Ellis, iii. 86. See also, for a repetition of Wagner's error, Hadow, *Studies in Modern Music*, i. 312–320 ; and Krehbiel, *Studies in the Wagnerian Drama*, p. 12.

opera ought to have warned him of the importance of sensuous tonal pleasure in music, and of the impossibility of ignoring it in any consideration of the future relations of music and poetry. When he himself writes an exquisite scene such as the love-duet in the *Valkyrie*, or Isolde's *Liebestod*, he is simply doing what Donizetti and Bellini did, though he puts a thousand times the force of brain into his compositions that they put into theirs ; he, like them, simply carries us along on a sea of sensuous delight. We are bound by our very constitution to appreciate the curve of a beautiful melody ; and the only difference between the curve of the *Liebestod* and that of *O mio Fernando* is that Wagner's is more complex and less obvious, and comes to us surcharged with greater experience of life. Psychologically speaking, however, he is appealing simply to the same faculty that Bellini and Donizetti and every other musician must appeal to—the faculty of cognising sounds in orderly and meaningful relations, and of enjoying them sensuously as well as intellectually. And the very fact that for so many generations men tolerated the absurdities of Italian opera ought to have shown him that there was something involved in this that could not be ignored, something that threw a light on the deepest recesses of æsthetic psychology. He ought to have recognised, in fact, that not only will more men be attracted by music than by poetry or the drama, but men will be and have been more tolerant of absurdities and incongruities in music than in drama or poetry ; there evidently being a quality in musical pleasure that can, upon occasion, override the dictum of the intelligence that the other constituents of the performance are nonsensical.

This is not a characteristic of the Italian opera alone. It would probably be impossible to point to a quarter of the globe of which it has not been true from time immemorial. One of the most curious features of

the music of savages is the way in which, in certain
performances, the pleasure given by the music itself
compensates for the absence of any meaning in the
words ; neither the singers nor the auditors, in many
cases, understanding the words, which may have belonged
to the now-forgotten tongue of their ancestors, or have
been borrowed, along with the music, from a foreign
tribe or from slaves.   At almost any savage song-
festival this phenomenon may be observed.

"These songs, for the most part," wrote a traveller of the
last century, "are filled with the fables of ancient times, the
heroic deeds of their nation, and are composed in an antiquated style—so old that they understand not what they say." [1]

Once more—

"Speaking of the Iroquois, Dr. Morgan says that their war-
songs are in a dead language, or, at all events, they are unable
to interpret them. . . . Mr. Baker, too, observed the meaning-
lessness of the Indian songs, making the additional remark
that primitive man could only be satisfied with such simple
utterances as long as his mind was too little developed.   I think,
however, this fact must have a deeper psychological source, for
even we sing our meaningless *tra la la*, &c., without being in
the least disturbed by its having no signification whatever." [2]

Everything, in fact, points to the fundamentally
satisfying quality of music itself, and to the existence,
even in the lowest psychological states, of that *pensée
musicale* which Wagner overlooked.[3]   In this connec-

[1] Père Lafitau ; *Mœurs des Sauvages*, quoted by Brown, *The Rise, Union
and Power, the Progressions, Separations and Corruptions, of Poetry and Music*
(1763), p. 30.

[2] Wallaschek, *Primitive Music*, pp. 173, 174.   Among the Australians,
Esquimaux, Bushmen, and others, again, "the melody is so far the chief
thing that the words are disarranged or mutilated to satisfy the rhythm, even
to the point of their losing all sense.   Our *traderidera tralala* have their
equivalent in the poetry of these races."—Ernst Grosse, *Die Anfänge der
Kunst*, quoted by M. Lucien Arréat, *Mémoire et Imagination*, p. 57.

[3] The explanation of our readiness to sing music either to paltry words
or to words we do not understand, is to be found not only in the fact that
the satisfying quality of music makes us insusceptible to the minor defects of

tion Dr. Wallaschek's conclusions are most interesting and significant :—

(1) "In primitive times vocal music is not at all a union of poetry and music. We find, on the contrary, vocal music among tribes which, owing to the insufficient development of language, cannot possibly have any kind of poetry. Thus the position of vocal music is quite independent of any other art.

(2) "It is impossible that in these cases music arose as a direct imitation of the natural accent ready made in speech, (3) because these texts are neither themselves a language, nor could the melody *alone* have been taken from a developed language, for in such a case the words would have been borrowed together with the music. Entirely meaningless words simply serve to facilitate the vocalisation." [1]

It almost reads as if Dr. Wallaschek were writing not of the music of savages, but of the Italian opera of the eighteenth and nineteenth centuries. Nor does the similarity end here.

" Another striking feature of these savage songs," he continues, "is *the liberty with which the composer treats the grammatical structure of the sentence and the logical order of words.* Thus in many of the Andamanese songs the words in their poetic form are so mutilated to suit the metre as to be scarcely recognisable. . . . If negroes sing they keep strict time, and do not allow themselves to be hindered by any obstacle in the use of words." [2]

its verbal accompaniment, but to the further fact—already dwelt upon—that musical conception and expression and verbal conception and expression have their own cerebral centres and their own nerve tracts. This affords an explanation of a curious phenomenon that must have been observed by all students of music—that when reading the score and text of a new opera for the first time, no clear or complete impression remains of the plot and action of the opera. To get this, as Dr. Wallaschek observes, we must read the text separately, with our eyes and brain unoccupied by the music.—*Ueber die Bedeutung der Aphasie*, p. 68. (See also Gowers, *Lectures on the Diagnosis of Diseases of the Brain*, pp. 122, 127.)

[1] *Primitive Music*, p. 174. Mr. Spencer also notes, without perceiving the bearing of the fact upon his own theory, that when singing, the East African "contents himself with improvising a few words without sense or rhyme, and repeats them till they nauseate."—*Essays*, ii. 434.

[2] *Ibid.*, pp. 174, 175.

Or as Père Lafitau observed of the Iroquois—

"Every one hath his particular song; that is, an air to which he adjusts a very few words, which he repeats as often as he pleaseth. I have observed that they even retrench or strike off some syllables from their words as if they were verses or measured words, but without rhyme."[1]

The evidence seems conclusive, then, that in the earliest, least theoretical, least sophisticated form of union of words and music, to which Wagner is so fond of referring for his own purposes, the music is found so satisfying in itself that all kinds of liberties are taken with the words—perfectly meaningless syllables being used, syllables being cut off anywhere to suit the rhythm of the music, or the chant accompanied by words the meaning of which is unknown to the singer. And a further link in the chain of evidence is the fact, now agreed upon, that so far from music springing from speech _viâ_ recitative— according, for example, to Mr. Spencer's and Wagner's theory—choral and melodic music precede recitative in historical sequence—the latter, indeed, being possible only among tribes whose language is fairly developed.

"The union of words and music," writes Dr. Wallaschek, "assumes at times a quite different form, resembling our 'recitative.' Upon the fact that this recitative does not occur in the _most_ primitive state of culture I have to lay special emphasis, if for no other reason than that it requires a comparatively developed language. . . . Examples like this form one of the strongest arguments against Mr. Spencer's speech-theory, according to which music arose from emotional speech, and the recitative was its most primitive form."[2]

Theodor Baker,[3] he further remarks—

"has shown by numerous musical examples the existence among North American Indians of two different forms of

---

[1] In Brown, _op. cit._, pp. 31, 32.   [2] _Primitive Music_, pp. 180, 181.
[3] _Ueber die Musik der Nordamerikanischen Wilden_, p. 47.

music — the recitative and the rhythmic choral song. In his opinion the latter is the older form of the two for the following reasons :—

"(1) The characteristic feature of primitive song was the collectiveness of amusement. (2) We find an unbroken line beginning with simple rhythmic songs up to accomplished strictly-measured airs. . . . (3) The rhythmic form has been mentioned by almost every writer upon the subject of North American Indians. (4) Such recitatives have a flow of words and a clearness of expression which are both incompatible with primitive song." [1]

From all this there arises the one conclusion, that Wagner went hopelessly astray in omitting to notice the great part played in opera by the mere sensuous quality of the sound, and by the musical imagination *per se* apart from poetry. I have already shown how little pleasure he experienced from ordinary symphonic music, which to him had an insufficient "poetical basis"; that is, he was unable to receive from specific music a specifically musical pleasure. It is interesting to compare any of Wagner's opinions upon symphonic music with the opinion of such a man as Edmund Gurney, who may here be taken as expressing the attitude of the normal musical mind.

"Music," writes Gurney, "in its abstraction and aloofness from visible and intellectual subject-matter, is naturally the one where reason soonest deserts the field; and, as a rule, the ex-

---

[1] *Primitive Music*, p. 186. In ancient Greece it was only in the later stages of the evolution of the arts that recitative began to take the place of melody. "Aristotle informs us that in his time the rhapsodists, whose profession it was to sing the poems of Homer and Hesiod, were beginning to make inroads into the ancient practice ; and now recited those poems which in former times had been always sung" (Brown, *op. cit.*, p. 117, referring to Aristotle's *Poetics*, Part V. 2). Brown, it may be noted in passing, combats the theory of Du Bos (*Réflexions Critiques*, Part III. c. 13), that declamation was employed in the episode of the ancient tragedy. See also note 269 in Twining's edition of the *Poetics*; Plutarch, *Concerning Music* (in Plutarch's *Morals*, Boston, 1878, vol. i. p. 107) ; and Athenæus, *Deipnosophists*, iii. 989 (Bohn's ed.).

pository efforts so common in musical programmes, after telling
us all the composer had in his mind, and *meant* to say, end by
naïvely admitting that what concerns us is, after all, what he
did say—to wit, *a certain self-justified succession of tones, appreci-
able only by means of a particular faculty which knows no law but
its own.*" [1]

Which passage constitutes, though Gurney did not
mean it to do so, an admirable criticism of Wagner
and his "poetical-basis" theory. Even more instructive as to the psychology of the musical mind that is
the direct opposite of Wagner's—and the mind, I
repeat, that is really the normal musical mind, for
Wagner's was an abnormality—is the passage in which
Gurney contends that not music, but poetry, lends
itself to the riot of the imagination in arbitrary
"explanations."

"It is naturally when we come to poetry," he says—"the
art which deals not only with visible aspects of life, but
with all life, with the whole sphere of the concrete, and not
only has this as its subject, but has words themselves as its
material—that verbal exposition finds its freest scope. Here
it is that reasoned criticism will go furthest towards covering
the field; and in proportion to the extent which it will really
cover, and to the amount of excellent and illuminating work
that it can do and has done, is the danger that the part which,
like the essence of music, cannot be explained or argued about, will
be ignored." [2]

Evidently to Gurney music was pure sensuous enjoyment of pure tonal form and colour, untroubled by
any suggestions from the realms of poetry and prose.

Even the aberrations of musicians and theorists
who have been guilty of overstatement in the contrary
direction to Wagner's do but prove how abnormal

---

[1] *Tertium Quid*, ii. 122, 123. Gurney's theory is perhaps slightly wrong
in parts. For a correction, see M. Combarieu's book already cited.

[2] *Tertium Quid*, ii. 124.

was his method of cognising music.   Helmholtz, for example, at the conclusion of his *magnum opus*, lays it down that music "does not seek to reproduce any natural truth, and cannot express any real object."[1] His argument is that music is not at all a "state of the soul," and that its effects can all be explained on purely physiological lines.

"In music," he writes, "the pure sensation plays a greater part than in the plastic arts; painting, for example, touches the eyes in order to awake certain images in the soul; at the same time that it produces an impression on the senses, it calls forth an act of intelligence which links that impression to an object external to us.   Now music is incapable of representing objects; the sounds which it employs have no other *raison d'être* than themselves, and produce their effect independently of any relation of imitation with any object whatever.   It results from this that the physiological study of sound plays a leading part in musical æsthetic, far greater than that of the study of light or of perspective in painting.   What in the other arts is only a means is here both end and means."[2]

There can be no question, of course, that Helmholtz is overstating the case here.   Our appreciation of music is something more than physiological delight in an orderly arrangement of sound ; it involves also an intellectual mode of receptiveness.[3]   This would probably have been admitted by him in later days, in the light of the criticism which the æsthetic portion of his great work from time to time encountered.   But divesting his theory of its extravagant trappings, we have to recognise the important truth running through it, that our appre-

---

[1] "In der Musik wird keine Naturwahrheit estrebt"; *Sensations of Tone*, pp. 3, 4.

[2] *Sensations of Tone*, p. 4.   Compare with this the extreme opinion of M. Victor de Laprade, who in his *Contre la Musique* pronounces music to be "the least human of the arts," because mathematical and physiological laws reign supreme in it, and the free intellect co-operates less than in any other art except architecture.   See also Ch. Beauquier, *Philosophie de la Musique*.

[3] See the criticism of Helmholtz by M. Combarieu, *op. cit.*, pp. 3–7.

ciation of music differs from our appreciation of poetry in the fundamental particular of sheer delight in the sensuous material of which it is composed. Of similar significance is the treatise of Hanslick on *Musical Beauty*,[1] in which he argues that the distinction between the form and the content of music is altogether false, and goes so far as to say that "the sorrowful impression which a melody makes on us comes, not from the real sorrow of the musician, but from the *intervals* between the notes of the melody; not from the anguish of his soul, but from the tremolo of the cymbals; not from his longing, but from chromatic progressions."[2] Hanslick, of course, represents an order of musical mind diametrically opposite to that of Wagner, his book being, indeed, designed to combat what he held to be the errors of the Wagnerian æsthetic; and in his zeal to discredit all attempts to look upon music as anything but music, he undoubtedly exaggerates, as Helmholtz does, the purely formal pleasure of the art. But underlying his extravagant exposition is the psychological truth one feels compelled to insist upon as against Wagner—that he is hopelessly astray in omitting to recognise the satisfying quality of musical sound *per se*, the self-sufficiency of the musical imagination in its own domain, and the extent to which his theory of poetry, music, and music-drama will consequently have to be modified.

What now is the explanation of this æsthetic blindness on Wagner's part? Bearing in mind all that has been said as to the distinct cerebral tracts that are con-

---

[1] *Vom Musikalisch-Schönen.*

[2] *Op. cit.*, p. 58. M. Combarieu (*op. cit.*, p. 14, *note*) points out that similar ideas had been put forward in the last century by Boyé, in his *L'Expression musicale mise au rang des chimères* (Amsterdam, 1779). Boyé "maintains that the expression is a matter of indifference, and 'bears the same relation to the words as the decoration to a room'; he goes the length of trying to prove that 'the music which approaches most nearly to expression is the most wearisome,' the *airs*, for example, being much more agreeable than the recitatives."

cerned with speech and music, it seems probable that
in Wagner these tracts were in closer correspondence
than in most men, thus causing him to flood his sensations of the one art with sensations derived from the
other. His brain, indeed, seems to have been in many
ways abnormal, and to have touched upon derangement
at many points—though kept from actual derangement
by the approximate balance of all the faculties. He
himself has told us, in his *Autobiographical Sketch*,[1] how
he used to have visions in which chords " seemed to
take on living form "—how he used, that is, to visualise
an auditory impression.[2] His mind, indeed, paid the
usual penalty of extraordinary fleetness of sensation and
ease of communication between its different parts ; he
was sometimes subject to the delusions that ensue when
one tract of the brain signals its message to another,
and the higher inhibiting power is incompetent to point
out how unreal is the phantom thus evoked. Read, for
example, his own curious account of what happened
when he was making the funeral speech over the
remains of Weber, which had, in 1844, been brought
from England to be buried in German soil. He seems
to have fallen into a kind of hypnosis, induced by the
sound of his own voice ; and he not only *heard* himself
but *saw* himself in front of the audience, and waited
expectantly for what was to come, as if he were another
being than the speaker, until the curious silence and the
sight of the faces turned towards him recalled him to
himself.[3]

The brain of Wagner thus seems to have been one
in which certain centres communicated more rapidly

[1] G. S. i. 6 ; Ellis, i. 6.

[2] A great many people, of course, *analogise* (if I may coin a word) music in
this or similar ways, some conceiving a musical sequence in terms of line,
others in terms of colour. But in its pronounced forms it is decidedly an
abnormality. See the brilliant and instructive study of music-madness in Mr.
Stanley V. Makower's story *The Mirror of Music*.

[3] See the G. S. ii. 45.

with each other than they do in the majority of individuals, and we have only to look at the matter in this
way to see the real reason of his blindness to many of
the effects of music and of poetry, as well as of his
exclusive preference for that order of music that had
poetical associations.   In ordinary men the mental
spheres that are severally concerned with the perception
of poetry and music remain for the most part separate,
so that music is cognised purely as music, poetry purely
as poetry.   But we have only to imagine a brain in
which these tracts were in closer intercommunication,
and we can see how such a brain would colour many
of its musical impressions with poetry, and many of its
poetical impressions with music.   Of this kind we may
conjecture Wagner's brain to have been.   Everywhere,
throughout his works and in his letters, we find him
looking at poetry as no poet would look at it, and at
music as few musicians would look at it ; railing at the
poets for cutting themselves adrift from music, at the
musician for striving to be independent of poetry ; reading poetical meanings into Beethoven, and stripping
poetry of everything that made it poetry ; and laying it
down that the musical art of the future should only be
allowed to develop in the direction of poetical art.   To
support positions like these he indulges in the most
extraordinary paralogisms, presenting, indeed, in his
constant apriorism, in the perpetual weakness of his
hold upon actual facts as they exist for the mass of
men, the spectacle of a mind enslaved to an inborn
hallucination.   There can, I think, be no question of
his being abnormal on this point, of his being utterly
off the ordinary line of human psychology ; and I trust
there is nothing extravagant in the hypothesis I have
put forward in explanation of it—that in his fine and
delicate brain poetry and music sang to each other
across the strands of matter, so that he never thought
of the one apart from the other, never knew in his own

soul what were the sensations of the lover of poetry as
poetry, or those of the lover of music as music. In no
other way can we explain all the aberration of conception and of argument in his theoretical work which
I have tried to emphasise in the foregoing pages.

VI

Let us now, for the sake of clearness, briefly
summarise the result of our criticism thus far. We
have seen that Wagner's great formula—" The error in
the art-genre of Opera consists herein : that a Means of
expression (Music) has been made the end, while the
End of expression (the Drama) has been made a means "
—is altogether erroneous. There is a primary fallacy
in the use of the word drama at all in this connection,
importing, as it does, alien meanings into opera ; for
the addition of music to poetry so alters the whole
complexion of the latter art, and gives rise to such
utterly different emotions, that if we now say the drama
is the " End " of the combination of poetry and music,
we must look upon the word as having quite a different
meaning from that which it has always had. Further,
when Wagner complains that in the old opera the poem
was written merely to suit the music, he forgets that
his own poems are written on the same adaptive
principle ; that upon this principle, indeed, in some
form or other, *all* poems must be written which are
intended for music. His complaint against the older
opera really amounts to this, that forms which men
had, by long experiment and by instinctive feeling,
discovered to be the best for music unaided by poetry,
were unthinkingly applied to music when associated
with poetry. Here, however, the very purpose of the
symphonic forms—to give coherence and intellectual
meaning to music that had not the support of words—
was distorted ; for a musical emotion reinforced by the

concrete suggestions of poetry has no need of these forms. The result of the imposition of unnecessary restrictions upon operatic music was necessarily to provoke a feeling of discontent in the intelligent hearer, for an alien form is not merely useless but a positive burden, hindering spontaneous delight in the art. Wagner is then wrong, both psychologically and historically, upon this point ; he attributes to the overweening pretensions of music in relation to poetry what should really be attributed to the mistaken use of certain more or less conventional forms. As a matter of fact, in his own operas, as in all vocal music, the main pleasure comes from the music rather than from the words ; and his failure to perceive the immense importance of the sensuous element is a fundamental blunder on his part. Nor is there any "pretension" on the part of the older composers which is not repeated by himself. He also shapes the words to suit the music ; he also lingers lovingly over a beautiful theme for the mere satisfaction it gives. His own procedure is simply that inevitable to every composer, due to the very nature of music itself ; the only difference being that he is less formalistic, less consciously swayed by custom and convention.

Further, when, as in the two long letters to Uhlig, he states at length his own conceptions of poetry and music, we find him falling into the most extraordinary fallacies. We were forced to conclude that he knew nothing of purely musical pleasure and purely poetical pleasure as other men experience them ; that in him, by some curious structure of brain, music and poetry were more closely intertwined than in other men ; and we sought a physiological explanation of this. Finally, by examining the practice of primitive tribes—where we found music *as* music satisfying the mind in spite of any incongruities in the words, just as in modern Italian opera—and the opinions of certain musical

æstheticians—who, in spite of the exaggerations of
some of them, show the normal psychological conditions of musical appreciation—we came to the conclusion that the element of delight in music for its own
sake, which Wagner (in theory) so strangely neglected
or despised, is of the utmost importance in any theory
of opera.

One or two points connected with Wagner's theory
still remain to be discussed. It has been argued in
the preceding pages that no one art or combination of
arts can now satisfy humanity, and take the place of
all the different arts, for the reason that these have
developed to their present form in obedience to a
diversity of intellectual and emotional wants ; and until
humanity changes so far as to lose these wants, each
of them can be satisfied only by the particular art that
has been born from it. The truth of an earlier argument must, I think, be admitted—that the man who
can take up Wagner's standpoint only does so because
he really knows nothing of the distinctive pleasures of
the arts. He knows, that is, nothing of the poetical
pleasure *I* feel when I read an ode of Keats, and still
less of my pleasure in reading a dramatic lyric of
Browning ; he knows nothing of the pleasure *I* experience when hearing a simple melody played upon the
piano, or of the pleasure given to *me* by the line and
colour of painting. Pleasure in these things of course
Wagner may have found ; but the point I am insisting
on is that it was not the pleasure of other men, not the
complete, wholly satisfying delight that craves no re-
inforcement from any other art.[1] And pushing the
analysis a little further, it becomes more and more
evident that Wagner, as I said in the earlier stages of

[1] M. Schuré speaks of "the confused aspiration of poetry towards music,
and of music towards poetry—*the desire for the other muse-sister felt by every
true poet and by every musician*" (*Le drame musical*, i. 287). One wonders
what can be the mental state of people who can spin theories in this way,
without the slightest regard for the facts that contradict them.

the present chapter, controlled poetry by music just as effectually as any of the composers whom he was never tired of condemning. He did not do it consciously, but his unconsciousness of the procedure made it none the less effectual. He was merely unconscious of it, indeed, because the musical mood from which this procedure came was the very foundation of his nature. Hence at once his blindness to it, and his ignorance of the very different standpoint from which other men regard poetry and music.

His own opera-poems, it may easily be shown, are for the most part not poetry at all in the proper sense of the word ; they are simply verses adapted for music. In writing them he adapted his poetry to his music as flagrantly as any previous composer could have done. The explanation of it is that the emotion from which he started out into expression was *not a poetical but a musical*[1] *emotion*. It was vague, expansive, lyric, tonal. It was from a mental state of this quality that his creative thought took rise. *This* was what he wanted to shape into utterance, and he unconsciously, instinctively, moulded his words to run in harmony with its possibilities. The reader of his prose works notices that architecture, sculpture, and painting seem scarcely to have appealed to him, the three "human" arts, as he calls them, being Dance, Tone, and Poetry. The beginning of the second part of *The Art-Work of the Future*, again, proves conclusively that Wagner's own emotions were fundamentally *musical*, and that all his reasoning upon music and the drama is vitiated by the fact that the mass of men take a quite different view of the arts. See, for example, the passage already quoted on p. 65, and compare the following :—

---

[1] The reader, of course, must understand the term "musical" here in the sense I have already given to it in connection with Wagner ; that is, as implying a state of mind less abstract and more objective than that of the "absolute" musician.

"Through this enforced renunciation, through this giving up of all delight in the physical element of his own utterance—at least of that degree of pleasure which the corporeal- and the emotional-man experience in their method of expression—the intellectual-man attains the faculty of giving by means of his speech-organ that certain utterance in seeking which the former found their bounds, each in his own degree. His capability is unlimited: he collects and sifts the universal, parts and unites according to his need and pleasure the images which all his senses bear him from the outer world; he binds and looses the particular and general even as he judges best, in order to appease his own desire for a sure and intelligible utterance of his feelings, his reflections, or his will. Yet he finds once more his limit where, in the agitation of his feelings, in the living pulse of joy or the violence of grief—there, where the particular and arbitrary draw back before the generality and spontaneity of the feeling that usurps his heart; where from out the egoism of his narrowed and conditioned personal sensations he finds himself again amid the wide communion of all-embracing world-emotions, a partaker in the unconditioned truth of universal feeling and emotion; where, finally, he has to subordinate his individual self-will to the dictates of Necessity, be it of grief or joy, and to hearken in place of commanding—he craves for the only adequate and direct expression of his endlessly enhanced emotion. Here must he reach back once more to the universal mode of utterance; and, in exact proportion as he has pressed forward to his special standpoint, has he now to retrace his steps and borrow from the emotional-man the physical tones of feeling, from the corporeal-man the physical gestures of the body. For where it is a question of giving utterance, immediate and yet most certain, to the highest and the truest that man can ever utter, there above all must man display himself in his entirety; and this whole man is the man of understanding, united with the man of heart and man of body—but neither of these parts for self alone."[1]

This passage alone is sufficient to show how closely Wagner's theories were dependent upon his own peculiar psychology. For him, no doubt, "the highest and

[1] *Art-Work of the Future;* G. S. iii. 65, 66; Ellis, i. 93, 94.

the truest that man can ever utter" found expression in sound; but it is not so for thousands of other men. To refer to our modern poetry as merely the language of the understanding, and therefore not an expression of the whole man, is begging the question. A poet or a lover of poetry might very well make Wagner the rejoinder that poetry gives utterance to more and deeper things than music can do. Is not the conclusion unavoidable that while Wagner was deeply stirred by music, he knew practically nothing of the emotions engendered in other men by other arts?[1]

On almost every page, indeed, of *Opera and Drama* we can see the same tendency to glorify music as being able to express almost all that men can say, simply because it expressed almost all that Wagner had to say. When he girds at "word-speech," as "the organ of the understanding," for not being able to satisfy "the feeling," it is evident that he was unaware that word-speech in poetry *does* satisfy millions of human beings far more completely than music can do. What he really means by "the feeling" is that peculiar impulse to generalised expression which can find vent only in music—that peculiar receptive faculty which in music alone can find satisfaction.[2] Take one or two examples at random :—

"In the Interest of this man all outward differences are to be raised into one definite thing; in which, however, the Interest must reveal itself according to its greatest, most exhaustive

---

[1] In the *Beethoven* again he wrote that "Drama towers above the bounds of Poetry in exactly the same manner as Music above those of every other art, and especially of plastic art, through its effect residing solely in the sublime" (G. S. ix. 105; Ellis, v. 106). Here he certainly overrates the possibilities of his own art. Plastic art gives us a thousand emotions which music cannot give, but which are none the less indispensable to us.

[2] This may be realised from passage after passage of *Opera and Drama.* See, for example, G. S. iv. 89, 90, 96, 99, 100, 101, 104, 120, 122, 127, 136, 137, 141, 142, 197, 198; Ellis, ii. 222, 229, 233, 234, 239, 257, 259, 264, 274, 275, 280, 343.

compass. But this is as good as saying that from this Interest all which savours of the particularistic and accidental must be taken away, and it must be given in its full truth as a necessary, purely human *utterance of feeling.*"

"A great conjuncture of phenomena—through which alone they are individually explicable—is only to be displayed, as we have seen, through a concentration of these phenomena; this concentration (*Verdichtung*), as applied to the phenomena of human life, means their simplification, and for its sake a *strengthening* of the moments-of-action—which, again, could only proceed from motives likewise strengthened. But a motive can gain an access of strength only through the ascension of the various intellectual moments contained in it, into one decisive ' moment '-of-feeling; while the word-poet can arrive at imparting this convincingly, only through the primal organs of the soul's inner feeling —through *Tone-speech.*"

"*A Tone-speech to be struck into from the outset* is therefore the organ of expression proper for the poet who would make himself intelligible by turning from the understanding to the feeling. . . ."

So far as passages of this kind merely have in view the undeniable fact that in any dramatic form, whether poetical or musical-poetical, the multiplicity of actual life must be concentrated and focussed in order to make an artistic effect, Wagner was simply expounding an æsthetic commonplace as old as Aristotle. His novelty consists in arguing that "the poetising understanding," through its medium of expression—word-speech—cannot present this focussed, concentrated "moment" to us in its true reality, and that this can be done by "the feeling" only, through *its* organ of expression—tone-speech. Clearly the state of mind that generated a theory such as this was at bottom merely a musical one. This is evident again from all his remarks upon the function of the vowel in the expression of the truly-human, and the necessity of its being uplifted to the higher emotional plane of music. It is evident once more when he discusses the present relations of music and poetry. Music, as he rightly says, does as it pleases with the rhythm of poetry, breaking it up or prolonging it according to its own necessities;[1] while the rhyme of poetry is either drowned in sound or totally disregarded as a division of the phrase. For this reason, in his own drama there shall be no discrepancy between the rhythm of the verse and that of the music. But he does not perceive that in writing verses such as his he is really controlling poetry by music just in the ordinary manner. For why do we not grumble when a

[1] He has pointed out how, in Greek poetry, the speaking-accent was interfered with at will to suit the exigences of musical accent, but he failed to perceive that this was precisely what music always has done and always will do with speech. He is right in saying that modern poetry cannot be made to proceed upon the basis of a sequence of classical "longs" and "shorts," though he does wrong in trying to enlist this fact in the service of his own theory of coincidence of musical and poetical accents. The true solution of the difficulty is that modern poetry is *not* quantitative in the sense in which Greek and Latin were—or are supposed to have been. The subject is too wide for discussion here; but for light upon the hopeless chaos of the current notions upon "accent" and "quantity" in ancient and modern verse I may refer the reader to Poe's essay on *The Rationale of Verse*, the appendix (on "Accent, Quantity, and Feet") to Mr. John M. Robertson's *New Essays towards a Critical Method*, Steele's *Prosodia Rationalis* (1779), Roe's *Principles of Rhythm, both in Speech and Music* (1823), Sidney Lanier's *Science of English Verse*, Professor Sylvester's *Laws of Verse*, J. Addington Symond's *Blank Verse*, Mr. T. S. Omond's *English Verse Structure*, and Mr. Robert Bridges' *Milton's Prosody*. Wagner betrays the very grossest ignorance of what constitutes poetical rhythm when he approves the action of the German actress—he calls her "intelligent"—who "had all her rôles written out in prose, so as not to be tempted *by their look* to exchange the natural speaking-accent for a sense-destroying scansion of the verse." Evidently neither she nor Wagner had any ear for the beauty and the variety of poetical rhythm. He tells us that "the secret of this Iambic has become patent on our acting stages. Intelligent actors, concerned to address the hearer's understanding, have spoken this verse as naked prose; unintelligent ones, unable to grasp the content of the verse by reason of its beat, have declaimed it as a sense- and tone-less melody, alike unintelligible as unmelodious." It is evident to any one who knows how to read poetry properly, that it should sound neither like unrhythmical prose nor like mechanical sing-song—that it has, in fact, a very subtle and constantly variable rhythm of its own. The point is interesting as affording yet another proof that Wagner knew nothing whatever of what constitutes poetry; that he was insusceptible to it; and that he saw real artistic beauty in music alone.

musician plays havoc with the rhythm of a poem? Why do we allow different composers to set the same poem to music of different rhythms? Why should a lyric of Heine go equally well in $\frac{2}{4}$, in $\frac{3}{4}$, in $\frac{12}{8}$, or in common time, with the syllables lengthened to any extent that the music may demand? For the simple reason that the musical rhythm takes such complete possession of the senses that the poetical rhythm is wholly disregarded. It is useless for Wagner to say that we *ought* to look upon this procedure as inartistic.[1] The plain and sufficient answer is that we do not; that extreme delight even can be given by a word being made to stretch over two or three musical tones—the music, which is the main source of our pleasure, atoning for everything. Now Wagner's own procedure is on a par with this; the only difference being that whereas another composer *musicalises* (if I may coin the word) the verse after it is written, Wagner treats it in this way before it is written. The amount of genuine *poetical* pleasure that is given us by his later opera poems is exceedingly small; they can hardly, indeed, be said to exist as poetry, their whole *raison d'être* being the music. Their primitive rhythm, for example, is a very poor substitute for all the wealth of rhythm of modern poetry; and since Wagner manages to make his lines acceptable to us by dowering them with all the beauty and variety of musical rhythm, it is evident that in *his* opera music has the upper hand in relation to poetry as effectually as in the operas of any other composer. Nor, in face of the many passages, such as the *Parnass und Paradies* of

---

[1] In his paper *On Operatic Poetry and Composition* he pointed out some blunders on the part of Weber and others in the union of poetical and musical accent and rhythm. He is quite right as far as he goes. Where we really feel that a verbal absurdity is being perpetrated for the sake of giving free play to the musical phrase, our æsthetic sense is of course outraged. But if no absurdity of this sort is committed, we do not mind whether a lyric poem is set in $\frac{2}{4}$ or in $\frac{3}{4}$ rhythm—the musical rhythm taking the poetical up into itself.

the Prize-Song in the *Meistersinger*, where the one syllable is made to extend over several musical moments, quite in the style of every other man who has written vocal music, is it easy to see the justice of his sweeping condemnation of the music that does as it likes with the rhythm and the accent of the words. The plain truth is that Wagner was grievously deluded when he imagined that in *Opera and Drama* he was vindicating the claims of poetry as against the pretensions of music. What he was really doing was to assert, more imperiously than ever, the claims of music as against those of poetry, *for the "feeling" to which he wished the art-work to appeal, and from which he wished it to take its rise, was really not a poetical but a musical frame of mind.*

VII

More particularly can it be seen how in Wagner's operas, as in those of other men, the music does the bulk of the work, and not only blinds us to the imperfections of the verse but carries us over chasms that would be appalling were the music not there, by an examination of his own practice in connection with the theories of previous æstheticians. We have seen how clearly the best writers upon music in the eighteenth century marked out the difference between the drama and the musical drama, and showed how the drama must be modified, both in form and in scope, by its union with music. There are two poles of expression in opera—the lyrical, and what can only be called, in contradistinction, the non-lyrical. Poetry may be said to cover the latter field,[1] while the former is best occupied by everything we include in the term "Song." Not only can the girl sing her lost love better than the

---

[1] The reader will gather from the sequel in what sense I here use the terms "lyrical" and "non-lyrical," without my defining them at greater length.

miser could sing his lost money-bags, but she can sing her passion more poignantly, more beautifully than she could speak it—this, indeed, constituting the peculiar strength of opera, where the great primary human passions are raised to their highest artistic power. But a song does not make a drama, nor would twenty songs make one. Some connective tissue must be run between the lyrical portions, this tissue being concerned with the narrative and conduct of the drama. There are thus two planes of emotion in opera—the lower, on which is enacted all that goes to make the drama a connected and intelligible picture of human life, and the higher, on which the characters pour forth the lyrical utterance of their passions in moments of intense excitement. The question is, what is to be the character of the music to which this non-lyrical connective tissue is to be set? Obviously it must not be passionate, self-existent music, for between the exalted beauty of this and the more commonplace significations of the words there would be so obvious a difference in emotional pitch that the hearer's æsthetic pleasure would be partially destroyed. But since the drama cannot get on without these connective passages, there are only two alternatives: they must be spoken, or they must be set to music of some kind. That they should be spoken, as in *Der Freischütz*, has been proposed in our own day by M. Charles Beauquier in his *La Musique et le Drame*,[1] a work of much value in spite of its frequent self-contradictions. M. Beauquier, who is somewhat reactionary in his attitude towards the Wagnerian opera, holds that recitative is a bastard and essentially false form of expression, which had better be banished altogether from the opera,[2] to be replaced by spoken words, as in the operas of Weber. He is forced to admit that the shock of falling from lyrical music to mere speech is

---

[1] Paris, 1884.
[2] Work mentioned, pp. 102, 103.

somewhat distressing, and one surmises that he was betrayed into so false a position in relation to recitative by sheer reaction against everything that is anathema to him in Wagner. Few will now be found to maintain that spoken words have any place in opera. They sound *banal* enough in Weber ; and placed between the glorious lyrical moments of such modern music as *Tristan* they would remind us rather too unpleasantly of the grit in the plate of strawberries.

To music, then, this connective tissue must needs be set. The question is, to what kind of music ? Even in the eighteenth century it was seen that while certain parts of it approached closely to lyrical music, other portions were necessarily so bald and unilluminative that music of any degree of formal, independent beauty must seem incongruous with it. Let me illustrate the eighteenth-century opinion on this point from Brown's *" Letters upon the Poetry and Music of the Italian Opera, addressed to a Friend."* [1]

"The Italians," he says—contrasting them with English writers in this respect—"have with great propriety considered that the speeches in the drama, whether in dialogue or soliloquy, must be either such as are expressive of passion and sentiment, or such as are not so. On this real distinction, and not, as with us, on the mere caprice of the composer, is founded their first great division of vocal music into *recitative* and *air*. It is evident, on the slightest consideration, that in the progress of the drama many passages must necessarily occur, such as simple narration of facts, directions given, plain answers made to plain questions, sometimes abstract truths or moral reflections—none of which, as they contain nothing of passion or sentiment, can ever become the subject of musical expression. Simply to have spoken these

---

[1] The "My Lord" to whom the Letters are addressed is, I should say from internal evidence, Lord Monboddo. They are in the most approved polite style of the eighteenth century. Mr. John Brown might have been the subject of the classic story of the lecturer on chemistry who is reported to have said, " The gases will now have the honour of combining before your Royal Highness."

passages, however, and then abruptly to have set up a singing, when any pathetic part presented itself, would have produced exactly that barbarous jumble of prose and poetry, of music and dissonance, which characterises the English comic opera.[1]   To avoid this, and at the same time not idly to bestow the charms of fancy and feeling where embellishment and expression would be improper, the Italians have invented that species of singing termed by them *simple recitative*.   Its name almost sufficiently explains its nature: it is a succession of notes so arranged as to coincide with the laws of harmony, though never accompanied but by a single instrument, whose office is merely to support the voice, and to direct it in its modulations.   Though, for the sake of this accompaniment, recitative is, like other music, divided into bars, yet are not these bars, as in other music, necessarily of equal lengths; the notes of which they are composed being sub- jected to no precise musical measure, but regulated, in this respect, almost wholly by the natural prosody of the language. Thus this kind of recitative answers completely its end, and it detains the audience very little longer than the spoken recital would do; and, being music itself, the transition from it to the higher and more interesting parts is perfectly natural and agree- able to the ear."[2]

Further—

"The Italians have observed that all those passages in which the mind of the speaker is agitated by a rapid succession of various emotions are, from their nature, incompatible with any particular strain or length of melody; for that which constitutes such particular strain is the relation of several parts to one whole. . . . But while the Italians conceived such passages to be incompatible with that regularity of measure and that unity of strain which is essential to air, they felt, however, that they were of all others the most proper subject for musical expression; and, accordingly, both the poet and musician seem, by mutual consent, to have bestowed on such passages their chief study; and the musician, in particular, never fails to exert on them his highest and most

---

[1] This was *not* written in 1898.
[2] *Letters upon the Poetry and Music of the Italian Opera*, pp. 2–5.

brilliant powers.   It is to them they adapt that species of
recitative termed *recitativo istrumentato, or recitativo obbligato,
accompanied recitative. . . .*"[1]

In the eighteenth century, then, quite as much as in
the nineteenth, there was felt to be some incongruity in
writing very beautiful music to the more commonplace
portions of the libretto.   Nor do their attempted solutions of the difficulty seem to me to have been altogether
successful.   There are, of course, many fine examples
of *obbligato* recitative in the works of the older opera-
composers ; but the general disrespect into which
recitative had even then fallen in the estimation of the
musical public, shows clearly enough that after a lyrical
outburst of passion we cannot take very much interest
in ordinary musical declamation.   What, then, is the
solution of the difficulty, if spoken words be summarily
rejected ?   Obviously to take the bull boldly by the
horns, and *sacrifice everything in order to satisfy the most
important element in opera—the music*.   We already tolerate
in a musical drama a score of weaknesses and incongruities that would be sufficient to damn any spoken
drama ; we put up with wretched verses, paltry plots,
absurd incidents, and attacks on our sense of the
ludicrous, all for no other reason than that the music
moves us too deeply, pleases us too completely, for
these minor objections to have their full value in the
mind ; the music compensates for everything—providing, of course, a certain limit of absurdity or banality
be not passed.   To maintain the even current of our
delight, then, there must be no very perceptible disparity between the emotional planes of the lyrical and
the non-lyrical portions of opera.   Some difference, of
course, there must be ; Walther's colloquies with Hans
Sachs cannot have the same kind of music as his Prize-
Song.   But the difference must not be too great ; it
must never go so far as to suggest to us that it has

[1] *Letters upon the Poetry and Music of the Italian Opera*, pp. 13, 14.

ceased to be a mere difference of degree and become a
real difference of kind.   If once it does this it is inevitably lost ; we no longer wish to listen to it.   Thus the
great interest of Wagner's operas consists in this even
flow of the musical-emotional current throughout—or
almost throughout.   And, curiously enough, he himself
has given the most instructive proofs of the truth of the
æsthetic position here maintained.   Let us take one
example.   In the first act of the *Meistersinger* occurs
Pogner's beautiful and noble address to the Meistersingers—a long passage of ordinary communicative
speech which by any other composer would, beyond a
shadow of doubt, have been set to ordinary recitative.
It has in it nothing whatever that demands beautiful
lyrical treatment.   I will quote it in Mr. Corder's
English translation, in order that the reader may the
better see the point I am driving at—merely stating
that there is no special beauty in the German original
that could make the quotation of it in an English translation at all unfair :—

> St. John's most holy festal day,
> You know we keep to-morrow ;
> In meadows green among the hay,
> With song and dance and merry play,
> Each heart will gladness borrow,
> And cast aside all sorrow,
> So each will sport as best he may.
> The Singing-school we Masters here
> A staid church-choir will christen ;
> From out the gates, with merry cheer,
> To open meadows we will steer,
> While festal banners glisten :
> The populace shall listen
> To Master-songs with layman's ear.
> For those who best succeed in song
> Are gifts of various sizes,
> And all will hail, full loud and long,
> Both melodies and prizes.

> I am, thank God, a wealthy man ;
> And, as each giveth what he can,
> I've ransacked every coffer
> To find a prize to offer,
> To shame not to be brought.
> Now hear what I've bethought.

No one, I think, will allege that there is any especial reason why words of this kind should be set to music at all ; they are merely what I have called connective tissue, essential to the carrying on of the drama, but not demanding emotional musical treatment in the same way that a passionate lyric does. Yet these very words, which another composer would have set to conventional recitative, are set by Wagner to very beautiful music to which the ear listens in continuous delight. The succeeding words of Pogner's address, however—

> Through German lands when I have roved,
> It pained me, as I listed,
> To hear the Burghers are not loved,
> Deemed selfish and close-fisted.
> In low life as in Courts the same,
> I always heard the bitter blame,
> That only treasure and gold
> The Burgher's thoughts can hold—

are set to recitative of the most wearisome and commonplace order ; while lyric — or semi-lyric — beauty is once more given to the closing words—

> That we in all the kingdom's bounds
> Alone Art have promoted,
> I fancy they scarcely have noted.
> But how in this our honour redounds,
> And how with proudest care
> We treasure the good and rare,
> What Art is worth, what it can do,
> Now I have a mind to show unto you.

So hear, Masters, what thing
As a prize I mean to bring.
The singer to whose lyric skill
The public voice the prize shall will,
On John the Baptist's Day,
Be he whoe'er he may,
I, Veit Pogner, an Art-supporter,
A townsman of this quarter,
Will give, with my goods and gold beside,
Eva, my only child, for bride.

Will any one allege that there is the slightest difference in the emotional value of these three sections?
Surely not.   Yet, while Wagner has made the first and
last exceedingly beautiful, he has deliberately made the
second exceedingly dull and wearisome.   There can be
only one conclusion possible—that not only must the
composer swell the emotional significance of the words
in the lyrical portions of the opera, but even in the
non-lyrical portions he must, if he is to engage our
æsthetic interest, give music of a certain degree of
emotional beauty to words that have not a shadow of
emotional beauty of their own.   But, in face of a conclusion like this, it is surely idle to dispute the position
we have reached upon so many other lines of argument—that music, and not poetry, is from first to last
the dominant, the tyrannous factor in the musical
drama.[1] Grétry, I think, once said that if put to it
he could set the *Belgian Gazette* to music.   This is, of
course, exaggeration ; there is a certain line over which
words will simply not bear musical treatment ; one
could not very well listen to a speech on Welsh Dis-
establishment even if set to the finest music.   But such
words as form the connective tissue between the lyrical

---

[1] See, in this connection, Wagner's *Prologue to a reading of the Götterdämmerung before a select audience in Berlin*, G. S. ix. 308–310 ; Ellis, v.
305, 306.

portions of opera, though they suggest little or no
lyrical feeling, can yet be allied without incongruity
to music that is emotionally beautiful; and to do this
is the business of the musician, if he wishes his work
to please and to interest. The eighteenth-century view
of the functions and powers of recitative was only a
stage in the æsthetic problem. In the state of operatic
music at that time no other conclusion, perhaps, was
possible. In our own day it becomes more than ever
clear that in any combination between poetry and
music in opera, the latter art must be the shaping
factor almost throughout, for it occupies our attention
almost exclusively. It is certainly significant that while
thousands of poor or mediocre poems live in virtue of
their being set to beautiful music, mediocre music will
not be listened to even if associated with the finest
poetry.

Wagner himself, in his confused and roundabout
way, has pointed out that since the lyrical moments
themselves cannot tell the story, and therefore cannot
make the drama, there must be a connective tissue of
less emotional value, which must be set to less
emotional music, but still to music.

"In this Tone-speech," he writes, "must the dramatic person
speak, if we are to understand him with our kindled Feeling:
but he must also speak in such a way as to *determine* the
emotions roused in us; and our vaguely roused emotions can
only be determined by their being given a fixed point round
which they may gather as human Fellow-feeling, and whereat
they may condense themselves to a specific sympathy for this
one man, involved in this particular plight, influenced by this
surrounding, ensouled by this will, and engaged in this project.
These necessary conditions for displaying an individuality to the
Feeling, can be convincingly set forth in nothing but Word-
speech—in that language which is instinctively intelligible to
ordinary life, and wherein we mutually impart a plight or Will

such as must be resembled by those laid bare by the dramatic person, if these latter are to be *understood* by us at all. As our kindled mood, however, has already claimed that this word-speech shall not be one at total variance with that tone-speech which has so lately moved us—as it were the interpreter, but alike the partner, of the roused emotion—so by this very fact, the Content (*Inhalt*) to be set forth by the *dramatis personæ* is prescribed as one as much uplifted above the matters of our daily life, as the Expression itself is raised above the language of that life." [1]

All this, in plain language, simply means that if you are to present a story in an opera, you must have non-lyrical as well as lyrical portions. Now it has been recognised from the very beginning of opera that the non-lyrical portions cannot bear the same kind of music as that which fills the more impassioned moments. Caccini in 1601 was trying to find "a kind of melody by which it would be possible to *speak* in music"; and Jacopo Peri also sought to "utilise the accents which we unconsciously employ in moments of deep emotion." [2] Wagner, with his "intensification of ordinary speech," is simply travelling along the same line. In practice, however, we find that so far as his non-lyrical portions are music they are in no way, as he wrongly thought, developments from or intensifications of speech; while in so far as they are not music they are simply boredom insufferable. We have seen, in the *Meistersinger*, words of simply no beauty at all rendered palatable to us by lovely music that has not the remotest affinity with speech. Let us now look at an opposite case, where words in no way better or worse than those I have quoted from the *Meistersinger* are set to something that is *not*

---

[1] G. S. iv. 195; Ellis, ii. 340, 341.

[2] See E. de Bricqueville, *L'Opéra de l'avenir dans le passé*, pp. 71, 72. See also Hubert Parry, *The Evolution of the Art of Music*, p. 127.

music. Look at the following passage from the 1st Act of *Parsifal* : [1]—

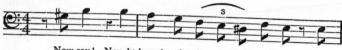

Now say ! Nought know'st of all I have asked thee, then

Say what thou know'st ; of some-thing must thou have knowledge.

In the name of all that is artistic, who wants to listen to dreary stuff of this kind ?   The boredom here arises from the fact that while the tones are not beautiful enough to give us any musical pleasure in themselves, the aridity of the words is too plainly forced upon our consciousness ; whereas the same words, if set to beautiful music, would scarcely be noticed as commonplace, the mind being wholly interested in the musical current.   Wagnerians have told us that Wagner by the use of this " speaking music " avoids both the error of making the non-lyrical portions too highly emotional, and of introducing merely spoken words with their terrible lapse into the commonplace.   Mr. Hadow, for example, writes that " the only alternative is to intensify the tones of ordinary speech until they reach the minimum of tonality which is compatible with their being embodied in musical notation and accompanied by the melodies of the orchestra.   This is precisely what Wagner has done.   In general his *aria parlante* is a marvellously devised system of musical equivalents for the actual tones and cadences of the speaking voice." [2]   That seems to me wholly fallacious. As soon as the sounds acquire tonality and are accompanied by harmony they cease to be *spoken*, and cease to appeal to the faculty by which we appreciate the

---

[1] Vocal score, p. 55.   [2] *Studies in Modern Music*, i. 314.

intellectual meanings of words ; they become music
and appeal to the musical faculty in the first place.
If a passage such as that I have just quoted from
Parsifal is " a marvellously devised system of musical
equivalents for the actual tones and cadences of the
speaking voice," how comes it that it bores us so
dreadfully ?   If the words were spoken we would
listen to them with a certain amount of interest ; and
we would still listen to them with interest if they
simply intensified the speaking accent.   The fact that
they now bore us indicates clearly that we judge
them by a different standard, because we are listening to them in another mood and from a different
standpoint of expectation ; we listen to them as words
set to music, and are wearied because we hear the
banal words instead of being charmed with the accents
of music.   And if they *were* set to beautiful music, the
words might be ten times as *banal* as they are without
that fact troubling us in the least.

   But this fact has an important corollary.   If the
passages in Wagner's operas that most interest us are
those that contain beautiful music,[1] and if our interest
shades away gradually as the music becomes less fascinating, down to the point of absolute boredom, it
follows that the more lyrical tissue a composer can
put into his opera the better.   We do not, in these
days, agree with the older critics who thought the
second and third acts of the *Valkyrie* almost unmiti-
gated dulness ; but who, among the most ardent
admirers of Wagner, would not have preferred these
two acts in the style of the second or third act of
Tristan—had it been possible to write them in that
manner ?   Thus we see that the ideal opera would

---

[1] I do not, of course, mean beautiful music merely in the sense of shapely
lyrical passages of melody or harmony.   I include under the phrase all his
finest dramatic passages so long as they can keep us interested in the performance—such as the tarn-helm motive, or Alberich's curse, or the scene between
Alberich and Hagen in the 2nd Act of the *Götterdämmerung*.

be one in which the non-lyrical portions would be reduced to the minimum compatible with presenting a connected dramatic action.[1] *Tristan* comes the nearest of all operas to this ideal ; and we may suppose that it is impossible to construct an opera-poem with less waste matter than this contains. But on these terms not only is it quite clear that, in opera, music must necessarily determine the drama, instead of the drama determining the music, as Wagner thought, but the limitations imposed by this musical domination become plainly evident. It is seen at once how greatly the range of drama becomes restricted ; how a thousand subtle shades of thought and emotion, that are capable of expression in the poetical drama, become quite out of the question in the musical drama. And here we light once more upon that peculiarity in Wagner's mental constitution that made all other forms of art but the musical drama seem inefficient to him, simply because he was a musician and nothing more.

"Let us finally," he writes at the conclusion of *Opera and Drama*, "denote the measure of poetic worth as follows : As Voltaire said of the opera, 'What is too silly to be said, one gets it sung'—so let us reverse that maxim for the drama which we have in view, and say, ' *What is not worth being sung, neither is it worth the poet's pains of telling.*'"[2]

Perhaps not, when the "poet" is of Wagner's calibre ; but there are other kinds of poets in the world.[3]

Clearly then, it was the musical quality of Wagner's

---

[1] Wagner's theory that the myth is most suited for musical-dramatic purposes, because it avoids the multiplicity of detail of "historical" subjects, was anticipated by Beaumarchais, in the preface to his opera *Tarare* (1787) : "Il m'a semblé qu' à l'Opéra les sujets historiques devaient moins réussir que les imaginaires."   The whole preface is well worth reading.

[2] G. S. iv. 208 ; Ellis, ii. 355.

[3] Mr. James Oliphant thinks " there is no denying that had destiny ordered his course so, Wagner might have become chief among the masters of spoken drama (Article on "The Place of Poetry in a Music-Drama," in the *Scottish Art Review*, 1888). Wagner would have been the first to reject this flattering estimate.

mind, the vagueness of his conceptions as compared
with those of a poet proper, that led him to exalt
the musical drama as he did. In the same way
Walter Pater regarded music as the most perfect of
the arts simply because his own nature leaned towards
the art in which there is the most perfect absorption
of idea in form ; and upon a similar attitude towards
life and art Nietzsche based his theory that the
ancient Greek tragedy was born from the spirit of
music.[1] These solutions of the æsthetic problem can
only be valid for minds whose whole outlook upon
art is from the standpoint of music ; they fall lamentably short of the truth for all whose artistic needs
are of quite another order. Let any one who has
seen Shakespeare's *Othello* and Verdi's *Otello* upon the
stage recall his impressions of the drama and the
opera, and he must be struck by one thing that shows
clearly how music alters the mood in which we regard
a drama. One of the most impressive episodes in the
spoken play is that in which Iago relates to Othello
his discovery, during Cassio's sleep, of his passion for
Desdemona. Now in Verdi's opera, though the words
at this juncture are practically the same as in Shakespeare's drama, the dramatic effect is shorn of half its
impressiveness and half its terror by the beauty of the
music. The composer, of course, cannot write ugly
music for the scene ; if he is to add music at all to the

---

[1] On these subjects I may refer to my articles on "Walter Pater on Music,"
in the *Musician*, 29th September 1897 ; and the "Wagner-Nietzsche View of
Drama," in *Music* (Chicago), May 1898. It is of a piece with Wagner's theory
that the Greek drama showed a progressive decline from song to speech, from
an appeal to the feeling to an appeal to the understanding, that he should
join in the current unthinking disparagement of Euripides at the expense of
his two predecessors. To the modern mind, the work of Euripides is intensely
human, and the dramatist himself a most interesting psychological study. For
a sane appreciation of him, as well as of Æschylus and Sophocles, see Mr.
Gilbert Murray's recent volume on *Ancient Greek Literature*. Once more it
is apparent that Wagner depreciated the intellectual and artistic world of
Euripides simply because his brain was not of an order to appreciate any world
but that of music, or of poetry that had some psychological affinity with music.

words it must be of an order to capture our interest and to please us æsthetically. But this feeling of sensuous pleasure comes into conflict with the horror of the poetical situation in a manner to which there is no parallel in the spoken play. All art, of course, must wrap up its terror in beauty or it would not be art ; but the peculiarity of music is that its sensuous beauty is so great as to dull the nerves somewhat to impressions of dramatic terror. Iago in an opera cannot possibly be the evil compound he is in Shakespeare's play. Music, in fact, is powerless to mate itself with a thousand subtle dramatic emotions of the highest interest ; while it has the power of raising the great primary emotions to extraordinary heights of expression. This is its strength, these its limitations ; and they explain at once the secret of Wagner's success in practice and of the failure of his theory.[1]

Taking his theory as a whole, with its dictum that all the scattered arts ought to be reunited in the musical drama, one might say, even without any acquaintance with its details, that it was an utterly vain dream. We can no more set back the hands of time in art than we can in social life. If the arts have developed along divergent lines, it is because the human brain has in the course of the centuries become more complex ; if poetry and music have become self-dependent arts, needing no assistance from each other, it is because there are deep fountains of specialised emotions in us, each of which can only be put into play by

---

[1] For an admirable analysis of the psychological and æsthetic possibilities of opera and drama, see Professor Sully's article on "The Opera," in vol. 26 of the *Contemporary Review* (1875). For some weighty criticism of the Wagnerian theory see the chapter on "Opera" in Edmund Gurney's *Power of Sound*. In chapter vi. of the present volume I have endeavoured to find a *via media* between Gurney's mind and Wagner's. The reader may derive a little innocent amusement from reading Bitter's book *Die Reform der Oper durch Gluck, und R. Wagner's Kunstwerk der Zukunft*, which is anti-Wagnerian, along with Ludwig Nohl's *Gluck und Wagner: Ueber die Entwickelung des Musikdramas*, which is *very* Wagnerian.

poetry or by music. *A priori*, then, we are entitled to say that Wagner's attempt to satisfy humanity with an art-work that shall be a fusion of all the arts is necessarily foredoomed to failure. Much as his art-work may do for us, this at all events it cannot do. Whether we consider the theoretical psychology of poetry and of music, or their actual conditions of existence to-day, or the manner of their exercise in the past, it is indubitable that no one art can now be found to do the work of both of them. As Dr. Wallaschek has expressed it—

"It would be contrary to all laws of development that the accomplished arts should once more form as organic union as they might have formed in their primitive state. Therefore the attempt to unite the accomplished arts in equal rank to a single art is theoretically a contradiction and practically an impossibility. The result of such an attempt was always that the composer either spoiled his art by a theoretical prejudice, or practically acted contrary to his rules. Wagner's artistic genius was never in doubt for a single moment which way to go, and therefore his theory has remained an intolerable chaos, while his art has flourished in unrivalled splendour." [1]

This, seemingly, must be the verdict of posterity upon him. His notion of an art-work, a combination of the arts, that is to take the place of the arts in separation, is simply a melancholy delusion. We cannot be so easily persuaded to remove our old landmarks; we cannot, merely at his bidding, forego our old delight in poetry and music because he was incapable of feeling this delight. The upshot of our analysis must be that he was just an opera-composer like the rest; greater than any that went before or any that have come after him, but still of their craft and lineage; his art being stronger, finer, firmer, lovelier than theirs, but still a rational development of theirs and not a new art-work.

[1] *Primitive Music*, pp. 215, 216.

CHAPTER VI

THE RING OF THE NIBELUNG

I

IT was in the full flush of enthusiasm over his new ideas on the musical drama that Wagner set to work on the huge tetralogy that occupied him, in one way and another, for more than twenty years. In 1848 he wrote his prose-sketch *The Nibelungen myth arranged as a drama*, which plans out the play practically as we have it now. Later on in the same year he dramatised the final portions of the myth, under the title of *Siegfried's Death*, which corresponds in the main with the present *Götterdämmerung*. He soon saw, however, that *Siegfried's Death* was imperfect, by reason both of its containing much in narrative form that ought to be visually present in the form of drama, and of its assuming too great a knowledge on the spectator's part of the preceding portions of the myth. Accordingly, in 1851 he wrote the drama of *The Young Siegfried*—the prototype of the present *Siegfried*. Then, feeling again that the poem was not so clear to the spectator as it should be, he prefixed to *The Young Siegfried*, in 1852, the *Valkyrie*, and to this, later in the same year, the *Rheingold*. The music was written in the reverse—that is, the natural—order. *Rheingold* was written in 1853 and 1854, the *Valkyrie* between 1854 and 1856, part of *Siegfried* in 1856 and 1857, and the remainder in the years between 1865 and 1869,[1] and the *Götterdämmerung* between 1869 and 1872.

---

[1] The musical setting of *Siegfried* was finished in 1869, but the scoring was not completed until 1871.

No work of Wagner's—probably no work of any man except Shakespeare—has been the starting-point of so much discussion as the *Ring*. One curious fact must have struck the student of the Wagnerian literature of late years : while there is coming to be less and less discussion of his music or of his musical system, there is an increasing body of writings on the ethical import of his dramas. I have already argued that Wagner is not to be taken quite so seriously on the intellectual side as many of his admirers would like him to be ; and perhaps the *Ring* will furnish as good a text as could be desired for that sermon. Here, as in so many other instances, the best way to study Wagner's theories is in connection with the circumstances of his own life. It was characteristic of him, as we have seen from his æsthetic theories and from his three earlier operas, that he should try to elevate his own idiosyncrasies into norms of thought and action for the rest of the world. One of the most curious features of Wagner's mind was this passion for holding up his own peculiar and *à priori* ideas as laws of life or laws of art for others, in the most perfect unconsciousness that his ideas were born of an organism not only physiologically abnormal in many ways, but radically incapable of sane objective thinking. From his first work to his last he presents a pathetic picture of the hopeless idealist in conflict with external forces too vast and too complex for him to understand. His writings on social subjects—particularly his early ones—are sometimes *à priori* to the verge of absurdity ; scarcely another man, we may safely say, could have been found in Europe to advocate so earnestly, with such sincere conviction, a return to the social and artistic ideals of the Greeks. That vain dream, clung to by Wagner with extraordinary tenacity, is typical of the unreal, fantastic cloudland in which the great musician lived. He himself—the sincerest and most unselfish artist of his day—wanted only, as he used to tell Liszt and his other correspondents, a competency sufficient to free him from the ignobler cares of existence, and to enable him to compose for the benefit of his race and its culture ; and upon this personal desire, and upon the fact of the dramatic representations of the Athenians being, in a sense, the work of the community, he built the strange philosophy of life and art that we have glanced at in *Art and Revolution* and *The Art-Work of the Future,* and that has gone so far to reveal the incompetence of his mind to deal with questions of the positive and the actual. I have already tried to show the dependence of this social creed upon his own congenital ideas and his pecuniary circumstances, by comparing his letters of the period immediately following his flight from Dresden with the above-named treatises. One brings, of course, no charge against him of casuistry or deliberate self-seeking ; the very naïveté both of the theories themselves and of their correspondence with his own personal needs is conclusive as to Wagner's sincerity in the matter. He was simply a man of enormous musical power, filled with peculiar notions as to the importance of the musical drama in the development of culture, and with too little objective outlook upon the world and too little capacity for impersonal reason to allow of his seeing the utter unreality and apriorism of most of his theories for all other men. In later life he partly came to recognise some of his deficiencies in this respect— admitting to Roeckel, for example, that though he read and wrote so much of philosophy, he had little head for philosophic thinking. And on one notable occasion —when he had given birth to a more than usually preposterous theory as to our duties in relation to vegetarianism—he admitted that his suggestions belonged to the sphere of " phantasms." [1] But taking his prose works and his letters on their face-value, the most

---

[1] See the final chapter of the present volume.

cursory reading suffices to show how abnormal he was in many respects, how he dwelt with exaggerated emphasis upon theories and suggestions that appear to us hopelessly *à priori*, how he argued in the most sincere unconsciousness from the desires and needs of Richard Wagner to the supposed desires and needs of civilised mankind. This we have seen in connection both with his theories of life and his theory of the drama ; and it is of the utmost importance not only in the diagnosis of his character but in the attempt to comprehend his musical works. One has only to become acquainted with his correspondence during the twenty-three years he spent upon the *Ring*, to realise that he meant that work to be something more than a mere opera, a mere story of gods and men, of love and hate, and life and death ; that he intended it as a serious contribution to the philosophy of the universe. In the case of the *Dutchman, Tannhäuser*, and *Lohengrin*, we have been able to understand the dramas better by becoming acquainted with Wagner's ideas upon art and life at that time. Hence also the need of studying the *Ring* in connection with some of the theories expressed in his prose-works and elsewhere. We do not, of course, necessarily invalidate, *à priori*, the philosophy of the drama by showing its dependence upon Wagner's innate ideas and his outward circumstances ; but we undoubtedly obtain a better standpoint from which to view the scheme of philosophy put forward, and to judge its objective value as a contribution to human knowledge.

The biographies of Wagner contain so many accounts of *The Ring of the Nibelung* that it is unnecessary to tell the story once more here. It is perhaps sufficient for present purposes to remind readers and opera-goers of the main features of the drama—the attainment of the gold by Alberich by the denial of love ; the curse that follows it and devolves upon each successive possessor of the Ring ; the contest, in the person of Wotan, between authority and moral right; the need for renunciation on his part; the means by which he effects this renunciation; the advent of Siegfried as the liberator, and of Brynhild as the incarnation of love the conqueror; the murder of Siegfried, the voluntary death of Brynhild, the restoration of the Ring to the Rhine-maidens, and the final dissolution of the gods. The "problem" of the drama, as it has been stated by a recent writer, is the revolt of the "natural individual" against constituted authority as embodied in conventions and formulas. The *Ring* "and all Wagner's sayings and writings of this period maintain enthusiastically the inherent goodness of nature and man, and the glory of physical vitality. Laws, imposed by the few on the many, first made sin possible. Man, to work his way out of the possibility of sinning, had to cast off the restraints of the law. The *Ring* is thus solely occupied with a conflict between the assumed right of traditional authority and the natural instinct in man to satisfy his desires." [1]

[1] See Mr. David Irvine's *Wagner's Ring of the Nibelung and the Conditions of Ideal Manhood*, chapter i. Mr. Irvine makes some curious blunders in his exposition of this "problem" of the *Ring*. Whenever he comes across the word "authority," for example, he assumes it to mean authority in the external sense in which Wagner conceived it. Thus he quotes from Mr. Balfour's *Foundations of Belief*, "We must not forget that it is authority rather than reason to which in the main we owe not religion only, but ethics and politics," and rejoins that "the mere existence of liberalism, which consists of relaxing instead of tightening the strain of constituted authority, is a standing denial of this assumption." But Mr. Balfour, in the passage in question—as indeed throughout the *Foundations of Belief*—never means "*constituted* authority" when he speaks of "authority." When he argues that such beliefs as "God exists," or "There is an external universe," or "Matter is extended," are held on "authority," not on "reason," he means that they are based on non-rational processes of the mind, *i.e.* they are quasi-instinctive convictions with which reason has nothing to do. Thus "authority" in Mr. Balfour's sense is equivalent to "necessity" in Wagner's sense. Each holds up the instinctive promptings of "natural man" as against his "reason" or "understanding"; so that Mr. Balfour's position, instead of being opposed to that of Wagner as Mr. Irvine imagines, is really one with it. (See the telling criticism of Mr. Balfour's book in Mr. Hugh Mortimer Cecil's *Pseudo-Philosophy at the End of the* 19*th Century*.)

One need not follow Mr. Irvine and his fellow-commentators into those jungle-depths of interpretation where every character in the drama becomes a personified abstraction of some social or political or moral tendency.[1] One has no desire to multiply Gervinus-literature in England on musical subjects ; that way Wagner - madness lies. But without out - Heroding Herod in the fashion of the modern Wagnerian "interpreter," without reading into the *Ring* more pseudo-philosophy than it has the misfortune to contain already, one can see clearly enough from a mere perusal of the poem, that in that drama Wagner was preaching a social evangel which, with characteristic seriousness, he held to be of prime importance to mankind.

Now one has only to go back to his prose-works and his correspondence to see the theories of the *Ring* in all their naïveté, free from the glamour in which they are enveloped, in the tetralogy itself, by the wonderful art of the musician. Hearing or studying the music, one almost feels inclined to subscribe to the theorems of Wagner, just as *Tristan* tempts to the longing for Nirvana, and *Parsifal* to asceticism ; one gets a clearer notion of the ideas and their objective value by contemplating them in their plain prose expression. And looking at the matter in this way, one gets new proof that Wagner was a man of high spirit and generous sympathies, acutely sensitive both to his own miseries and those of others, but quite incapable of thinking any social problem out, or of doing anything more than offer the most *à priori* solutions of it. We have

---

[1] Mr. Irvine tells us, for example, that Mime is "that spirit which superficially appears as the educator of mankind, and when intelligence begins to perceive that nature is its true educator and the other a mere charlatan, with which it has nothing in common, then craft and subterfuge are called into requisition in order to turn this step, leading to a truer knowledge of things, into the further service of self-interest. Mime is thus the craft which finds its best soil in the Church, impressing every one in early youth, before judgment is ripe, with the belief that it is a spiritual father and mother."—*Ibid.*, pp. 66, 67.

only to look at his correspondence of 1849, just after his flight from Dresden, when he was confronted with the problem of compromise between artistic desires and plans and the earning of one's daily bread, to realise that the philosophy and the portraiture of the *Ring* are only objectivations of the personal problem of his own existence. In his correspondence with Uhlig he not only foreshadowed the theories of his *Art and Revolution* and *The Art-Work of the Future*, but unconsciously sketched out, as it were, the moral theme of the *Ring* and some of the characters. Just as we can recognise much of Wagner himself in Walther of the *Meistersinger*, so one can see that Siegfried in the tetralogy is just a peg whereon to hang certain theories he then held as to the wholesome vitality of the "free individual"— the theories expounded in his letters to Uhlig, already quoted in chapter iv. It is a kind of philosophising that has gone sadly out of fashion, the day being past when vaporising about the free individual, and inner necessity, and man being that which he is by virtue of his inner essence, and the rest of the windy jargon of the dreamer, can do much more than make us yawn. The passage is only of interest for the light it throws upon the philosophical scheme of the *Ring*. At the end of *A Communication to my Friends* (1851), when Wagner was relating the steps of his musical and intellectual development, he told how in the drama as he had then worked it out he had found expression for his inmost philosophy of life.

"With the conception of Siegfried," he wrote, "I had pressed forward to where I saw before me the Human Being in the most natural and blithest fulness of his physical life. No historic garment more confined his limbs; no outwardly-imposed relation hemmed his movements, which, springing from the inner fount of Joy-in-life, so bore themselves in face of all encounter, that error and bewilderment, though nurtured on the wildest play of passions, might heap themselves around until they threatened to destroy him, without the hero checking for a moment, even in the face of death, the welling outflow of that inner fount; or ever holding anything the rightful master of himself and his own movements, but alone the natural outstreaming of his restless fount of Life. It was Elsa who had taught me to unearth this man; to me, he was the male-embodied spirit of perennial and sole creative instinct (*Unwillkür*), of the doer of true deeds, of *Manhood* in the utmost fulness of its inborn strength and proved loveworthiness. Here, in the promptings of this Man, Love's brooding wish had no more place; but bodily lived it there, swelled every vein and stirred each muscle of the gladsome being, to all-enthralling practice of its essence." [1]

This ill-conceived abstraction was the type of man Wagner had held up for admiration in his writings and in his letters; it was the type to which he himself wished to conform. He was oppressed with a sense of the hardness of the world and the restraint which our modern society, based on commerce and industrialism, imposes upon the artist; and he was filled with vague longings for a condition of things more favourable to art. Thousands before and after him have felt the same weariness and cherished the same desires; but him they always impelled to random philosophising, to weaving cloudy schemes of social and political and artistic improvement. There is consequently from first to last in his works—outside the department of music—hardly one suggestion as to art and life that is worth attention—or at least any more attention than one usually gives to the earnest and sincere but unpractical prophet; hardly one that shows the slightest sense of the reality of things. It is a somewhat saddening spectacle, this of the sensitive artist quivering under the blows of the huge unfriendly world; feeling dimly that in the evolution of mankind, he, whose business is with heart and soul alone, has become inextricably entangled with the limbs and the

[1] G. S. iv. 328; Ellis, i. 375.

O

viscera of the race; but able to offer towards the diminishing of the grievous burden nothing more than petulant outcries, and sad looks upon the past, and vain hopes that the wheels of evolution will stand still that the universe may be built again according to the plans of the idealist. He lived, we must always remember, in a time of obscure social and political ferment, and in a country where the tendency has always been to philosophise *in abstracto*. Everything— his own nature, his training, his associates, his enemies —combined to make him a mere declaimer upon themes that require anything but declamation to elucidate them. He always states just that half of any problem which serves the end of his own artistic theories; anything like a sanely comprehensive view of the intermixture of good and evil in the world is impossible to him. "Our god is Gold," he cried; "our religion the Pursuit of Wealth."[1] Modern art is a mere product of Culture, not of Life itself; therefore, being simply a hot-house plant, it cannot take root in the natural soil, or exist in the natural climate of the present. There is really no meaning in talk of this kind; it is windy rhetoric pure and simple—the mere sad declamation of a frustrated artist, in a world of dark complexities whose meaning and whose interconnection he cannot fathom.

The mood in which Wagner thought out the philosophy of the *Ring*, then, was one of emotional revolt against the resistance of modern life to the impulses of the artist—a revolt determined in its form and theories by the musician's idealism, and by his lack of objective vision and of impartial reason. The part played by the Ring itself in the tetralogy can be clearly seen to be an expression of Wagner's own passion for attributing most of the evils under which art now suffers to its dependence upon gold and commerce.

[1] G. S. iii. 28; Ellis, i. 51.

"This is art as it now fills the entire civilised world!" he cried, in *Art and Revolution*. "Its true essence is industry; its ethical aim the gaining of gold; its æsthetic purpose, the entertainment of those whose time hangs heavily on their hands."[1]

In the famous *Vaterlandsverein* speech of 1848, mis-inspired no doubt by some of the economists of the time whom he had read and only half understood, he fulminated against the evil wrought among men by gold.

"When all the classes hitherto at enmity, and parcelled off by envy, have been united in the one great class of the free Folk, embracing all that on the dear German soil has received its human breath from God — think ye we first begin in earnest! For then must be taken firmly and deedfully in eye *the question of the root of all the misery in our present social state*—then must be decided whether Man, that crown of the creation, whether his lofty spiritual, his artistically stirring bodily powers and forces, were meant by God to serve in menial bondage to the stubbornest, the most lifeless product in all Nature, to sallow Metal?"[2]

And finally, among his theories of this period was that of the necessity of the downfall of the State. In *Opera and Drama*, after a long "interpretation" of the *Œdipus* of Sophocles, in which the action of Antigone is taken to mean "the annulling of the State by her love-curse," he proceeds in a passage that shows how prone he was to read extraneous meanings into certain artistic products, and at the same time throws light upon the kind of subtle theorems he tried to incorporate in his own dramatic works.

"To-day," he writes, "we only need to faithfully expound the myth of Œdipus according to its inmost essence, and we in

---

[1] G. S. iii. 19; Ellis, i. 43.
[2] The *Vaterlandsverein* speech, in Ellis, iv. 138.

it win an intelligible picture of the whole history of mankind, from the beginnings of society to the inevitable downfall of the State. The necessity of this downfall was foreboded in the Mythos. It is the part of actual history to accomplish it. . . . With this concrete State—whose substance Louis XIV. correctly designated as himself—we need not further occupy ourselves : its kernel, also, is bared us in the Œdipus-saga ; as the seed of all offences we recognise the rulership of Laïus, since for sake of its un-diminished possession he became an unnatural father. From this possession grown into an ownership, which, wondrously enough, is looked on as the base of all good order, there issue all the crimes of myth and history.—Let us keep our eye upon the abstract State alone. The thinkers of this State desired to plane down and equalise the imperfections of actual society, according to a thought-out ' norm' ; yet that they retained these very imperfections as a given thing, as the only thing to fit the sinfulness of human nature, and never went back to the real man himself — who from his at first instinctive, but at last erroneous, views had called those inequalities into being, exactly as through experience and the consequent correction of his errors he must also bring about, quite of itself, the perfect Society, *i.e.* one answering to the real needs of men, this was the grand error through which the Political State evolved itself to the unnatural height whence it fain would guide our Human Nature far below ; that nature which it did not understand at all, and understood the less, the more it fain would guide it. The Political State lives solely on the *vices of Society*, whose *virtues* are derived solely from the human *individuality*. Faced with the vices of society, which alone it can espy, the State cannot perceive the virtues which society acquires from that individuality. . . . The essence of the Political State is *caprice*, whereas the essence of the free Individuality is necessity. From out this Individuality, which we have recognised as in the right in its thousand-years' battle with the Political State—from this to *organise* Society, is the conscious task imposed upon us for the future. But to bring *the unconscious part* of human nature to *consciousness within Society*, and in this consciousness to know nothing other than *the necessity common to every member of Society*, namely of *the Individual's own free self-determining*—this is as good as to say, *annul the State;* for through Society has the State marched on to a denial of the free self-determining of the Individual—upon the *death* of that has it lived." [1]

This was Wagner's method of dealing with problems of the philosophy of history—merely declaiming a number of pseudo-propositions that explain simply nothing. It is a typically Teutonic method, requiring for its most perfect exhibition nothing more than a half-comprehension of any question under the sun ; and it is somewhat strange that Wagner's panegyrists should have followed his lead so blindly in discussions of this kind, and have sung pæans in his praise as a great and original thinker. Nothing could more clearly prove his incompetence to handle a philosophical question than this innutritious rhetoric about the "annulling of the State," "the free self-determining individual," and the rest of it. Civilisation is, of course, faced with the perennial problem of the respective spheres of activity of the individual and the State ; how far the State is morally justified in restraining the impulses and desires of the individual, and how far these impulses and desires are morally right as against those conventions of the State which alone make individual existence possible—these are problems that have indeed pressed for solution from time immemorial. But no one with a grain of philosophical ability will set about the business in the manner of Wagner, retailing empty platitudes instead of arguing, verbalising instead of thinking, and maundering for pages together about those precious entities "the State," "Society," and "the individual." [2] There

[1] G. S. iv. 65–67 ; Ellis, ii. 191–194.

[2] The peculiarity of the problem is that it must for ever remain insoluble. While on the one hand our social and other laws are justified by the fact that they represent a working compromise between the opposing desires of individuals — being, indeed, simply one phase of the struggle for existence and the survival of the fittest—on the other hand, individuals are perpetually in revolt against laws and conventions that seem to limit their freedom too

is no special merit in multiplying darkness in this
way in quarters where there is already too little light ;
and it is a hopeless absurdity for a musician, with
no ratiocinative ability to begin with, no habits of
cool, persistent, objective thought, and no training
in the special subject he is so fain to meddle with,
to inflict his frothy rhetoric upon an unoffending
world. One blames him and his thoroughgoing worshippers only in so far as they attempt to handle
subjects with which they are quite incompetent to
deal ; and one's objection to their voluminous writings
is not that they expound wrong or doubtful theories,
but that their pseudo-demonstrations are mere shoddy,
having as little relation to the subjects they are actually
concerned with as a seventeenth-century divine's commentary on Genesis has with modern science. With
the best will in the world, indeed, and with all one's
admiration for Wagner's stupendous musical genius,

much. As soon as we attempt either to defend "Society" or "the Individual" by means of reason, we are landed in a series of logical difficulties,
simply because the actions of neither party are really based upon reason.
Thus nothing is easier than for the conservative to show the immorality of the
individualist, or for the individualist to show the stupidity of the conservative.
This latter has been delightfully done by Mr. George Bernard Shaw in his
little book on *The Quintessence of Ibsenism*, where the conceptions of "God,"
"reason," and "duty" are proved to be merely idealist veils thrown by
society over the face of reality. But any one—say Mr. Shaw himself—could
just as easily show that the "realist," who imagines that he is fighting for
what he calls truth against what he calls convention, is as much the victim of
an idealist delusion as any Philistine of them all. Mr. Shaw terminates his
book with a quotation from Wagner : "Man will never be that which he can
and should be until, by a conscious following of that inner natural necessity
which is the only true necessity, he makes his life a mirror of nature, and frees
himself from his thraldom to outer artificial counterfeits. Then will he first
become a living man, who now is a mere wheel in the mechanism of this or
that Religion, Nationality, or State." Wagner did not know, and Mr. Shaw
knows but will not tell, that any amount of following " inner natural necessity "
will not alter the constitution of things. Since individuals are of different
natures, if they are to live together at all they must compromise—that is,
repress their individualities to some extent. In this way Society and its conventions have come into being ; and if individuals *could* act upon Wagner's
advice, the ultimate outcome would be a state of affairs precisely similar to
that we no   have.

it is sometimes hard to feel well-disposed towards him
when reading his prose-works. To say that the root
of all our social misery is money, and that in "property" originate "all the crimes in myth and in
history"—to carry on a brazen trade in facile half-
truths of this kind, is to place oneself almost outside
the pale of serious discussion. Mr. Houston Stewart
Chamberlain has recently told us that "with Wagner
the faculty of negation went hand-in-hand with a rare
faculty of affirmation." It did indeed. The trouble
is that mere "affirmation" is not what we want from
a musician who insists on importing his untrained
imagination into questions of philosophy and sociology
and economics.

II

It will be admitted, I think, on the basis of the
above citations from the prose-works and the letters,
that in the *Ring* Wagner was simply preaching a scheme
of philosophy purely personal to himself. Most artists,
of course, tend to express in their works their own
congenital or acquired leanings towards this or that view
of life. The difference between these and Wagner is,
however, enormous. One does not urge it against any
artist that he sings his own moods and desires, so long
as these are capable of being bent towards and comprehended in an artistic effect. We read certain things
of Baudelaire and Verlaine, for example, not because we
admire the inverted eroticism of their temperaments,
but because they manage to make their faults of mood
and impulse lyrical, emotional, artistic, beautiful in
their form of presentation. With Wagner the case is
precisely the opposite. The unfortunate part about
Wagner's *Ring* is that he does not merely voice the
mere crude notions of his own organism, but that these
notions step outside the circle of art into those of

philosophy and politics, and therefore provoke criticism from other than artistic sides. A novel that is a tract is bad enough ; a poem that is a tract is infinitely worse ; but what shall be said of a musical drama that is a tract ? The thorough-going Wagner-worshipper may object to the term as being irreverent, and missing its mark by over-statement ; he prefers to speak of the "philosophy" of the *Ring*. "Philosophy," however, is a somewhat more dignified word than suits the occasion. Most art-works that set out to "prove" something are flawed at the commencement ; if you take them as works of art, ignoring the argumentation, the latter seems somewhat superfluous ; while if you find that the premisses of the work do not really lead to the conclusion the author has aimed at, you resent his having chosen an artistic medium for a mere piece of bad philosophising. As Flaubert said, the objection to writing a novel to prove something is that any one can sit down and write a novel to prove just the opposite ; you have only to select and ignore the material at your discretion. But when the "philosophy" of the work is forced down your throat, and you are compelled to make some effort to digest it, and you find yourself disagreeing with it for reasons that are patent to any one who will think, you are not inclined to be very "reverent" to the philosopher or to his admirers.

Now the scheme of the *Ring*, in so far as it leaves the broad currents of human passion, and affects to preach a social or philosophical evangel, is essentially a childish one. Wagner has shown considerable art in the way he has welded the various sagas together in his poem ;[1] it was not an easy task, and he has performed it for the most part with signal success. The music, again, in its best moments is unapproachable, and even

---

[1] On the relation of Wagner's poem to the mythical sources from which he compiled it, see Dr. Ernst Koch's *Richard Wagner's Bühnenfestspiel Der Ring des Nibelungen.*

in its lapses from its highest standard is interesting in a way that is without parallel in operatic music. But Wagner would have been offended at the suggestion that the *Ring* was to be looked upon merely as a good dramatic poem set to immortal music. If there was one point upon which he was more positive than any other, it was the stupidity of regarding his works as mere operas—as mere combinations of music and poetry. They were *dramas;* and not merely dramas in the ordinary sense of the word, but lights upon man and the universe, elucidations of problems of life and art and conduct. He was a born preacher ; and if you did not care to pay attention to the matter of his sermon, he did not wish you to listen to his words and his accents as you would simply to a fine oratorical performance. All his life he fought the German theatres, the German performers, and the German public upon this point, insisting that he who only heard beautiful music and expressive orchestration at a performance of one of his operas had not even made an approach to understanding it. I have often wondered how much his worshippers, or the public, or the performers, would have understood of his operas, in the sense he intended them to be understood, had he not given the key to his intentions in his prose works. Let any one, as an experiment, who is well acquainted with *Tannhäuser* and *Lohengrin,* sit down and write out his ideas as to the psychology of the characters in these two operas, and then compare his reading of them with the analyses Wagner has given in " *The Performing of Tannhäuser* " and " *A Communication to my Friends,*" [1] and he will, I venture to think, agree with me that nine-tenths of the treatises upon the philosophy of Wagner's dramas are based not upon the dramas themselves, but upon the prose-works and the letters. Wagner's own delusion upon the point was really something abnormal ; but

[1] See the remarks already made in Chapter iii.

one can pardon in him what one cannot pardon in his worshippers, for in him it was part of the very structure that made him so wonderful a musician. He saw things in music that no one else can see there; it aroused in him suggestions of concrete things; it spoke to him of definite thought and action, where to us it is only beautiful and vague emotion. Hence the folly of his worshippers, who are by no means built upon his cerebral pattern, in attempting to make his philosophy of music theirs. This aspect of mind may be illustrated from his attitude towards *Tannhäuser*. For the benefit of all concerned with the performance of that work, he wrote a small treatise giving the most valuable hints to all who took part in the performance, as well as an analysis of the character of Tannhäuser as he conceived it. Now it is quite safe to say, as a piece of æsthetic psychology, that no living man or woman can have the slightest notion of the philosophy of that or any other opera *except from the words of the poem*. The music may enforce the emotions aroused by the words, and the leading-motives may throw many side-lights upon the utterances of the characters; but to no one whatever can the music give an insight into the psychology of the characters further than that given by the poem. No one, I think, not under the sway of Wagner's theories, and not merely echoing, parrot-like, Wagner's ideas as to the psychological power of music—ideas, be it remembered, that were perfectly natural to his abnormal brain—can dispute the truth of this. Now Wagner held that a piece of psychological portraiture that was impossible to the mere actor, dependent as he is upon mere words, was rendered possible to the singer by the expressive power of the music.

"I declare," he writes, "that not even the most eminent actor, of our own or bygone times, could solve the task of a perfect portrayal of Tannhäuser's character on the lines laid down in the above analysis; and I meet the question: 'How could I hold it possible for an opera-singer to fulfil it?' by the simple answer that to *Music* alone could the draft of such a task be offered, and only a dramatic *singer*, just through the aid of Music, can be in the position to fulfil it. Where a Player would seek in vain, among the means of recitation, for the expression wherewithal to give this character success, to the Singer that expression is self-offered in the music."[1]

And that this passage bears out the interpretation I have put upon it—that it correlates with a hundred other passages of unconscious self-revelation—may be seen from the fact that Wagner regarded *the music* of the *Ring* as affording the true key to the comprehension of its philosophy.

"I now realise myself," he wrote to Roeckel, "how much of the whole spirit and meaning of my poem is only made clear by the music; I cannot now for my life even look at the words without the musical accompaniment."

This does not mean merely that by the system of leading-motives a light that would otherwise be lacking is thrown upon certain scenes and incidents. One has only to understand the peculiar psychology of Wagner, and the exaggerated stress he laid upon the power of music in the drama, to see that to *his* mind the philosophy of the *Ring* was not only revealed by the music, but made clearer, more convincing, more universal than could possibly have been done by words.[2]

Upon this point Wagner certainly deceived himself. At the risk of repetition, let me say once more that from beginning to end of his career, he laid down for universal acceptance ideas and theories that were purely personal to himself, and that he was unable to conceive how the whole world, when it came to its senses, could think differently from him. We have seen him declaring Lohengrin to be the type of the

---

[1] G. S. v. 155, 156 ; Ellis, iii. 201, 202.

[2] See the later remarks, in the present chapter, on his use of leading-motives in the *Ring*.

only true tragedy of modern times. Now he avows
to Uhlig his belief that the poem of the *Ring* is "the
greatest ever written"; and to Roeckel he writes that
he is certain the hearer will see the philosophy of the
drama as the composer has conceived it. His faith in
his own philosophical ideas, his belief in their importance for the regeneration of the universe, would surely
be grotesque if it were not so pathetic. His purely
musical gift, which has never been equalled among
men, he seemed to lay comparatively little stress upon;
while he constantly troubled himself, his correspondents, his readers, and his hearers, with speculations in
philosophy and other subjects for which he had only
the most mediocre capacity. One sometimes rises
with a feeling of sadness from a study of the *Ring*
and all Wagner's writings connected with it—a feeling
of pity that this man should have spent precious year
after year of his life gnawing at his own heart to no
purpose, embittering his days and nights with long
meditation on questions that any clear-headed schoolboy could quickly have settled for him. For it must
be reiterated that Wagner had no more capacity for
philosophical speculation than the average curate. He
hung upon the fringe of every great question, half
understanding it and half perverting it, falling a victim
to the most elementary of verbal fallacies, twisting
everything into a kind of forced harmony with his
own preconceived notions, but reaching no conclusion
by dint of solid thinking, and in the long run adding
nothing to the sum of human knowledge. He fell an
easy victim, first to Feuerbach, then to Schopenhauer.
In the case of the latter philosopher, he was unable
to detect the simplest of his errors by reason of his
lack of real metaphysical training; and he maundered
on in his terribly serious way about the Will, and
Time, and Space, and Causality, and the rest of it,
without ever a suspicion that he was following the

lead of Schopenhauer in the merest verbal absurdity. And he confesses withal that he can only understand even Schopenhauer by a kind of intuition, not by real assimilation of the argument—evidently regarding one of the simplest and clearest of writers as a thinker almost too profound for the comprehension of ordinary minds.

" I cannot pretend," he writes to Roeckel, "that I am at all times able to follow the process of the solution of this mighty problem, still less to expound it clearly. The clear realisation of the subjective character of time, space, and causality, as mere forms of perception, *argues a mental process of so sublime a nature that, as Schopenhauer proves beyond dispute, it can only be possible to an abnormally organised brain, and under conditions of peculiar excitement.*" [1]

The man who is capable of a performance of this kind had really better leave metaphysics alone ; one begins to wonder whether he did not see something rather profound in the multiplication table or in Euclid's Elements. Yet this was the man, and this the mind, that preached in season and out of season upon questions of philosophy, and economics, and history, and æsthetics, and sociology ; that really felt a mission to give to the world, not only in prose but in a drama, the true solution of the problem of human existence.

III

For that, finally, is what the *Ring* pretends to do. Enough has already been said to show what were Wagner's views upon certain great questions of human life during the years when he was thinking out the drama. He was living, as he always did, in a mental world of fog and mist, wherein everything took the strangest of forms. His essay on *The Wibelungen*, written at that time, is still worth reading as an

[1] *Letters to Roeckel*, p. 129.

example of the most approved Teutonic apriorism; a purely historical subject is treated from the point of view of the most abstract dialectics, and historical events, depending upon all kinds of economic, social, and military forces, are made to stand as "moments" in a development that follows its dialectical course like a piece of prearranged clockwork. He was not alone in this manner of writing history in Germany just then; other men were doing it almost as serenely and as absurdly as himself. The only things worth wondering about are, first, how a musician who could treat history and sociology in this, the easiest, the most primitive, the most *banal* of all possible methods, could ever have been held up to men's adoring gaze as a great thinker; and second, how it is that those who have shrugged their shoulders in quiet tolerance over Wagner's world-philosophy as expressed in the *Wibelungen* and other prose works, should have failed to pass a similar criticism upon the philosophy of the *Ring*.

For surely one has only to read that poem with one's eyes open to be convinced that Wagner was labouring under the most pathetic delusion when he thought he was contributing anything of the slightest value to the intellectual store of the race. It is quite unnecessary for his disciples to take such infinite pains to prove that he was a Schopenhauerite before ever he read a line of Schopenhauer. That is just the trouble; he had already certain vague innate notions as to renunciation and redemption, and Schopenhauer, so far as Wagner could understand him, simply gave a support to these notions. He took the philosopher up, not because of his interest in philosophy, but because of his interest in his own ideas.

"In accepting unreservedly the profound truths of his teaching," he wrote, "I was able to follow my own inner bent; and although he has given my line of thought a direction somewhat different from its previous one, yet only this direction harmonised with the profoundly sorrowful conception I had already formed of the world."[1]

The confession was quite unnecessary; the impression one gets from all his prose works is that of a man who could assimilate only so much of other men's ideas as happened to harmonise with his own—he being curiously like Schopenhauer himself in this respect. There was no correction or readjustment of view by the clash of other men's opinions; if he changed at all, it was merely in obedience to the changes in his health, or in his personal relations to the world.

The programme of the *Ring*, in its final form, was not exactly what Wagner intended it to be in the beginning. At first the hero was Siegfried, the man of the future; in the drama as we now have it the real hero is Wotan. Wagner's curious explanation of this reversal of mood—optimism giving way to pessimism, or what looks very like pessimism—is that in the first sketch of the drama he was obeying his intellectual instead of his artistic nature. The latter, he assumed, was always correct in its intuitions; the former was liable to error.

"I made my most remarkable discovery in this respect," he wrote, "with my Nibelung drama. It had taken form at a time when, with my ideas, I had built up an optimistic world on Hellenic principles; believing that in order to realise such a world, it was only necessary for man to wish it. I ingeniously set aside the problem, *why* they did not wish it" [which is as good a criticism as one could desire on *Art and Revolution* and *The Art-Work of the Future*]. "I remember that it was with this definite creative purpose that I conceived the personality of Siegfried with the intention of representing an existence free from pain."[2]

---

[1] *Letters to Roeckel*, p. 124.
[2] *Ibid.*, p. 149.

The drama was, in fact, simply a moral treatise on the wrongness of wrong and the rightness of right—not a particularly illuminative philosophy. As he went on, however, he discovered, according to his own account, that he was

"unconsciously being guided by a wholly different, infinitely more profound intuition, and that instead of conceiving a phase in the development of the world, I had grasped the very meaning and essence of the world itself in all its possible phases, and had realised its nothingness; the consequence of which was, that as I was true to my living intuitions and not to my abstract ideas in my completed work, something quite different saw the light from what I had originally intended."

This "something quite different" was the making of Wotan the centre of the whole drama, as the embodiment of the principle of renunciation. Wagner, in fact, was suffering from a very bad attack of Schopenhauerism, partly congenital and partly induced. There is undoubtedly a touch of old-world grandeur even in the more metaphysical portions of the *Ring;* but that effect is produced mainly by the nobility of the music. On the purely philosophical side, upon which Wagner laid so much stress, the scheme is hopelessly mediocre in conception ; it is just a very dull sermon on liberty and law. Fricka, as the representative of conventional law and order, is as hopeless a lay figure as one could meet in drama ; and all the other characters, in so far as they do not interest us on the purely human side, in so far as they merely pose as symbols of various parts of the social structure, are not only dull but foolish. For what is the great "tragedy of renunciation" which Wotan accomplishes of his own free will ? As Wagner expresses it, the lesson that "we have to learn from the history of mankind is to will what necessity imposes, and ourselves to bring it about."[1] Well, the comment

[1] *Letters to Roeckel,* p. 97.

upon that kind of thing is that it is painfully reminiscent of the dialectic of the young curate.   What *is* necessity in nature ?   If there is " necessity," can it be opposed ? and if it can be opposed, ought it to be called necessity ? Wagner's doctrine was that " we must will the inevitable, and accomplish it spontaneously."   What conception could he have had of the inevitable?   If you can will whatever you like and get it, then necessity is not inevitable ; and if you cannot get what you want by willing—if you can only get what inevitable necessity has predestined for you—then it is somewhat superfluous to talk of "accomplishing freely what necessity wills."   Wagner, in fact, was not only trying to treat in music a subject for which music is quite unfitted, but he was setting about to preach a new philosophy of society with only the merest smattering of knowledge, and only a mediocre capacity for thinking.   Undoubtedly there is, and always has been, a conflict between the interests and desires of the individual and the laws of society.   But who is going to treat with even average respect a theory that affects to settle the whole complex question by mere rhapsodising about the "free individual," and the necessity of " willing the inevitable," and the rest of that airy jargon? If a musician must needs preach a social evangel in his operas, have we not a right to expect of him some little logical preparation for his task ?   Who cares for all this vapouring about "the individual," and "constituted authority," and the "immorality of convention " ? who wants the characters of an opera to be a procession of dull abstractions drawn alternately from anarchistic and socialistic handbooks ?   To repeat once more, Wagner was not contributing one iota to the knowledge or the wisdom of mankind ; he was simply throwing at our heads the crude and primitive ideas of an organism radically incapable of patient and profitable thinking. He perpetually rambles, in his confused and amateur way, about the superiority of "instinct" to "abstract

P

knowledge," of the feeling to the understanding. One does not, in the year 1898, set oneself to combat primitive psychological blunders of that kind ; it is sufficient to note the phenomenon as being of importance in a diagnosis of Wagner's character. Holding these ideas, he argued, as he always did, from the particular to the general ; because he could see no further than this himself, he failed to perceive that to other people his "philosophy" was only arrant nonsense. His Wotan, for example, was meant to typify a being "who has wished to drink at the fountain of wisdom—to be guided by the counsels of sovereign reason" ; while "Siegfried, on the contrary, always obeys the primordial law of instinct." Who takes any serious interest in these crude metaphysical antitheses ? and who, above all, wants them embodied in music ? Or take again his lay figure of Fricka, as the guardian of the conventional marriage-law, and his Brynhild as the upholder of Love against traditional morality. Even the most thoroughgoing revolutionary must draw back in amazement at this childlike mode of settling a huge social question. Has "traditional morality" no justification ? Are we to have all our doubts allayed by this sentimental rhapsodising about Love, and by the assurance that if we were all actuated by no other motive than Love we should all be very happy ? No doubt ; but that is not a particularly profound philosophy, nor does one need it preached at him in a four-barrelled opera.

That the so-called "philosophy" of the *Ring* is merely the crude sentiment of a man incapable of thinking out the great problems he was interested in, must, I think, be the verdict of every one who considers it on its merits, apart from the glamour of the music. It was only natural that a mind of this kind should be impervious to criticism ; the ideas not being got at through solid thinking—being in fact nothing more than the irresponsible self-expression of the artist—

were not likely to be affected by the views of other men. So that it is not surprising to find Wagner writing to Roeckel that

"it was not so much the obscurity of my version of the poem, as the point of view which you persistently adopted in opposition to mine, which was the cause of your failing to understand many important parts of it. Such mistakes (*sic*) are of course only possible in the case of a reader who substitutes his own ideas for those of the poet, while the simple-minded reader, perhaps unconsciously to himself, takes in the matter more easily, just as it is." [1]

In other words, you must not criticise the poem by bringing to bear upon its philosophical and social theories your own knowledge of philosophical and social problems. That is " substituting your own ideas for those of the poet " ; what you have to do is to be a " simple-minded reader," open your mouth and shut your eyes, and take in the matter " just as it is." Well, Wagner has had followers enough of that order ; but to the outside mind the letter to Roeckel has its touch of pathos. From an intelligence of this kind no light could possibly come upon concrete matters of life and art ; and we may surmise that the shrewd Roeckel had an intuition of this, and hinted as much to Wagner.

"You must not take it ill," we find the musician replying, "if I only smile at the advice you give me to tear myself away from dreams and egoistic illusions, and to devote myself to what alone is real, to life itself and its aspirations. For I, on the contrary, believe that I am devoting myself to absolute Reality, in the most effective, deliberate, and determinate way, by carrying out my own views, even those that entail the most suffering, and by dedicating every one of my faculties to this end."

The self-delusion was complete. The man with no notion of reality believed that he alone saw reality as

---

[1] *Letters to Roeckel*, pp. 94, 95. Compare p. 104.

it actually was ; the man whose every conception was abstract and *à priori* lamented the tendency of other men to live in abstractions ; the man whose powers failed ignominiously whenever he came to touch a concrete question must needs attempt to deal with the most intricate of all concrete questions in the most unsuitable of all possible mediums.

It was probably some such reflection as this that was in Roeckel's mind at the time of his correspondence with Wagner. Knowing the man's enormous musical gift and the mediocrity of his talent in other directions, he must have regretted the one flaw in Wagner's mind, the one malign gift his natal fairies had bestowed on him—this desire to make his musical genius the mere mouthpiece of his crude philosophical notions. That is the regret that fills the minds of some of Wagner's admirers to-day, and that will probably be dominant in men's minds a century hence, when the metaphysics and sociology of Wagner and his era shall have become as utterly alien to the race as those of the sixteenth century are to us. In those days, when Wagner's prose-works will be reprinted only in short extracts and summaries, and men will recall, as they listen to his music, vague traditions of certain pseudo-philosophical notions which the operas are supposed to embody, they will regret that he did not choose somewhat less grandiose and somewhat more human subjects for his muse to work upon. That is what a great many of us feel to-day. We do not want a composer to give us tracts instead of operas, particularly when the tracts themselves are uninteresting to a degree. Fifty years ago, A. B. Marx, reviewing in a not unsympathetic spirit such of Wagner's works as had then seen the light, called attention to the fact that some of the composer's ideas were so far off the ordinary line of human psychology as to be almost incomprehensible to the majority of men. In the case of *Lohengrin*, for example, he remarked that few people could take much interest in a man who leaves the woman who loves him simply because she asks his name. It is what a great many other auditors of *Lohengrin* have felt ; but it was an aspect of the question that had never presented itself to Wagner. He was concerned with Lohengrin as the representative of certain social and personal ideas which were of profound interest to the composer, but of little interest to any one else ; and he failed to perceive that other people, whose notions of life were not congenitally coloured by these prepossessions, would look at the tragedy of the drama in a very different way. Had Marx been acquainted with the *Ring* he would, I think, have had an even better text for his sermon. These musical dissertations on freedom, and convention, and the marriage laws, and necessity, and renunciation, and regeneration, have little interest for any one but those constructed somewhat upon Wagner's pattern. To the vast majority of us they are merely dull.

IV

It is to Wagner's preoccupation with his moral scheme, again, that we have to attribute some of the artistic faults of his work. It has led him to write page after page of matter that is quite unsuitable for music, and in which the pseudo-music that accompanies the words is padding pure and simple. He has also inserted scenes that might well have been dispensed with, though he was hampered here by the fact that his poem was written in the reverse order of the drama, repetitions being thus almost forced upon him. The scene between Mime and the Wanderer, for example, in the 2nd Act of *Siegfried*, would have served the purpose, if no previous drama had existed, of acquainting the reader with all that had happened before the opening of *Siegfried;* but it is almost entirely superfluous after the *Rheingold* and the *Valkyrie*, where the events discussed between Mime and the Wanderer have been already presented upon the stage. A similar criticism applies in great part to the scene of the Norns at the commencement of the *Götterdämmerung*, which was justifiable in the first sketch of *Siegfried's Tod*, but mainly superfluous here. There is no need, again, for Wotan to tell Erda, in the 3rd Act of *Siegfried*, what we already know from the *Valkyrie;* while the later scene between Siegfried and Wotan might have been shortened with advantage. Apart from difficulties of this kind, placed in his way by his constant reshaping of the poem, Wagner's intentness on his moral scheme is answerable both for his dramatic blunders and his absurdities. The unsophisticated hearer who wonders why Erda should pop up now and again, and discuss metaphysics and cosmogony with Wotan, can only allay his dissatisfaction if he submits blindly to Wagner's guidance through the scheme of the drama. Unfortunately the bulk of us cannot do this; we are not sufficiently hypnotised to take this kind of thing very seriously. All that Wotan has to do with Erda in the 3rd Act of *Siegfried* is to tell her he sees the approaching end of the gods and is resigned ; and simply for this purpose there is really no need to drag a dreary old abstraction upon the stage and expect our dramatic sense to be interested in it.[1]

---

[1] An enthusiastic lady who has recently published a guide to the *Ring* gives us the following analysis of Erda :—

"The Impersonation of the *Earth*.

All the secrets of Nature and Destiny are known to her :

But she has no power to change either the one or the other.

Her voice is only heard as a warning against evil.

She is vanquished by the Will of Wotan, to whom she reveals herself ;

And to him she imparts knowledge and wisdom.

She furnishes him with the means by which to combat hostile forces :

But her wisdom and foresight vanish before the power of Wotan's Will ;

And at his bidding she sinks again (*sic*) into eternal (*sic*) sleep."

(*The Epic of Sounds*, by Mrs. Freda Winworth, p. xxxiii). Absurdly as this reads, it is really a fair transcript of Wagner's notion of Erda, and the reader

Wagner, in fact, for all his anxiety to teach the world what did and what did not constitute drama as distinct from literary poetry, quite failed to apprehend the difference himself. Philosophical poetry may be made extremely impressive only so long as there is no pretence of an appeal to the visual sense. A poet may present philosophical ideas as incarnated in human figures, but he can only do so as long as the figures appeal simply to the internal imagination ; the impressiveness vanishes when an attempt is made to represent these personifications to the eye. Just as the huge bulk of Milton's Lucifer could not be depicted upon canvas without becoming absurd instead of terrifying, so the personification of a moral or philosophical concept becomes unimpressive when taken from the inner imagination and set visibly before the eye. We immediately judge it by a different standard of probability, and the ludicrous contrast between the merely human figure and the vast cosmic forces which it is supposed to represent, not only prevents any belief in the figure itself, but weakens the philosophical effect that might be had from the mere reading. Erda, as the embodiment of the forces of the earth, might be made a solemnly impressive conception in the hands of a fine poet ; but Wagner's Erda—a woman rising from a hole in the rock, to the accompaniment of blue light—simply jars on the artistic sense.[1] She may utter such pseudo-profound jargon as "Whatever was, I know ; whatever is, whatever shall be, also I do see ; the endless world's

can estimate from it how inappropriate the conception is to a drama. The good ladies and gentlemen who spell "Will" always with a capital W, and fancy they are philosophising when they write of the wisdom and foresight of the Impersonation of the Earth vanishing before the power of Wotan's Will, could surely find more scope for their great powers in another medium than that of the drama. *C'est magnifique, mais ce n'est pas le drame!*

[1] The stage directions in *Siegfried* are—"A bluish light glows in the rocky chasm. Illumined by this, Erda very gradually rises from the earth. She appears covered with hoar-frost ; her hair and garments emit a glittering light."

all-wise one, Erda, speaks to you "—but we never for a moment believe in her as an artistic creation. She is a pure abstraction, and has no place in acted drama.

Once more does Wagner's artistic sense blunder when he brings the dragon upon the stage in the *Götterdämmerung*, and when he makes Alberich go through his transformations into serpent and toad in the *Rheingold*. Here again what is valid in a poem or tale intended merely for reading is quite invalid in a dramatic representation that is set before the eye. The dragon is particularly absurd. No spectator with any real artistic sense could take quite seriously the scene between the dragon and Siegfried ; there is a touch of pantomime that is inseparable from it, that even refuses to vanish at the bidding of the music. Wagner, in fact, was always making the strangest lapses as a dramatist, partly because of his childish seriousness in face of certain elements of the old myths, and partly because of his tendency to use the dramatic picture or action as a mere pretext for a moral or metaphysical treatise. Thus the scene between Siegfried and Wotan, where the god attempts to bar his path to Brynhild's rock, only becomes intelligible, and it is only saved at times from puerility, by a knowledge of what Wagner intended it to symbolise—the last ineffectual stand of constituted authority against the young, untrammelled individuality of the future. Wotan has already, in the preceding scene with Erda, told us very categorically that the end of the gods was drawing nigh, that Siegfried would attain to Brynhild's fire-girt rock, that Brynhild would subsequently achieve the redemption of the world, and that he himself looked towards the end with calm resignation. On these terms there hardly seems any particular reason why he should go through the farce of attempting to bar Siegfried's path.[1] The only valid explanation

---

[1] The current Wagnerian view is that Wotan's action is the last dying spark of his Will—the last kick of the mule, as it were, if the simile be not too

seems to be that Wagner wanted to enforce the moral
scheme at this point—to show visually to the spectator
the result of the conflict between old authority and free
individuality. It takes all the seriousness we can sum-
mon up for this conception to suppress hilarious thoughts
at what actually happens on the stage—an old man,
wearing a large hat, stretching out a spear, getting it
chopped in two, quietly picking up the pieces and walk-
ing off with them, remarking to Siegfried, " Advance !
I cannot stop thee ! " That is what the eye sees ; and
Wagner has made a mistake in putting upon the stage
a scene whose symbolism loses most of its impressiveness when made visible. The spear as the symbol of
constituted authority is a purely imaginative conception,
and should appeal to the imagination alone ; when
stretched out before our eyes across the stage it has an
unfortunate tendency to look merely like a piece of
ordinary wood.

Wagner, as we know, always regarded the theatre
in a very serious light ; but his dramatic sense, fine
as it was at times, was always prone not only to
artistic blunders but to childish lapses. Nothing, for
example, could be more absurd than the scene where
the corpse of Siegfried lifts its hand to stop Hagen
from seizing the Ring. The dramatist's dilemma is
of course apparent ; it is necessary for the purposes
of " redemption " that the Ring shall not go to Hagen
and Alberich but to Brynhild, and through her be
restored to the Rhine. Yet now that Siegfried is lying
dead, and Gunnar has just fallen by Hagen's sword,
there is really nothing whatever to prevent Hagen
wrenching the Ring from Siegfried's finger ; and the
only device open to Wagner is the dreadfully indigent

irreverent—and that he is particularly roused to anger at the thought of his
beloved Brynhild falling into the hands of Siegfried. That is quite a rational
view, as far as it goes ; but it seems to me that this explanation still fails to
square with the previous scene between Wotan and Erda. Wagner has
simply pieced his drama together unskilfully.

one of making the corpse raise its hand in warning. A dramaturgist is occasionally reduced to great straits in order to pave the way for his closing scene; but it is characteristic of the peculiar weakness of Wagner's dramatic sense that he should insert this mere piece of melodrama in a work that, as a whole, is an attempt to deal with life intellectually instead of sensationally. Of a similar order is the sinking to the level of the old legends in the use of the magic potion in the *Götterdämmerung,* that takes away Siegfried's memory of Brynhild and causes him to love Gudrun. One feels that there is something crude in the episode, playing, as it does, so important a part in the evolution of a drama that is elsewhere worked out on such philosophical lines; while the singing dragon and the speaking bird are also sore trials to our sense of verisimilitude—even the sense of verisimilitude as affected by stage conditions. We are told, of course, that we are not to be too critical, too modern in our attitude towards these elements in the *Ring;* that *Siegfried*

"is a fairy tale, and Wagner expects his adult hearers to take it in the way adults generally take a fairy tale—in a humorous or semi-humorous way. Even children do not believe you are a bear when you 'play bear' with them; they are half frightened, half amused when you pursue them on all-fours; and for grown children it is not necessary to take the dragon seriously in order to be delighted with the scene."[1]

Mr. Finck opines that

"no scene ever written has given the musical experts more opportunity to show their habitual lack of poetical feeling, of naïveté, and sense of humour, than this. . . . A man who cannot see the exquisite combinations of humour and pathos in this fairy scene for grown children, cannot be helped by argument, however much we may pity him."

---

[1] Finck, *Wagner and his Works,* ii. 351.

It is decidedly amusing to be told, by the good souls who take the dragon-nonsense quite seriously, that *we* object to it because *we* lack the sense of humour! The truth is that the scene is only made tolerable to the audience by its musical accompaniment — thus showing once more that in Wagner's operas, no less than in those of previous composers, the beauty of the music makes us less critical of the substance of the play than we would be towards prose or poetical drama—makes us tolerant of exhibitions of childishness that would be sufficient to damn a real play. The Wagnerians naïvely imagine that incidents of this kind show the superiority of the musical to the spoken drama, in that things are possible in the former that would be impossible in the latter. In reality, they simply show that the intellectual level and critical standards of opera are much lower than those of drama, and that consequently no combination of music and poetry—not even Wagner's—can ever take the place, among men of civilised and educated minds, of the real drama. One begins to understand Wagner's antipathy towards the more intellectual work of other men, and his failure to comprehend it, when we see the primitive level at which his own dramatic sense existed. It may have satisfied him, and it may now satisfy Wagnerians, to have the problems of life presented to them in the form of fairy tales; but we are not all constituted like that. In any case, if the drama is to be a fairy tale, let it be a fairy tale pure and simple—not a combination of pantomime heroics and the children's story-book with long dissertations on the will, and the basis of social obligation, and the conflict between Authority and the free Individual of the Future.

V

We may put the matter succinctly by saying that Wagner was not a dramatist but a musical dramatist. He himself did not see the absurdity of a great deal of the *Ring* because his mind was intent not so much on the objective aspects of the drama as on the musical forms and phrases in which the drama was conceived. There can be no proper understanding of the complex problem which Wagner's brain presents, if we do not recognise how entirely different it was from that of all other musicians. He lived, as we have seen, in an ideal world of politics and economics—a world having few points of contact with that of other men. We need to recognise, further, that his dramatic conceptions also were denizens of an interior world whither we are unable to follow them ; the most we can sometimes do is to see that his mental pictures were creations peculiar to himself. This becomes very clear when we examine the leading-motives of the *Ring* and their various uses throughout the tetralogy. We have to remember all along that Wagner did not build up the score by means of leading-motives because of certain abstract notions on the subject, or because he was unable to compose continuous music throughout the work : as far as the latter point is concerned, no one who knows his musical powers can doubt that he could have written five beautiful operas in the ordinary style with less trouble than any one section of the tetralogy must have cost him. He took so kindly to the principle of the leading-motive [1] because it was the natural outcome of his peculiar imagination, the natural vehicle of expression for a brain constituted like his. He

---

[1] It is probably unnecessary to remind readers that the convenient term "leading-motive" is not Wagner's own.

saw human life and character, the outward world, the interplay of force with force, of element with element, all in terms of music. Those who are acquainted with his scores stand astonished at the rare felicity of some of his conceptions, his power to sketch character in a musical phrase, to write descriptive music —such as the forest-scene in *Siegfried* or the fire-music in the *Valkyrie*—that can only be described as marvellous in its pictorial quality ; and no less wonderful than the veracity of these pictures is the unerring colour-sense that gives that "inevitable" quality to his orchestration—gives us the feeling that ear and eye are interchanging their functions, that the music of the orchestra is only another aspect of the person or the scene upon the stage. Wagner could have achieved these results only in virtue of a cerebral constitution that was unique ; and the manner in which he thus saw external life in terms of music helps us to understand his failure, in his prose-works, to get outside the circle of his own musical prepossessions.

Not only, however, did he conceive man and nature in terms of music, but the inter-relations of one with the other were symbolised for him in the inter-relations of the musical phrases in which they were expressed. A musical phrase once created, as the representative of some character or motive in the drama, became henceforth for him a thing of flesh and blood, a living thing that played its part in the orchestra in the manner of its prototype upon the stage ; significant in its speech, in its silence, in the countless transformations it was made to undergo ; suffering defeat, rising triumphant ; a warning from the past, a prophecy of the future ; a proclamation of things invisible and unspoken. At the end of the *Götterdämmerung* it is not Brynhild or the Gibichung spectators who have the final word in this vast and complex drama ; it is the orchestra that mingles the song of the Rhine-maidens, Alberich's

curse, and Wotan's lust for power, in one fierce contest, from which there emerges at the last the triumphant strain of redemption by love. Wagner had no
need of words for the construction of many of his
dramatic pictures ; using the musical phrases as symbols, he could present dilemmas or strike conclusions
into the auditor's mind merely by his manner of
combining them.

But his existence in this world of music had its
drawbacks as well as its advantages. If it sometimes
led him to results hitherto undreamt of in opera, it also
tempted him to things that no reasoning can justify.
His memory of a dramatic character would be along
the lines of music rather than of the more objective
aspects of the character ; and hence in his preoccupation with the musical phrases he sometimes relies too
implicitly on the similarity of other men's conceptions to his. One example will make this clear. In
the 2nd Act of the *Rheingold*, Wotan and Loge ask
Alberich to show the magic powers of the Tarn-helm
by assuming the form of a serpent. Alberich does so,
and the appearance of the monster is accompanied in
the orchestra by a heavy unison phrase which, in the
strange clumsiness of its turnings, is a perfect analogue
of the motions of the unwieldy monster on the stage.
As a piece of musical description it is decidedly clever,
but one never expects to meet with it again in the
course of the drama. What then is our surprise to
find that in *Siegfried*, when a phrase has to be found
for Fafner, who has now turned himself into a dragon,
it is this old phrase from the *Rheingold* that is made to
do duty ! The amazed hearer asks himself on what
grounds Wagner or his disciples can justify so strange
a procedure as this. It is quite true that both Alberich
and Fafner have converted themselves into serpents by
the magic of the Tarn-helm, and that therefore there
is a faint connection between the two circumstances

in this respect. But that is quite insufficient to justify the mechanical transference of the motive that represents Alberich as serpent to the figure of Fafner as serpent. A German critic once compared the leading-motive to the labels that one sees issuing from the mouths of persons in old pictures, informing us of their names and qualities. That of course is a very shortsighted view of the leading-motive as Wagner generally uses it; but it is singularly appropriate to the particular case we are now considering. Even the Wagnerians who accept so unquestioningly all that the master has done, must admit that this use of the Alberich motive in connection with Fafner is bound to lead to confusion. Whenever it occurs in *Siegfried* or the *Götterdämmerung* we are, of course, supposed to refer it to Fafner. But why? If it has once been appropriated to Alberich, why should it not again carry the mind back to him? Surely to use leading-motives in this way is to create the very uncertainty which they were introduced to avoid.

Wagner, in fact, here as elsewhere, was unable to look at his drama through the eyes of other men, because his thought travelled along musical by-paths where no breath of outside criticism could reach him. He probably used the same serpent-motive for Alberich and Fafner because he conceived the two characters not as concrete beings, but as symbols of the one order of sub-human life. In the same way we may account for his giving to the bird-voice in *Siegfried* a form of melody that is very similar to that of the Rhine-maidens.[1] Dramatically there is no justification for this; the hearer is simply puzzled at first by the similarity, and wonders what reminiscence of the Rhine-maidens Wagner wishes to arouse by this echo of their song. The explanation of his procedure seems to be that he conceived both the Rhine-maidens

---

[1] See Wolzogen, *L'Anneau des Nibelungen*, p. 93.

and the bird as representations of pure nature, each serviceable to Siegfried in its own way ; and that he accordingly wished to indicate their equality of level in organic life by giving a similarity of form and phrase to their music.[1] These are attempts to convey to the hearer mystic significances to which he is quite indifferent.

The earlier operas had prepared us for the spectacle of a mind living among its own preconceived ideas, and incapable of assimilating the ideas of other men ; but it is in the *Ring*—the work conceived in the full flush of Wagner's first consciousness of all the heights and depths of his new theory—that we get the most instructive light upon the peculiarities of his psychology. Particularly in regard to his handling of the eighty or ninety motives of the *Ring* do we see how liable his system is to abuse, and how he himself has frequently misapplied it. This may seem a very bold assertion ; but I believe that no one can go through the score of the tetralogy with his eyes open, without becoming conscious that Wagner frequently makes a double error—that of expecting from the leading-motive more than it can possibly perform,[2] and that of employing it where it is quite unnecessary. One or two examples may suffice to make this clear. When, at the end of the *Rheingold*, Wotan sees the future unfolded before him, and recognises the danger that threatens the gods if Alberich should again become possessor of the *Ring*, he looks towards Valhalla, raises his sword, and cries " *So* greet I the castle, secure from fear and terror !" The orchestra gives out a theme that has never been heard before, and which first becomes significant in

[1] We know, in the case of the Rhine-maidens' song, that he wished to convey by it a suggestion of the innocence and simplicity of primitive nature.

[2] See Mr. J. D. Rogers' appendix to Mr. Bosanquet's History of Æsthetic (1892), for some remarks on Wagner's misapplication of the motive principle in the *Meistersinger*.

the *Valkyrie*, where we learn to associate it with the sword. We are told by the Wagnerians that the " *So !*" accompanied by the gesture, immediately informs us of what is passing in Wagner's mind—of his resolve to combat the schemes of Alberich by raising a race of free heroes, who shall get the Ring into their possession and lift from the world the curse that lies upon it.

" The ' *So*,'" writes Mr. Chamberlain, for example, "is a thought which for the present only finds, and can find, expression in the gesture, and which through the gesture attains a vastly higher significance than if Wotan indulged—as he would do in a spoken drama—in a long soliloquy about a thought which has only just at that moment entered his mind as a sudden inspiration. The spectator is not left for an instant in doubt about the meaning of that *so !* the gesture has told him everything; it is : 'heroism against gold.' The working out of the thought had to be deferred till later; but in this sudden resolve lies eternal truth, the source of everything which Wotan could and must achieve." [1]

Now with all respect to the gentlemen who indulge in this kind of æsthetics, one has to say that it is simply ultra-Wagnerian nonsense. Neither the gesture, nor the " *so*," nor the musical phrase, can for a moment tell us the plan that Wotan is revolving in his brain ; if it could, it would surpass the significance of Burleigh's famous nod in the *Critic*. The Wagnerians are simply following Wagner's lead in utter blindness when they profess to see meanings of this kind in music or in situations where no such meaning can really be discovered. Mr. Chamberlain did not, could not, grasp the significance of the passage *until he had been through the other three sections of the tetralogy*. It is only when, with the knowledge of the events of the *Valkyrie*, *Siegfried*, and the *Götter-*

[1] *Richard Wagner*, p. 316.

Q

dämmerung in our minds, we come back again to the *Rheingold*, that we see what Wagner meant this passage to signify. If he had died after completing the *Rheingold*, without leaving any indication of the future development of the *Ring*, neither Mr. Chamberlain nor any one else would ever have discovered the meaning they now see in the passage ; and if they *had* begun trying to find the inner significance of it, there would certainly have been as many guesses as there are Wagnerians.

Yet there can be no question that Wagner intended the passage in question to bear this interpretation ; and the cause of his blunder—as will be explained more fully in a later chapter—was his predisposition to see in musical phrases all sorts of meanings that do not exist for other men. When he was writing the *Rheingold*, he would have before his mind's eye the whole subsequent development of the story, together with the music of the leading themes.[1] He knew what use he intended to make of the sword-motive in the succeeding dramas ; and with all the later associations clustering round it in his mind, he failed to perceive that to us who hear it for the first time at the end of the *Rheingold*, it has no associations whatever. It is to us two bars of music and nothing more. When, like him, we are acquainted with all that subsequently happens, when we have seen the part played by the sword and its theme in the three dramas, we can then, like him, look beyond the musical phrase and Wotan's gesture, and see with prophetic eye the whole future contest between Alberich and Wotan's offspring. But until we know all this, the phrase cannot mean a tenth of what Wagnerians imagine it to mean ; and Wagner

[1] Wilhelm Tappert tells us that from the first conception of the *Ring* Wagner had in his mind some of the musical phrases that were to accompany salient features in the Drama (*Richard Wagner, sein Leben und seine Werke*, p. 76). It was, in fact, his practice to conceive the character and action musically in the first place. See the preceding chapter.

must be held guilty of a palpable misuse of his own system.

Other examples crowd upon the recollection. In the 2nd Act of *Siegfried*, when Mime takes the hero to Fafner's cave and tells him that here he shall learn what fear is, the orchestra gives out the slumber-theme from the 3rd Act of the *Valkyrie*. We are told that this signifies, "in a beautiful way," that it is not from Fafner but from Brynhild that Siegfried is destined to learn what fear is. How can that be? The phrase in question might mean a dozen different things. We know, of course, *after* Siegfried has penetrated the flames, that this use of the slumber-theme meant that he would ultimately reach Brynhild's rock and rouse her from her slumber; but will any one venture to say that upon the first hearing of the 2nd Act of *Siegfried*, ignorant of what happens in the 3rd Act, he would immediately seize the significance of this motive? He might or he might not—probably not; but the mere fact that there can be any doubt in the matter is fatal to Wagner's theory, since the very object of the system of leading-motives was to make the past and present and future of the drama intelligible to a degree that was impossible by any other means. If there is any room for doubt as to the meaning of a musical reminiscence, it might as well have been omitted from the score. Similarly Wagner must be said to have missed his mark in several other cases, where either the form of the motive or the use to which he puts it leaves the hearer simply puzzled. The theme known as "the triumph of the Nibelung," that is compounded of the Valhalla theme and that of Loge,[1] is particularly fruitful in confusion. Wolzogen tells us that this motive is based on "the second part of the Valhalla theme, which Alberich has really annexed. . . ." To it "Loge will afterwards add, when, a little latter, he will dupe

[1] See the *Rheingold*, vocal score, p. 145.

the proud one by means of his own pride, the mocking leaps of his own motive, expressive of an ironic joy of victory." [1] The difficulty attendant on making a motive out of two others, in this manner, is that not only is its first appearance somewhat perplexing, but one is never quite clear afterwards as to whether we have the motive or not. On page 146 of *Siegfried*, for example, there is a phrase that might be either a modification of the theme of the Nibelung's triumph, or of the fire-motive ; while the confusion is increased by the fact that the words give no positive indication of what is signified in the music.[2] Wagner must have had some purpose in his mind at the moment ; but he has quite failed to make his scene self-explanatory by the use of the leading-motives.

Even more numerous, however, than the cases in which he has missed lucidity in the employment of the system, are the cases in which the score is quite unnecessarily burdened with motives that simply tell us nothing we do not know already. Let us take, as a salient example, the two phrases associated with the dragon—the serpent-theme already mentioned, and one formed by a slight modification of the giant-theme from the *Rheingold*.[3] There is probably no motive which Wagner has employed with such unnecessary frequency as these. The object of a leading-motive is to acquaint the hearer with something not revealed either in the words or on the stage, by the use of a phrase in the orchestra that carries the mind back to some previous character or circumstance. When Sieglinda, for example,

---

[1] *L'Anneau des Nibelungen*, p. 42.

[2] The same remark applies to the use of Fafner's motive, in the preceding bar.

[3] The first three notes are the same as in the *Rheingold* phrase, the fourth a semitone lower. An unconscious French humorist informs us that "in this way Wagner apprises us that Fafner, by changing himself into a dragon, *has descended one degree in the scale of beings.*" One welcomes the suggestion, although one would have thought the difference between a giant and a serpent was more than that.

in the 1st Act of the *Valkyrie*, is telling Siegmund of
the mysterious old man who struck the sword into the
ash-tree, the orchestra gives out the majestic Valhalla-
phrase. Sieglinda herself does not know who the old
man was ; but the spectator learns at once from the
orchestra that it was Wotan. This is a quite legitimate
use of the leading-motive principle ; but there is surely
no necessity to employ a motive that refers to a certain
person, when the audience already knows who is being
referred to—nay, even has the character before its
eyes upon the stage. In the scene between the Wanderer and Alberich, in the 2nd Act of *Siegfried*, the
Wanderer speaks of the hero who is shortly to slay
Fafner and take possession of the Ring. "Wouldst
thou know more ?" he continues. "There lies the
dragon ; warn him of his doom, and he perhaps will
give you the toy." [1] What earthly necessity is there for
the Fafner-motive to be sounded in the orchestra here,
and again throughout all the ensuing colloquy between
the dragon and Wotan ? We have the dragon visibly
before our eyes ; we know him to be Fafner trans-
formed ; what then can the leading-motive add to our
comprehension of the scene ? On very few of the occasions, indeed, on which Wagner uses the Fafner-motives,
can we say that they are really required. Without
discussing in detail any other cases in which they are
thus unnecessarily dragged into the score, I may refer
the reader to pages 76, 163, 185, 186, 224, and 265 of
Siegfried, and pages 29, 50, 66, 136, 138, 186, 247, 255,
and 260 of the *Götterdämmerung*. A Wagnerian may
answer that Wagner, by the use of the motives, intends
to remind us not so much of the dragon himself as of
his qualities—his ethical significance in relation to the
Ring. That rejoinder is quite invalid in all the cases I
have cited. Fafner is being spoken of ; the mention of
him recalls his appearance and all the incidents in which

[1] Vocal score, pp. 152, 153.

he has taken part ; and the orchestra simply tells us nothing more of him than we know already. Let any Wagnerian who thinks Wagner justified in the use of the Fafner-motives in the places I have mentioned, read through the score and imagine these motives absent wherever they now occur, and he will realise that they add nothing whatever to our understanding of the drama.

Other instances are not far to seek. Apart from many passages that might be cited in which it is only after long reflection that we can grasp the significance of a motive, there are cases where themes are used as unnecessarily as those of Fafner. I do not for a moment deny that in some of these cases there may be a slight justification pleaded for the themes. The principle by which to test them, however, is this—Do they or do they not tell us something we would otherwise be ignorant of—as in the case already cited, of the use of the Valhalla motive in Sieglinda's recital ? That is the true function of the leading-motive ; it is by his unequalled skill in using it in this manner that Wagner has made it so important an element in the musical drama. If it cannot justify its existence in this way it is quite superfluous—a mere label stuck on a character or an object, as a child writes across its drawing, " This is a horse." It seems to me that Wagner has made this unnecessary use of the Ring-motive on pages 8, 58, and 155 of *Siegfried;* of the gold-motive on page 206 of *Siegfried* and page 16 of the *Götterdämmerung.* In *Siegfried* the Valhalla-motive is superfluous on pages 61 and 313 ; the Volsung-motive on page 67 ;[1] the

---

[1] Wotan asks Mime, " What is that race that Wotan dealt so hardly with, and yet loves so dearly ? " This is a case in which the Wagnerian may say that the use of the Volsung-phrase in the orchestra tells us clearly which race is being referred to. But we would know it with equal sureness if the phrase were not used. The answer to Wotan's question has been given in the whole three Acts of the *Valkyrie;* and the Volsung-phrase on page 67 of *Siegfried* is therefore quite superfluous. In this and the next case (p. 71), the use of the phrase would have been justifiable had no other drama preceded *Siegfried.*

sword-motive on page 71 ; Mime's motive on page 228 ; the Wanderer's motive on page 245 ; Wotan's farewell on pages 252 and 253 ; the Valkyrie-motive on pages 287 and 289 ; the bird-motive on page 332. In the *Götterdämmerung*, the Volsung theme is unnecessary on page 49 ; the forge-song on page 65 ; the Tarn-helm-motive on pages 67 and 185 ;[1] the Rhinemaidens' theme on page 327. In all these cases, I think, our understanding of the drama is not in any way assisted by the leading-motives ; Wagner has simply ridden his hobby to death.

On the other hand, the number of cases in which a motive has been used judiciously and legitimately is, of course, legion ; and the reader who wishes to see the distinction between a merely mechanical use of the motive-principle and a use that really helps to elucidate the drama, may compare the passages I have just cited with the employment of the curse-theme on page 200 of the *Rheingold*, pages 191, 222, and 223 of *Siegfried*, and pages 18, 61, 72, 75, 77, 85, 125, 126, 182, 190, 215, 296, 314, and 337 of the *Götterdämmerung*. Any one who will take the trouble to go through the scores of the *Ring*, and note the various ways in which Wagner has employed his motives—wrongly, confusedly, unnecessarily, and judiciously—will light upon a significant fact. He will see that while the musician has frequently blundered in the use of themes that refer to persons or events, he is quite unerring in his use of themes that refer to what we may call the invisible forces of the drama. Thus while the Fafner-motive is constantly being thrust upon us where it is not needed, the motive of Alberich's

---

[1] Here again Wagnerians will hold that the motive of the Tarn-helm informs us, while all the occupants of the stage are perplexed, how Siegfried obtained the Ring from Brynhild. But we know all this from what has already gone before ; and not a spectator in the audience needs the information given him by the motive in the orchestra.

curse keeps recurring always at the most appropriate moment, always adding to our knowledge of what is going on upon the stage. It is by such achievements as this that Wagner has made his leading-motives such a marvellous instrument in the dramatic effect. It is necessary, for our comprehension of the evolution of the drama, that we should have the curse upon the gold suggested to us whenever its fruits are seen upon the stage ; and the orchestra can not only do this where the characters cannot, but can speak with far greater dramatic effect than words can do. At the end of the *Rheingold*, for example, Fafner and Fasolt, having acquired the gold that has only a little while before been wrested from Alberich, immediately begin to quarrel for possession of the Ring ; and Fafner strikes his brother dead with his staff. No words could thrill us with such tragic terror as now descends upon us when the orchestra gives out the sombre theme of the curse, amid the solemn silence of the characters upon the stage. And throughout the remaining dramas of the *Ring* the motive of Alberich's curse plays the same eloquent part of prophecy and retrospect. It is more than a character in the drama —more significant than any living character could be ; it seems to be the symbol of forces too vast, too terrible for visible representation, the silent, implacable cosmic forces, proceeding with their inexorable work through all the mutations of individual life and circumstance. It is by such uses as this of the leading-motive that Wagner has made his drama a living thing, that can stand unashamed among the finest artistic products of all the ages.

VI

Of the *Ring* as a whole it is impossible to speak with any attempt at completeness within the limits of a single chapter ; a proper consideration of it would involve the writing of a work almost as huge as itself. The more one studies it the more one stands astonished not only at the enormous expenditure of mental energy that must have gone to its creation, but at the striking originality of Wagner, his unequalled gift for musical-dramatic writing, the unique structure of brain that by device after device makes the most volatile and least intellectual form of art coherent, vital, surcharged with quintessential meanings. To attempt to show by mere description the almost incredible heights and depths of expression to which Wagner attains in the music, or the Titanic force with which he urges all this unwieldy matter towards the one consummation, would be but a vain task. Nothing short of an intimate knowledge of the scores can give even a faint idea of what the work really is ; the work that occupied Wagner more than twenty of the strongest years of his life is not to be discussed without our having studied it with some share of his own eternal patience and unflagging enthusiasm. There is nothing like it in art, nothing to equal the marvellous results Wagner has obtained from this mass of the most unpromising material with which a musician ever had to deal.

That it is a failure, in the artistic sense of the word, will probably be the verdict of posterity. From its very nature it could not help being a failure, for no one could fill that libretto and its philosophy always with the warm breath of musical inspiration, and no one but Wagner could have brought it so near to success. The really wonderful parts of the score are not the glorious lyrical moments—the superb love-music of the *Valkyrie* and *Siegfried;* the solemn *Trauermarsch*—that seems too vast, too universal for association with mere human death, that seems rather to be such music as the spirit of the universe might hear when world crashes into world at the end of time ; the exquisite music descriptive of fire and flood and forest ; the great triumphant theme that wins its way through all things and crowns the drama at the last. These are beautiful as no other music is beautiful ; but to the observant eye they are not the greatest things in the work. The unapproachable Wagner is seen in the non-lyrical portions, where there seems to rage a perpetual conflict between the spirit of music and all that is most antipathetic to her. It is these portions, which any other musician would have shuddered at the idea of setting to music, that Wagner has filled almost throughout with life-blood by his own peculiar art. The eloquent orchestra courses through it all, carrying us over sand and rock and stone by its own sheer force. Of necessity these passages cannot be always beautiful ; there are times when one catches the breath with wonder at the magic of this alchemist, who can turn the hardest and strangest things to gold ; there are times when the alien elements refuse to answer to the charm, and instead of the gold in the crucible we see only a turbulent mass of half-compounded matter. But if Wagner has not achieved everything he strove for, it is certain no other musician could have achieved half as much. When he fails, it is due to no defect in his powers as a musician, but because of the utter unsuitability of certain passages of the poem for any kind of musical treatment.

The extent to which his mind worked along musical lines, representing character to itself by sound rather than by speech, may be seen from his curious effort to make each leading-motive tell its own tale, and not only speak its own philosophy but throw side-lights on the philosophical meanings of other themes. His disciples, of course, have been his posthumous enemies in this as in every other matter, exaggerating his theory to the point of downright absurdity.[1] He was unfortunate enough to say, in one of his letters to Roeckel, that there was scarcely a bar of the orchestral music that did not develop out of previous motives ; and the bare hint, of course, has been suffi-cient to start his worshippers on their usual career of absurdity. They would have us believe that each leading-motive is simply a modification of a kind of basic theme that exists potentially in each of them. To a certain extent they are right ; one can readily see that the theme with which the *Rheingold* opens, Erda's motive and its opposite, the sword-motive, the Valhalla-motive, and perhaps one or two more, are in a sense thematically akin. But to push the analogy beyond nine or ten motives at the outside is to run headlong into folly ; and no one but the typical un-critical Wagner-worshipper could profess to believe that there is any thematic connection between some

---

[1] "Suffice it to say," remarks Mr. Frank Parkinson, "that the whole of the music is thematically developed, and worked up from the first, which is characteristically called, from its mythical (*sic*) attributes, 'the motive of the primeval element'" (*A Commentary upon "The Nibelung's Ring,"* pp, 25, 26. See also Mr. David Irvine's book, already cited, chapter v.). Passages like the following are quite common in the Wagnerian literature upon the *Ring* : Wotan, as "the type of Creed, and an incarnation of Will," has "two motives assigned to him, one called by the name of Walhall, over which he rules as Supreme God ; the other is his Wanderer-motive, performed by the same instruments in *Siegfried*, but its element of repose is gone, for it is absolutely devoid of definitive key-colour." . . . "In the *Dutchman*, the curse is brought on by a defiance of the laws of Nature, and the music which paints it has its spirit imbued with the sternness of her command . . . but in the *Ring* the curse attaches itself because there has been a want of regard to the dictates of custom and society ; moreover, the theme which represents this idea is as unswerving as its nature is destructive . . . further, this motive is in its musical structure as pitilessly relentless as it is lowering and debasing in its effects" (Frank Parkinson, work cited, pp. 24, 25).

of the motives they quote.[1] Even if there were any such connection between the themes, it could only puzzle the hearer in five cases out of six. One may, by a stretch of the imagination, see in the Ring-motive a kind of degenerate form of the Valhalla-motive ; and we may listen with constrained seriousness when we are told that each theme represents power, but that the power typified by the former is of a baser, more worldly kind than that typified by the latter—as, indeed, befits a power based upon mere gold.[2] But when the ear suddenly notes a remarkable thematic similarity between the motive of " Siegfried the Volsung" and the motive of Alberich's curse, how is it to discover the hidden significance of this resemblance ? I have no doubt that Wagner meant the themes to be similar in their

[1] The Wagner-guides are as amusing in this respect as in every other, particularly when they disagree as to the derivations of certain themes. Mr. Irvine is quite sure that "the chief source of the motives peculiar to *Siegfried* and the *Dusk of the Gods* is found in the Horn-motive of Siegfried, which does not adapt itself readily (*sic*) to any of the motives already provided in the *Rheingold* and *Valkyrie*." On the other hand, he hastens to tell us, "Albert Heintz finds room for its subsequent introduction in the cadence of the Sword-motive, which in the earlier drama, the *Valkyrie*, discloses the Volsungs' distress theme ; but even in this case there is obviously no development of the Horn-motive. Wolzogen connects it in some way with the first rhythm of the ride of the Valkyries, and an inversion of the first notes of Siegfried's heroic Volsung theme" (*The Ring of the Nibelung*, &c., pp. 242, 243). One is at a loss which to admire most—the desire of all these gentlemen to find an analogy by hook or by crook, or the charming unanimity of the results they obtain. In any case, a perusal of much of the esoteric literature upon the *Ring* makes it comprehensible how Wagnerians come to take such an interest in the pantomime dragon.

[2] Mr. Irvine shall again be our instructor : " There is another form of the *Valhalla*-motive, as unrealisable as that of the aspiration to rule worthily by means of coercion, but equally sought after by man—in short, part and parcel of coercive rule. That is the power of gold. The *Ring*-motive possesses all the rhythm of the *Valhalla*-motive. It is, however, devoid of majesty. It is empty, dispiriting, and unworthy (*sic*). The *Valhalla*-motive, which must always be regarded as transcendent, never realisable—in short, an ideally egoistic aim of the few—has its ignoble counterpart in the *Ring*-motive" (Work cited, pp. 258, 269). I confess that, for my part, I am unacquainted with the ethical meanings of sounds, and do not know when a musical phrase is morally worthy or unworthy. But so far from the Ring-motive being dispiriting, it has always seemed to me particularly bright and cheery.

difference ; his mind, as I have already attempted to show, thought in musical phrases as other minds think in words, and probably he had some concept of the moral interconnection of the Alberich and Siegfried principles that was self-evidently expressed —for him—in their themes. But it is a stark impossibility for any one else to see these things as Wagner saw them ; even those who know the *Ring* through and through are frequently puzzled at some of the thematic resemblances that suggest themselves. To claim that we can see the moral problem of the *Ring* incarnated in its musical motives is pure affectation. When Wagner combines two themes, or makes one follow another in a peculiar way, he is probably bent on expressing in this way a struggle for mastery between the principles represented by the themes. In some cases we can catch his meaning ; in other cases the key is lacking. The phrases may have been as definite, as clear, as concrete to Wagner as figures of sculpture or of painting to other men ; but to us, as we hear them, they may mean any one of a dozen things. Edmund Gurney has told us that he listened with close attention to "the wonderful passage where Siegfried is breaking through the ring of fire." The Wagnerian may ask himself where there occurs *any* passage descriptive of Siegfried breaking through the fire ; and he may find Gurney's later note somewhat instructive :

"Alas for the uninitiated ! Having been forewarned of this passage, I felt my pleasure in listening to it distinctly increased by the idea that the hero's advance through the flames was typified by the manner in which the melodic strain seems again and again to force its way through the changing harmonies. What, then, was my chagrin, on consulting the *Guide through the Music*, to discover that the strain was the 'slumber-motive,' and that what was really being typified was Brynhild's repose."[1]

---

[1] "Wagner and Wagnerism," in *Tertium Quid*, ii. 44.

That experience must surely be what we have all
gone through on listening to Wagner for the first
time ; the leading-motives have not always told their
own tale, because we had not the key to their concrete
significations. Afterwards, of course, when we have
had the opportunity to view the *Ring* from every side,
and to think out Wagner's intentions in detail, we have
learned the secrets hidden in the thematic web. But
this is to prophesy *after* the event ; if the very object of
the leading-motives is to make easier our path through
the psychology of the drama, a motive in the *Rheingold*
ought to deliver its message direct to us, and not need
elucidation afterwards from *Siegfried* or the *Götterdämmerung*. One needs only to recognise that Wagner's
abnormal brain saw in a musical phrase things that *we*
can only express in words, in order to find the *tertium
quid* between the Wagnerian who pushes his "interpretations" to the point of absurdity, and the anti-
Wagnerian to whom the leading-motives suggest
nothing because they are not symphonic in form and
content. Thus we can now see that Gurney was as
wrong when he denied the right-to-exist to the motives,
as the Wagnerians are when they see moral worth in
one musical phrase and moral unworthiness in another.
The psychological and æsthetic truth lies between the
two parties.

"The ear's strictness," writes Gurney, "is thus at once accounted for and justified. It must take kindly to the strains
which salute it, and find in them the coherent stuff that it
wants, before it will at all credit them with emotional messages
or pass those messages on further. It must frankly enjoy the
label before it will permit the slightest artistic appreciation of
the labelled idea. . . . No outside signs of expression, no noisy
stamps of determination, no spasms of exaggerated intervals,
will take it in ; no juggling with the labels, or mixing them up
together, will move it to more than scornful amusement, unless
the juggling be the true magician's juggling, and produce the

musical magician's prime result—beauty. And inasmuch as this beauty is essentially an attribute of form, and musical forms are built, just as much as human ones, out of definite elements, the substitution in Opera of the dramatic *stream* for the symphonic *structure*—however rightly descriptive of the general arrangement of the larger musical sections—is a perpetual trap. For that most intimate and organic sort of structure which lies in the constant vital necessity of each bar as it stands to its neighbours as they stand, can never be abandoned while the ear holds the keys of emotion—a musical ear being nothing more or less than one which is percipient of such structure." [1]

The æsthetic analysis of the preceding chapter will, it is hoped, afford a basis of compromise between the Wagnerians and the anti-Wagnerians. It is quite true that the ear demands specific musical beauty in a phrase of absolute music before it can enjoy it ; but on the other hand the demand for strictly formal structure in the phrase diminishes when dramatic rather than symphonic elements enter into it. Gurney, in his insistence upon the need of pleasing the ear first and last, forgets the all-important psychological fact that we do not hear with the ear alone, but with the brain ; and that music may appeal either to a purely subjective sense—as in symphonic music, or to a more objective sense—as in dramatic music set to words, placed in the mouths of living characters, and accompanied by action upon the stage. No composer, not even the most un-Wagnerian who ever lived, has written operas without putting in them many bars of music whose effect is wholly dissimilar to that of symphonic music, that appeal to a different sense, and are justified by a different law. The mere fact of the existence of these "dramatic" passages, with their power to move us in their own peculiar manner, proves that both ear and brain stand towards them in an attitude of expectancy quite different from that in which they stand towards absolute music.

[1] Essay cited, pp. 35, 36.

The composer, indeed, inserts them because just then his mind is intent on some more concrete image than usual—something whose sharp significance cannot be suggested by a form of music born of more subjective, more abstract moods. Now Wagner's mind is simply that of the ordinary opera-composer pushed to its logical extreme. Instead of being spasmodically dramatic, it is dramatic from start to finish ; instead of being able to find merely for an utterance here, an episode there, the musical form and colour that will suggest an external thing rather than create simply an internal mood, Wagner is able to conceive in musical phrases *all* characters, *all* episodes, *all* the internal play of force upon force. We, however, who listen, cannot always pierce through the envelope of music to the concrete suggestion that lies inside ; though in most cases we are enabled to do so by the aid of either the words or the scenic action. Thus while the æstheticians of Gurney's school are altogether wrong in maintaining that Wagner's motives are merely "outside signs of expression, noisy stamps of determination, spasms of exaggerated intervals," on the other hand the hearer must sometimes take in the music merely *as* music, instead of as the outward and visible sign of an inward dramatic action. The verdict, of course, is finally in Wagner's favour as against his detractors. Strike off the cases in which he has assumed too readily that a musical phrase that had a definite meaning for him would have a like definite meaning for every one else, and there remain a thousand happy examples of his use of the leading-motive that speak to us with a positiveness beyond question. It is, indeed, one of the clearest proofs of Wagner's unapproachable superiority as a dramatic composer that he should be able to suggest all kinds of shades of thought and mood by harmonic and rhythmic variations of a motive. Any one who will follow up the themes of the *Ring* in all their uses cannot fail to realise this. Wagner can employ the Valhalla-motive, for example, in such a way that while recognising it as the symbol of Wotan's power, we can read in it also the story of Wotan's frustration, as in the particularly fine passage in the 2nd Act of the *Valkyrie*.[1] Again, one has only to compare the theme at the beginning of the 3rd Act of *Tristan* with the form in which we heard it in the prelude, to be conscious, almost as clearly as if we had been told in words, that the love of Tristan and Isolde has brought them to the uttermost ends of woe ; the phrase has lost its feverish unrest, its suspense, and breathes now only of the weariness of pain and grief. If an æsthetician cannot see or hear these things, and a thousand others like them, one can only say either that he is criticising a form of art which he is constitutionally unfitted to assimilate, or else that he is framing his opinions upon the mere blind, inconsiderate sensations of the moment —Gurney's criticism coming perhaps under both these categories.

In any case, setting aside all those passages in the *Ring* that require a Wagnerian brain to appreciate them, there is surely music enough of the most "musical" kind, to satisfy even those who want an opera to be merely a succession of highly interesting moments of sensation. There is scarcely an emotion of which human nature is capable that does not find expression somewhere or other in this encyclopædic score—and what expression ! One only realises the musical power of Wagner when one comes to compare him point by point with other operatic writers, and notices the imaginative truth of the expression of each scene, as contrasted with the more or less conventional handling of other men. For each emotion, each situation, he seems to have found the one expression that was inevitable for it, from the grandeur of the Valhalla music

[1] Vocal score, p. 134.

R

to the horror of Alberich's and Hagen's, from the lyric
rapture of Siegmund and Sieglinda to the poignant
simplicity of the dialogue between Siegmund and
Brynhild.　Everything and every character is in heroic
size.　Even the defects of *ensemble* of the work seem to
have a paradoxical fitness ; the figures and the canvas
being so large, so remote from all our ordinary conceptions, that even the asymmetry and unwieldiness of the
whole scheme gives a certain sensation of grandeur.
The work is like some immense quarry with huge
figures of gods and men and beasts standing sculptured
in the rock, not statuesque, not plastic, not submissive
to the ordinary canons of the sculptor's art, sometimes
fascinating, sometimes terrifying, sometimes unpleasant,
but always impressive by reason of their strength, their
strangeness, their suggestiveness of the whole range of
human and sub-human and superhuman life.　Against
such a work the ordinary formulas of criticism are
impotent : we may tell the creator of it that he did
wrong in conceiving it, but it holds us and draws us
back for all that.　When criticism has said the worst it
can against the *Ring*, there remains nothing but to bow
the knee and worship.

CHAPTER VII

WAGNER AS GERMAN

EDGAR ALLAN POE, in a little note on German Literature, suggested by La Motte Fouqué's *Thiodolf the Icelander*, once found occasion to make some remarks on the state of German thought which are as essentially true to-day as when he wrote them :—

"This book could never have been popular out of Germany. It is too simple, too direct, too obvious, too *bold*, not sufficiently complex, to be relished by any people who have *thoroughly* passed the first (or impulsive) epoch of literary civilisation. The Germans have not yet passed this first epoch. It must be remembered that *during the whole of the Middle Ages they lived in utter ignorance of the art of writing*. From so total a darkness, of so late a date, they could not, *as a nation*, have as yet fully emerged into the second or critical epoch. Individual Germans have been critical in the best sense, but the masses are unleavened. Literary Germany thus presents the singular spectacle of the impulsive spirit surrounded by the critical, and, of course, in some measure influenced thereby. . . . For my own part I admit the German vigour, the German directness, boldness, imagination, and some other qualities of impulse, just as I am willing to admit and admire these qualities in the first (or impulsive) epochs of British and French letters. At the German criticism, however, I cannot refrain from laughing all the more heartily the more seriously I hear it praised. Not that, in detail, it affects me as an absurdity, but in the adaptation of its details. It abounds in brilliant bubbles of *suggestion*, but these rise and sink and jostle each other until the whole vortex of thought in which they originate is one indistinguishable chaos of froth.

The German criticism is *unsettled* and can only be settled by time. At present it suggests without demonstrating, or convincing, or effecting any definite purpose under the sun."[1]

The critical reader is forcibly reminded of these words when he comes to the study of Wagner's writings dealing with Germany and the Germans, their place in culture-history, and their influence upon other nations. In a series of writings, not particularly noteworthy for any intrinsic value of thought, but interesting and illuminative in a study of Wagner's mind as a whole, he enlarges on the themes that German culture is mainly independent of all other cultures, and that German art is to be the salvation of modern Europe. There are traces of this way of looking at things in his earlier literary works, though it was only in later years that he gave a connected form to his thoughts on these questions. *Judaism in Music* (1850),[2] though ostensibly a demonstration that the Jews can never create vital art, by reason of their being an alien race among the European nations, is really concerned, in a negative sense, with the topic of nationalism; while more extended treatment is given to the question in *German Art and German Policy* (1867), and *What is German?* (1865).[3] All three treatises are interesting, not only as aids to the study of Wagner, but for the light they throw upon the intellectual condition of a large part of the German artistic world in the middle of the century.

There was, indeed, a time when, as he himself has it, "Deutschland schien mir nur ein sehr kleiner Theil der Welt"; this was in his young days, when he was in

---

[1] *Marginalia*, No. 76, in Works, iii. 387, 388.

[2] A reference to the Synthetic Table will show that *Judaism in Music* was written for the *Neue Zeitschrift für Musik* in 1850, under the pseudonym of "K. Freigedank," and published in pamphlet form under Wagner's own name in 1869.

[3] Written in 1865, but only published in 1878, in the second number of the *Bayreuther Blätter*.

that state of sensuous excitability that gave birth to *Das
Liebesverbot*.

"I was then twenty-one years of age, inclined to take life and
the world on their pleasant side. *Ardinghello* (by Heinse) and
Das Junge Europa (by H. Laube) tingled through my every
limb; while Germany appeared in my eyes a very tiny portion
of the earth. I had emerged from abstract mysticism, and I
learnt a love for matter. Beauty of material and brilliancy of
wit were lordly things to me: as regards my beloved music, I
found them both among the Frenchmen and Italians. I for-
swore my model, Beethoven; his last Symphony I deemed the
keystone of a whole great epoch of art, beyond whose limits no
man could hope to press, and within which no man could attain
to independence." [1]

It was in this state of mind that he fell a victim to
Bellini's *Romeo and Juliet*—or, more probably, to the
acting and singing of Madame Schröder-Devrient in
that opera; and in the enthusiasm of the moment he
wrote an article in which he lauded Italian music and
referred to the German in somewhat depreciatory terms.[2]
Malicious critics have contrasted this with his later
attitude, but to do so is to attribute a very exaggerated
importance to the youthful lucubration. It was probably no more than a momentary enthusiasm, such as
musicians at the age of twenty—and afterwards—are
all too subject to. On the other hand, his specifically
German sympathies were from the beginning a matter
of comment among his friends. Laube remarks in his
"Memoirs" that "according to Wagner's conversations
at the time, he had already, at the age of twenty (1833),
formed the intention of creating a German dramatic
genre that should surpass the French";[3] and his Teutonic enthusiasm grew in depth and ardour until in 1872,

[1] G. S. i. 10; Ellis, i. 9.

[2] See a quotation from the article in Glasenapp, *Richard Wagner's Leben
und Wirken*, i. 48.

[3] S e Freson, *L'Esthétique de Richard Wagner*, i. 38, *note*.

when writing the Introduction to the third and fourth volumes of his *Gesammelte Schriften*, he was convinced that—

> "According to the high opinion which this great thinker [Carlyle] has proclaimed, of the destiny of the German nation and its spirit of veracity, it must be deemed no vain presumption that we recognise in this German people—whose own completed *Reformation* would seem to have spared it from the need of any share in Revolution—the pre-ordained 'Heroic Wise' on whom he calls to abridge the period of horrible World-Anarchy. For myself, I feel assured that just the same relation which my ideal of Art bears to the reality of our general conditions of existence, that relation is allotted to the German race in its destiny amid a whole political world in the throes of 'Spontaneous Combustion.'"[1]

The general movement in Germany towards political union, and the vague sense that a united Germany might be a power among the nations, must have had some influence in the formation of Wagner's patriotic theories. But here again, as in his general views upon art and civilisation, we must probably look into his own personal history for the main force that generated his theories. His early experiences in Dresden must have gone far to imbue him with his detestation of foreign influences in music—a detestation that at times was simply insensate. Ever since 1817 Weber at Dresden had been trying to stem the tide of the Italian domination, and to establish German opera;[2] and Wagner's boyish admiration of Weber would enlist his adolescent sympathies in the cause for which the great German master was fighting. At a later stage he himself was destined to feel the power of the Italian rule in Dresden. It took him two years to get *Rienzi* brought

---

[1] G. S. iii. 7 ; Ellis, i. 29.

[2] See the *Life of Weber*, by his son, vol. ii. chap. 2. Though conductor at Dresden, Weber found it impossible to produce *Der Freischütz* there until a year after it had been performed in Berlin.

out there—it being put off on one occasion in order
that an Italian opera of Reissiger, the Dresden conductor at that time, might be brought out. Afterwards,
when Wagner obtained a kapellmeistership at Dresden, in succession to Morlacchi, he had to take up
the battle in which Weber had been defeated. The
Dresden opera-stage, like every other stage in Germany, was over-run by Italian composers, while the
great native masters could scarcely obtain a hearing.
Even in 1845 (the year in which *Tannhäuser* was
produced), says Mr. Finck—

"Bellini, Donizetti, and Rossini had thirty-three performances
together, while Mozart, Beethoven, and Weber combined had
only twenty-four.[1] How much the great German composers
needed such a champion as Wagner, may be inferred from the
extraordinary fact that two of the finest productions of German
genius—Marschner's *Hans Heiling* (that gloomy but splendid
opera which cast its shadow on the *Flying Dutchman*) and
Gluck's *Armida*—had never been heard at Dresden till Wagner
brought them out, though Marschner's masterwork was eleven
years old, and Gluck's sixty-six."[2]

At an earlier date Wagner himself had been unable
to get his youthful opera *Die Feen* performed in
Leipzig, owing to the abnormal demand for Italian
music at that time. All through his early struggles,
indeed, down to the culminating period of his exile,
he must have felt that the Italian domination was fatal
to new and original German dramatic music. It was
not long, indeed, before his rapidly developing mind
saw that even some of the finest of his countrymen's

[1] One gets a curious sensation in reading, at the present time, some of the
high eulogiums which were passed upon men like Rossini, Meyerbeer, and
Bellini in their own day. See, for example, Balzac's *Gambara* and *Masimilla
Doni*, and Heine's *Florentine Nights*.

[2] Finck, *Wagner and his Works*, i. 157, 158, going upon the statistical
tables given in the *Wagner Jahrbuch*, 1886.

work was flawed by the foreign influences;[1] and his own aim was to create an opera that should be truly German :—

"That this opera" [*The Flying Dutchman*], he wrote to Heine in 1846, "not only in Dresden, but especially in Cassel and in Riga, has gained for itself so many friends, and even won the favour of the larger public, appears to me a finger-sign pointing to show us that we must only write just as the poetic sense inborn in our German hearts dictates, never making the least concession to foreign modes, and simply choosing out our stuff and handling it as it appeals to ourselves, in order to be surest to win the pleasure of our fellow-countrymen. In this way may we win for ourselves once more a German School of Original Opera; and all who despair of this, and import foreign models, may take an example from this *Dutchman*, which certainly is so conceived as never a Frenchman nor Italian would have dreamt of conceiving it."[2]

It was in this spirit that Wagner had come to regard art and life in the period of his greatest literary activity ;[3] and it was partly under the influence of these ideas that he wrote his *Judaism in Music*. One

[1] "Yesterday," he writes to Uhlig, in 1852, "I saw Marschner's *Vampyr* [at Zurich] . . . This time the music *quite* disgusted me : this duet, trio, and quartet singing and drawling is downright stupid and devoid of taste, as it does not even charm the senses, and so only offers so many notes played and sung. I willingly grant that there are some exceptions to be made ; but now first I see how far above this so-called 'German' manner *my* operas stand. Heaven knows this is only a German-soled-and-heeled Italian music, impotent sophistry; nothing more nor less" (Letter 59 to Uhlig; Eng. trans. p. 209).

[2] Letter 8 to Heine ; Eng. trans. p. 457. See also the letter of 24th Jan. 1844 (recently published for the first time), in which Wagner tried to induce Breitkopf and Härtel to publish the score of the *Dutchman*. "Finally, listen to the voice of patriotism within you, and remember that it is an ORIGINAL GERMAN OPERA." See Mr. Shedlock's translation of the letter in the *Musician*, 17th Nov. 1897.

[3] There was, it must be remembered, what might be called a wave of Germanism in Germany at that period. See, for example, Heine's *Religion and Philosophy in Germany*, where, in the closing words, Heine indulges in a piece of portentous braggadocio at which he himself must surely have smiled cynically in his wiser moments. See also his laudation of German poetry in

has always to remember that the Semitic question in
Germany and Austria has an importance to which
there is no analogue in England ; and we need also
to bear in mind that the German press of that epoch
was largely in the hands of the Jews, to whose hostility
Wagner attributed, rightly or wrongly, a great deal of
the opposition he had to encounter, and a great many
of the attacks that were made upon his art and life.
The historical interest thus possessed by Wagner's
pamphlet is not by any means equalled by its intrinsic value as a contribution either to æsthetics or to
sociology. His thesis is that whereas we at one time
emancipated the Jew, it is now our turn to seek
emancipation from him, inasmuch as he rules all
Europe by his financial power. That may or may
not be an exaggeration ; it is more to our purpose to
consider Wagner's dictum that the Jew is "incapable
of any artistic utterance of his inner essence." The
Jew, he maintains, is always an alien, immiscible
element in our modern nations, preserving his mental
as well as his physiognomic peculiarities, never becoming an integral, organic part of the national life of any
country. This holds good even of the cultured Jew,
who cuts himself off from his commoner fellows, but
does not thereby become any better assimilated to the
race among whom he is living ; he is an alien "in the
midst of a society he does not understand, with whose
tastes and aspirations he does not sympathise, whose
history and evolution have always been indifferent to

---

his essay on *Don Quixote*—a passage in which the racial conceit is clearly
seen to be due to the fact that German literature is of comparatively recent
origin. Nations with centuries of fine literature behind them do not pat themselves on the back in this self-complacent manner. Note also the passage in
his *Confessions*. "It is much to be a poet, especially to be a great lyric poet,
in Germany, among a people who in two things—in philosophy and in poetry
—have surpassed all other nations." And once more in the *Religion and
Philosophy*—"We Germans are the strongest and wisest of nations." Every
nation can and does talk in this foolish way when the fit is on it.

him." Thus the culture even of the educated Jew is doomed to remain inorganic, infertile.

"Our modern arts had likewise become a portion of this culture, and among them more particularly that art which is just the very easiest to learn—the art of *music*, and indeed *that* music which, severed from her sister arts, had been lifted by the force and stress of grandest geniuses to a stage in her universal faculty of Expression where either, in new conjunction with the other arts, she might speak aloud the most sublime, or, in persistent separation from them, she could also speak at will the deepest bathos of the trivial. Naturally, *what* the cultured Jew had to speak, in his aforesaid situation, could be nothing but the trivial and indifferent, because his whole artistic bent was in sooth a mere luxurious, needless thing. Exactly as his whim inspired, or some interest lying outside Art, could he utter himself now thus, and now otherwise; for never was he driven to speak out a definite, a real and necessary thing, but he just merely wanted to speak, no matter what; so that, naturally, the *how* was the only 'moment' left for him to care for." [1]

Correlative with this phenomenon was another. No man can ever learn a foreign language, says Wagner, so thoroughly as to be able to speak it like a native; least of all can he learn it so intimately as to be able to compose poetry in it. Now the Jew, though he adopts the speech of each country in which he finds himself, never learns to speak its tongue otherwise than as an alien; and since every language is thus to him an acquired language, he can never express himself in it with perfect idiomatic ease and freedom, in such a way as to give utterance to the whole of his nature.

"A language, with its expression and its evolution, is not the work of scattered units, but of an historical community; only he who has unconsciously grown up within the bond of this community, takes also any share in its creations. But the Jew has stood outside the pale of any such community, stood solitary

---

[1] G. S. v. 74; Ellis, iii. 88.

with his Jehovah in a splintered, soilless stock, to which all self-
sprung evolution must stay denied, just as even the peculiar
(Hebraic) language of that stock has been preserved for him
merely as a thing defunct. Now, to make poetry in a foreign
tongue has hitherto been impossible, even to geniuses of highest
rank. Our whole European art and civilisation, however, have
remained to the Jew a foreign tongue; for, just as he has taken
no part in the evolution of the one, so has he taken none in that
of the other; but at most the homeless wight has been a cold,
nay more, a hostile looker-on. In this speech, this Art, the Jew
can only after-speak and after-patch—not truly make a poem of
his words, an art-work of his doings." [1]

This inability to handle the language at first-hand also
debars the Jew from song, for "Song is just Talk
aroused to highest passion."

The latter statement has already been criticised in a
previous chapter ; here it must be said that not only is
the Jew not incapable of music on this account, but his
comparative independence of each nation among which
he lives is no *à priori* hindrance to his becoming a poet.
Wagner's argument, indeed, is throughout a mixture of
misstatement and overstatement. A Frenchman, it is
true, who learns English in mature life is not likely
to be able to handle it so idiomatically as an English-
man ; but a Frenchman brought up in England from
his infancy will speak the language as purely and as
idiomatically as a native ; and, if he be of poetic
temperament, will not find any check placed either on
his imagination or his expression, by the fact that his
ancestors lived on the other instead of on this side of the
English Channel. Few Englishmen have handled the
language so easily, so imaginatively, so beautifully, as
Dante Gabriel Rossetti, who "in blood . . . was three-
fourths Italian, and only one-fourth English ; being on
the father's side wholly Italian (Abruzzese), and on the

[1] G. S. v. 70, 71 ; Ellis, iii. 84, 85.

mother's side half Italian (Tuscan) and half English."[1]
A man brought up as Rossetti was is English to all
intents and purposes. In his blood there would of
course be certain hereditary predispositions from his
Italian ancestry; but in everything that concerned the
shaping of thought into speech he was at no more
disadvantage than one whose ancestors had lived in
London for a thousand years. Similarly the Jew,
though mentally and physiognomically different in
some respects from the Germans among whom he
lives, can certainly handle the German language as well
—frequently far better—than nine true-born Teutons
out of ten. If Heine and Lassalle are not to be recognised as masters of idiomatic German, it is difficult
to know where to look for that commodity. It is nonsense to assert that to employ a language with perfect
ease, in order to express oneself to the utmost, and to
get the greatest artistic finish upon the speech, one's
ancestors must have grown up for centuries within this
particular "historical community." All our Welsh,
Scotch, and native Irish poets, novelists, and thinkers
would, on the lines of Wagner's argument, be incapable
of making a "true art-work" in the English language.
The fact that they are writing and speaking in a tongue
which is not that of their ancestors is no more bar to
the flow of their artistic imagination than the fact that
French is the native tongue of half the Canadian people
hinders them from equalling the English inhabitants
in literature and art. Wagner's formula is a puerile
absurdity, only surpassed in this respect by the correlative formula that the Jews cannot hope to become
original musicians.

There can be no question, indeed, that here, as in
so many other cases, Wagner was merely rushing from
a particular fact to a supposed general principle. The
main factor in the production of his thesis—apart from

[1] See Mr. W. M. Rossetti's preface to his brother's Poetical Works.

the influence of the Jews upon the press—seems to
have been his dislike of the music of Mendelssohn and
Meyerbeer.   One has only to bear in mind Wagner's
peculiar view of post-Beethoven instrumental music in
the one case, and his detestation of the meretricious
French-Italian opera in the other, and the further fact
that the leading representative of each of these despised
forms of art was a Jew, to comprehend the psychological
genesis of his treatise.

"At present," he wrote, "no art affords such plenteous
possibility of talking in it without saying any real thing, as that of
Music, since the greatest geniuses have already said whatever
there was to say in it as an absolute separate-art. When this had
once been spoken out, there was nothing left but to babble after;
and indeed with quite distressing accuracy and deceptive likeness,
just as parrots reel off human words and phrases, but also with
just as little real feeling and expression as those foolish birds."

This of course was his normal view of the post-
Beethovenian symphony.   As has been abundantly
shown in Chapter V., he was insusceptible to a great
deal of the charm other men find in instrumental
music—even missing, in this respect, the beauty of
some of Beethoven's work that was off the line of what
he would call "poetical" development.   And if his
opinion of the lack of originality of a great deal of the
symphonic music that followed Beethoven had been
put forward merely as a critical judgment, one would
not have found very much reason to quarrel with it.
It *was* imitative, derivative, a second-hand repetition of
things that had already been said, it being the peculiarity
of music—due to the sensuous factor of sound—that
this kind of thing is more tolerable there than in any
other art.   One does not see anything particularly
profound, for example, in the slow movement of
Mendelssohn's Violin Concerto ; yet any one—with
the exception of Wagner—could listen to it with real

pleasure. Certain turns of melody, certain harmonic combinations, certain instrumental effects in it *must* delight us so long as our auditory nerves remain what they are ; and there are innumerable compositions that hold their place in virtue of these qualities, not in virtue of any particular originality or profundity of thought. But Mendelssohn was neither the first nor the last musician to live by retailing other men's wares. That he missed greatness, that he was too frequently commonplace, was due to the defects of his artistic nature, not to the fact that he was a Jew. Wagner says very truly that

"in hearing a tone-piece of this composer's, we have only been able to feel engrossed where nothing beyond our more or less amusement-craving Phantasy was roused through the present-ment, stringing-together, and entanglement of the most elegant, the smoothest and most polished figures—as in the kaleidoscope's changeful play of form and colour—but never where those figures were meant to take the shape of deep and stalwart feelings of the human heart."[1]

Quite so ; but are there not a thousand composers in Europe to-day of whom exactly the same thing can be said, not one of whom is a Jew ? Why put down to a man's Hebraic origin what is solely due to the fact that he has a mediocre brain ? The plain truth is that the circumstance of Mendelssohn and Meyerbeer being Jews counted for a great deal in Wagner's pseudo-demonstra-tion of the incapacity of the Jew to write great music. Demonstration, in the strict sense of the term, there is none at all ; Wagner starts out with the blind assump-tion that the Jew is artistically impotent *quâ* Jew, and all the pretended argumentation is simply the finding of bad reasons for a worse theory. His bias is plainly seen when he tells us that *had* the Jews been able to do anything in music, this would simply prove that *we*

[1] G. S. v. 79; Ellis, iii. 94.

were stagnating—"we should merely have had to admit that our tarrying behind them rested on some organic debility that had taken sudden hold of us," a delightful way of settling the controversy, but not a very convincing one. Finally, coming to defend his dictum that "the Jews have brought forth no true poet," this is how he disposes of Heine :—

"At the time when Goethe and Schiller sang among us, we certainly knew nothing of a poetising Jew: at the time, however, when our poetry became a lie, when every possible thing might flourish from the wholly unpoetic element of our life, but no true poet—then was it the office of a highly-gifted poet-Jew to bare with fascinating taunts that lie, that bottomless aridity and jesuitical hypocrisy of our Versifying, which still would give itself the airs of true poesis. His famous musical congeners, too, he mercilessly lashed for their pretence to pass as artists ; no make-believe could hold its ground before him : by the remorseless demon of denial of all that seemed worth denying was he driven on without a rest, through all the mirage of our modern self-deception, till he reached the point where in turn he duped himself into a poet, and was rewarded by his versified lies being set to music by our own composers. He was the conscience of Judaism, just as Judaism is the evil conscience of our modern civilisation." [1]

For lunacy of this kind the most ironic condemnation is probably the simple quotation of it. It might have interested Wagner to learn that poetical Europe thinks, and will continue to think, more of Heine's "versified lies" than of the libretto of *The Ring of the Nibelung;* and that there are certain dull moments in that musical masterpiece which we would gladly barter away for some of the musical settings of Heine's lyrics. One is forced to the conclusion that Wagner knew no more what constituted real poetry than he knew of politics or philosophy ; and that the blind eagerness he shows to discredit, by any means he can think of, any-

[1] G. S. v. 85 ; Ellis, iii. 99, 100.

thing that fails to appeal to him, ought to be charac-
terised occasionally by a stronger term than mere
stupidity.[1]

It goes without saying that the man who could
make so sorry an exhibition in his handling of an
ethnical problem that is not particularly abstruse, was
bound to blunder serenely when he came to discuss the
influence of one national culture upon another, and the
sociological problem of international contact. His thesis
may briefly be said to be this: that the "German
spirit"—to which is due everything that is noble and
original in German art—has developed out of the
German folk by a natural process of evolution, different
from that of the French, for example, in that the people
owed less to their princes.   French civilisation is
materialistic ; and the German princes who try to bring
about the triumph of that civilisation over the German
spirit, will find that their days are numbered.   The
Germans, in fact, are the intellectual and artistic kins-
men of the ancient Greeks ; they are "a nation of high-
souled dreamers and deep-brained thinkers."   Further,
"ever since the regeneration of European folk-blood,
considered strictly, the German has been the creator
and inventor, the Romanic the modeller and exploiter;
the true fountain of continual renovation has remained
the German nature."

The last extraordinary passage may be serenely
disregarded; not in this mood of blind and ignorant
self-confidence is the history of European civilisation
to be written.   But it is worth while to give a moment's

[1] It is distinctly refreshing to read, in the appendix to the edition of 1869,
that Wagner felt aggrieved at the hostility the Jews showed towards him after
this!   A friend—a Jew, but of course "an undoubtedly very gifted, truly talented,
and intellectual writer"—who had conceived an admiration for the poems of
The Ring and *Tristan*, wished to publish his views about them, but found his
co-religionists would not let him do so.   Nothing could more clearly show
Wagner's childlike lack of all sense of reality than his open-mouthed astonishment of this fact.   The man who thinks he can attack as he did without being
attacked in return exhibits an idealism so naïve that it almost disarms criticism.

consideration to the proposition that Germany owes very little to other nations. Wagner dogmatises to the effect that the princes have been an un-German element. That they imbibed foreign culture, so far from being, as he thinks, a clause in the indictment of them, is really a strong point in their favour. One almost blushes to have to say in cold print that there is no such thing as "*the* German spirit," seeing that the German national character, like every other, must needs be a medley of all kinds of conflicting thoughts, passions, and ideals. To pick out the noblest elements of human nature, and style these "the German spirit," as Wagner does, is amateurish to the verge of stupidity.[1] Goethe and Schiller, he thinks, held up the banner of the German spirit on the stage, in opposition to the crude inanities of dramatists like Kotzebue. Well, but were not Kotzebue and his fellows also Germans? If Schiller and his actors exhibited "the German's aptitude for the ideal," what are we to call the extreme aptitude for the other thing exhibited by nine-tenths of Germany? Was this *not* German? Wagner himself admits that the universal rage for vulgar and foolish drama enabled the wretched dramatists to live in clover. Who did this for them, if not Germans? The point is that no one but a clumsy thinker or a rabid partisan would think of selecting a handful of able and earnest men as the true types of the German spirit, when what gave point to their own attempts at reform was the crude materialism of taste exhibited by the German nation at large. On Wagner's method you could prove any proposition you set yourself to prove ; could show, for example, the beauty of the monarchical system by selecting the best types of monarchy and quietly ignoring the rest. The hundred pages of Wagner's *German*

---

[1] Wagner forgot that the very Beethoven whom he regarded as the typical representative of the German spirit, owed almost every strong feature in his character to his Flemish ancestry.

S

Art and German Policy contain little in the way of
argument that rises above this transparent fallacy;
while as for his contention that German civilisation
has developed directly from the people, that proposition could only be put forward by a man ignorant at
once of the really vital forces of culture, and of the
historical debt which Germany owes to other countries.
A nation develops in civilisation and culture through
the stimulus of a thousand external forces, the influence
of which is not to be disposed of by the mere amateur
rant of a great musician about "the true German
spirit" and "the Folk." One wonders what Goethe
would have said to all this cheap and narrow-minded
laudation of the German race—the wise Goethe who
saw how little he or any man could owe to the mere
fact of his being born in one country rather than
another, and how much to the vitalising touch of all
the thought and art of all the nations that have been
under the sun, each, like coral insects, leaving its
deposit of culture to be built upon by others.[1] Even
at the beginning of the seventeenth century France was
exerting an influence upon the culture of the best
German families, and this influence persisted for something like two hundred years. In the early eighteenth
century, almost the whole of the history of belles lettres,
such as they were, is concerned with the struggle
between the school of Gottsched, who modelled himself on the French, and that of Bodmer, who looked
for light to Milton; even the German historians of

---

[1] Goethe did, indeed, upon one occasion deny that the French had any
influence on his productions (Conversation with Soret, 6th March 1830). But
this must have been in one of those moments of patriotic hysteria when men
are inclined to underrate their debts to other nations. It was the saner
Goethe who said to Eckermann (14th March 1830): "How could I, to whom
culture and barbarism are alone of importance, hate a nation which is among
the most cultivated of the earth, and to which I owe so great a part of my
own cultivation?" (Bohn's ed. ii. 259). See also the conversation of January
3, 1830.

the present day admitting that the literature before the accession of Frederick the Great was poor and taste-less. When we come to the great German names of the eighteenth century, the influence of France and England—to say nothing of that of antiquity—is clearly marked. Lessing's acquaintance with English literature, though not equal to his acquaintance with French, had certainly something to do with the im-provement of his taste in dramatic matters ; while his own earliest model in playwriting was Molière.[1] In dramatic criticism he undoubtedly profited by French example ; even his own movement towards naturalness and directness—which critics of the Wagner type would attribute to his "German heart"—being stimulated, even if not generated, by French critics like Marmontel and Diderot.[2] In his æsthetic theories again, Lessing certainly owed something to—among other books—the *Refléxions Critiques sur la Poésie et la Peinture* of Du Bos. Herder, like every other thinking man of the epoch, was deeply indebted to the nature-movement of which Rousseau was the great moving force ;[3] and Herder in his turn led Goethe to Rousseau and to Shakespeare. Goethe's intellectual life in particular was the product of influences from every quarter—from ancient Greece,

---

[1] Sime's *Life of Lessing*, i. 49. See also p. 61.

[2] See the *Hamburgische Dramaturgie*, No 14 ; and Mr. John Morley's *Diderot*, i. 310 &c. Mr. Morley remarks, "It has been replied to the absurd taunt about the French inventing nothing, that at least Descartes invented German philosophy. Still more true is it that Diderot invented German criticism." On the influence of Diderot upon Lessing's art-criticism see ii. 80–82.

[3] In his *Beethoven* (1870) Wagner wrote : "We know that it was the 'German spirit,' so terribly dreaded and hated 'across the mountains,' that stepped into the field of art, as everywhere else, to heal this artificially induced corruption of the human race"—the "rescuers from that corruption" being Lessing, Schiller, Goethe, and the rest. It is a peculiarly offensive form of national vanity that blinds men like Wagner to the influence of France upon Germany in the eighteenth century. On Herder's debt to Rousseau, Swift, Richardson, Fielding, Sterne, and Goldsmith, see Mr. Sime's *Life of Goethe*, p. 39.

Italy, France, England, and the Netherlands ; influences which he, the most cosmopolitan man of his time, would have been the last to deny. Even without adding further evidence, it can be seen that Wagner's high-sounding thesis breaks down at every point. Germany has been influenced and stimulated by foreign culture at least as much as any other nation; and the racial vanity that can see anything degrading in such intellectual influence is a fitting companion to the glib ignorance that denies one of the most evident of historical phenomena. The fertilising seed of foreign culture must, during the seventeenth and eighteenth centuries, have been working in a thousand ways towards the literary, artistic, and scientific efflorescence of the Germany of the present day. And as for Wagner's contention that the German princes, being under French influence, were antagonistic to the true German spirit, that is of a piece with his whole argumentation. It is the dictum of a man who knows nothing of how national changes come about ; who can only indulge in wild rhetoric about that undiscovered entity "the Folk." So far as the French influence tended to stereotype artificial customs it was harmful ; but no one would ever contend that any foreign influence can work the maximum of good without any admixture of evil. What remains certain is that without the French influence the period of Germany's barbarism would have been indefinitely prolonged, and the system of princely patronage, though it certainly had its bad side, yet on the whole must be said to have wrought for good in Germany.[1] Wagner himself, when his thesis was not the glorification of Germany, but the need of providing adequate opportunities for the culture of art —as in the *Report to his Majesty King Ludwig II. of Bavaria, upon a German Music-school to be founded in*

[1] See Note, p. 138.

Munich—could very readily admit German debts to Italy and France, even saying that

"it is the peculiar mark of the German cycle of culture that it takes its form and motive mostly from without, consequently that it tries to digest a conglomerate culture whose elements lie primarily remote from it, not merely in space, but also in time. Whereas the Romanic nations abandon themselves to a dubious life of the moment, and, strictly speaking, have a sense of nothing but what the immediate Present offers them (*sic*), the German builds his world of the Present out of motives from all zones and ages." [1]

He further admits, after implying a score of times that the German princes were inimical to German civilisation, that they did a great deal of good in the eighteenth century by sending their protégés to Italy for musical instruction.[2] His culture-thesis is, in fact, utter chaos whichever way we look at it. He had no grasp of sociological problems, no real understanding of the subtle interplay of the forces that control national life and art; so that when he came to treat of these questions he could do no more than ignore every historical fact that told against him, and give the rein to the cheapest and crudest spirit of national self-laudation. We cannot afford to let pass in silence Wagner's writings upon these questions, bad as they are. Not only are they significant elements in the diagnosis of the man as he really was—showing how hopelessly unfitted he was to treat of any but musical subjects—but they are so far backward steps towards social barbarism that one is compelled to combat them, more especially as the vogue of his prose-works is now so great among his more unintelligent admirers. He and they need to be told that this crude spirit of national

[1] G. S. viii. 136; Ellis, iv. 183.
[2] G. S. viii. 141; Ellis, iv. 188.

vanity is a mark of the beast rather than, as they suppose, of the angel; and that moralists who are so very anxious for the rehabilitation of the "purely-human" may be sometimes reminded, to their own advantage, that their moral fervour does not appear quite so "purely-human" to others as it does to themselves.

CHAPTER VIII

TRISTAN AND ISOLDE AND DIE MEISTERSINGER

I

A GLANCE at the Synthetic Table will show that *Tristan and Isolde* and *Die Meistersinger* belong to the middle of the period during which Wagner was engaged on the *Ring*, the tragedy being written between 1857 and 1859, and the comedy completed in 1867 ; both works thus coming between the composition of about half of *Siegfried*, in 1857, and the remaining portion in 1869. The biographical details are, in brief, that Wagner undertook these two fresh works in order, for pecuniary reasons, to have something produced immediately upon the stage—there being very little prospect in 1857 of the *Ring* ever being performed. In March 1857 he received an invitation from the Emperor of Brazil to write an opera for Rio de Janeiro, and at first he thought of offering *Tristan* for this purpose ; but the notion was soon abandoned. His hopes that the opera might be quickly produced in Germany were, however, doomed to bitter disappointment. The intrigues of his enemies combined with the difficulties of the work itself to keep it from performance. Even so important an operatic establishment as that of Vienna rehearsed the opera fifty-four times, and then gave it up as unplayable ; and it was not until 1865, more than six years after its completion, that it had its first performance, at Munich. The *Meistersinger*, again, was first sketched out by Wagner in 1845, immediately after *Tannhäuser ;* but other plans intervened, and the subject

was only taken up again in 1861, the opera being completed six years later. It was more fortunate than
Tristan on the practical side ; its first performance took
place in the year following its completion.

The two operas are thus seen to fall between the
years 1857 and 1867, when Wagner was for the first
time the real Wagner as we now know him. One
period of his development may be roughly said to close
with *Lohengrin;* and any one who compares that opera
as a whole with any of the later works will see how
enormously Wagner's brain had grown in complexity
since 1847. There are, it is true, certain resemblances
to be noted between *Lohengrin* and the *Rheingold*,[1]
although the advance as a whole is very great from
1847 to 1854 ; while in the *Valkyrie*, and still more in
Siegfried, one sees Wagner's musical style becoming
less and less like that of any previous or contemporary
composer—becoming less formally melodic, more homogeneous, and at the same time more complex. A comparison of the love-duet in the 1st Act of the *Valkyrie*
with the love-duet in the 3rd Act of *Siegfried* will serve
to show how, even on the side of lyrical and impassioned
beauty, Wagner's style was moving from every point
of contact with that of other musicians, and becoming
distinctly his own. Beyond the point represented by
Siegfried his mind did not develop so much. There
are, of course, in the *Götterdämmerung* and *Parsifal*,
visions of worlds of music that are not to be had in
Siegfried; but in everything that concerns the handling
of his forms and his material, it may be said that *Siegfried* shows us the fully developed Wagner, thoroughly
conscious of his own aims and ideals, and more perfectly equipped for the realisation of them than at any
previous period of his life. So that in *Tristan* and the
Meistersinger, written as they were in the plenitude of
his artistic powers, we may expect to find Wagner deal-

[1] See, for example, in vocal score of the *Rheingold*, pp. 68–76, 88, 89.

ing with the musical drama as he had never done before, drawing from his peculiar form of it more than he had previously been able to draw, when his intuitions and his reasoned ideas of its possibilities were as yet unmated with the strong and easy hand of the mature craftsman.

It was probably some kind of revolt, conscious or unconscious, against the enormous mass of material with which he had burdened himself in the tetralogy, that led him to the simplicity of outline and clearness of content of *Tristan;* while the ardour with which he threw himself into the work may have been partly due to the desire of the artist to see something grow into actual life under his pen—a desire, born of the apparently unending labour of the *Ring*, to find artistic joy and new energy in some work that should stand before his eyes complete, harmonious, and alive.

"For the sake of that most beautiful of my life-dreams, *Young Siegfried*," he wrote to Liszt in 1854, "I shall have to finish the *Nibelungen* pieces after all. . . . As I have never in my life felt the real bliss of love, I must erect a monument to the most beautiful of all my dreams, in which, from beginning to end, that love shall be thoroughly satisfied. I have in my head *Tristan and Isolde*, the simplest but most full-blooded musical conception; with the 'black flag' which floats at the end of it I shall cover myself to die."[1]

He was impelled to the composition of *Tristan* with an urgency rare even with him, the apostle of "Need"; his interest in the story, the place of love in his philosophical system, the gloom of his outward circumstances, the need of self-expression, and the influence —then at its strongest—of Schopenhauer's pessimistic theories—all combined to make the new opera personal and vital in the highest degree.

After the huge canvas of the *Ring*, the scheme of

---

[1] *Correspondence of Wagner and Liszt*, Eng. tran. ii. 54.

Tristan is of course simplicity itself ; and Wagner showed once more the general rightness of his intuitive sense as to the essentials of good music-drama, in his reduction of the mass of material in the old Tristan-legends to the particular form to which he has set his music.[1] The tendency to drop into the epic or narrative form, which at first troubled him in writing the poem of the *Ring*, is here almost entirely avoided by the skilful weaving of all the events anterior to the drama into the structure of the drama itself, so that although these earlier events are communicated to the spectator in the narrations of the characters themselves, they are for the most part not mere pieces of narration grafted on to the drama, but vital elements in the dramatic action, woven into the general texture in an extremely skilful way, by the use of certain leading-motives. As for the general structure of the poem and the music, and their congruence with his theories, Wagner himself has told us that he was quite willing to allow it to be submitted to the severest test of this kind ; and while he did right thus to challenge investigation, we, on the other hand, may find evidence in *Tristan* to confirm us in the belief that he erred when he imagined himself to be asserting the claims of the poet against those of the musician, and again when he ranked the musical-drama so high above all other arts. In the "*Zukunftsmusik,*" after laying it down that operatic subjects should be chosen from the myth, in order that the action, being hindered by a mass of extraneous incident, might develop solely along the lines of inner necessity, he proceeds to trace his artistic progress in this respect from the *Dutchman* upwards, and finds the culminating point in *Tristan.*

---

[1] On the relation of Wagner's version of the legend to that of Gottfried von Strassburg and others, see Mr. Chamberlain's *Richard Wagner*, pp. 307–310, and his *Das Drama Richard Wagner's*, pp. 63–67 ; and M. Gaston Paris' article in the *Revue de Paris*, 15th April 1894.

"Here," he writes, "in perfect truthfulness, I plunged into the inner depths of soul-events, and from out this inmost centre of the world I fearlessly built up its outer form. A glance at the volumen of this poem will show you at once that the exhaustive detail-work which an historical poet is obliged to devote to clearing up the outward bearings of his plot, to the detriment of a lucid exposition of its inner motives, I now trusted myself to apply to these latter alone. Life and death, the whole import and existence of the outer world, here hang on nothing but the inner movements of the soul."[1]

And with his usual curious misunderstanding of the trend of his own theories, he supposes that the development from the *Dutchman* to *Tristan* has consisted in the superior place given to the *poet*, whereas the real truth is that the advance has been in the direction of making the *musician* the real shaper of the drama —his error once more arising from his supposition that he was altering the psychological relations of poetry and music in opera, when he was only altering the external form which music had there assumed.

"In looking through the poems" [*i.e.* from the *Dutchman* onward], he wrote, "you will readily notice that I but very gradually grew conscious of the advantage just referred to,[2] and but gradually learned to profit by it. Even the outward volumen, increasing with each poem, will afford you evidence of this. You will soon perceive that my initial bias against giving the poem a broader reach sprang chiefly from my keeping at first too much in eye the traditional form of opera-music, which had hitherto made a poem impossible that did not allow of numberless word-repetitions. . . . Perhaps in the execution of this poem [*Tristan*] much will strike you as going too far into subtle (*intime*) detail; and even should you concede this tendency as permissible to the poet, you yet might wonder how he could dare hand

---

[1] G. S. vii. 122; Ellis, iii. 330, 331.

[2] *i.e.* the advantage afforded by the use of legendary subjects, whereby the action was simplified externally, and more space given to the development of the "inner springs of action."

over to the musician all this refinement of minutiæ, for carrying out. In this you would be possessed by the same bias as led myself, when drafting the *Flying Dutchman*, to give its poem nothing but the most general of contours, destined merely to play into the hands of an absolute musical working-out. But in this regard let me at once make one reply to you: whereas the verses were there intended as an underlay for operatic melody, to be stretched to the length demanded by that melody through countless repetitions of words and phrases, in the musical setting of *Tristan* not a trace of word-repetition is any longer found, but the weft of words and verses foreordains the whole dimensions of the melody, *i.e.* the structure of that melody is already erected by the poet."[1]

What really suggests itself to the outside mind, on reading these passages, is that Wagner was quite blind to the true circumstances of the case. In the first place, it is altogether wrong to say that the older opera exacted from the poet "numberless word-repetitions," for an opera could easily be put together, even in the conventional form of aria, recitative, *ensemble*, and the rest, that would proceed simply and naturally without *any* repetitions. The operatic aria was, in its typical form, a lyrical outburst, a highly emotional expression of some mood of more than ordinary intensity. In this respect it resembled the modern non-operatic song; and the finest achievements in the modern song are in no way dependent upon word-repetition for their effect. Grant the supposition that an ordinary opera must contain detached arias, and it does not at all follow that the words need be stupid in matter or conventional in form. We can easily conceive an opera that should take all the strong points of the Wagnerian theory and exhibit them in the older operatic frame; that is, it might choose a very simple, emotional subject; it might develop, psychologically, upon the line of "internal" instead of "external" issues; and, while main-

[1] G. S. vii. 121, 123; Ellis, iii. 329, 331.

taining the old plan of division into aria, recitative, and *ensemble*, might avoid, as Gluck said, "too great a disparity" of emotional pitch between these various parts, and at the same time make their junction easy, fluent, and natural.   An opera built up on these lines would make a total impression very little less than that made by one of Wagner's—given, of course, Wagner's rare musical gift in the composer.   The world has seen few operas constructed in this way ; but that has been mainly because each successive opera-composer and opera-poet followed blindly the old conventions, instead of thinking out the problem of form and expression anew for himself.   It is one more illustration of the fact pointed out in a previous chapter, that Wagner imagined he had discovered a defect in the psychological relations of poetry and music in the ordinary opera, whereas he was only dealing with a historical convention that left the general question of the relations of poetry and music quite untouched.

For in the second place, he altogether misses the real significance of the changes in his own manner of writing opera-poems, from the *Dutchman* to *Tristan*. There are two ways in which a poet can allow the musician to give the fullest possible expression to a given emotion : he may write a poem of a few lines, and allow the musician to repeat these, or parts of them, again and again, thus exhausting all the emotional possibilities latent within that particular mood ; or he may spread his phrase out in a much thinner medium, allowing the musician to occupy just as much time in the development of his own particular forms of expression, but mating each new phrase of the music with a new phrase of the poem.   The former method was that of the *Dutchman* and of the ordinary opera ; the latter the method of *Tristan*.   The psychological relations of poetry and music remain, however, quite unchanged throughout each of these two modes of combination.   It

is the music that leads and controls ; anything not congruous with the nature of music will not be tolerated ;
while in the case of any words that *can* be combined with
it, one requires only to grasp so much of the meaning
of them as will give a more definite character to the
somewhat vague expression of music. So that Wagner's
progress from the *Dutchman* to *Tristan* was really along
two lines. In the first place, he made the mental current seem more continuous, more organic, by adopting
a more continuous and more organic form of expression, by discarding the set divisions of aria, recitative,
and *ensemble,* which exist on different planes of æsthetic
psychology, and in the passage from one to another
of which the hearer's mind experiences a sense of
emotional discontinuity. But this development was not
a revolt, as Wagner thought, against " absolute-musical
working-out " on the part of the musician, but simply
an attempt to restore to this form of art a homogeneity
of medium that ought never to have been destroyed,
that had been destroyed only through the stress of
definite historical circumstances, and towards whose
restoration every earnest composer had striven. Wagner
himself is forced to admit at times that there had been
attempts of this kind to give more unbroken continuity
to the stream of music in opera.[1] On the one side, then,
his advance was only a logical development from the
best efforts of previous composers, but made consistent
and successful by his enormous musical gift and his
consciousness of a definite purpose—the two points in
which he so greatly surpassed his predecessors. In the

---

[1] See, for example, G. S. vii. 133, 134 ; Ellis, iii. 341, 342. " Though the
hideous juxtaposition of absolute recitative and absolute aria is retained
almost everywhere, preventing any finished style, and everlastingly breaking
and barring the musical flow (through the fundamental error of a faulty poem),
yet in our great masters' finest Scenas we often find this evil quite overcome ;
to the Recitative itself there has been given already the stamp of rhythmic
melody, and it opens imperceptibly into the broader structure of the melody
proper."

second place, his librettos, from the *Dutchman* to *Tristan*,
were becoming more and more *musical* in quality ; that
is, they were more adapted for being set to music.   The
climax was reached in the poem of *Tristan*, where, as
we saw in a previous chapter, the words can no longer
be described as poetry, but merely as " words intended
for music."   Wagner might have spared himself and us
much elaborate discussion had he recognised that music
is the controlling factor in opera, determining what
shall and what shall not be said in the course of the
so-called " drama."   He could only arrive at a conclusion coinciding with this in substance, though differing
from it in appearance, by the circuitous path of an
analysis of the myth.   His attempt to diminish the rôle
of external circumstance in the opera was due to the
perception that the ideal nature of music debarred it
from participation in anything but the broadest of
dramatic motives.   His own handling of the Tristan
legend for the purposes of opera shows at once the
peculiar strength and the peculiar weakness of the
musical drama.   On points where poetry and music
can unite in the one expression, the power of the
musician must enormously exceed that of the poet ;
in the love-duet of the 2nd Act, for example, and
the terrible delirium of the sick man in the 3rd Act,
the musician's power to move us is a thousand times
greater than anything the poet could achieve.   But on
the other hand, precisely because music has this power
of intensifying a particular emotion and dwelling upon
it far beyond the point where the poet would have
wearied us, it is incapacitated for taking part in the
drama as we ordinarily conceive it, where a greater
number of moods are generated, each being dwelt
on a much smaller time than in opera.   No one will
question that *Tristan* is an almost ideal poem for
music-drama—at any rate the finest specimen that
musical literature possesses ; but for that reason it is

only in the minutest degree a drama.   M. Lichtenberger opines that *Tristan* is "the somewhat paradoxical type of the Wagnerian drama," inasmuch as it is "a subject entirely interior, entirely *musical*." [1]   Quite so; but precisely on that account it is a musical drama and not a drama—a distinction which Wagner was incapable of making, but which is fatal to his pretension that the drama as he conceived it was the supreme summation of all the arts.

Thus *Tristan* is in some respects the most instructive of all Wagner's works in the light it throws upon his theories; and it certainly bears out the analysis of a previous chapter, wherein it was shown that the musical stream of thought is the most important factor in opera, and that given a satisfaction of the æsthetic sense in this respect, the poem may for the most part go hang.   After the great stress that Wagnerians have laid on "the restoration of the poet to the supreme place in musical drama," it is certainly refreshing to meet with their naïve admissions that not only is *Tristan*—the work which Wagner himself regarded as the incarnation of his theories—built up on the poetical side simply to suit the exigencies of the music, but that in many passages the words might just as well be non-existent.

"As the interior action of the drama," says M. Lichtenberger, "is essentially musical and based on feeling, and poetry is, by its very essence, incapable of revealing the intimate nature of the emotions which agitate a human soul, to note the supreme ecstasies of love and despair, it cedes at every instant the first place to the music.   There are in *Tristan* long passages *where the verse is resolved, so to speak, in the music; where it is reduced to being merely the support, almost indifferent by itself, of the chanted melody;* where the poet, conscious of his impotence to express in clear and logical ideas the pure sentiment that

---

[1] *Wagner, Poète et Penseur*, p. 329.

sings through his melodies, replaces the regular phrase by a series of broken interjections, exclamations with scarcely a link between them, *and offering to the intelligence only a sense extremely vague.*" [1]

Well, that is precisely what has been contended for in the present volume as the main argument against Wagner's claim that the drama must be resolved into the musical drama; the great objection is that though music has an intenser life than words, its range is far more limited; that more complex arts than music have come into existence simply because the human brain has grown more complex since the day when man's first vague emotion found outlet in a cry; and that for the satisfaction of our more specialised needs we must have recourse to more specialised forms of art. We can imagine no musical drama more beautiful, more terrible, more profoundly moving than *Tristan;* only when one compares it with *Ghosts*, or *Hamlet!* Wagner may have been so constructed that poetry, as poetry, had little charm for him; but are *we* to surrender our intellectual delights on that account? The poem, says the French critic just quoted,

"shocks the taste . . . by the obscurity of a most elliptical form of speech, which exasperates in general both philologists and men of letters, and in which it is almost impossible, indeed, to discover the least charm as soon as the poetical expression is separated from the musical." [2]

---

[1] Wagner, *Poète et Penseur*, pp. 330, 331.

[2] *Ibid.*, p. 331. Mr. Finck, however, tells us that *Tristan* is "a poem for poets" (*Wagner and his Works*, ii. 144). He goes on to the effect that "although poetic imagery is less essential in a musical drama than in a literary drama, because there the music supplies the appeal to the feelings for which a poet usually resorts to similes, Wagner's *Tristan* poem, nevertheless, is full of exquisite imagery which alone would put him in the front rank of German poets." To praise a libretto for being full of the very things that are not essential to a libretto seems rather contradictory. Most people, however, who have read the poem of *Tristan* would have some compunction about placing Wagner "in the front rank of German poets."

T

On these lines it is difficult to see the force of the favourite Wagnerian contention that the musical drama combines each of the arts just at the point where its own expression fails, and demands the assistance of the other. Test the theory by the poetry and music of *Tristan*. Besides the lines I have already quoted in a previous chapter, look at a few others :—

> " sie zu suchen,
> sie zu sehen,
> sie zu finden,
> in der einzig
> zu vergehen,
> zu entschwinden
> Tristan ist vergonnt."

. . . . .

> " O süsse Nacht !
> Ew'ge Nacht !
> Hehr erhab'ne,
> Liebes-Nacht !
> Wen du umfangen,
> wem du gelacht,
> wie—wär' ohne Bangen
> aus dir er je erwacht ?
> Nun banne das Bangen,
> holder Tod,
> sehnend verlangter
> Liebes-Tod !
> In deinen Armen,
> dir geweiht,
> ur-heilig Erwarmen,
> von Erwachens Noth befreit.
> Wie es fassen ?
> Wie sie lassen,
> diese Wonne,
> fern der Sonne,
> fern der Tage
> Trennungs-Klage ?

Ohne Wähnen
sanftes Sehnen,
ohne Bangen
süss Verlangen ;
ohne Wehen
hehr Vergehen,
ohne Schmachten
hold Umnachten ;
ohne Scheiden,
ohne Meiden,
traut allein
ewig heim,
in ungemess'nen Räumen
übersel'ges Träumen.
Du Isolde,
Tristan ich,
nicht mehr Tristan,
nicht Isolde ;
ohne Nennen,
ohne Trennen,
neu Erkennen,
neu Entbrennen ;
endlos ewig
ein-bewusst :
heiss erglühter Brust
höchste Liebes-Lust ! ' "

Now let any one remember that these words are
from the duet in the 2nd Act, and that they are set
to some of the most beautiful music in the whole
opera, and it will at once be evident that the musical
drama does *not* consist in a union of poetry and music
just at the point where each demands the aid of the
other in order to extend the field of its own expression.
The music in *Tristan* is in many respects the most
complex, the most subtle, the most modern, that we
possess ; three centuries of development were necessary before music could attain to such depth of imagination and such control of form.   Compare with this

music the "poetry" to which it has been set—verse that deliberately casts away almost every literary beauty which poets have been slowly developing through century after century. It has nothing but the most *banal* rhythm, rhymes irritating in their closeness and their frequency, and a terseness that is generally fatal to any poetical beauty whatever. And this jargon, this bald prose chopped up into lines and adorned with the most obvious rhymes, this is what Wagner would have us regard as poetry developed so far that the expressive power of words can no further go, poetry that in its dire need for completion calls imperatively for the helping hand of music! Such a union as this of the two arts may perhaps have seemed to Wagner one in which poetry and music met on equal terms, neither attaining expression at the expense of the other; but to the outside mind the reconciliation seems to be of the kind attained when the lamb lies down inside the lion. Can there be any doubt that Wagner's brain was, in nine-tenths of its structure, the brain of a musician pure and simple; and that although there was in his musical imagination an infusion of more concrete impressions than usually go to the making of music, he was not a poet in any but the vaguest sense of the word, having neither the verbal, the rhythmical, nor the imaginative gifts that make the poet as distinguished from the mere versifier? Poems he did *not* write; what he wrote was simply words for music.[1]

Tristan is indeed for the most part simply a huge achievement of the musical imagination, to which the words have contributed in a very slight degree. As has already been pointed out, Wagnerians themselves

[1] Mr. Chamberlain tells us that he "has been able to study the very first sketches of *Lohengrin*; they furnish documentary proof that all the principal motives of the drama formed themselves in Wagner's mind simultaneously, while the poem was still an unfinished sketch" (*Richard Wagner*, p. 288, *note*). That is precisely what we should have expected.

have admitted that in long stretches of the opera the
poem is altogether "resolved into the music."   Even
Mr. Chamberlain, who regards Wagner's theory as
a very important contribution to musical æsthetics,
appears to the non-Wagnerian mind to surrender the
case entirely.   Wagner felt, he writes,

"that for the complete realisation of his poetic intent he must
make use of every means of expression, that he could no more
do without the 'indispensable foundation' of language than without the 'realising aid' of music." [1]

Observe the confusion and contradiction of terms even
within the limits of this short sentence ; because a
musician employs words to which to set his music, he
must be credited with a "poetic intent"—as if music
could not be, and as if Wagner's music frequently was
not, set to the merest prose.   The "poetic intent"
which looms so largely before Mr. Chamberlain's vision
is simply what plain people would call the story of the
opera, not necessarily poetical either in conception or
in form.

"When we are dealing with the creative soul," continues Mr.
Chamberlain, "the distinction between poet and musician is
purely artificial ; the musician is 'the poet revealing his purpose
in its deepest meaning'; the poet can only grasp this purpose
(that of directly representing so deeply emotional a subject-
matter) in so far as and because he is in the depth of his heart
a musician.   And the more he attains perfection in his art, the
more impossible it becomes to draw a line and to say, here ends
the work of the poet, here begins that of the musician.   In conception, in the main lines of the words, a poem like that of
Tristan has sprung as truly from music as Aphrodite, the goddess
of perfect beauty, has sprung from the waves of the sea.   Whether
therefore we consider the pastoral play of his boyhood, or the
master-works of his mature age, we shall always find 'word-poet'
and 'tone-poet' to be one and the same person in Wagner." [2]

---

[1] *Richard Wagner*, p. 243.   [2] *Ibid.*, p. 243.

Was there ever such a chaos of fallacy and self-contradiction in so limited a space? Mr. Chamberlain
first of all contends that in Wagner's mind there was
a poetic picture to be realised, which could only be
realised by calling in the aid of musical expression.
In the next breath it appears that there is no such
division of imagination as this; that, in fact, "the
distinction between poet and musician is purely artificial"—that is, if words mean anything, in *Tristan*
we should be unable to say, "This is the part of the
poet, this the part of the musician," which is precisely
what Mr. Chamberlain has been saying all along.
Then, when we have arrived at the proposition that
we cannot draw a line, and say, "Here ends the work
of the poet, here begins that of the musician," we are
suddenly told that the poem of *Tristan* (*i.e.* the part
which is indistinguishable in separation from the music),
has sprung from the music (*i.e.* the part which is merely
the realisation of the poem), as Aphrodite has sprung
from the waves of the sea. And all this mass of
absurdity, this perpetual see-saw from one opinion to
another, is due to neither Wagner nor his disciples
having perceived that there is *no* poem, in the true
sense of the word, in *Tristan;* that there are, as I have
already remarked, simply a number of words for music.
The proper phrasing of the Wagnerian theory that the
poem of *Tristan* is born from the music, is simply that
Wagner, having his mind filled with the musical expression of certain great emotions, and needing a sub-
stratum of words in order to give definiteness and
coherence to the music, set the music to a simple old
story told in the smallest possible number of words.
A story of some kind is indispensable to an opera,
but if the mere fact of there being a story is to lead
to the composer being credited with a "*poetic* intent,"
there is no limit to the fallacy that lies open before us.
We have simply to substitute "verbal" for "poetic,"

" verse " for " poetry," " versifier " for " word-poet," in
all cases where these terms are used by Wagner, in
order to see the real æsthetic bearings of the relation
of poetry to music in opera.   Mr. Chamberlain himself has admitted that in one portion of the opera—
the warning uttered by Brangæna from the tower, in
the 2nd Act—the words are necessarily indistinguishable, by reason mainly of the long-drawn notes to
which they are set, the turmoil of the orchestral accompaniment, and the fact that the singer is not, properly
speaking, on the stage at all ; here, he admits, the
human voice comes to us simply in the form of a
cry, a vague lamentation.[1]   Well, to that Wagnerian
admission there require to be added the further facts,
(1) that in many other parts of the opera the intellectual signification of the words is absolutely sunk in
the musical expression, and (2) that in still other cases
the words are quite superfluous, the music being all
that the mind cares to take in.[2]   If in the face of these
facts the Wagnerian still refuses to admit that in Wagner, just as in other composers, the music is the dominant factor from first to last in opera—though Wagner
avoids some of the technical errors of his predecessors
—one can only rejoin that to these æstheticians the

[1] *Das Drama Richard Wagner's*, pp. 80, 81.
[2] For example, in the following passage from the love-duet :

> Du Isolde,
> Tristan ich,
> nicht mehr Tristan,
> nicht Isolde ;
> ohne Nennen,
> ohne Trennen,
> neu Erkennen,
> neu Entbrennen ;
> endlos ewig
> ein-bewusst ;
> heiss erglühter Brust
> höchste Liebes-Lust.

Let any one recall the fact that these are the concluding words of the duet,
and are set to the most passionate of music, and he will realise how entirely
superfluous they are.

terms under discussion must mean something very different from what they mean to the rest of the world.

II

When one comes to the discussion of the music itself, however, the voice of criticism is almost silenced. The opera was written at one of the most feverish epochs of Wagner's life, when his brain was vibrating to all sorts of new impressions, emotional and intellectual; and the passion of his mental life at that time is plainly reflected in the music of *Tristan*. It would perhaps be incorrect to say that there is no other of his operas in which the inspiration is so continuous, for there are scenes in *Lohengrin*, in the *Meistersinger*, and here and there in the *Ring*, that are perfectly conceived and perfectly executed, models of artistic synthesis, and of a beauty that is homogeneous throughout; but none of the other operas are quite equal in *ensemble* to *Tristan*. Here the fever of the man's soul seems to have burnt its way into almost all his feeling and all his thought, fusing the strands into one glowing mass; and upon this molten material the plastic hand of the intellectual craftsman has been laid, casting it into mould after mould of the clearest and most vivid form, complex in the highest degree, yet sane and orderly and lucidly synthetic throughout. To examine some of the scenes, first in separation and then with an eye to their relation to the whole, is to stand amazed at the genius of the man who could bring the thematic elaboration of dramatic music to so high a pitch of perfection. The use of the leading-motive is of course not carried to such proportions as in the *Ring*; here the simplicity of the action, minimising as it does the threads of psychology the musician has to keep in hand, allows of a more continuous texture of the music, and at the same time of a synthesis of the

motives that might be called symphonic in its completeness and its grasp, were not that word too impotent to
convey a notion of the intellectual coherence of almost
every part of *Tristan*. As we listen to the opera,
parallel with the line of imagination along which we
follow up the motives in their more obvious dramatic
and emotional significance, there runs a line of appreciation of the formal structure of the work—an appreciation musical in its essence, but made curiously
complex and subtle by the perpetual sense that the
endlessly changing beauty of the thematic picture is
only the outward symbol of some vast drama of the
emotions, that complicates and vitalises the purely
musical sensation with suggestions of wider issues.
Take, as an example, the strangely melancholy motive
first heard at the beginning of the 3rd Act, and afterwards wrought so subtly into the texture of the vocal
and orchestral material during Tristan's monologue.
One can realise how other composers would have
treated this scene ; and to realise that is to see at a
flash the enormous superiority of Wagner to other
operatic writers, not only in sheer musical power—the
power of emotional representation—but in the vital
quality of brain that enables him to bend everything
to the imperious will of the creative dramatic artist,
to the concrete, plastic realisation of the inward vision.
He plays with his theme as the symphonic composer
plays with his "subjects," but yet in a manner that is
peculiarly his own. To no other musician has it been
given at once to realise all the aspects of a given
emotion, and to light intuitively upon so perfect a
medium for the exhibition of every change in it. As
we listen to the moan of that strange phrase inter-
twining itself with the plaint of the wounded man, the
mind feels that not only is a consummate musical
artist casting his magic over the phrase, manœuvring
it with an eye to showing all the varied musical beauty

of which it is capable, but with each new light in which the phrase is presented there comes a suggestion of some new phase of the man's psychology. One feels in a case of this kind the rare value of Wagner's method, and its vast superiority over the merely absolute-musical method of his operatic predecessors. With them the mere interest of the moment was predominant, and with its passing away there vanished also the significance of all that had previously been said. With Wagner the state of mind in which individual musical pieces are written for themselves alone has given place to the state in which a whole scene or a whole act is conceived organically, the artist's mind looking before and after, so that not only is each phrase comprehensible only by association with the rest, but each raises the other to a potency it could never attain to alone.

Considered in detail, of course, *Tristan*, like the *Ring*, exhibits one or two lapses of the artist's mind, particularly in the misuse of the leading-motives. It has always seemed to me, for example, that there was no adequate preparation for the use of the motive signifying the love-potion, at the juncture when Isolde and Tristan pledge each other in what is thought to be the cup of death. Immediately after the draining of the goblet, the well-known phrase is heard in the orchestra :[1]—

---

[1] Vocal score, p. 74.

Now how are we to learn from this phrase that what
Tristan and Isolde are really drinking is the love-
draught, and not, as Isolde supposes, a draught of
poison ?   Where has it been heard before ?   It occurs,
of course, at the beginning of the prelude, where, however, there cannot possibly be any indication of what is
symbolised by it.   Its next appearance is in the scene
between Isolde and Brangæna, where it may seem to
some that the clue is given to its meaning, although it
appears to me that this is only read into it *afterwards*,
when the drama has been completed, and that were it
not for this after-knowledge we should be in ignorance
of what was signified by the phrase.   Isolde has just
remarked that she must in future live near Tristan, and
"loveless ever languish."   Brangæna rejoins, "What's
this, my lady ?   Loveless thou ?   Where lives there
a man who would not love thee ?   Who could see
Isolde and not sink at once into bondage blest ?   And
even if it could be any were cold, did any magic
draw him thence, I'd bring the false one back to
bondage, and bind him in links of love."   There
then resounds in the orchestra the following broken
phrase :—

And Brangæna continues, "Mindest thou not thy
mother's arts ?   Think you that she who had mastered
these would have sent me o'er the sea without assistance
for thee ?"—the accompaniment being based on the
phrases of the first fourteen bars of the prelude.   When,

after some intervening words, Isolde bids Brangæna bring the casket, the maid sings, "It holds a balm for thee. Thy mother placed inside it her subtle magic potions; there's salve for sickness or for wounds, and antidotes for deadly drugs; the helpfullest draught I hold it here"—the orchestra again recapitulating certain phrases of the prelude.[1] It has never seemed to me that the symbolisation here is quite as lucid as it should have been. No one, I think, coming to the work for the first or second time, would be able to grasp from the music, the words, or the action, the fact that Brangæna possessed a potion having the power to create love in all who drank it. Later on in the same scene, when Brangæna recoils with horror from Isolde's command to mix the draught of poison, Isolde cries, "Pity thou me, false-hearted maid! Mindest thou not my mother's arts? Think you that she who had mastered these would have sent thee o'er the sea with no assistance for me? A salve for sickness doth she offer, and antidotes for deadly drugs: for deepest grief and woe supreme gave she the draught of death."[2] To the first half of this the accompaniment is again founded on the potion-motive, the musician's purpose being apparently to indicate that though Isolde is meditating on the cup of death, Brangæna's "assistance" will take the form of the love-draught that is destined to bring Isolde and Tristan together. Whether Wagner was justified in the belief that the hearer would read all this significance into this particular scene, whether it does not fail as a true psychological preparation for the scene where the potion is quaffed, and whether those who believe the psychological preparation to be quite adequate are not unconsciously reading into it their later experience of the opera—these are questions it is impossible to settle positively. Each student

[1] Vocal score, pp. 42–45.
[2] *Ibid.*, pp. 54–55.

must resolve them for himself; to me at any rate it has always seemed that here Wagner's use of the leading-motive broke down just on the very verge of success— when a little more clearness in the preliminary indication would have justified it beyond dispute. It must be remembered that Wagner's claim for his form of drama was that it made an immediate appeal to the unsophisticated intelligence, and that the use of the leading-motives made quite clear the organic connection of all parts of the work. It is obvious that if the motives are not properly prepared for, the hearer will be practically no better off than if the system of leading-motives were discarded altogether. To take an example from my own experience, I had had ten years' intimate acquaintance with the score of *Tristan* without it ever having struck me that there was any peculiar significance in the phrase that accompanies the entry of Tristan, in the fifth scene of the 1st Act. What then was my astonishment to learn from Mr. Krehbiel that at the beginning of this scene,

"the entrance of Tristan is proclaimed in a manner that leaves no doubt as to the meaning of the first of the two phrases [from the prelude] now under investigation. The melody there appears extended, in augmentation, as the musicians say. It stands for the hero of the tragedy."[1]

Now the phrase in question appears, in the prelude, in this form :—

[1] Krehbiel, *Studies in the Wagnerian Drama*, p. 49.

And I would like to take a census of opinion among a number of people who are listening to the opera for the first time, with the object of discovering whether they can spontaneously correlate the music at the beginning of scene 5, Act i. with this phrase from the prelude. Even now that I am informed that the music at Tristan's entry *is* based upon the phrase just quoted, I cannot quite see it, although the 12th and 13th bars of scene 5 reproduce bars 22nd and 23rd of the prelude—which is quite another matter. Altogether, one arrives at the conclusion that the true Wagnerian, in his dealings with the question of the leading-motive, is gifted with an internal vision that is denied to other men. In this same scene, for example, Mr. Krehbiel finds an orchestral proclamation of Tristan in his character as a fully developed tragic hero—this, be it observed, almost before any suggestion of the coming tragedy has been thrown out. How is this done?

"Observe," says Mr. Krehbiel, "how by augmenting the simple phrase, the orchestra increases the stature of the knight; but also how, though he looms up in Isolde's doorway like a demi-god clad in steel and brass, a knight capable of overthrowing the choicest spirits of Arthur's round table, and scattering thirty of King Marke's knights, the fateful harmonies in their chromatic descent (which have their model in the melody of the wounded Tristan), *published his doom with a prophetic forcefulness that cannot be misunderstood.*" [1]

Well, the mere outsider can only say that the downward chromatic passage is no more like the melody of the wounded Tristan than it is like any other downward series of chromatics; while the mind that can see in it a foretelling of the doom of Tristan must really be gifted with a power of vision denied to ordinary mortals— unless, indeed, the association of these passages with the future course of the drama comes not from what

[1] Krehbiel, *Studies in the Wagnerian Drama*, p. 59.

has gone before but from the memory of what has come after, the "prophecy" thus being nothing more than a philosophising *after* the event, as prophecy generally turns out to be upon examination.

There can surely be no unwisdom in frankly recognising that the great master of the leading-motive could sometimes blunder in its use. We must remember that to Wagner, with the picture of the whole past, present, and future of the dramatic action in his mind, a certain phrase would mean a great deal more than it can possibly mean to us, who have no internal picture of the drama to begin with, and who have to piece together the action out of the fragments into which the dramatist has dispersed it. We have only to ask ourselves the simple question, "What is the use of a Wagnerian overture?" in order to realise this. Let any one, for example, listen to the prelude to *Tristan* for the first time, without any knowledge of the opera to which it forms the commencement, and then compare his impressions of it with those of one who knows the whole of the music of the opera, and who, as he looks back upon the prelude, sees it in the light of this ampler knowledge. What can the prelude signify to the first of these men? It will indeed tell him to prepare himself for a tragedy and not for a comedy, but that is all. The man with an experience of the opera itself, on the other hand, sees all kinds of dramatic significances in the prelude; when he hears the draught-motive, for example, it rouses in him a mental picture of the scene on the ship and all that follows from it; while the merely vague awe that the uninstructed hearer feels is made definite by its association with particular scenes and particular words in the opera. And as the hearer who knows the opera can see more things in the prelude than are really there, so Wagner, in the composition of the opera, would imagine certain thematic indications

to be far clearer to the auditor's mind than they
really are, their logical connection being quite evident
to him, but insufficiently made evident to us.[1]

Certain of his uses of the leading-motive are, of
course, as in the *Ring*, models of subtle dramatic
suggestion, such as the quiet rising from the orchestra
of the tones of the potion-motive, as sole reply to
King Marke's mournful query, " The unexplained and
hidden cause of all my woes, who will to us disclose ? "
In the 3rd Act, again, Kurvenal is bending over the
wounded man, and, in reply to Tristan's question, tells
him of all that happened since Melot dealt him the
blow in Cornwall. " Thy wound was heavy ; how to
heal it ? Thy simple servant then bethought that she
who once closed Morold's wound, with ease the hurt
could heal thee that Melot's sword did deal thee. I
found the best of leeches there ; to Cornwall have I
sent for her." Here the first words are accompanied in
the orchestra by the phrase that accompanied Isolde's
recital, in the 1st Act, of her previous nursing of Tristan
in Ireland—thus furnishing a beautiful anticipation, before Kurvenal can complete this story, of the news that
he has sent for Isolde. Again, when in his death-agony
he hears her voice without, and his failing brain reverts
to the scene of the garden-meeting, the orchestra
pours out a reminiscence [2] of the exquisite phrase
that sang throughout the beginning of the 2nd Act,
when it was Isolde who was waiting for the beloved
one [3]—but now altered in its harmonies, with all its
former placid rapture turned to bitterness. These are
indeed the points that show forth Wagner's genius

---

[1] One of the most refreshing little bits of unconscious humour in *Opera
and Drama* is the passage in which Wagner tells us that " every man of
common sense must know that these tone-pieces [*i.e.* the modern *operatic*
overtures] should have been performed *after* the drama, instead of *before* it,
if they were meant to be understood." It never occurred to him that a *tu
quoque* was possible.

[2] Vocal score, p. 237.   [3] *Ibid*, p. 91.

so triumphantly. Unthinking critics have objected to his incessant repetition of certain phrases, and have imagined that it indicated nothing but the poverty of his mind, and his inability to invent new musical utterances. Had their knowledge of Wagner been a little more profound, they might have seen that his repetitions are an essential part of his scheme for giving organic coherence to the dramatic action, and that by the ever varied forms in which the motives are repeated he throws ever new light on his characters and situations. The astonishing art with which he can present a motive in a form that enables us to recognise the occasions of its previous use, and yet alter it in harmony and in rhythm in such a way as to change entirely the mental mood it arouses in us, can only be realised by those who have studied the thematic texture of his greatest works. If the phrase "musical painting" is ever justifiable it is surely here, for one really has a series of pictures made almost objective in their definiteness by the exhibition of the same musical phrase in a score of forms.

On the whole, *Tristan* is perhaps the finest example of Wagner's art, the action being simple, the unmusical portions reduced to a minimum, and the musical portions of extraordinary beauty. There are, perhaps, one or two dramatic and psychological flaws in the opera. Into the much-debated question of the love-potion I do not propose to enter in great detail. Some critics have maintained that no true intellectual tragedy can be based upon an action in which the evil springs from the mere drinking of a magic potion— the love of the fated pair being thus, as some one has expressed it, shown as a purely chemical product. To this it has been rejoined that in Wagner's version of the story Tristan and Isolde really love each other before the opera commences, and that the love-draught is not the cause of their love, but simply the element

U

that makes the scales fall from their eyes, so that they realise their situation and confess their love. There is a little to be said for both views of the matter; and perhaps one may say, without prejudice, that the use of the love-potion is a slight flaw in the composition of the work, even after every argument has been brought up in its favour. Mr. Krehbiel's view that

"the love exists before the dreadful drinking, and the potion is less a maker of uncontrollable passion than a drink which causes the lovers to forget duty, honour, and the respect due to the laws of society"[1]

—seems to suggest that the troubles of the ill-fated pair came about through their being under the influence of drink.

"It is a favourite idea of Wagner's," continues Mr. Krehbiel, "that the hero of tragedy should be a type of humanity freed from all the bonds of conventionality. It is unquestionable in my mind that in his scheme we are to accept the love-potion as merely the agency with which Wagner struck from his hero the shackles of convention."

But falling in love with another man's wife or bride is surely the most conventional of all proceedings, and if this is to be the passport to dramatic immortality a good many of us might figure as "types of humanity." The truth of the matter seems to be that we object to the love-potion episode simply because here, as in the *Ring*, the interposition of the element of mediæval magic disturbs our more modern psychology; we cannot look at the tragedy of two human souls in the same homogeneous frame of mind if the misfortune that should come from purely human actions and passions comes partly from the drinking of a magic potion. We do not object to the love-philter in the old story, because the manner in which

---

[1] *Studies in the Wagnerian Drama*, p. 70.

it is spoken of there is congruous with the whole psychological scheme of the story; but to preserve it in all seriousness in a work that is entirely modern in every other respect is to break the force of the purely human tragedy.

From the purely theatrical side, again, it must be conceded that the popular sense is right in its objection to the long speech of King Marke at the end of the 2nd Act. The music is singularly noble and beautiful, and all that is said by the King is not only essential to the comprehension of the drama, but presents him in a better light than in any of the older versions of the story—Wagner's alteration of the legend at this point being one of the finest features of his work. But the pit objects to the length of the recital, and the pit is mainly right. It is bad policy to keep the spectators' attention occupied at all after the frenzy of the culminating passages of the love-duet; for sheer physiological reasons the scene ought to end then or shortly after. The sense of contrast is usually grateful, but here the contrast is not sufficiently strong to rouse a fresh interest at all comparable to that with which for half-an-hour we have listened to that delicious duet; besides which, the length of the Marke-recital and the subsequent passages given to Tristan and Isolde increase the feeling of anti-climax. The whole conclusion of the 2nd Act is from the dramatic standpoint at once justifiable and unjustifiable; upon the intellectual side it is necessary to complete our knowledge of the action of the drama, while upon the musical side it palls upon us, in spite of its purely musical beauty, through the physiological reaction ensuing upon the love-duet. If Wagner could have found some means to end this Act with the musical excitement at its height, as he has ended the 1st and 3rd Acts of *Tristan* and the 1st and 3rd Acts of the *Valkyrie*, our final sensations

would have been somewhat happier. As it is, the
pleasure given us, when we read the score, by all
that follows the termination of the love-duet gives way
to weariness when witnessing a stage-representation—
the actual strain upon the hearer's system during the
duet being greater when the voice and orchestra are
heard instead of being imagined, and the subsequent
reaction being correspondingly greater. It was probably a miscalculation of this kind of the purely
physical effect of the scene that led Wagner into his
érror of anti-climax. In the same way, though in a
slighter degree, a feeling of weariness comes now and
again upon us during all that ensues between the
death of Tristan and the final lyric outburst of Isolde.
Here again all that happens is essential to the dramatic
structure of the work, and one little stroke in particular—the participation of the "chorus" in the scene
without their uttering a word—shows in its quiet way
the superiority of Wagner over the ordinary opera-
composer as a dramatic thinker.[1] But in its own way
this scene also is felt as a slight anti-climax, though
the memory of it is quickly forgotten in the death-
song of Isolde that terminates the opera.

Into the question of the supposed influence of
Schopenhauer upon Wagner's thought at the time he
was writing *Tristan*, and the correspondence between
the "philosophy" of the opera and that of Schopen-

---

[1] It is probably the consideration of passages of this kind in which Wagner
has avoided some of the absurd conventionalities of structure of the older
opera, that has betrayed him and his disciples into the error of supposing that
with him "the drama" is the paramount consideration. What is really foremost in his thought, however, as I have tried to show, is not the drama, but
the drama as modified by music. The spirit of music determines what the
drama shall be—determines its ranges of character, of action and psychology ;
though of course *within* these limits Wagner tries, as in the above-cited case,
to avoid anything that would be dramatically inappropriate or absurd. See,
in this connection, Wagner's own account of how he came to give up the set
operatic forms, in the *Communication to my Friends*, G. S. iv. 321, 322 ;
Ellis, i. 368.

hauer, I do not wish to enter. Those whose taste is for intellectual diversions of this kind need assuredly be in no lack of material wherewith to gratify it, for no Wagnerian has ever written on *Tristan* without adding something to the discussion—the degree of light thrown upon the question ranging from something almost approaching candlelight to the "trebly cataphractic invisible." Perhaps we may be allowed to anticipate the action of posterity in sweeping aside all considerations of whether *Tristan* does or does not embody the philosophy of Schopenhauer. It is quite certain, let me repeat, that had Wagner written no letters and no prose-works, and had we been left to discover the "philosophy" of *Tristan* as best we could from the poem and the music, there would have been no profound treatises written showing the connection between the opera and *The World as Will and Idea*. Of course, if you are on the lookout for "correspondences" of this kind you can very easily find them anywhere ; and I for one am prepared to maintain that the schoolboy's lines,

> "The reason why I cannot tell,
> But I don't like thee, Doctor Fell!"

are the incarnation of a philosophy of fatalism, and that profound philosophic and economic lessons may be drawn from the story of Old Mother Hubbard. But if you wish to discover these things you must bring them with you ; and I am constrained to believe that the Wagnerians who saw Schopenhauerism in *Tristan* also brought it with them, and that had they had the poem only to draw upon we would have been spared a goodly number of pseudo-philosophical treatises. Posterity will probably say that it cares little what dull metaphysician is supposed to have inspired the poem of the opera, so long as the music is beautiful and the passion human. Even a sane Wagnerian like

M. Lichtenberger can be found to tell us that the passion of the lovers

"discloses to them the fact that its true domain is not *life*, the *daylight*—or, to borrow the formulas of Schopenhauer, the world of phenomena, of sensible appearances, the world of plurality, where the Will appears split up into innumerable individualities —but rather *death*, the *night*—or, in philosophical language, the domain of the absolute, the unconscious, the one."[1]

Alas that men should ever have thought it necessary to see in *Tristan* anything more than a superb musical drama : that they should have thought it necessary to mar the divine beauty of that great duet by associating it with these uninteresting tags of pseudo-philosophy ! If when Tristan sings, "Those who death's dark night boldly survey, those who have studied her secret way, the daylight's falsehoods, rank and fame, honour and all at which men aim, to them are no more matter than dust which sunbeams scatter," we are not moved by the beauty of the music, we are hardly likely to have our interest retained by the fact that these lines can be tortured into a resemblance to the philosophy of Nirvana. There is tenfold more philosophy, in the proper sense of the word, in Schumann's *Faust* than in *Tristan ;* yet it will hardly be disputed that what we return again and again to Schumann's great work for is its exquisite expression of certain deep human emotions, not the fact of the musician having chosen a few philo- sophical commonplaces as the medium through which to make his music reach us. *Tristan* must finally stand or fall without Schopenhauer's help or hindrance, as a piece of musical artistry ; and on these lines there is no reason to fear the verdict of posterity. If in the Valhalla of musicians there be a system of rewards and punishments, and if one good deed may be

---

[1] *Wagner, Poète et Penseur*, p. 338.

allowed to wipe out the memory of a number of bad ones, the composition of *Tristan* will surely be held to absolve Wagner from the crime of having written so much prose that was foolish and so much more that was dull.

III

Though the *Meistersinger*, as we have seen, was composed during the same epoch of frustration and misery as *Tristan*, it has throughout a peculiar serenity that would in itself lead us to think it the product of the happiest period of Wagner's life. When he first sketched it out in 1845 it was intended as the comic pendant to *Tannhäuser*, somewhat in the manner of the "jovial Satyr-play" that at Athens followed the tragedy. Having drawn out the scheme of the opera, however, he gave up it in obedience to the more urgent need to compose *Lohengrin*. The reason of this surrender of the opera was, according to his own later account, his sudden sense that

"the cheerful mood which sought to vent itself in the conception of the *Meistersinger* . . . took alone the shape of *Irony*, and, as such, was busied more with the purely formal side of my artistic views and aims than with that core of Art whereof the roots lie hid in life itself."[1]

His object was to criticise life mirthfully but not ironically, and finding himself incapable at that time of the objectivity necessary for this, he laid his would-be Satyr-play aside. By a curious irony of fate, he was destined to take it up again when the outward circumstances of his life were much more unfavourable to mirth than they were in 1845; and the tone of the *Meistersinger* as we now have it is a testimony to the artist's wonderful power of self-detachment. It

---

[1] *A Communication to my Friends*, G. S. iv. 286, 287; Ellis, i. 331.

is the most delightful piece of work that ever came from Wagner's pen—delightful both in its ease and mastery of workmanship and its pervading colour of *gemüthlichkeit*. Written, as we have seen, in the prime of his musical powers, and therefore exhibiting on the purely formal side the rare command of technique that is seen in *Tristan* and in *Siegfried,* all its enormous musical strength seems to be made delightful to us by its good-natured association with the smiling mask of comedy. We have the matured genius that went to the making of *Tristan,* but with breeze and sunlight and open meadow in place of the storm and darkness and elemental fury of the earlier work ; and one sometimes wishes that, appropriate as *Parsifal* is in many ways to be the final work of Wagner, he could have given his last message to the world in the *Meistersinger,* where we have him at his best and wisest, and with all his strenuous emotions turned to serene and lofty kindliness. Had it been the final work of his life we could have regarded it as we do Shakespeare's *Tempest,* as the last word of the great artist who has risen superior to the shocks of fortune, and looks towards the end in a mood of calmest peace, thrilled with the sense of deep-lying kinship with all created things. Not only do genial wisdom and broad tolerance breathe through every line of the poem, but the music also is at once noble and sweet as no other music is.

With the experience of the years after 1845, Wagner came to see that his first sketch of the comedy had several serious defects ; and the changes he effected in it were all in the direction of making Sachs the centre of the play. As we have it now, not Walther, as is popularly supposed, but Sachs is the real hero of the drama ; and Wagner has "internalised" the action, according to his own principles of music-drama, by making all its essentials take place in the heart of Sachs, who himself loves Eva, and who surrenders her in favour of the younger man. It goes without saying, of course, that Wagner tries to achieve by use of the leading-motive more than can possibly be done by its means. The best example of this failure in the *Meistersinger* is the prelude to the 3rd Act, about which so much has been written, and which Wagnerians have put forward as a marvellous example of Wagner's power to make clear the inner action of his drama by means of music. And this particular passage, by its clearness and its isolation and the use that has been made of it by Wagner and his disciples, may serve as an excellent text upon which to base a sermon. Let us transcribe Wagner's own analysis of it :—

"In the third stanza of the cobbling-song in the 2nd Act there is first heard the motive given out by the strings; there it expresses the bitter moan of the resigned man, who presents to the world a strong and serene countenance. Eva had understood this secret lament; and so deeply had her heart been pierced by it that she wished to fly from him, in order not to hear any more of this song that in outward appearance is so cheerful. Now, in the prelude to the 3rd Act, this motive is sounded and developed by itself, dying away in resignation; but at the same time, and, as it were, from a distance, the horns give out the solemn chant with which Hans Sachs greets Luther and the Reformation, and which has won unparalleled popularity for the poet. After the first strophe the strings take up again, very tenderly and in a long-drawn-out manner, a single snatch of the true cobbler's song, as if the man had turned his eyes upward, away from his daily toil, and lost himself in sweet and tender dreams. Then the horns, with greater fulness of tone, continue the master's hymn, with which Hans Sachs, upon his entering on the scene of the Festival, is greeted by the whole of the people of Nuremberg in a unanimous and thunderous outburst. Next enters again the first motive of the strings, with its large expression of the emotions that move a profoundly thoughtful soul ; now, calmed and appeased, it attains the extreme serenity of a tender and holy resignation."[1]

---

[1] Wagner, *Entwürfe, Gedanken, Fragmente*, pp. 104, 105.

Now with all respect to Wagner and those who have followed him in his view of this matter, the Vorspiel to the 3rd Act cannot possibly, by itself, express all this. The curtain has not risen, and the orchestra is playing the Vorspiel. How, in the first place, is any one to know that this Vorspiel, if it has any connection at all with one of the characters of the drama, is to be understood as being associated with Sachs? In the second place, how are we to know that the first theme—

represents "the bitter moan of the resigned man, who presents to the world a strong and serene countenance"? We are informed that we can understand this by the fact of its occurrence in the 2nd Act, in the third stanza of Sachs' song. But even if the phrase itself, heard there, could inform us exactly what it meant, or what Wagner intended it to mean—which is pure assumption—how many people can even distinguish the theme in its place in the 2nd Act? It is a mere contrapuntal episode of a few bars in the heart of a complex score;[1] and the fact that Kleinmichel, who reduced the full score, has not been able to show the theme in the voice-and-piano arrangement, shows how small are the chances of the hearer even distinguishing the theme at the movement of its apparition, to say nothing of grasping its psychological significance and carrying it in the memory, out of all the complex music of the 2nd Act, to the beginning of the 3rd.[2]

[1] The theme is given out by the oboes, clarionets, and horns, while the strings and brass maintain the cobbler-song.

[2] As a matter of fact, we first realise the meaning of this phrase in the Vorspiel later on in the 3rd Act, in Sachs' celebrated monologue *Wahn, Wahn, überall Wahn*, where the *words* give the key to the music.

In the third place, how are we to grasp the meaning
of the next phrase—

Wagner tells us that this is "the solemn chant
with which Hans Sachs greets Luther and the Reformation," and which is sung by the populace at the
entry of Hans Sachs at the end of the 3rd Act.   But
until it *is* sung there, and some indication given us
that the people are singing in Sachs' honour one of
his own songs, how are we to know that this phrase
in the prelude signifies, according to Mr. Chamberlain,
that the lament has given way to "the thought of
his own artistic creations . . . as if the eternal part
of a great human breast were striving against the
temporal"?[1]   And of course it goes without saying
that the further uses of these themes in the prelude
cannot possibly signify to the unilluminated intelligence

[1] *Richard Wagner*, p. 285.

what Wagner intended them to signify. What can we say then except that the Vorspiel is a gigantic blunder from the standpoint of the very criticism to which Wagner would wish it to be submitted, a pathetic example of his failure to see that the indefinite character of music makes it impossible for any one else to discover, from the music alone, the mental picture of which Wagner meant it to be a transcript? One might listen to it for years, and, if one is ignorant of the rest of the 3rd Act, never have the slightest suspicion even that Wagner intended it to be something more than just a very beautiful piece of music. Of course when we know what it is supposed to symbolise, and, as each phrase floats upward from the orchestra, conjure up before us Sachs in meditation, and imagine the fluctuating currents of his thought, the Vorspiel becomes even more beautiful to us, and expressive in a way that we had never realised before. But I reiterate that the meaning of it cannot be fathomed merely from itself, and that it must be held to fail entirely as a revelation of Sachs' thoughts preparatory to the 3rd Act. We should probably have more light thrown on this and other questions of Wagner's use of leading-motives, if Wagnerian writers, instead of chattering after each other the old legend as they had it from the composer's prose, would only ask themselves whether they could have arrived at this interpretation of the Vorspiel if they had not had the master's prose to guide them. The question, let us remember, is not one of merely declaring Wagner right or wrong ; it really goes much deeper than that, and is concerned with a problem of æsthetic psychology. As we saw in the *Ring*, and again in *Tristan*, one cause of Wagner's failure was the fact that while we have to take the music in the order in which it comes to us, and construct the total drama from all its fragments, moving, as it were, from points in the periphery to the centre, he conceived the drama centrally in the first place, and worked, with this central conception in his brain, to the periphery. Thus when writing the Vorspiel he would have the whole course of events in the 3rd Act in his mind—would see all the circumstances that attended Sachs throughout the Act, and the moods they generated in him. Wishing to indicate prophetically, in the Vorspiel, that Sachs will find in his art a consolation for his troubled soul, he expressed this by the influx of that grand choral song into the world of pain and discouragement represented by the first theme of the prelude, and again by the exquisite softening of this theme in its final form. But he forgot that no one else could possibly interpret the Vorspiel as he would, without the help of a prose explanation,—and on Wagner's own terms, the music ought to be so clear, so definite, so organic in its union of part with part throughout the whole opera, that the hearer ought never to be in doubt as to what were the dramatist's intentions. It is surely evident that, from the dramatic standpoint, the Vorspiel to the 3rd Act of the *Meistersinger* is a pure superfluity.

In spite of whatever faults of this kind that we may find with it, however, the *Meistersinger* is a stupendous work, wonderful alike for the qualities in which Wagner enters into competition with other musicians and for those that are peculiar to himself. As pure music, nothing could surpass such things as the two trial-songs and the prize-song, the prelude to the 3rd Act, the great quintett, Pogner's address, the reading of the Meistersinger rules by Kothner, the exquisite little song—to the words of the historical Hans Sachs—in which the populace greet the old master, and the meditation of Sachs in the third scene of the 2nd Act. Really charming also in its way is Beckmesser's sere-

nade in the 2nd Act—an admirable parody of the
Italianised German operatic serenade of Wagner's day,
with its fairly obvious melody, the guitar-like strum of
the orchestral accompaniment, and the dreadful dislocation of the verbal accent to suit the exigencies of
the musical phrase. The opera is full of exceedingly
beautiful touches — the persistent recurrence of the
warm theme of Walther's first song in the sober meditation of Sachs, the quaint old melody of the night-
watchman, and the still quainter sound of his oxhorn
after the riot in the 2nd Act—a delightful touch of
mediæval crudity ; the moonlit street of the earlier
scene, with Sachs' jovial song trolling out, broken
every now and then by the passionate accents of
Walther and Eva, who are concealed in the shadow ;
the scene where Eva and Sachs listen in rapture while
Walther pours out his glorious dream ; the soberly
philosophical address of Sachs to the folk of Nuremberg after the success of Walther.   In the characteristics, again, in which Wagner stands alone among
operatic composers, one easily recognises the technical
mastery which appears in all his writings at this time.
Particularly beautiful is the accompaniment to the
dialogue between Hans Sachs and Eva in the 2nd Act,
where the music, to adopt a simile of Wagner's own,
courses through the scene like blood through a living
body, always fluent, always vital.   In the same way he
presents in a thousand new lights the phrase, from
Walther's first song, that accompanies the comments
of the masters upon the performance—the varying
dramatic sentiments seeming to float upon the waves
of sound as upon the sea. As for the opera as a whole,
one need not take it too seriously as a piece of auto-
biography, nor as a dissertation upon the relative merits
of conservatism and radicalism in art. If it inculcated
a moral twice as wrong as its actual one is right, that
would not make the slightest difference to our enjoy-

ment of it.   I am probably expressing only a personal
opinion, but it seems to me that the *Meistersinger* is
after all the loveliest and perhaps the profoundest of
Wagner's works—the one to which we go back again
and again with undiminished enthusiasm and ever-
increasing admiration.   There is only *Tristan* that can
be compared with it for intensity and continuousness
of inspiration ; and *Tristan* is at times almost *too* intense
—the emotion seems at times too violent, too disturbing,
for art ; seems, as in the 3rd Act, to be a veritable representation of the agony of real life.   One feels now and
again, in *Tristan*, that this music has taught us more of
the dreadful capacity of our poor human nature for
pain than all our actual experience of life has done ;
one feels shattered, cowed ; one realises what a penalty
one pays for being human, for being clothed as we are
in "this muddy vesture of decay."   There is no such
strand of nervous or of philosophic pain in the delight
with which we listen to the *Meistersinger*.   Wagner was
never greater than in this divine music ; and to look
out upon the world from the height to which he lifts us
is to feel superior to all pain, all doubt, all enmity with
life.   The old master had grown if not intellectually at
least emotionally wise ; and it is this emotional wisdom,
this seer-like intuition of the hearts of men, that makes
the *Meistersinger* so broad, so deep, so tolerant, so peace-
giving.   Even in the saddest moments of the work, as
when, during Sachs' monologues, one feels that the
man's heart is full almost to bursting, the dominant
sensation in us is that curious one of pain tempered by
strong philosophy that becomes so strangely uplifting a
pleasure.   If ever there was music to which the term
"philosophical" might be applied, it is the whole score
of the *Meistersinger*.   Wagner has here emancipated
himself from the tyranny of the strange old legends to
which he had been so long enslaved.   His subject is
one of purely human interest, the joys and griefs of

men merely as men, not as symbols or personified abstractions; and the humanism of the dramatic action and motives is reproduced in the humanism of the music. No better example could be given than the exquisite scene in which Walther tells Sachs of the lovely dream that has come to him. Note how the atmosphere of delicious languor that steals upon the scene with Walther's opening words spreads itself over the majestic theme of Sachs, as the old shoemaker proceeds to read the young man that tender little sermon on art and life and tolerance of the frailties of human nature. "In words I scarce dare touch its theme," says Walther, in reply to Sachs' request that he will relate the dream, "for fear it all should fade away." "My friend," rejoins Sachs, "that is just the poet's art—to give life and shape to dreams. Believe me, the best ideas of men come to them in dreams; all poetry is nothing but the truth of dreams made manifest." Here is a situation, here a thought, nearer to us and more beautiful than the primeval world of the *Ring* or *Lohengrin*; and Wagner has rendered them into music that deepens the sweet and gentle philosophy of the words, emotionalises it, makes it truer and more lovely than mere words can do. Well might the master lay stress upon the fact that the centre of the dramatic action of the *Meistersinger* was the heart of Sachs. There is no more definitely drawn character in the whole range of musical drama, nor any in all Wagner's work so beautiful and so human. There can be set beside him only the grand and tragic figure of Wotan, who is also a conception not only remote from those of all other dramatists, but possible only in music such as Wagner's. But the plain old cobbler of Nürnberg is nearer and dearer to us than the All-father of the grey old North. He touches warmer springs of feeling in us; he does not tend, like Wotan, to become at times only a philosophical abstraction; he is human, and

more universal even than the god. Alas, that Wagner
should have been so blind to the possibilities that lay
within the art of which he was so unapproachable a
master ! One sometimes feels, as one compares the
Meistersinger with the *Ring*—as one sees, in the latter
work, the heroic struggle of music to breathe the breath
of life into that huge mass of inartistic matter, and, in
the former, the perfect marriage of music with so much
that is beautiful, and wise, and noble in the hearts of
men—one feels that had Wagner made all his dramas
as "purely human" as the *Meistersinger*, he would have
been some steps nearer Shakespeare than he is even
now. However, there is at least the *Meistersinger* to be
grateful for. If I were confronted with the old question
as to which of Wagner's scores I would save from
general destruction if only one were allowed to me, I
think it would be this. The others would not be sur-
rendered without many pangs ; but I would console
myself with the reflection that the *Meistersinger* is after
all the most human of all Wagner's works, and therefore—though perhaps he did not know it—the most
Wagnerian ; while all the best qualities of his mind have
gone to make the music the noblest, the profoundest,
the most philosophical music in the whole range of
opera.

x

CHAPTER IX

SOME LATER PROSE-WORKS

I

THE years between 1860 and 1870 were about equally apportioned by Wagner between musical and literary composition. Between 1853 and 1860, besides working assiduously at the *Ring*, he had completed *Tristan and Isolde*, while his literary compositions were comparatively few and unimportant. During the next ten years, he almost completed the *Ring*, as well as producing the *Meistersinger*, while his literary work comprises the lengthy *"Zukunftsmusik," State and Religion, What is German? Report to his Majesty King Ludwig II., German Art and German Politics*, and *On Conducting*, besides a number of smaller writings. In the following five or six years he composed very little music, his time being occupied partly with the efforts to establish Bayreuth, and partly with literary works, the number and details of which may be seen by reference to the Synthetical Table.

It is in the essay on Beethoven (1871), perhaps, that one sees Wagner at his best. It has, it is true, many of the faults of his other prose-writings, being frequently obscure and diffuse, *à priori* in method, and unduly prone to the besetting sin of Wagner's writing —the tricking-out of a very ordinary piece of reflection in the flowing garments of metaphysic. But it has also many good qualities, prominent among them being the truly admirable insight it shows into the psychological origins of some of Beethoven's work, and the qualities that distinguish this work from that of his predecessors. Even here one may not feel inclined altogether to agree with Wagner, for to many of us it seems that he finally makes a very good piece of culture-criticism go to the establishing of a somewhat weak theory of music and the drama ; but on the whole the article gives the student of Wagner's prose-works more pleasure than anything that came from his pen.

Apart from the æsthetic criticism of Beethoven's work, the main object of the essay is to enlist Schopenhauer's philosophy, together with Shakespeare's plays and Beethoven's music, into the service of Wagner's own theory of musical drama. According to Schopenhauer, whereas the other arts only give us presentations of the "Ideas" of the world, music gives us at first hand the world-Idea itself, "since he who could entirely translate it into abstract concepts would have found withal a philosophy to explain the world itself." Our consciousness is to be regarded as having two sides—the one turned outward to external things, the other turned inward towards one's own self. The plastic arts, dealing with external objects and their relations, never succeed in depicting more than phenomenal appearances ; music alone, taking its origin from the inward-facing side of consciousness, expresses the thing-in-itself, because the character of the thing-in-itself is one with our own Will. Thus "the *individual will*, silenced in the plastic artist through pure beholding, awakes in the musician as the *universal will*, and—above and beyond all power of vision—now recognises itself as such in full self-consciousness" ; the musician's state being similar to the internal ecstasy of the saint. For this reason music is not to be judged by the canons of plastic art ; that is, it is not the function of music merely to generate *pleasure in beautiful forms*. The only category by which it can be judged is that of the sublime. Whereas plastic art merely effects "the [temporary] liberation of the intellect from service to the individual will through our discarding all relations of the object contemplated to that will," music effects this freeing of the will at her *first entry*, "inasmuch as she withdraws us at once from any concern with the relation of things outside us, and—as pure Form set free from Matter—shuts us off from the outer world, as it were, to let us gaze into the inmost essence of ourselves and all things." The peculiar power of Beethoven comes from this quality in his music; it stands to the more external music of other men somewhat in the relation that Religion stands to the Church. And since music does not, like the other arts, portray "the Ideas inherent in the world's phenomena, but is itself an idea of the world—it naturally includes the Drama in itself." Music towers above every other art just as the Drama towers above every form of poetry; and as a drama

"does not depict human characters, but lets them display their immediate selves, so a piece of music gives us in its motives the character of all the world's appearances according to their inmost essence. Not only are the movements, interchange, and evolution of these motives analogous to nothing but the Drama, but a drama representing the [world's] Idea can be understood with perfect clearness through nothing but those moving, evolving, and alternating motives of Music's. We consequently should not go far astray, if we defined Music as man's qualification *à priori* for fashioning the Drama." [1]

If we compare Shakespeare's world of shapes with Beethoven's, we feel that each contains the other. Beethoven's *Coriolanus* overture, for example, sets be-

[1] G. S. ix. 106; Ellis, v. 106. The reader will observe how this bears out the psychological analysis of the preceding chapters. Nothing could more clearly show how Wagner tended to cognise musical phrases merely as symbols of concrete things; which accounts both for his passion for reading these concrete things into certain musical compositions, and for his insensitiveness to much beautiful music that did not happen to stimulate these centres of symbolical associations.

fore us the inmost essence of the drama as vividly as
does Shakespeare's play. The perfect art-form, then,
must take its rise from the point where the spheres of
Shakespeare and Beethoven meet. As in dreams a
stimulus may be transmitted from the brain to the
sense-organs (in the opposite direction to the ordinary
manner of transmission, during waking life, from sense-
organs to brain), thus giving the effect of externality to
what is really internal, so the musician can pass from
the realm of sound to that of light—the shapes that are
born of music thus becoming visible in the form of
dramatic motives and actions. Thus will be effected
the union of Beethoven and Shakespeare in *the most
perfect Drama*. It is not the verses of a text-writer that
can determine Music. "Drama alone can do that;
and not the dramatic poem, but the drama that moves
before our very eyes, the visible counterpart of Music,
where word and speech belong no more to the poet's
thought, but solely to the action."

The peculiar theory of æsthetics here put forward
has already been criticised in another connection.
Here it is only necessary to point out how completely
Wagner's statement of his æsthetics in the *Beethoven*
enforces the argument of the previous chapters, that
so far from the drama—as other men understand it—
being made by him the dominating factor of his art-
work, it is really music that shapes the drama. For
the sake of clearness it may be well to recall the
points, (1) that in arguing for the claims of "the drama,"
Wagner is unconsciously using that word simply to
denote the only kind of drama *he* could conceive—
namely, the musical drama; (2) that for him to tell
us this is the *true* drama is a mere begging of the
question, since there are scores of psychological points
of interest in the literary drama which music cannot
possibly attain to; (3) that Wagner thought the
musical drama the true drama merely because he

was a musician of gigantic power and enormous com-
prehensiveness, all his thought running spontaneously
into the mould of music ; (4) that consequently this
fact has to be allowed for in estimating his theories,
his claim that the musical drama towers above every
other form of art being met by the majority of men
with a simple flat denial ; and (5) that no matter how
much he may have theorised as to the subordination of
poetry and the drama to music in the earlier opera,
everything—from the choice of subject to the treatment
of it—is in his own dramas planned, consciously or
unconsciously, in accordance with the demands of the
musical imagination, and to suit the expressive powers
of music.   It is no rebuttal of this argument to point
out that Wagner states, in so many words, that he is
not setting a text *to* music, but expressing a dramatic
concept *in* music.   The fact remains that there are
innumerable moods, all of deep dramatic interest, that
are quite incapable of a musical setting, and for the
expression of which we must look to the other arts—
the assertion that the musical drama "stands high above
the work of poetry" being thus seen to be an exaggeration.[1]   Moreover, since only the broader and more
generalised emotions can be expressed in music,[2] only a

---

[1] He speaks in the *Destiny of Opera* of the "musically-conceived drama."
It never seems to have occurred to him that a drama conceived in terms of
music was necessarily a drama only in a very small degree, and an opera in a
very large degree.

[2] In the *Destiny of Opera*, again, he argued that Shakespeare's art was so
lifelike because it was a "fixed mimetic improvisation of the highest poetic
work" ; that is, the true dramatic author, "mapping out a plan of action for
the improvising mime," ought to stand "in much the same relation to him as
the author of an operatic text to the musician." Following upon this, he
remarks that Shakespeare "gives us a glimpse into the nature, and more
especially the method, of the genuine dramatist.   Mysterious as we found the
most part of this matter too, yet we saw that the poet was here entirely at one
with the art of the mime ; so that we may now call this mimetic art the life-
dew wherein the poetic aim was to be steeped, to enable it, as in a magic
transformation, to appear as the mirror of life. *And if every action, each
humblest incident of life displays itself, when reproduced by mimicry, in the*

man whose own mental constitution was built up of these emotions could for a moment think that music could supply "the perfect art-work." Wagner was such a man ; but to tell us others in all seriousness that a simple old myth turned to the purposes of third-rate metaphysic and set to music, can satisfy the aspirations of modern men for the drama, would be an insult to our intelligence, did we not perceive the psychological limitations that account for Wagner's theory.

Nor does the case stand much better with the other portions of the essay on *Beethoven.* Even with all the goodwill in the world, one finds it difficult to take Wagner quite seriously in his metaphysical moments, and some of his more enthusiastic admirers would really be doing his memory a service if they laid rather less stress upon his contributions to metaphysic. Even a student of opposite tendencies can still read Kant with respect—though the fallacies seem to stare him in the face at every turn—because Kant's was at any rate an individual and original performance, and because no one can question the dialectical power that is embodied in it ; but when one comes to Kant's greatest error as made worse by Schopenhauer, and then to Schopenhauer's mixed metaphysic,

---

transfiguring light and with the objective effect of a mirror-image . . . in further course we shall have to avow that this mirror-image, again, displays itself in the transfiguration of purest Ideality so soon as it is dipped in the magic spring of music and held up to us as nothing but pure form, so to say, set free from all the realism of Matter" (G. S. ix. 146 ; Ellis, v. 146, 147). It is hardly necessary to point out that this is an absolute *non sequitur.* Wagner is right in saying that where two ideas can be expressed either in music or speech, the musical setting will affect us the more powerfully ; but he forgets that the *range of expression* of music is necessarily much smaller than that of words. Hence music cannot possibly produce a drama so comprehensive as he would wish. To expect, as he did, that in the new art-work "the sublimest inspirations" of Shakespeare and Beethoven "should live with an undying life, as the essence of the world displayed with clearness past all measure in the mirror of the world itself" (G. S. ix. 149 ; Ellis, v. 150) is to exhibit a very imperfect comprehension of other men's notions of what constitutes "the essence of the world."

blind assumption, and verbal blundering, utilised as the basis of Wagner's philosophy of music and the drama —one really feels slightly prejudiced against the *Beethoven* at the outset. There is, alas! nothing very wise in saying that music expresses the essence of things, nor is there anything very original in it. It is a platitude, in no way illuminative, and not even new. Ever since men began to try to give voice to the extraordinary rapture into which music threw them, they have looked upon the art as revealing the very secret of the universe. They did not know what they meant by that very high-sounding phrase, any more than Schopenhauer or Wagner, or any of their perfervid disciples, knew what they meant when they said that music expresses the essence of things ; they merely felt that any phrase but the biggest of all was quite incompetent to do justice to the power of sound. The phrase, or the mood that gives birth to the phrase, is as old as Socrates at any rate : and Schopenhauer and Wagner simply take their place with Schelling, with Carrière, with Lamennais, with Vischer, and with every other æsthetician who has talked of music revealing a secret that is only partially made known to us by the world of concrete objects. The phrase, I repeat, is sonorous, but it is meaningless ; however charming it may be in the mouth of a poet, the philosopher is not much assisted by it in his quest for a true philosophy of music. In any case, no matter what justness of idea a man may sometimes attain to even when dealing with merely platitudinous phrases, very little can be expected from a philosophy such as that of Schopenhauer, with its sometimes grotesque nonsense about the Idea, its unscientific handling of Time and Space, its arbitrary division of our consciousness into two sides—"in part a consciousness of *one's own self*, which is the will ; in part a consciousness of *other things*, and chiefly then a *visual* knowledge of the outer world, the apprehension of objects "—and its always primitive jargon about the will, a relic from the days of prescientific psychology. Schopenhauer is, perhaps, the most readable of all German philosophers, a fact that has probably gained him a greater vogue than the intrinsic merit of his work would have done ; but in the history of philosophy he is certainly a negligeable quantity.[1]

Yet, just as Wagner himself occasionally arrives at a truth in a most extraordinary and roundabout way of his own, so there is in Schopenhauer's theory something that really does bear upon the philosophy of music, though not exactly in the way he intended. To make clear the following criticism upon his theory and upon Wagner's use of it, it will be as well to lay before the reader the briefest possible statement of that theory in Wagner's own words :—

"It was Schopenhauer who first defined the position of music among the fine arts with philosophic clearness, ascribing to it a totally different nature from that of either plastic or poetic art. He starts from wonder at Music's speaking a language immediately intelligible by every one, since it needs no whit of intermediation through abstract concepts (*Begriffe*) ; which completely distinguishes it from Poetry, in the first place, whose sole material consists of concepts, employed by it to visualise the *Idea*. For according to this philosopher's so luminous definition, it is the Ideas of the world and of its essential phenomena, in the sense of Plato, that constitute the 'object' of the fine arts ; whereas, however, the poet interprets these Ideas to the visual consciousness (*dem anschauenden*

---

[1] Professor Sully, in his undeservedly neglected book *On Pessimism*, easily disposes of Schopenhauer by the simple process of making him define his terms. Professor William Wallace in his *Life of Schopenhauer* (pp. 122, 123) admits that "the absolute antithesis which he insists upon between will and intellect can hardly be maintained." But on these terms Schopenhauer's whole doctrine must go by the board. The distinction between will and intellect is the essence of his theory.

Bewusstsein) through an employment of strictly rationalistic concepts in a manner quite peculiar to his art, Schopenhauer believes he must recognise *in Music itself an Idea of the world,* since he who could entirely translate it into abstract concepts would have found withal a philosophy to explain the world itself.[1] . . . In making use of this material supplied us by the philosopher, I fancy I shall do best to begin with a remark in which Schopenhauer declines to accept the Idea derived from a knowledge of 'relations' as the essence of the Thing-in-itself, but regards it merely as expressing the objective character of things, and therefore as still concerned with their phenomenal appearance. 'And we should not understand this character itself'—so Schopenhauer goes on to say—'were not the inner essence of things confessed to us elsewhere, dimly at least and in our feeling. For that essence cannot be gathered from the Ideas, nor understood through any mere *objective* knowledge; wherefore it would ever remain a mystery had we not access to it from quite another side. Only inasmuch as every observer is an Individual withal, and thereby part of Nature, stands there open to him in his own self-consciousness the adit to Nature's innermost; and there forthwith, and most immediately, it makes itself known to him as *Will!*' If we couple with this what Schopenhauer postulates as the condition for entry of an Idea into our consciousness—namely, a temporary preponderance of intellect over will, or, to put it physiologically, a strong excitation of the sensory faculty of the brain without the smallest excitation of the passions or desires, we have only further to pay close heed to the elucidation which directly follows it—namely, that our consciousness has two sides: in part it is a consciousness *of one's own self*, which is the Will; in part a consciousness *of other things*, and chiefly then a *visual* knowledge of the outer

---

[1] I need hardly point out that this sentence is quite meaningless. It looks like an argument, but is really pure assertion. The "since," for example, has no value whatever. All that comes after "since" is simply a repetition, in another form, of what goes before it; and there is only the appearance of reasoning. To say that Music is an Idea of the world *because* if translated into concepts it would provide a philosophy of the world, is simply to say that Music is an Idea of the world because it is. Like the bulk of Schopenhauer's philosophising, the sentence is simply a piece of pompous dogmatism, and without any meaning at that.

world, the apprehension of objects. 'The more the one side of the aggregate consciousness comes to the front, the more does the other retreat.' After well weighing these extracts from Schopenhauer's principal work, it must be obvious to us that musical conception, as it has nothing in common with the seizure of an Idea (for the latter is absolutely bound to physical perception of the world), can have its origin nowhere but upon that side of consciousness which Schopenhauer defines as facing inwards. . . . If this consciousness, however, is the consciousness of one's own self—*i.e.* of the Will, we must take it that its repression is indispensable, indeed, for purity of the outward-facing consciousness, but that the nature of the Thing-in-itself—inconceivable by that physical [or visual] mode of knowledge—would only be revealed to this inward-facing consciousness when it had attained the faculty of seeing within as clearly as that other side of consciousness is able in its seizure of Ideas to see without." [1]

Wagner then proceeds to correlate with this Schopenhauer's dream-theory, according to which,

"as the world of dreams can only come to vision through a special operation of the brain, so music enters our consciousness through a kindred operation."

Into the fallacies of Schopenhauer's metaphysical theory I do not propose to enter in detail. It is enough to point out that the talk about "The Thing-in-itself" and "The inner Essence of Things" is merely verbal wandering; that it is an error to divide consciousness into an inner and an outer; and that Wagner goes astray in separating musical conception from the objective world, because, forsooth, sound is not perceived by sight. Consciousness is one and homogeneous, and the philosopher who bases an æsthetic theory upon an arbitrary division into inner and outer is not to be seriously argued with at this

[1] G. S. ix. 66–68 ; Ellis, v. 65–67.

time of day.[1] But what I chiefly desire to call attention to is the fact that whatever truth there is in
the Schopenhauer-Wagner theory can be accounted
for on simpler and less metaphysical lines than theirs ;
and that along with this explanation goes the further
explanation of what some people call the paradox of
Beethoven—the paradox consisting in the union of
the highest genius and the utmost artistic conscien-
tiousness with so strange an incapacity for ordinary
mundane life.

To begin with, Wagner is right in calling attention to the facts of the clairvoyant condition of the
musician's brain in the act of composition, and the
paralysis of vision that comes upon us when we are
listening to music that affects us profoundly. The
two facts are correlated, and have really the same
explanation ; not a metaphysical explanation, however,
but a physiological one. There is no need to talk
sonorous nonsense about the essence of things, or
about the inner and the outer consciousness. The
explanation of the fact that during the performance
of fine music we fail to see many things that would
obtrude themselves upon our attention at other times
—such as the antics of the conductor and of the
instrumentalists—is that consciousness is momentarily
abstracted from the visual organs. It is not the eye that
sees but the brain—as any one can understand who has

[1] When this argument appeared in the *Musician*, a critic called me to book
for this sentence, and quoted Professor Croom Robertson to the effect that
there is such a thing as outer consciousness—as when we look at a scene—
and such a thing as inner consciousness—as when we close our eyes and
imagine the scene. No one disputes *that ;* and it was hardly necessary to
call up the ghost of Croom Robertson to tell us so self-evident a truth.
My point is not that there is no distinction of this kind between inner and
outer consciousness, but that all our "inner" mental pictures are derived
from "outer" ones—as, indeed, is apparent from the very passage cited by
my critic. To support the theories of Wagner and Schopenhauer, one has
to believe that the inner mental life is something distinct, in nature and in
origin, from the outer ; which position, I repeat, is not to be seriously argued
against.

looked at his watch and not noticed the time; and if anything occurs to divert the energies of the correlated brain-centres, impressions are not registered by the peripheral sense-organs. Any strong mental disturbance will suffice to effect this; the callousness of martyrs or of hypnotised persons to pain, indeed, being due to the consciousness being wholly occupied in other directions, so that no message can pass between a brain-centre and a particular limb. Without drawing at all upon any metaphysical theory, then, it is easy to understand the temporary paralysis that falls upon our visual organs during the performance of great music.[1]

A somewhat similar explanation will apply to the other fact, that during composition the musician is in a state similar to that of the clairvoyant, with the vision blind to the outer world, but with an intense life surging and palpitating within the brain. To begin with, neither Wagner nor Schopenhauer need have assumed a "dream-organ" for the production of dreams.

"As dreams must have brought to every one's experience," writes Wagner, "besides the world envisaged by the functions of the waking brain there dwells a second, distinct as is itself, no less a world displayed to vision; since this second world can in no case be an object lying outside us, it therefore must be brought to our cognisance by an *inward* function of the brain; and this form of the brain's perception Schopenhauer here calls the dream-organ."

This is merely obscuring the case quite needlessly. There is no concept in the brain during sleep that has not been generated therein during previous waking hours, by contact with the external world; and the

---

[1] Sensuous pleasure, especially if rhythmical in character, has always this tendency to close up the outward-turned faculties. The sending of a baby to sleep by the rocking of a cradle, and the closing of the eyes in a cat or dog when it is stroked, are familiar examples.

brain, being almost entirely an automatic organ, can produce at any moment pictures of its past experience in response to a stimulus. Here particularly Wagner goes astray in supposing that

"as the dream-organ cannot be roused into action by outer impressions, against which the brain is now fast locked, this must take place through happenings in the inner organism that our waking consciousness merely feels as vague sensations."

Any one's experience will tell him that the "dream-organ" *can* be roused into action by outer impressions; for a noise, a light, a touch, will be sufficient to start a dream in the sleeper's brain. And the so-called "inner" impressions are really one in nature with the "outer" impressions, for all are external to the brain itself. A disturbance of the digestive organs, for example, or an accelerated or retarded beat of the heart, may stimulate the brain to dreams—the impression in this case being as really "external" to the brain as a sound in the ear or a touch on the hand. Wagner and Schopenhauer, in fact, are so painfully anxious to drag in the theory that the "inner" life of man answers to the "inner" life of nature—whatever that piece of vague metaphysic may mean—that they quite unnecessarily exaggerate the significance of one of the commonest of phenomena. The object of the exaggeration appears in the next sentence:

"But it is this inner life through which we are directly allied with the whole of Nature, and thus are brought into a relation with the essence of things that eludes the forms of outer knowledge, Time and Space. . . ." [1]

---

[1] This sensation of being "allied with the whole of Nature" is explicable by the fact that music deals with emotion in its vaguest and most generalised form. It may be somewhat fanciful, but I have always thought it stands in somewhat the same relation to the other arts as a "law of Nature" stands to science. Mr. Karl Pearson puts it that what we call a law of nature is just a conceptual symbol of things, a kind of shorthand summary of a great

I repeat that this is simply meaningless; nothing is easier than to philosophise in this inexpensive manner, the jungle of metaphysic being indeed malodorous with these dead flowers of rhetoric. One must just sweep all such vague platitudes aside, and come down to the fundamental fact that in the dreamer, the clairvoyant, and the somnambulist, the mental life seems for the moment to be greatly increased both in power and in liberty, many of the fetters of waking life being struck away, and the spirit apparently endowed with wings.

Now this plainly comes from the fact that in the dream or clairvoyant condition the sense-organs that open out upon the world are momentarily sealed up, thus allowing freer play to the synthetising inner centres of the brain. The true state of the case can be most easily seen by looking at some of the phenomena of hypnotism. The rationale of hypnotism seems to be that while certain centres of the brain are momentarily laid to sleep, other centres are stimulated into abnormal activity; the energy liberated from the former probably overflowing into the latter. Thus many men become better actors in the hypnotic state than they could possibly be in the waking state; a man who is told he is the great Napoleon, for instance, going through a whole series of correlated movements in a manner that would be beyond him in his normal condition.[1] Evidently the abstraction of consciousness from certain centres gives temporarily an added energy to the others; and further, no inhibiting messages coming from the outside organs, the whole of the brain is given up to the idea of the moment. This accounts for all the cases in which the brain, in the hypnotic or somnambulistic conditions, performs prodi-

many existences and impressions (see his *Grammar of Science*); hence its universality. We may similarly regard music as the rapid summary of many emotions, in which the more individual features of our emotional life are passed over, and the more fundamental features are generalised.

[1] See Moll, *Hypnotism*, for examples of this kind.

gies that would be impossible to it in the waking state[1]—
as when a mathematician solves in his sleep a problem
that had baffled him when awake, or a somnambulist
walks in safety over a narrow ledge. We have only to
apply this to the case of the musician to see that the
same explanation holds there also. The composer sinks
into the clairvoyant condition, not because while in
that condition his inner life becomes "one with the
essence of things," but because while in that condition
his whole brain, undistracted by external impressions,
can work harmoniously in the one direction upon
the one material. All artists exhibit the same phenomenon, the musician being simply the extreme of all
the other cases. The practical, active man is one
whose brain is instantaneously alive to every external
impression: his dreaming, imaginative, artistic powers
being therefore at a minimum. The opposite order
of mind is that of the artist, wherein external facts
have not the same value, and which, by its faculty
of self-hypnotisation, can make all the cerebral forces
co-operate towards the one imaginative end. Among
prose-writers the same antithesis may be observed;
there standing at one side a Spencer, with his quick
mental readjustments following upon every stimulus,
and at the other side an Amiel, whose brain was in
a chronic hypnosis, and in whom, consequently, while
the imaginative life was luxuriant and the imaginative
vision at times superb, the faculty of will, which is
pre-eminently concerned with the external world, was
utterly paralysed.

A recourse to the ordinary phenomena of physiology
and psychology suffices, then, to explain the "clairvoyant" state of the musician without indulging in
empty verbalising about "the essence of things." And
the very fact that artists are so frequently unfit for the

[1] See a collection of phenomena of this kind in J. A. Symond's *Miscellanies*
(1871), and Dr. Andrew Wilson's *Life and Sense*.

daily commerce of life is an added proof of the fact
that their brain runs along a hypnotic groove, insulated
from the real facts of the world. They can only pay
for their strength in one direction, indeed, by lacking
strength in another. In Wagner himself, for example,
while the musical faculty was at least equal to anything the human brain has ever contained, the faculty
for cool, persistent, impartial thought was extremely
meagre. And in the case of Beethoven, so far from
our being surprised that, as Wagner says, his mind
on any other subject than music was of the ordinary
bourgeois order, there would have been reason for
surprise had the case been different. The hypnotic
faculty for artistic dreaming and the logical faculty for
clear cut-and-thrust comprehension of the world can,
from the very nature of things, be only in the very
rarest cases united in the same organism.[1] So that
poor Beethoven's failure as an ordinary social being
was really of service to him as an artist. That he was
so brusque and so lacking in tact in his relations with
men, came from the circumstance that his clairvoyant
brain did not properly respond, as other men's brains
have to do, to the innumerable stimuli of the outer
world. Thereby he had so much more mental energy
to devote to his imaginative work ; and his music
consequently became richer and deeper. Great art
comes from great suffering ; and it may well be that
the unreasoning anger of Beethoven at the most trivial
things may have generated in his organism such storms
of passion and despair as come to other men through
the real blows of fortune. His art was fed in this way
as other men's art might be by sterner troubles.
And then, when the real troubles came, with the grim,
pathetic mockery of that deafness, and the anguish
caused him by the unworthy nephew, his soul had
surely the deepest well of sorrow to draw upon.

[1] See the final chapter of the present volume.

Everything threw him inward upon himself, making the inner work of the brain so much the easier from the fact that the outer universe made so little demand upon it. If the President of the Immortals had wished to torture that divine soul into the noblest expression that art had ever witnessed, he could not have chosen a surer method than this of depriving it of all the qualities that help to make the lives of average men comfortable and full of ease.

II

The prose-works that immediately follow the *Beethoven* are not of very great interest, either in themselves or for the aid to the study of Wagner. The exceedingly stupid pseudo-satire *A Capitulation* scarcely deserves mention, and should not be reprinted by admirers of Wagner; not because it reflects on the musician's character, but because it reflects on his intelligence—which is a far more serious matter.[1] On the other hand, such writings as *The Destiny of Opera*, *Actors and Singers*, *Letter to an Actor*, and *A Glance at the German Operatic Stage of To-day*, do not call for special discussion in a volume like the present. We see running through them all Wagner's strong predilection for his own art, and his strange belief that humanity was somehow or other to find redemption in opera. His insusceptibility to other forms of art, and his incompetence to see the real relation of these to actual life, are shown in his remark that though the opera is accountable for the downfall of the theatre, " yet . . . by it alone can our theatre be raised again." The dramatic stage has undergone no deterioration through the follies of opera, except in so far as dramatic genius

[1] Mr. Ellis, in the note prefixed to his translation of the dreadful thing, opines that it "reminds one very forcibly of the grim humour of Aristophanes." It does—in the same degree as a Christy Minstrel interlocutor reminds us of Congreve.

has been unable to get a hearing from a public too
much inclined to cheap music; while the modern
revival of the stage under Ibsen and the realists owes
about as much to opera, or even to the Wagnerian
music-drama, as it does to the man in the moon.
Wagner of course would say that Ibsen's was not real
dramatic art—that he shows man under "State-historical
conditions" instead of in the guise of the purely-human;
but this kind of æsthetic is not very impressive.   Moreover, whenever Wagner discusses his own theory of the
drama we see the truth of the facts already so much
insisted on in the preceding chapters, that his notion
of drama corresponded to what we would call merely
the musical drama ; that instead of making the drama
determine the music, as he thought, he was really
allowing music to determine the drama; and that
although he was so constituted as to see in music-
drama a sufficient embodiment of all the arts, other
men regard it simply as one art among the rest.   He
himself, arguing for a certain phase of his own theory,
admits in one place that

"there is a side of the world, and a side that concerns us most
seriously, whose terrible lessons can be brought home to our
minds on none but a field of observation where music has to
hold her tongue." [1]

That is true in a far larger sense than Wagner ever
thought ; and not only would all other men regard
painting and sculpture, as well as poetry, as satisfying
a thousand needs which music or poetry and music
cannot minister to, but they would object to Wagner's
view that in opera [2] you can get a union of "the
Beethovenian music and the Shakespearian drama." He
would hold that so much of the Shakespearian mode

[1] *The Destiny of Opera*, G. S. ix. 153; Ellis, v. 153.
[2] It may be necessary for me to say that in this, as in a number of other
cases, I include under the term "opera" Wagner's own work.

of conception as was incompatible with the spirit of Beethoven's music was somewhat inessential ; other people are inclined to tell him that if he really thought this he may have known a great deal about Beethoven, but really knew very little about Shakespeare or the drama in general. At a later date he wrote that by the efforts of the great German musicians

"we have arrived at uniting Music so completely with the Drama's action that this very marriage enables the action itself to gain that ideal freedom—*i.e.* release from all necessity of appealing to abstract reflection—which our great poets sought on many a road, to fall at last a-pondering on the selfsame possibility of attaining it through Music."[1]

What Wagner conceives as "abstract reflection" is the very essence of other men's appreciation of poetry ; and that absurdly depreciatory term simply proves how little he knew of other modes of æsthetic appreciation than his own. When, in the same paper, he spoke of reading

"in guise of a bare dramatic poem a work *that owes its origin to nothing but the feasibility of carrying it out completely in Music,*"

he was expressing the true facts of the case, and throwing a light on the limitations of opera by which his followers, if not himself, might have profited. He believed he

"might submit it as a play in dialogue to the same judgment we are wont to invoke with a piece indited for the Spoken Play."

Technically he is right ; that is, in his poem, instead of there being the conventional operatic divisions of aria, recitative, duet, and so forth, the dialogue runs continuously through it as in the spoken drama ; but if he imagined that this technical similarity between

[1] *Prologue to a Reading of the " Götterdämmerung" before a Select Audience in Berlin;* G. S. ix. 309 ; Ellis, v. 305, 306.

the poetical and the musical drama brought his poem upon anything like the same psychological level as the former, he was grievously deluded.

III

The still later prose-works have an interest of their own quite independent of their actual contents ; they exhibit the decadence that from this time until his death was going on in Wagner's purely intellectual faculties—a decadence that was correlative with an increased sensitiveness upon the side of music pure and simple. Weak as are the philosophical writings of his earliest period, those of his last years are decidedly weaker ; the man was plainly losing even the little grasp he ever had upon the plain facts of the world and their logical connection, while at the same time his purely intellectual concepts were dissolving into emotion. His system was slowly settling into the precise pathological form necessary for the writing of *Parsifal;* his humanitarian impulses were as strong as ever, but his outlook upon the world and his actual proposals for reform were becoming more and more phantasmal, the exhaustion of his nervous tissue that accounts for this fact accounting also for the correlative strengthening of the artistic expression of these humanitarian feelings. Throughout all his prose-work there runs a strong vein of sympathy with suffering ; in his last epoch this takes a less militant, a more submissive form, culminating in the " pity " that is so exquisitely expressed in *Parsifal.*

It was only to be expected that as his life advanced and his brain became more rigid, he should exhibit all the intellectual vices and all the limitations of his earlier years in a more pronounced form. Thus while, as we shall presently see, his latest writings on his own form of opera are among the most interesting things that ever came from his pen, full of the clearest perceptions of what his own system was and what it exacted of the musician, his outlook upon the other arts was even more astonishingly restricted than it had been at the beginning of his career. Setting out, in *Religion and Art* (1880), with the most *à priori* theories as to the dependence of art upon religion, he can see nothing but degeneration in the history of painting since the time when, under the great Italians, the Christian religion was the source of the artist's inspiration.

"Now," he writes, "in respect of plastic art it is palpable that its ideally creative force diminished in exact proportion as it withdrew from contact with religion. Betwixt those sublimest revelations of religious art, in the godlike birth of the Redeemer and the last fulfilment of the work of the Judge of the world, the saddest of all pictures, that of the Saviour suffering on the cross, had likewise attained to its height of perfection ; and this remained the archetype of the countless representations of martyred saints, their agonies illumined by the bliss of transport. Here the portrayal of bodily pain, with the instruments of torture and their wielders, already led the artists down to the common actual world, whose types of human wickedness and cruelty surrounded them beyond escape. And then came 'Characteristique,' with its multiple attraction for the artist ; the consummate 'portrait' of even the vulgarest criminal, such as might be found among the temporal and spiritual princes of that remarkable time, became the painter's most rewarding task ; as, on the other hand, he had early enough taken his motives for the Beautiful from the physical charms of the women in his voluptuous surroundings." [1]

One can understand a man, for purely religious reasons, ranking religious art very high ; but when he regards as mere degeneration the passage from the conventional types of portraiture in Italian religious paintings to the vitalised study of human character in individual

[1] *Religion and Art*, G. S. ix. 220; Ellis, vi. 221, 222.

portraits, it becomes evident that he can have very little appreciation and very little knowledge of the art he is discussing.

"Suffice it to say," continues Wagner, "that that art which was destined to reach its apogee in its affinity with religion, completely severing itself from this communion—as no one can deny—has fallen into utter ruin."

The statement that the plastic arts have fallen into utter ruin must read very curiously to those who recall the wonderful beauty of so much modern sculpture, and reflect that painting is the art that seems to have the greatest future before it, inasmuch as it is really more virgin soil than any of the other arts ; there being to-day a thousand fresh problems of form and colour awaiting their artistic solution. It is amusing, too, to reflect that the Münich in which Wagner hoped to found a music-school for the study of the musical drama as *the* art of life,[1] is now the home of a school of young artists who are occupied with problems of how to make their art vital and true, and who work with an energy and an intelligent seriousness that are extremely rare among contemporary musicians. The plain truth is that Wagner knew nothing of painting, and was as incompetent to pass an opinion upon that as upon so many other questions. In one's first moment of irritation at these wild and foolish generalisations of his, one is tempted to call them mere literary impertinences. It is only when we try to regard the man as a whole that we see their dependence upon the very qualities of brain that make him so titanic in other respects. He believed he was preaching a gospel of pressing importance to men ; and the very strength of his innate prepossessions hindered him from seeing how

[1] See his paper on *A Music-School for Münich;* G. S. viii. ; Ellis, iv.

grotesque are the majority of his views upon art and life.

His power of calm thinking, never very great, was indeed becoming weaker and weaker as he advanced in years. His brain was filled with a medley of ill-assorted and half-digested ideas; any theory that seemed to him to help out his own peculiar notions was something to be written about in his own distorted way; while his excursions into metaphysics sometimes became positively ludicrous. In *The Public in Time and Space*, for example, where he is arguing that while the birth of great minds is governed by mysterious, hidden laws, they are tragically dependent during life upon the laws of time and place, we get such a gem as the following :—

> "For us, our first concern must be to trace the tragedy of that relation" [*i.e.* the relation of genius to its surroundings] "to the individual's subjection to the rules of time and place; whereby we may find those two factors assuming so strong a semblance of reality as almost to upset the 'Criticism of Pure Reason,' which ascribes to Time and Space no existence but in our brain."[1]

The unconscious humour of this gem of metaphysic is something too delightful for words; one remembers nothing that can even approach it except the passage on Moses in Berkeley's *Principles of Human Knowledge*. Verily, what little philosophical capacity Wagner ever had was fast becoming exhausted when he could seriously pen such sentences as these. The failure of the intelligence upon the purely intellectual side may be seen again in any of the later writings that concern themselves with positive and practical matters. He was very strong on vegetarianism at this time, and therefore has no difficulty in attributing the decline of modern nations to their having adopted a flesh diet. He is not very clear as to what constitutes a decline of nations,

[1] G. S. x. 92; Ellis, vi. 86. See also pp. 91, 92.

nor as to the beneficent results of vegetarian and maleficent results of animal food ; but he is quite positive, for all that, that the modern world *is* in a state of decline, and that flesh food is the main cause of the degeneration.   Correlative with this failure of his faculties in the spheres of calm thought and accurate knowledge, was his habit of prolix declamation against everybody and everything associated with pursuits that were distasteful to him.   Thus we have him telling us that

"the world soon managed to abolish sin entirely, and believers now look for redemption from evil to Physics and Chemistry."

And again—

" It certainly may be right to charge this purblind dulness of our public spirit to a vitiation of our blood—not only by departure from the natural food of man, but above all by the tainting of the hero-blood of noblest races with that of former cannibals now trained to be the business-agents of society "

—and much more vapid nonsense of the sort. Throughout all the work of this epoch, to even a greater extent than in the earlier work, there run that irritating assumption of knowledge and that fatal tendency to empty philosophising that have earned for him in certain quarters the reputation of a great thinker. In *Hero-dom and Christianity*, for example, he quotes with admiration a perfect specimen of Schopenhauer's most hopeless apriorism, and proceeds to impress it into the service of his own theories.

"From what blood, then," he writes, "could the ever more consciously suffering genius of mankind bring forth a saviour, seeing that the blood of the white race was manifestly paling and congealing?—For the origin of natural Man our Schopenhauer propounds an hypothesis of well-nigh convincing power: going back to the physical law [Mariotti's] of increase of force under compression, he explains the unusual frequency of births of twins after abnormal periods of mortality as if the vital force were doubling its exertions under pressure of a pestilence that threatened to exterminate the species; which leads him to the theory that the procreative force in a given type of animals, threatened with extinction by opposing forces through some inherent defect in its organism, may have become so abnormally augmented in one mated pair that not merely does a more highly organised individual issue from the mother's womb, but in that individual a quite new *species*. The blood in the Redeemer's veins might thus have flowed, as divine sublimate of the species itself, from the redemptive Will's supreme endeavour to save mankind at death-throes in its noblest races." [1]

There is no limit to the possibilities of nonsense of this kind, inasmuch as the writer, dealing as he is in pure speculation, cannot be brought up by any conflict with facts. There is a certain air of factitious plausibility about theories of this sort; yet they concern us no more, and are no more interesting to us, than what Huxley used to call "lunar politics." Let it not be thought that I am merely trying to discredit Wagner as a thinker by dragging into light a few of the more absurd of his utterances. His works are full of fatuities of this kind; and the point I am urging is that they prove him quite incapable of rational philosophising. No man with any sense of reality or any gift of reasoning could seriously think there was anything in these half-digested scraps of second-hand knowledge, these random flashes of crude intuition, these misty theories of life and art that evade all the problems of the one and do but touch the fringe of the other.

Yet, as I have said, while his brain was thus failing in its grasp of concrete issues, the purely imaginative life continued almost unimpaired. *Parsifal*, of course, exhibits no falling off either in technical power or artistic beauty; while the treatises *On Poetry and Composition*, *On Operatic Poetry and Composition*, and

---

[1] G. S. x. 282; Ellis, vi. 282. The passages to which Wagner is referring occur in Schopenhauer's *Zur Philosophie und Wissenschaft der Natur*, sec. 91 in *Parerga und Paralipomena*, ii. 166–170.

On the Application of Music to the Drama, are extremely
lucid and thoughtful.   Perhaps the last-named work is
the most valuable of the three, by reason of the fact
that Wagner is there dealing with a problem peculiarly
his own.   He points out how Beethoven's dramatic
writing was vitiated by his adherence to symphonic
form ; how, for example, after

"feeling impelled to introduce an actual stage-effect in the
middle of his *Leonora* overture, he still repeated the first
section of the tone-piece, with the customary change of key,
exactly as in a symphonic movement — heedless that the
dramatic excitement of the middle section, reserved for thematic
working-out, had already led us to expect the *dénouement.*"

After Beethoven, according to Wagner's well-known
theory, absolute music degenerated into mere note-
spinning ; while the correlative rise of programme-
music was an indication that composers were aiming,
in a tentative way, at giving dramatic reality to music.
Of this order were Berlioz and Liszt, whose error lay
in supposing that the dramatic picture they desired to
portray could be achieved by means of music alone.
They, however, have helped to reveal to us the real
problem of the application of music to the drama—
that is, to a definite presentation of human life and
action.   One law of formal technique is of prime
importance ; there must be the same organic unity of
structure in the musical drama as in the symphony.
This, however, cannot be attained in the former by
the mere importation of the rules of the latter ; the
unity of dramatic form is only to be attained by the
music spreading itself over the whole drama in one
continuous living tissue, by means of

"root-themes pervading all the drama, themes which contrast,
complete, re-shape, divorce and intertwine with one another as
in the symphonic movement ; only that here the needs of the

dramatic action dictate the laws of parting and combining, which were there originally borrowed from the motions of the dance."

He then proceeds to show that given this fundamental unity of musical conception, the music of the drama must no longer aim at effect for its own sake, but must be guided in every one of its developments by the necessities of the dramatic action. There is to be no turn of melody, no effect of harmony or instrumentation, employed simply to please the ear as it would in a symphonic composition; each effect is to be merely the outward and visible sign of a change in the thoughts of the characters or in the aspect of their surroundings. Thus the young men who brought Wagner their operatic scores and showed him truly "Wagnerian effects," received nothing but well-deserved censure. How could these "effects for effect's sake" please him, who had always shown the utmost restraint in his own scores?

"In the instrumental introduction to *Rheingold*, for instance," he writes, "it was impossible for me to quit the fundamental note, simply because I had no reason for changing it;[1] a great part of the not unanimated scene that follows for the Rhine-daughters and Alberich would only permit of modulation to keys the very nearest of kin, as Passion here is still in the most primitive *naïveté* of its expression."

I have already remarked that the imaginative mood that prompted Wagner's musical conceptions must have been very different in character from the moods of other composers, especially of those whose cast of imagination was purely symphonic. We can see this by comparing the orchestral preludes to some of Wagner's scenes with the overtures of other men;

[1] The reader will remember that the prelude to the *Rheingold* is built upon E flat, the one chord being simply repeated, in slightly different forms, through 135 bars.

while the latter are for the most part "self-justified successions of tones," appealing to the purely musical faculty, the former appeal to a more complex and less homogeneous faculty, and are justified only in terms of some concrete picture which they are intended to suggest. Wagner himself indicates this, pointing out how, for example, the simple cry with which the Rhine-daughters greet the gold is put through a hundred metamorphoses in the course of the drama, each being the tonal correlative of a new shade of psychological significance.

"One would have to follow this uncommonly simple theme," he writes,—"recurring in manifold alliance with almost every other motive of the Drama's widespread movement—through all the changes it receives from the diverse character of its resummoning, to see what type of variations the Drama can engender; and how completely the character of these variations departs from that of those figured, rhythmic, or harmonic alterations of a theme which our masters ranged in immediate sequence to build up pictures of an often intoxicatingly kaleidoscopic effect. . . . But neither a mere play of counterpoint, nor the most fantastic art of figuration and most inventive harmonising, either could or should transform a theme so characteristically, and present it with such manifold and entirely changed expression —yet leaving it always recognisable—as true dramatic art can do quite naturally.   Hardly anything could afford a plainer proof of this, than a pursuit of that simple motive of the Rhine-daughters through all the changing passions of the four-part drama down to Hagen's watch-song in the 1st Act of the *Götterdämmerung*, where it certainly takes on a form which—to me at least—makes it inconceivable as theme of a symphonic movement, albeit it still is governed by the laws of harmony and thematism, though purely in their application to the Drama.   To attempt to apply the results of such a method to the symphony, however, must lead to the latter's utter ruin; for here would appear as a far-fetched effect what follows there from well-found motives."[1]

[1] G. S. x. 189, 190; Ellis, vi. 187, 188.

This is quite true; the only pity is that the quality of mind that made Wagner so great in his own department, and gave him such clearness of insight into his own manner of working, should have also made him partially blind to the psychological processes of musicians of a different type. I have already sought to prove that he was curiously insusceptible to a great deal of musical pleasure to which other people are acutely sensitive, the reason being that he was only moved by music that either contained a dramatic motive, like his own work, or suggested a dramatic motive to him like some of the later works of Beethoven.[1] His mind was quite *sui generis;* and in view of the fact that so many of his young followers thought to write like him by merely using some of his effects, it is refreshing to note that he himself saw very clearly the danger of writing music like his where it was not plainly called forth by a dramatic need. In his earlier years he had seen, though perhaps not quite so comprehensively as he might have done, the evil of importing the symphonic modes of procedure into opera. He now points out the equal folly of putting into the symphony a kind of music that is only suited to the drama, illustrating his point by the music given to Elsa upon her entrance in the 1st Act of *Lohengrin*, where the modulation that is a psychological revelation when viewed in concert with the living motions and gestures of the character, would be merely bewildering if it

---

[1] Readers of his prose-works will recall the judgments he pronounced upon musicians; others will be found in Mr. Dannreuther's article in Grove's Dictionary. He assuredly had a small appreciation of certain great composers, while on the other hand he ranked Liszt higher than the majority of people would feel inclined to do. He once "spoke to Johann Svendsen very unfavourably of Schumann; when closely pressed, he confessed that he was not at all well acquainted with Schumann's greater works." (See Mr. Arthur Friedheim's article on "Past and Present," in the *Musician*, November 3, 1897.) The explanation probably is that Schumann's order of imagination being congenitally antipathetic to him, he would never go back to the music in order to correct his first impressions.

occurred in the slow movement of a symphony. All through this paper *On the Application of Music to the Drama*, indeed, there is the most admirable sense of the difference between his own ideals and those of other men. The only pity is that he did not, all through his life, give a little more time to writing on a subject in which he was thoroughly at home, and a little less to recording opinions that only showed how defective he was in certain æsthetic nerves that other men prize highly.

CHAPTER X

PARSIFAL

IN the preceding chapter we have seen that while
Wagner's purely artistic gift was quite unimpaired
even to the last, his brain was certainly failing
upon the intellectual side—his thought, which was
always at the mercy of his sensations and emotions,
now being simply dissolved in feeling. This diagnosis
is important both for the matter and the manner of
Parsifal—for the ethical motive he strove to incorporate in that drama, and for the music he wrote
for it. He was always a man of ardent sympathy,
but with little sense of the practical reality of things,
and in his later years the decay of his practical sense,
as exhibited in his last prose-works, was accompanied
by an increasing warmth of his sympathetic nature.
In this connection his *Open Letter* [on Vivisection] *to
Herr Ernst von Weber* has an interest to which its
own arguments do not entitle it. It may easily be
guessed what is Wagner's treatment of so complex
a subject as this : one is used to the outcry against
vivisection from well-meaning men whose affection
for domestic animals solves, for them, the whole problem. Wagner's Letter is of this order ; there is not
the slightest sense of the complexity of the question
as a whole, nor of the many points that the vivi-
sectionist can urge against his opponent ; there is
nothing but the usual stupid sneers at men of science,
and an impassioned expression of sympathy with
animals. Yet in spite of all its defects and all its
banalities, one cannot help feeling impressed by

Wagner's Letter. It moves us as the spectacle of a man labouring under strong and sincere emotion always will move us. The tremor of the man is so intense as he speaks of our duties towards the dumb world of animals, that we vibrate emotionally with him even while we are intellectually conscious of the flaws in his argument. It is worth noting that while every concrete subject which Wagner touches at this epoch —except that of his own music—is treated with the utmost dulness and with hopelessly unilluminative results, he rarely fails to impress and to move us when he plays simply upon our feelings. We may be intellectually out of sympathy with him ; but he has only to use his sensitive organism as an emotional instrument, and he can play upon it in a way that holds us for the moment against our better judgment.

It is herein that lies whatever strength the Letter on Vivisection has for non-partisan minds ; the warm humanitarian emotion of the man impresses us. We see him, as we read on through these closing works, becoming ever more and more sensitive to the suffering of living things, and ever more inclined to base all morals upon pity. Suffering is lauded because pity is its outcome. Guided by Schopenhauer, he sees in pity the final stage of a great cosmic struggle ; and though the philosophising is not remarkably clear or very noteworthy, one catches the vibration of the sensitive artist's soul through it.

"To feel that horror at himself so needful for his last redemption," he writes in *Religion and Art*, "this Man was qualified by just that knowledge, to wit the recognition of himself in every manifestment of the one great Will; and the guide to evolution of this faculty was given him by Suffering, since he alone can feel it in the requisite degree. If we voluntarily conceive of the Divine as a sphere where Suffering is impossible, that conception ever rests on the desire of something for which we can find no positive, but merely a negative expression. So

z

long as we have to fulfil the work of the Will, that Will which is ourselves, there in truth is nothing for us but the spirit of negation, the spirit of our own will that, blind and hungering, can only plainly see itself in its un-will toward whatsoever crosses it as obstacle or disappointment. Yet that which crosses it is but itself again ; so that its rage expresses nothing save its self-negation : and this self-knowledge can be gained at last by Pity born of suffering — which, cancelling the Will, expresses the negation of a negative ; and that, by every rule of logic, amounts to Affirmation." [1]

From the purely philosophical standpoint this is of course quite unilluminative ; it is only a verbal quasi-solution of a cosmic and ethical problem. But the general tone of the thought, so different as it is from Wagner's earlier tone, is very significant. We see clearly the collapse of his more militant qualities, the softening of his nature, and that certain sign of nervous weakness — the tendency of the sufferer to glorify suffering. Nietzsche has expressed it that "Wagner sank down, helpless and disjointed, at the foot of the Christian cross" ; and that in these latter days hatred of life got the upper hand in him. That of course is only partially true, being almost as unphilosophical as Wagner's own philosophising. A man does not necessarily show hatred of life in singing psalms to pity and suffering ; he is merely seeking self-expression —which is the formula for the affirmation, not the negation of life — in his own way. But upon the main point there can be no dispute. Wagner's nature towards the end was becoming ever more emotional and less intellectual ; and the physiological death of his old spirit of revolt forced him into those quieter by-paths, where the sufferer seeks consolation in the thought that he is better for his pain.

It was an attitude possible to few men so easily as to Wagner, by virtue not only of the reaction after his

[1] G. S. x. 244 ; Ellis, vi. 244.

years of frenzied struggle,[1] but of his constitutional
bias to flood every one of his thoughts with strong
emotion. Moreover, this mood of his last period was
one peculiarly suited for musical expression ; one
cannot imagine any utterance of tenderness, of pity,
or of pain, that will not be far more thrilling, far
more poignant, in music than in poetry. So that
upon this side everything was favourable to his new
music-drama, the great drama of suffering and balm
and consolation.

The point has hardly been sufficiently emphasised
that *Parsifal* is a purely Wagnerian subject, quite impossible to any one else. Almost all his works are of
course individual, and represent an original outlook
upon human life ; but his last work is "Wagnerian"
beyond any of the earlier ones. One has only to
consider the action and the characters of the drama
apart from the music in order to realise this. Looking at that strange group of beings, the like of which
have scarcely been seen upon the stage before or
since, one becomes vividly conscious of the genius of
the man who could breathe musical life into them,
and of the immense superiority of his dramatic gift
to that of any other musician. The work is a veritable *tour de force*. To take these shadowy characters
and give them dramatic life, to set before us this
half-metaphysical poem of sin and redemption, with
its current of ethical psychology so remote from that
of many of us, and yet to hold us as we are held
by perhaps no other work of Wagner's, to make us
feel that *Parsifal* is in many ways the most wonderful
and impressive thing ever done in music—this is surely
genius of the highest and rarest kind.

The birth of the work from the peculiar mental
world to which we owe Wagner's later prose-works,

[1] The cardiac trouble from which he suffered would help to lower his
vitality, and so affect his attitude towards life.

becomes clear upon a mere reading of the poem. The quiver with which he speaks of the sufferings of animals in his *Open Letter to Herr Ernst von Weber* is perceptible once more in the long homily which Gurnemanz delivers to Parsifal after the slaying of the swan, where a scene that would otherwise tend to make us smile becomes strangely impressive by the thrilling sincerity of Wagner's treatment of it. Again, we have a recrudescence in the drama of one of Wagner's favourite metaphysical speculations, in the passage at the end of the 1st Act, where Parsifal and Gurnemanz are supposed to be travelling from the wood to the hall of the Grail. The change is skilfully effected, like the similar one in the *Rheingold*, by means of a progression of painted scenes, that leads the spectator to imagine the characters on the stage are themselves moving. "I scarcely move," says Parsifal, "and yet we already seem to have gone far;" to which Gurnemanz replies, "Thou seest, my son, time here becomes space"—a piece of metaphysical crudity not only fatuous in itself, but doubly absurd as the accompaniment to a mere trick of sceneshifting. Wagner must have been very serious indeed over his Kant and his Schopenhauer to fail to see how ludicrous this passage is to the unhypnotised mind. And once more, we light upon a correspondence between *Parsifal* and the prose-works of the last epoch in the conception of Herzeleide (Heart's sorrow) as the mother of Parsifal—by which Wagner wishes to suggest his favourite thesis that pity is born of suffering—and in the strange figure of Kundry, who seems at times to be symbolical of the world under what theologians call "the old dispensation," waiting for the redeemer to come. Altogether, just as *Tristan* and the *Ring* are the dramatic embodiments of Wagner's social and ethical theories of earlier years, so *Parsifal* is the dramatic embodiment of his latest theories of sin and pity and redemption, the last fruit from an old tree.

The magic of the artist is shown not only in the fact that he has compelled our attention to so strange and untoward a subject, but that hearers of all schools of thought are equally held spell-bound by a music-drama which, viewed on its intellectual side, is an extremely partisan piece of ethical dogmatism. Even those of us who, had the poem alone been presented to us, would have been stimulated to only faint interest, or would probably have turned aside from it as an ethical treatise whose artistic merits did not compensate for its too patent didacticism, are enslaved by Wagner's work almost as completely as the greatest pietist could be. The truth is that Wagner the musician was so incomparably greater than Wagner the thinker, that the purely personal character of his philosophising is lost in the universal appeal of his music ; he unconsciously builded wiser than he knew. Hence it seems to me a limitation of the value of his work to attempt to interpret it in terms of some mere passing philosophy of the day. One able and sympathetic critic has told us that

"As Titurel represents the golden age of loving faith, and Amfortas the present iron age of loveless doubt, so Parsifal is a type of the coming Utopia, in which a new generation, born of sorrow, and therefore shielded from pain and sin, shall learn through fellow-feeling the secret of redeeming love, and shall restore the symbols of faith to those from whom they have been stolen and withheld."[1]

The objection to this form of interpretation of *Parsifal* or any other work is that it aims at an unwarrantable limitation of the artistic effect to those who hold by certain current formulas of thought. We have seen in the case of the *Ring* how the weakness and frequent puerility of the ethical scheme did not prevent many

[1] See Mr. C. T. Gatty's book on *The Sacred Festival-Drama of Parsifal.*

of us, who think nothing of that scheme, from being
profoundly moved by the music of the drama ; and in
Parsifal, as in the *Ring*, Wagner's art, if left to speak
for itself, probes much more deeply than his commonplace philosophy could ever do. We may be Christians
or Buddhists or Positivists in the second place, but in
the first place we are human beings. The quality of
great art is that its appeal is universal instead of
sectarian ; that it plays upon the intellectualised emotions of men purely as men, as sentient, joying, suffering, thinking human beings, not as mere seekers for
confirmation in this or that poor creed that must die
like every other creed the sun has looked down upon.
Nay, not only can the great artist move us without our
sharing his views upon life and death, without our
agreeing with him in his valuations of good and evil,
but he can hold us in the hollow of his hand all the
time that our reason is crying out against him. What
makes religious art survive is not the religion in it but
the beauty ; and no poem or picture that is not beautiful, that does not thrill our senses and our imagination
independently of its subject, can become a permanent
possession of the race. If it can do this, if it can give
us exquisite artistic emotions, it is sure of the gift of
immortality even from the hands of those who are no
more affected by its actual philosophy than by the
superstitions of a Hottentot. It is in this way that
Tennyson's *In Memoriam* thrills countless numbers who
have no sympathy with Tennyson's religious creed, and
that the fine image in *Maud* in which he expresses his
longing for war is admired by many who loathe and
despise that barbaric longing. And if the appeal of
poetry is thus to us in our quality of artistic beings,
not in our quality of ethical or social or philosophical
sectarians, much more is it in this way that music must
appeal to us. There are thousands who lay no store by
the philosophy of *Parsifal*, who yet are moved by the

work as nothing else can move them. They regard the
ethical subject with no more than the faintest interest;
they feel that this philosophy of sin and redemption
is only for bruised and broken souls, or for those
whose fight has brought them little else but grievous
wounds, not for those who love to live light in the
spring; and they feel inclined to say of Wagner what
Renan said of the similarly self-tortured Amiel—" He
speaks of sin, of salvation, of redemption, and con-
version, as if these things were realities." The robust
sense of the world declares that these things are not
real; that our terrible problems of life and society are
not to be solved by the melancholy dreamers with their
mere dream-formulas; that these are only phantasms
that beset the path of highly-strung men, not the real
shapes to which we owe our strife and suffering. Yet
the artistic sense must pass over these defects in the
artist's philosophy, so long as the more dynamic quality
of his art can shake us to our foundations. It is in this
that the power of *Parsifal* can be seen to lie. That
heartrending wail of Amfortas, that seems to express
the quintessence of agony, moves us not because we are
particularly interested in him as a type of one order of
sin, but because we feel for him as a human being. It
is superfluous to urge that to look at the drama in this
way is to fly in the face of Wagner's obvious purpose;
that he meant the drama to be a religious and Christian
one, and that admirers are therefore justified in reading
into it precisely that philosophy which Wagner intended
it should carry. That attitude would be correct enough
were we dealing merely with an argumentative treatise
upon Christianity. But we are not; we are dealing
with a work of art that appeals to thousands of human
beings who have no sympathy with the religious philosophy embodied in it. If this Christian drama touches
those who are not Christians as well as those who are,
the explanation can only be that its emotional appeal to

us as human beings is infinitely stronger than its appeal
to us as religious sectaries.[1]

For, in the last resort, the ethical world of *Parsifal*
is as alien to healthy modern minds as that of *Lohengrin*. Wagner was interested in these mediæval legends
because they presented him, as it were, with a shell of
dramatic substance, which he could fill with his own
peculiar philosophy of life and the world. But to us
—or to a great many of us—this philosophy is something entirely foreign. We cannot see eye to eye with
Wagner in this department ; and so we are left coldly
critical in presence of the resuscitated mediævalism of
the story, the characters, and the motives. Here, as in
the *Ring*, it is the humanism of the music that holds
our attention, while we are unable to regard the central
character of the drama quite as Wagner regarded him.
The most vivid picture that is burnt upon our brain is
that of the suffering Amfortas. Here the music speaks
directly to us, and we need no initiation into Wagnerian
or Schopenhauerian metaphysics in order to be penetrated by Amfortas' cry of anguish. But to think out
the character of Parsifal, and to attempt to understand
it as it was conceived by Wagner, is to realise the
sharp distinction between his view of ethics and ours.
Parsifal, of course, is the redeemer ; and following the

[1] One little point may be worth noting. Having expressed views similar
to the above in a review of Mr. Gatty's book on *Parsifal*, I was taken to task
by Mr. Gatty, and reminded that in reading Christianity into the drama he
was only taking out of it what Wagner had already put into it. This, of
course, I should not try to dispute, although, as will be seen from the argument
above, it somewhat misses my point. But the amusing part of the matter was
that Mr. Gatty was in turn attacked by Mr. David Irvine for reading *the
wrong kind* of Christianity into *Parsifal*, and for saying that the drama " pre-
supposes notions of a personal God." So that here are two Christians agreeing
that Wagner meant *Parsifal* to be a religious work, and yet unable to agree as
to what the religion is—or rather as to the precise shade of it. The outsider,
on the other hand, cries a plague on both their parties. Yet these three men
are equal admirers of *Parsifal !* What conclusion is possible, except that
from the artistic standpoint the particular philosophy of the drama is quite
immaterial ?

lines of the old legends, Wagner has depicted him, at
his first appearance, as being as innocent of knowledge
as he is of guile. He is the "pure fool," to whom
enlightenment can only come through pity for others.
Now whatever interest we may take in the guileless
youths of the mediæval legends is, to speak paradoxi-
cally, of a quite disinterested kind ; that is, we watch
them in their adventures in the most placid and objective of moods, since their psychology is purely fictive—
something plausible enough and coherent enough on
the lines of old romance, but altogether unconnected
with our own life and thought, and therefore unsuited
for serious modern treatment. As I have already expressed it in the case of *Tristan*, the lovers, *as* lovers, are
perennially interesting figures ; while the magic potion is
a feature in the old story that, if treated seriously in
a modern stage-version, breaks the continuity of our
modern ethical judgments upon the tragedy, and disturbs our artistic interest much in the same way as
would the use of barbaric colour upon the face of a
marble statue. If it is impossible for a cultured modern
mind to think itself back into the mediæval frame of
thought, as incarnated in the stories of innocent and
unworldly youths, it is also impossible for it to enter
with full sympathy into Wagner's conception of Parsifal
as the youth who knows nothing of either good or evil,
and who finally "redeems" others when enlightenment
comes to him through pity. What, let us ask ourselves,
does it all mean ? What conception can we have of
this youth in terms of our modern dramatic psychology ? What is the meaning of redemption—not the
meaning it had for the men of centuries bygone, living
in a different world from ours, but its meaning for us
in the nineteenth century, with our changed outlook
upon the problems of life ? Who will maintain that,
if the musical drama must concern itself with abstract
questions of ethics, the proper course of the dramatist

is to serve up before us these mystical, old-world problems of sin and redemption ?   Can his art not touch
our modern life more closely, more searchingly, than
this ?   The truth is that *Parsifal* fails as an ethical
drama because the ethical scheme is incoherent, dis-
continuous with our modern conception of life.   We
may not, perhaps, find too much difficulty in realising Wagner's meaning in the kiss of Kundry that
"enlightens" Parsifal—the surge of carnal passion in
him making him intuitively comprehend the agony of
Amfortas and its cause.   But when we are told, as by
Mr. Alfred Nutt for example, that "the strength of
the new-born knowledge enables him to resist sensual
longing, and thereby to release both Kundry and
Amfortas," one feels compelled to ask the meaning
of the words one is listening to.   How are they
"released"?   What strange world is this we are
moving in ? what mystical abstractions are these that
file before us in so shadowy and unreal a procession ?
What is the moral problem that is symbolised in this
"redemption" of Amfortas and Kundry by the ascetic
resolve of another human being ?   We are sent back
to mediæval and lower than mediæval concepts ; and
the modern imagination may well resent the attempt to
decoy it into this old net of ethical barbarism.[1]   To
Wagner, of course, the moral situation was intensely
real, because his own mental life, on the intellectual
side, was lived among theorems that the modern world
has long ago rejected.   Just as he was unable to propose any but the most abstract and ideal solutions of
some of our great social difficulties, because he had no
perception of the actual forces that are set in battle
against us, so his imagination could only conceive the
dark and complex problems of the moral life in the
abstract terms of the ignorant generations of the past.

[1] For a thoroughly mystical reading of *Parsifal* and its ethics, see Mme. E.
de Morsier's *Parsifal, ou l'Idée de la Rédemption* (Paris, 1893).

He attempted to solve the difficulty of the clash between the desires of the individual and those of society by the facile conception of his Siegfried, the "free individual" who "annuls the State"; he thinks to heal the moral diseases of men by a resuscitation of prehistoric notions of salvation and redemption, of men and women set free from sensualism by the ascetic renunciation of a redeemer. These concepts have no place in modern thought, and should have none in modern art. They are as truly things of the past as the blood-sacrifices that accompanied them among the poor savages who gave birth to them, and who, in their sad ignorance, knew no other way of escape from the moral burdens the world was beginning to feel.

Parsifal is then as unsatisfactory in its intellectual message as we found the *Ring* to be. Here, as there, what saves the drama is the music, that unapproachable music the peculiar colour of which was never seen before, even in the work of Wagner. The collapse of his intellectual life, to which I have already referred, undoubtedly had its compensations. It is to the insurgence of the emotional flood upon the nervous system, to the dissolution of the more purely intellectual processes into vibrations of feeling, that we owe the peculiar quality of the music of *Parsifal*, its power to heal us even while it wounds. Wagner's nervous system was too old at that time for pessimistic revolt against the hardness of human life. Suffering came to him now in the light not of an anomaly, an alien strand of darkness in the joyous web of human life, but of a sad inevitable necessity, something inwrought into the very constitution of the universe, and pointing out to us its own way of alleviation by the pity that is born of it. Hence the music to which he is inspired by contemplation of this suffering is no longer frenzied, insurgent, crying in the face of heaven, as it is in the 3rd Act of *Tristan*, but tender, resigned, compassionate, sweet and consolatory through all its sadness. The emotional peace that Wagner found in the strange philosophical conception of suffering that quietened his latter days, descends upon us as we listen to these accents of sorrow, pouring oil upon our wounds. Even in that long cry of Amfortas—surely the last word of human pain, where the music seems to voice the anguish of all the life that has suffered since the foundations of the world were laid—even here we feel no such laceration of the heart as during the delirium of Tristan ; we seem to realise that this grief is too large, too solemn, for our personal pain and terror to have any place in it ; that the cry comes not from a mere individual but from the travail of all organic nature, and that this sense of universality brings a strange balm with it. On the other hand, the scenes in which joy and peace are predominant have a calm beauty that is quite unexampled in music. In the wonderful *Charfreitagszauber* of the 3rd Act we have perhaps the most perfect evidence of the physiological change that I have referred to as characteristic of Wagner's last years. It needed a quite unusual state of the emotional life to write music so exquisite, so subtle, so imaginative as this, where the strange harmonic strife of the parts, resolving itself as it does into the most tender and consolatory harmony, seems symbolical of that philosophy of Wagner's wherein suffering found its completion and its anodyne in pity. Most remarkable of all is the way in which some of the earlier themes, such as that of the lament of Amfortas, are woven into the picture in a new form, softened and made tender, so that the memory of the former pain seems dissolved in benediction. In everything, in fact, that concerns the more imaginative side of his art, Wagner's touch in *Parsifal* is quite unerring. The less imaginative portions are at times uninteresting, mainly because of a strange monotony of cadence in the "recitative," that ultimately strikes us as merely conventional.[1] But the purely musical portions of the work are beyond criticism. Wagner's perfect absorption in his own emotional world of phantasms is nowhere made more evident than in this wonderful series of tone-pictures, that have a veracity to which no other dramatic musician could ever have attained. Once more I may reiterate that whatever strength, whatever beauty there is in Wagner's work from first to last, is due to the fact that before all things he was a musician, with an unrivalled power of conceiving life and character in terms of music. Such figures as Parsifal, Kundry, and Amfortas are representable in no medium but that of sound, and within the scope of no musician's brain but Wagner's. They are the projection into objective life of a seething world of thought and emotion that does not exist in the purely "musical" musician. The standing wonder is how Wagner has been able to seize these dim and abstract conceptions, and give them forth again in the guise of living music. One of the most precious qualities of Wagner's mind was its power of persistent musical thought—his power to follow up in sound all the phases and all the mutations of a thought or of a feeling, as a logician follows up a proposition from its premises to its uttermost conclusion. In *Parsifal*, by reason of the shadowy nature of the story and the characters, not only the emotional but the dramatic nexus of moment with moment has to be sought in the music. With what success that is done can only be discovered from the music itself; it lies beyond the power of speech to express.

[1] In the recitals of Gurnemanz, in particular, a very monotonous and irritating effect is produced by an unmeaning fall of the voice at the end of almost every verbal phrase. See, for example, pages 32, 33 of the vocal score.

CHAPTER XI

GENERAL CONSIDERATIONS

WAGNER stands quite alone among musicians in respect of the manner in which he touched upon life on other sides than that of music. There have, of course, been "intellectual" musicians before and since his time; but none of them has quite the interest which Wagner has for the student of psychology as a whole. Not that his brain worked with equal ease in the more concrete fields of thought. "Compulsion alone forced me to become an author," he wrote to one of his friends;[1] and he made, as we have seen, the further avowal that though he was compelled, in some of his investigations into the nature of music, to concern himself with philosophical subjects, his gift for philosophy was only slight. I have tried to show, indeed, in the foregoing pages, how singularly little light he threw upon any of the great questions which he undertook to discuss. On matters connected with the practical side of his own art—as in his treatise *On Conducting* and his notes on the manner of performance of certain musical works—he is of course always interesting, illuminative, and original. But off his own special domain he rarely rose above the commonplace; nor do the intense earnestness and the obvious sincerity of the man compensate for the general mediocrity of the thought. He was always too ready to undertake intellectual labours for which he had neither the logical capacity nor the special training; and the inevitable

[1] *Letters to Roeckel*, p. 55.

result was a wild mass of *à priori* dogmatism that at times repels the student, and forces him into unsympathetic opposition. He seems to have clung, like Schopenhauer, to a certain number of what for him were unquestionable truths, and to have made every fact and every fancy square with these. His acquaintance with certain departments of *belles lettres* seems to have been tolerably extensive ; but all his judgments upon literature were flawed by his prepossessions, which made him distort every impression in the effort to prove some favourite thesis.

In social and political matters he was but a preacher crying in the wilderness, more successful, as the preacher always is, in cursing than in diffusing new light. We have seen, too, that even in matters of musical philosophy—as in his *Beethoven*—he really had no grasp of the psychological problem, and could hit upon no solution but one of verbose platitude and sonorous commonplace.

It will hardly be disputed, then, that along with his great musical gift there went a quite distressing mediocrity in most other directions. The total mental energy must have been enormous ; but on every other issue than that of sheer musical imagination the brain did not work sanely, broadly, or penetratingly. What seems to have set him writing on many subjects was some sudden wave of impulse, some breath of intuition, some artistic vision within him, some humanitarian emotion striving to justify itself in words. There was no corresponding development of the calmer, more objective qualities of the mind, no adequate training of the faculties in the patient accumulation and sifting of evidence ; and so his flashes remained nothing more than flashes, his intuitions never got beyond the stage of intuition, never clothed themselves in forms sufficiently universal to command the assent of others. Thus one can always see the first vague picture that set his mind working, at the same time that one notes his utter failure to purify his mere spontaneous intuition, to correlate it with others, and so to make it coherent.

So that although he touched upon life at many points, he has rarely handled any subject in a way that really illuminates it. On the question of racial gifts and " destinies," on the development of nations, on the qualities of Greek art, on the history of music, on the æsthetic psychology of music and poetry, on the significance of politics and religion, on the future of civilisation, on vivisection, on vegetarianism—on all these questions he has said a great deal without adding very much to our comprehension of them. Although there appears here and there in his prose-work something of the vast synthetic power of his musical imagination— such a work as *Opera and Drama*, for instance, finally compelling our admiration for its tenacity of purpose and the breadth of vision that sweeps so far before and after—the prose-works as a whole do no more than take up purely personal positions, for maintaining which he can give no adequate grounds. And in this respect his disciples have easily outdone him. I know no more distressing literary phenomenon than the abject prostration of the average Wagnerian before the opinions of Wagner. Being, as a rule, men of little critical ability themselves, they have abased themselves before even the most absurd of his theories in a way that would make us think the ages of scholasticism were with us again. One of the most considerable of his worshippers, Mr. Houston Stewart Chamberlain, has recently given us a work that really surpasses all previous manifestations of uncritical servility. One point alone may serve as an example of whither Wagner-worship may carry a man. It is well known that in his later years the composer became a vegetarian. There was really no reason for this except the purely individual reason that Wagner's physical system, racked as it was with years of nervous and digestive derangement, found a partially vegetarian diet most suitable to him. But flying immediately, as was the custom with him, from the particular to the universal, he must needs elevate his own peculiarity into a law of life for the whole civilised world. Because, as we have seen, he himself was so dramatically musical that other orders of music hardly appealed to him, he thought it the duty of all humanity to strive for the extinction of instrumental music wherever it was not tending towards the drama; and now that he finds himself in better health under a vegetable than under a flesh diet, it immediately becomes the duty of all mankind to go to any length in order to be completely vegetarian; and since he is compelled to admit that animal food may be necessary in our northern climates, he thinks that "the nobler races should undertake a migration, 'rationally organised,' into other parts of the world." Even Wagner, though he seriously puts this proposition forward, partly recognises the absurdity of it—recognises that this suggestion, like many more, belongs to the domain of "phantasms." But Mr. Chamberlain, not content with admitting the impracticability of such an idea, not content even with admitting that Wagner is wrong upon every historical argument by which he attempts to uphold his vegetarianism, must needs exhort us in the most solemn of tones to still give ear to the prophet. Since Wagner is everywhere wrong upon the question, we have to be told that "Wagner's *theories* of vegetable diet are a much weaker argument than his own conviction"; as if Wagner's "conviction" was of any greater value than that of any other constitutionally hasty and ill-trained intelligence. And further—

"These remarks are not brought as criticism"—for you must never criticise Wagner as you would other men—"but

2 A

in order to indicate a striking characteristic of Wagner's doctrine of regeneration, namely that just in the empiric or material portions the 'phantasms' everywhere predominate. And it might easily happen that too concrete a conception of things which are valuable only as arguments, as pictures, would give quite a wrong impression of the truth which lies at the bottom of them, but which neither history nor experiment can prove."[1]

That is, though Wagner can give no adequate reasons why you should follow him, you are to follow him unquestioningly ; you are to surrender your own judgment, and believe in the theory of the regeneration of the human race through vegetarianism and other things, because the theory comes from the musician who wrote *Tristan* and *Parsifal*. Mr. Chamberlain's notion apparently is that any one is at liberty to sing pæans to Wagner, but no one must raise his voice in opposition to him. Being Wagner, he must be listened to in reverent silence. "It does not follow," remarks his biographer, "that because we can often form no distinct logical conception of Wagner's teachings . . . they may not still express a truth." Of course not ; and if any reader of Wagner's "phantasms" is inclined to remark that Wagner is treating of problems of civilisation which he has neither the innate ability nor the scientific training to understand, he must follow the advice of Mr. Chamberlain, and "trust himself unreservedly to the leading of [Wagner's] great and lofty mind."[2]

[1] *Richard Wagner*, pp. 179, 180. I may remark, in passing, that though Mr. Chamberlain is so anxious that we should not "criticise" Wagner, he himself has no scruple as to criticising the composer's opponents, going so far as to apply the term "barbarians" to some of them, and to compare the attitude of one educated man, who admired Wagner's music but declined to swallow his theories, to that of a savage listening to something far beyond his comprehension. Thus does Wagner-worship make for "the truly human."

[2] Work cited, p. 21.

A paralysis of the intellect such as is exhibited in fetish-worship of this kind is really something more than a literary phenomenon. It is safe to say that the standard of musical literature is at present many degrees below that of all other literature ; and the reason seems to be that less brains being required to appreciate music than to work in any other department of art or literature, the profession of musical criticism attracts a number of intellectual derelicts whose faculties would be of little value to them in other fields of thought. A biography of Shakespeare or Goethe, for example, if planned on the lines of the average book on Wagner, would be quickly laughed out of existence. It all seems to point to the fact borne in upon us by so many other considerations—by the great effect of music upon the savage mind, by the susceptibility of animals to its influence,[1] by the existence of musical prodigies, who, at an age when Shakespeare or Shelley would be perfectly unintelligible to them, can play Mozart and Beethoven, and even compose for themselves—that music is really the least intellectual of all the arts, and requires both in the composer and the hearer less intellectual processes than are necessary in the other arts. And this is certainly an ironic reflection upon the claims Wagner made for the musical drama ; it certainly cuts away most of its assumed title to be *the* drama, the universal art that is to be the summation of all the arts, the expression of all that is "truly human." The objections to this view of the musical drama have been already developed at some length in the preceding pages, and there is no occasion to recapitulate them here. It is sufficient to observe how congruous this view of music is with the facts of Wagner's psychology as they must present

---

[1] See, on this question, the extremely interesting evidence given by Mr. Cornish, in the chapters entitled *Orpheus at the Zoo*, in his book *Life at the Zoo*.

themselves to any unprejudiced student. It may not, perhaps, be any real disparagement of music to call it the least intellectual of the arts, to point out that its conception in the mind of the composer and its sway over the minds of the hearers depend on the less specialised faculties of the brain.[1] As to its enormous power over us, there can be no question, whatever faculties in us it may appeal to. But if there be any truth in the theory that music springs not from the higher and more specialised portions of the brain, but from the lower centres that are concerned with the more primitive organic sensibilities of the organism ; and if the undisputed hypnosis of the musician in the act of composition is seen to be the result of the higher controlling tracts of the brain being quiescent, while the whole mental energy goes into the lower tracts ; then it is evident that only in the very rarest of cases can a brain of enormous musical capacity, of enormous power of dreaming, go along with an intelligence quick to grasp all the issues of concrete fact, quick to check one stream of thought by the impact of another.

À priori one cannot say that such a brain will never exist, but we can certainly say that it has never yet been seen. Broadly speaking, as I have pointed out in an earlier chapter, the two types of mind are antithetical, giving us the customary contrast between the inspired artist with no sense of the practical value or meaning of external things, and the analytic scientist, whose power of grappling with reality, with the hidden resemblances and distinctions of things, is in excess of his power to soar into the empyrean on the wings of artistic imagination. The two types, of course, shade into each other imperceptibly in actual life, many scientists having great appreciation of art, and many artists being able to reason acutely on certain

[1] See the preceding section on Wagner's *Beethoven*, and a paper by the author on *Walter Pater on Music*, in the *Musician*, 29th Sept. 1897.

subjects.[1]   But in the very nature of things the combination of extreme clairvoyant imagination in the world of the ideal with perfect grasp of the world of the concrete, must be the rarest of phenomena.   Certainly musicians, who represent the pyschological extreme of the hypnotic state which is at the bottom of all artistic imagination, and in whom, therefore, one would expect to find the strictly reasoning faculties least developed, have never shown any great signs of what we are accustomed broadly to call intellectual power.   Beethoven, whose concentration upon his music and whose hopeless lack of all sense of the practicable in actual life mark him out as the perfect example of artistic hypnosis, certainly seems to me to have exhibited none of the marks of great intellect with which he is confusedly credited by some of his biographers.   He had copied out the following sentences, which he had framed and kept always before him upon his writing-table :—

" I am that which is.
" I am all that is, that was, and that shall be.   No mortal man hath lifted my veil.
" He is alone by Himself, and to Him alone do all things owe their being."

One really cannot with any justice think very highly of the concrete intelligence of the man who made, as it were, a fetish of such commonplace stuff as this.   That he thought it wonderfully profound is evident ; and one sees in his admiration for it exactly what we saw in Wagner's admiration for Schopenhauer —an utter failure of the philosophic, critical, reasoning

[1] Imagination is, of course, an important factor in scientific discovery and scientific theory.   See Mr. Herbert Spencer's article on Tyndall in the *Fortnightly Review*, Feb. 1894 ; and on the point of the presence of analytic power in the artistic mind, see Baudelaire, *L'Art Romantique*, pp. 228, 229.

sense, an inability to distinguish between really profound thought and mere sonorous platitude. The peculiarity of the wholly musical mind—the inward bend of the imagination upon itself, the lack of understanding of the true relations of things in the world—comes out as clearly here as in the admiration which Beethoven is known to have felt for Plato's *Republic*, which he considered

"the model for all governments to establish in every quarter of the globe; this was a fixed idea which dominated him all his life, and on which he would never brook the least contradiction. . . . He was persuaded that Bonaparte, when first consul, had no other intention than to establish the republic of Plato in France."[1]

Similarly the biographer records of Mozart that

"the relation between what one calls the real world and the ideal world was reversed for him. His real world was art, this was his true and serious life; while the positive world was a shadow that amused him at times, without ever greatly occupying his attention."[2]

There is little need to multiply evidence of this nature, which must be tolerably familiar to all students of musical biography. Wagner shared the common characteristic of the musical mind in being unfitted for most practical affairs, at the same time that, through the very breadth of his nature, his enormous energy of being, and his sympathy with suffering, he was incessantly impelled to utter himself in prose upon a variety of subjects. But in his treatment of almost every question except those connected with

---

[1] Oulibicheff, *Beethoven, ses Critiques et ses Glossateurs*, p. 68. The simplicity of Oulibicheff's comments upon this is well worth noting. See p. 69.

[2] Oulibicheff, *ibid.* p. 69, quoting his own *Biographie de Mozart*. Compare the story told of Balzac, in Taine's *Nouveaux Essais*, p. 95.

the practical side of music, he exhibits a congenital lack of the sense of reality. It is worth while recalling that after the revolutionary troubles of 1848 and 1849, when the authorities were examining certain of the prisoners, Bakunin declared to the Court that he "knew Wagner at once for a visionary."[1] He himself declared, in later life, that his sole concern with revolutionary politics was from the standpoint of art ; and though there is a touch of pathos in the admission, one is compelled to reiterate the point that not only had he no grasp of the actual forces of politics, but his plans for the regeneration of art suffered from the same overwhelming bent towards unpractical idealism. There can, then, be no ground for gainsaying the fact that Wagner's stupendous musical gifts were the correlative of very mediocre qualities in other departments ; the vast volume of the musical imagination, indeed, being due to the comparative exhaustion of the more logical faculties.[2] We may say of him as Goethe said of Byron, "*So bald er philosophirt, ist er ein Kind.*"

And just as we saw that the bulk of his prose-work sprang from some sudden nervous impulse of the moment, some spark of intuition kindled by the feverish friction of his nerves, so this excitability of temperament, this hurry of the organic life, accounts for much both of his musical achievement and his daily suffering. There have been few men in whom the torch of life has burned so fiercely. In his early days he seems to have had that gaiety of temperament and that apparently boundless energy which men, in his case as in that of Heine, Nietzsche, Amiel, and others, have wrongly assumed to be the outcome of

---

[1] Hugo Dinger, *Richard Wagner's geistige Entwickelung*, i. 179.

[2] It is interesting to recall Wagner's own remarks upon the mediocrity of Beethoven's brain in all other departments than that of music. See G. S. ix., 93, 94 ; Ellis, v. 93, 94 ; and the present volume, Chapter ix.

harmonious physical and mental health. There is a pathetic deception in the outward lives of so many young men of genius, the bloom being, to the instructed eye, only the indication of some subtle nervous derangement, only the forerunner of decay. There was clearly the tendency to nervous disorder in Wagner, though his frame was so organically sound in other respects that it was able to bear a half-century of storms that would have annihilated many apparently stronger men. Of the frailty of his nervous and digestive systems there can be no question. His letters during his Swiss exile are full of laments over the broken condition of his health, and accounts of the various cures he tried from time to time. His physical and mental life seems to have been a series of violent oscillations between feverish illness and equally feverish health.

" I walk well," he writes to Uhlig in 1852, describing a tour he is making in the Bernese highlands, "and am sound in my legs ; as yet, however, I am not satisfied with my head; the nerves of the brain are terribly strained ; excitement and lassitude —never true rest! Shall I really never be much better? No cure in the world is of any avail where only one thing would help—viz. if I were different from what I am."[1] "I am glad to be able to tell you," he had written on a previous occasion, "that I have discovered the nature of my illness : it was, to a great extent, melancholy; at any rate a strained state of mind has brought my constitution into the present dangerous and excited condition."[2]

His nervous system is constantly breaking down :—

" I am somewhat knocked up, and am suffering from extreme nervous exhaustion."[3] "From this letter you will get an idea of my health.—Splendid !—feeble, full of pain, and unable to sleep !"[4] "My health is better; however, as yet I have no

---

[1] *Letters to Uhlig*, pp. 242, 243. [2] *Ibid.*, p. 34.
[3] *Ibid.*, p. 28. [4] *Ibid.*, p. 29.

real strength, and feel, for the most part, very tired; but the nervous complaint has much abated. Ah! let us above all things get healthy."[1] "I have nothing to complain of with regard to my bodily functions; but—my nerves! I grant that, of late, I have over-exerted myself with the cure. The misfortune was that I had no doctor in whom I placed confidence: my lively mood was principally the result of the over-excitement of my vital powers, for in spite of the liveliness, my agitation was intense. . . . Reaction naturally set in."[2] "I can only write to you to-day if I make up my mind to be *brief*. I am so fearfully overwrought and unnerved that the least bit of writing is a torture to me."[3] "You must not discuss theory with me any more; it drives me clean crazy to have to do with such matters. The nerves of my brain!—there's the bother! I have cruelly taxed them: it is possible I may yet one day go mad."[4] "If only my head were in a better state! I have done for myself again with that cursed pamphlet, which I rushed through in order to get everything finished in hot haste. A sharp knife often cuts into the nerves of my brain; besides which I am weak and feverish in all my limbs. But if my head recovers, then I feel better at once. On it—on this laboratory of the imagination—everything depends."[5] "Your dispassionate temperament preserves you, in the contact with your manner of life and occupation, from violent convulsive attacks, such as I from time to time am subject to."[6] "With me, for example, everything points to a death by wasting of the nerves: my special and characteristic mode of life consists, to a certain extent, in avoiding the necessity of this wasting."[7]

To Roeckel he writes in the same strain :—

"My health is not of the best, and though physically I appear sufficiently robust, my nervous system is in a very depressed state, gradually growing worse—the result of my self-abandonment to that feverish and excessive sensitiveness, in virtue of which I am the artistic being that I am. The nerves of my brain especially have been so worked upon by this constant dwelling in a

[1] *Letters to Uhlig*, p. 57.
[2] *Ibid.*, p. 170.   [3] *Ibid.*, p. 219.   [4] *Ibid.*, p. 253.
[5] *Ibid.*, p. 258.   [6] *Ibid.*, p. 277.   [7] *Ibid.*, p. 288.

world of imagination, with no reality to balance it, that now I am only able to work at long intervals and with frequent breaks, otherwise I should certainly fall into a state of constant and protracted suffering."[1]   "When I think of the pain and discomfort which are now my chronic condition, I cannot but feel that my nerves are completely shattered: but marvellous to relate, on occasion, and under a happy stimulus, these nerves do wonders for me; a clearness of insight comes to me, and I experience a receptive and creative activity such as I have never known before.   After this, can I say that my nerves are shattered? Certainly not.   But I must admit that the normal condition of my temperament—as it has been developed through circumstances—is a state of exaltation, whereas calm and repose is its abnormal condition."[2]

His nerves and his digestion were continually giving him trouble, and in addition he was subject to frequent attacks of erysipelas. One or other of his maladies would assuredly be brought on by anything that made against the even tenor of his artistic life. Thus the London expedition of 1855, which he undertook against his own desire, had a sorely disturbing effect upon him.

"Since last I wrote to you," he writes to Roeckel, " I have been pretty wretched.   The London expedition was a foolish inconsistency on my part, for which I have patiently submitted to punishment, even to the extent of remaining to the end of my engagement.   While there, all power of work left me.   I had meant to finish the score of the *Valkyrie*, but my memory of what I had meant it to be vanished.   I returned to Zürich ill, and in the course of the winter, during repeated attacks of erysipelas, completed the *Valkyrie* with difficulty (but, between ourselves, it is well done)."[3]

What appears from all this evidence is that Wagner's constitution was one of extreme delicacy but yet of

---

[1] *Letters to Roeckel*, pp. 54, 55.
[2] *Ibid.*, p. 111.
[3] *Ibid.*, pp. 154, 155.

great vitality. The strain upon it, from his early anxieties in Germany, his starvation in Paris, his Swiss trials and disappointments, his storm and stress at Münich, and his efforts to establish Bayreuth, must have been really enormous; and the wonder is not that he was so frequently ill and depressed, but that his system should have endured the allotted three score years and ten. He must indeed have worked with colossal energy; and no conscientious student of his life can withhold his admiration from the man who could achieve so much under so grievous a burden of ill-health. Most remarkable of all was his power of artistic detachment from his external circumstances—for the *Meistersinger*, with its noble serenity and geniality of temper, dates, as we have seen, from the epoch of his worst sufferings. That he was occasionally irritable, sometimes childishly unreasonable,[1] is a fact no sane person would think of condemning him for, when one considers the normal failings of the artistic temperament even when there is no ill-health to contend with and external circumstances have no power to sting. On the whole, considering the incongruity between Wagner and the outside world, and the unpractical idealism of so many of his most cherished ideas, he may be said to have borne himself with a dignity suited to the noble gravity of his art and his ideal. Many an artist and many a philosopher, placed as Wagner was placed, would have come through the ordeal with very much less credit.

Of the passionate liking felt for him by most of those who came into contact with him there can be no question; and at this distance of time from him we can afford to look with charity, and even with impartiality, at some of the peculiarities of his nature that most irritated his contemporaries. That he was luxurious in

[1] See the story related of him by Ferdinand Praeger—*Wagner as I knew him*, pp. 250, 251.

his personal tastes seems to be undisputed. He probably did not, as his enemies said, expend 6000 francs on a silk-embroidered couch ; but he certainly loved to have silks and velvets and satins about his chamber. There is probably something in the observation of Ludwig Nohl, that household decoration being somewhat cheap and inartistic in the Münich of the sixties, even a very slight display of artistic fabrics in Wagner's house would lead to an exaggerated notion of his Sybaritism ; [1] and Ferdinand Praeger thought that " Richard Wagner's house and decorations are far surpassed by the luxuriously appointed palaces of certain English painters, musicians, and dramatic poetasters " ; adding, however, " Wagner was fond of velvets and satins, and he knew how best to display them." [2] There is ample excuse for his extravagance—if extravagance it can be called—in relation to his under-garments ; for not only were his cutaneous sufferings intense during his attacks of erysipelas, but even in the intervals between the attacks he could endure nothing but silk next to his body. He "could not," says Praeger, " endure the touch of cotton, as it produced a shuddering sensation throughout the body that distressed him." And even in the other matters of personal adornment the moving cause seems to have been not so much mere vanity or idle luxuriousness as a sense of the heightening of the vitality through the medium of fabrics soft to the touch and beautiful to the eye. When Pohl, as an evidence of Wagner's "astounding talent for cosy arrangement and tasteful decoration," mentions that all the rooms [at Triebschen] were brilliantly lighted, partly by chandeliers, partly by wall-lamps ; in his bedroom a red glass lamp was burning"—one does not feel that these harmless indulgences are any indication of a tendency to riotous extravagance, however they

[1] *Neues Skizzenbuch*, p. 146.
[2] *Wagner as I knew him*, p. 318.

may have struck the unsophisticated Teutonic mind.
But Wagner's amusingly detailed instructions to his
dressmaker as to the shape, material, and decoration
of a pink satin dressing-gown, " stuffed with eider-down
and quilted in squares, . . . lined with light satin, six
widths at the bottom," and with " a padded ruching all
round of the same material," [1] certainly appear, at first
sight, to give some justification to the charge of oriental
luxury made against him so persistently by his enemies.[2]
He himself confessed to Ferdinand Praeger, " By nature
I am luxurious, prodigal, and extravagant, much more
than Sardanapalus and all the old Emperors put
together." But there is really no ground for the
frantic abuse which has been lavished upon Wagner
in this connection. Mr. Finck suggests that " no doubt
the silk and satin which Wagner wore on his person
by day and covered himself with at night exercised a
soothing effect on his nerves, overwrought by excessive
work and continual worries and disappointments." [3] It
may well have been so. Not only would the silk
clothing soothe his cutaneous irritation, but the bright
colours of the decorations in his room would tend to
raise his spirits when more than usually depressed. It
is now recognised that whereas bright colours have an
over-stimulating effect upon patients who tend to madness, they act as a heightener of vitality in the case of
patients predisposed to melancholia. Wagner, with his
constant physiological reactions and epochs of depression, must have found the colour and lustre of his
decorations of service to him in this respect. But his
fondness for silks and satins and velvets has probably a
deeper explanation. Everything that we know of him
points to an extreme susceptibility to sensuous impres-

[1] See the letter quoted in Finck's *Wagner and his Works*, ii. 192.
[2] See a detailed description (from an article of the time) in Glasenapp.
Richard Wagner's Leben und Wirken, ii. 163, 164.
[3] *Wagner and his Works*, ii. 194.

sions. The admitted excesses of his early student days [1]
and the "free and frank physicalism" of *Das Liebesverbot*,
as well as the wonderful sense of harmonic and orchestral colour which he possessed, are facts which reinforce
the inference drawn from his passion for beautiful
coloured fabrics. It seems highly probable that his
satin and velvet would not only soothe his irritated
system during illness or depression, but would, in his
normal condition, stimulate his artistic imagination. [2]
All artists need stimulants of some kind ; and the touch
of a fine fabric may have been necessary to send the
thrill of inspiration through Wagner's nervous system—
the thrill that other and less fortunate men have to get
from women or from wine. [3]

He was, in fact, a curious compound of sensuousness and intellectuality. Although his art was stimulated
and made luxurious by his highly sensuous physical
nature, it was yet held in restraint by a brain of considerable breadth of view and tenacity of grasp. One
may not agree with a great deal of his prose-work ; but
it is impossible not to recognise in it some of the best
qualities of his music—the far-seeing eye, the power to
handle many strands of material, and to interweave

[1] See the *Autobiographical Sketch*, and Praeger, p. 33. Athough Praeger's
testimony may be relied upon here, it may be necessary to warn the reader
that he is suspected of having eked out his really little knowledge of Wagner
by a generous employment of the inventive imagination—even going so far as
to fabricate letters from the composer. Mr. Chamberlain has examined
Praeger's book exhaustively in the *Bayreuther Blätter*. See M. T. de
Wyzewa's article on *Un Faux Ami de Wagner* in his *Beethoven et Wagner*
(1898).

[2] See, on this topic, Krafft-Ebing, *Psychopathia Sexualis* (*trad. franç.*),
p. 124.

[3] It seems as if his imagination required a really strong stimulus before it
could set to work. "It is therefore," he once wrote to Liszt, "with genuine
despair that I always resume art ; if I am to do this, if I am to dive into the
waves of artistic fancy in order to find contentment in a world of imagination,
my fancy should at least be buoyed up, my imagination supported. I cannot
live like a dog ; I cannot sleep on straw and drink bad whisky. I must be
coaxed in one way or another if my mind is to accomplish the terribly difficult
task of erecting a non-existing world" (*Letters to Liszt*, ii. 4).

them all into one great and complex fabric. In the
case of *Opera and Drama*, for example, only a brain of
considerable synthetic strength could have conducted
that prolonged inquiry with such unfaltering decision,
could have built up so heterogeneous a mass of material
into the one desired shape. The arguments may be
frequently wrong, the facts may have peculiar and alien
interpretations put upon them ; but at least there is
exhibited more than ordinary strength in the general-
ship of the forces. One feels towards such a work as
Opera and Drama very much as one feels towards the
Ring. At a score of points we find ourselves parting
company with Wagner, detecting in him weaknesses or
extravagances, noticing flaws of structure, failures of
coherence, lapses into downright triviality ; but the
ultimate feeling, when we survey the work as a whole,
is one of admiration, a sense that we are dealing with
the handiwork of a giant—not a giant of assured grace
and evenly tempered strength, but a giant for all that,
a master of many forces. His very defects of intellect,
indeed, were the correlatives of his qualities ; his quick
and many-sided intuitions could hardly, in the nature
of things, be mated with an equal faculty of cold,
impartial logic. Underlying all his intuitions again, in
his prose as in his music, was the ardent temperament,
predisposed to certain innate views of things, and flood-
ing all ideas and emotions with its own peculiar colour.
The organic life must indeed have burnt fiercely within
him from his earliest days until almost the last ; and,
sexual neuropath as he probably was, he was fortunate
in that the storm and stress of the physiological life
went mainly to the stimulation of his art. He was a
Rousseau, without the distressing physiological derange-
ments that, in Rousseau's case, turned the wine of life
into poison. The basis for such a judgment as to the
erethism of Wagner's nature is to be found not only in
his music, but in his prose-work. It is in the more

unconscious functions of the brain that a man's organic
tendencies will most clearly reveal themselves—in the
rapid exchange of impressions between one portion of
the brain and another, for example, that results in
simile and metaphor ; and no reader of Wagner's prose-
works can fail to have been struck with the constant
drawing upon the themes of love and sex for phrase,
or metaphor, or illustration. His well-known comparison of music to the bearing and poetry to the
fertilising organism, is only one example of a mental
habit that ran through all his work. The metaphor is
the man ;[1] and in this persistency of sexual allusion in
Wagner's prose writings, as well as in the music and
the philosophic schemes of certain of his operas, we get
the key to many of his physical and psychical processes.
There is even some slight justification for Nietzsche's
violent diatribe against the philosophy of *Parsifal*—
"it preaches chastity, and the preaching of chastity is
an incitement to anti-naturalness. I despise every one
who does not regard *Parsifal* as an outrage on morals ;"
and one understands Nietzsche's attitude again when,
speaking of what he believes to be the decadent
elements in Wagner, he finds the symptoms of decadence to consist in "impoverished vitality, the will to
perish, the great lassitude." In a sense one finds these
elements in *Parsifal*, which to the pathologist represents
the final efflorescence of the almost exhausted tree of
sensuous life. The philosophy of *Parsifal*, with its
stress on the virtue of chastity and the beauty of renunciation, and the music of the opera, with its exquisite tenderness and balm, are clearly due, as we
have seen, to the physiological changes induced in
Wagner, as the years went on, by sheer exhaustion and

---

[1] See, for example, the interesting remarks of Mr. W. H. Dawson upon
the metaphors of Lassalle, and their congruence with his nature : *German
Socialism and Ferdinand Lassalle*, p. 194. See also Mr. Havelock Ellis's
article on *The Colour Sense in Literature*, in the *Contemporary Review*,
May 1896.

reaction from the "free and frank physicalism" of his earlier days.[1] It was certainly in no way strange that the man who in 1836 wrote *Das Liebesverbot* should in 1882 produce *Parsifal*. What is fatal to objections such as that of Nietzsche, however, is the fact that art in general, and music in particular, ought not to be condemned merely in terms of the physical degeneration or abnormality of the artist. Some of the finest work in art and literature, indeed, has been produced by men who could not, from any standpoint, be pronounced normal. In the case of Flaubert, of Maupassant, of Dostoievsky, of Poe, and a score of others, though the organic system was more or less flawed, the work remains touched with that universal quality that gives artistic permanence even to perceptions born of the abnormal. And Wagner was further fortunate in that the nervous reaction from the moods of his earlier days could find artistic expression in music, instead of in some grosser material, such as words, where the preacher's message is apt to conflict with theories and aspirations of our own. Tolstoi represents a somewhat similar phenomenon to that of Wagner, his present obscurantism and pietism being clearly the outcome of degeneration ensuing upon early sexual excess ; but Tolstoi's physical weakness, finding expression as it does in didactic formulas, inevitably rouses the antagonism of all who think differently.

[1] Since the above was written, I find that Max Nordau has also taken the view that Wagner was a sexual neuropath. Nordau's opinion upon this question, as upon almost every other, is however vitiated by his curious inability to distinguish between a mere physical peculiarity and the artistic work that is born from it. On the general point of the extent to which Wagner had indulged the sensuous parts of his nature in early manhood, see Mr. Dannreuther's article in Grove's Dictionary, and the reference already given to Praeger's book. It has long been recognised that there is an intimate connection between the sexual and the musical instincts. See a number of cases of excessive erethism among musicians in Mr. Havelock Ellis's *Sexual Inversion ;* and, on the general question, an article by Mr. Orford Northcote on " Music, Religion, and Sex," in the *Adult*, vol. ii.

Wagner was more fortunate when the twilight came upon his nerves; from those vague and fugitive emotions was born a music so tender, so compassionate, so subtly ministrant to all our cravings for balm and consolation, that it will continue to thrill the better part of men so long as the race remains sensitive to the philosophy of music.

That stormy and feverish youth and early manhood, indeed, was bound to lead to a physical state in after years that should be accompanied by a changed outlook upon many things. In religious matters the reaction is clearly seen. Wagner began with a view of the Church and of religion which, though his animus was always more towards the former than the latter, was pronounced enough to be regarded by many of his friends as atheistic.[1] It is evident that in this as in so many other intellectual matters he had not arrived at his position by any process of clear and steady thinking, but rather took it in by the way, as it were, in his passage towards some desired ideal condition of art. With his ardent imagination and lack of logic he fell a ready victim to any high-sounding scheme of philosophy that for the moment seemed to echo his own thoughts or aspirations. It was thus that he came under the sway first of Feuerbach, and then of Schopenhauer; while in later years his attitude became pronouncedly religious,[2] and his final outlook

[1] See the orthodox article of Dr. Anton Seidl on "Richard Wagner's Relation to Christianity," in the *New Quarterly Musical Review* for August 1894: "There is no doubt that Wagner at a certain period of his life went in an altogether anti-Christian direction, that he lived through an atheistical period." Mr. Ashton Ellis, on the other hand, seeks to show by quotations from Wagner's works that he was always fundamentally religious. The truth seems to be that Wagner's was not the brain to ever know very clearly *what* it thought on matters such as these. His intellectual utterances were no more than mere expressions of the emotion of the moment; hence it is possible for partisans or enemies to extract from them almost any religious philosophy they choose.

[2] See the *Life of Villiers de l'Isle Adam*, by Vicomte Robert du Pontavice de Heussy, chapter xiii., where Villiers gives a long statement of what pur-

upon life, as may be seen in *Parsifal*, was from that standpoint of tremulous emotion that is clearly the last precipitate of the waters of a strenuous life.[1]

Yet Wagner, as I have said, was fortunate in that his medium of expression was music instead of prose or poetry ; and whatever fluctuation of opinion he may exhibit in matters of philosophical thought, it must be recognised that he was consistency itself in everything that affected his art and his artistic ideals. It is not easy to draw the line between consistency and obstinacy, not easy to fix the point up to which adherence to a fixed ideal is quite commendable, and beyond which it seems to denote inaccessibility to new light. The view taken in the preceding pages of the present volume is that a great many of Wagner's ideals were wrong, considered from the point of view of their congruence with actual fact. But setting that aside, with just so much censure upon the short-sightedness of some of his notions as appears to be justifiable, we have to recognise that his consistency—his obstinacy, if we prefer that word—was a phenomenon that really moves us to admiration. There is sadness, perhaps, in the thought of the abnormal musician spending his painful hours in the vain attempt to convert other people to his own abnormality of view ; but as the suffering for his defects fell entirely upon himself, all that remains for us to do is to admire and wonder at the singular courage of the man, that could keep alive for so long his belief in the ultimate triumph of his principles. With the hope that sprang from that belief he fought poverty and wretchedness and the contumely

ports to be a confession of religious and artistic faith made to him by Wagner, ending with the words—" As for myself, since you ask me, *above all things I am a Christian*, and the accents which touch you in my work owe their inspiration to that alone." The whole passage, however, has a touch of hysterical sentimentalism that is clearly the work of Villiers.

[1] See, for example, the peculiarly emotional ending of Dostoievsky's *Crime and Punishment*, that affects us somewhat like highly nervous music.

of men as no other artist of our day has done ; and his honesty to his own ideals is something almost unparalleled in the history of art. It was one of his cardinal principles that his operas should not be heard apart from their stage setting ; and when he did consent to the arrangement of a few excerpts from them for concert use, in order to raise a little of the money he so sorely needed, it was with the utmost reluctance, and with a shamed feeling of apostasy such as other men may experience when they sell a political party, or renounce before all the world the social and moral ideals they have hitherto held. It is on record that he refused to allow his operas to be given at theatres where he knew they would not be given according to his wishes, although it was upon the receipts from theatrical performances that he mainly relied at that time to keep the wolf from the door. During the stormy years, filled with defeat and frustration and hopes that were born only to be strangled at their birth, when he was hungering for the realisation of the dream of his life—the performance of his great tetralogy—and when the schemes for the foundation of Bayreuth were falling through for mere lack of money, he refused offer after offer of financial help that did not carry with it a recognition of his artistic and social ideals.

"A company calling itself 'Wagneriana,'" says Mr. Chamberlain, "was formed in Berlin in 1873, and offered him a million thalers (?)[1] to have his festival plays in Berlin. Two hundred and twenty thousand thalers (more than twice the sum which had been obtained for Bayreuth with great labour in two years) were subscribed so quickly that there could be no doubt about the project being successful if only Wagner could have been

---

[1] Mr. Chamberlain adds in a footnote : "It would seem from the context that thalers (one thaler = three shillings in English money) are meant, but the passage in Wagner's letter is not quite clear."

prevailed upon to depart from his course of pure, disinterested art. Similarly tempting offers came from London and Chicago. The absolute ideality of his Germanism is shown by a letter written in that winter of 1873, that winter so hopeless, and yet 'so rich in millions,' if he had only chosen to accept what was offered. He writes: 'My object is to arouse the dormant powers of the Germans; this is almost more important than the success of my undertaking in itself.'"[1]

During the composition of the *Ring*, again, though he was in the utmost poverty, he refused an offer of $10,000 for the conducting of concerts for a few months in America, fearing that the uncongenial labour would spoil the music of his beloved work. Even when, seemingly defeated in the heroic struggle, he was on the point of throwing down his arms, his solution of the problem of existence was not the obvious one of writing popular music—which he could have done with the utmost ease—but the extraordinary one of going out to India as tutor to an English family. His wife and some of his friends could not understand why he would not consent to bend his proud spirit just once or twice, and write operas that would be quickly accepted, easily sung, and lavishly remunerative. Our own verdict, half a century later, is that we would not only have thought no less of him had he done so, but would have been glad to see a specimen of his work in this field, if only as an answer to those who asserted his musical incompetence. As we look back upon his operas, we can readily imagine what his essays in the popular *genre* would have been like, and with what consummate ease he could have outdistanced all his competitors among the quick or the dead. If arias were required, he could have filled his operas with heaven-born things like the Prize-Song; if duets, with long moments like that incomparable duet in *Tristan*,

---

[1] *Richard Wagner*, p. 358.

where, as Mr. Krehbiel finely says, beauty rests upon the scene like a benediction ; if concerted music, the brain that could imagine the *Meistersinger* quintett could have made an audience delirious with lovely *ensembles*. Point for point he could easily surpass any other opera composer on his own ground ; and if we think now that it would have been selling nothing of his birth-right to enter the theatre for once as other men were glad to enter it, we cannot wonder that his friends marvelled at his deliberate rejection of the sorely needed mess of pottage.   But Wagner was unyielding ; his idealism was impregnable, his purpose unalterable, his resolution unshakeable, from first to last.   Call it fanaticism if we will, from the standpoint of a more utilitarian balancing of the claims of the real and the ideal in this world ; but we must still recognise that the fanatic who can face his Gethsemane day after day, year after year, with so constant a courage as Wagner's, is a phenomenon that thrills us deeply in our better moments.   The scavenger-dogs who prey upon the refuse of musical as upon other literature, have dragged before the world the passages from his letters in which Wagner asks Liszt and other friends, time after time, for loans or gifts of money ; and they have painted him as an inveterate sponger, wilfully self-isolated in his own egoistic world, and desiring his friends to labour that he might indulge his dreams in idleness. One sometimes feels tempted to vary Baudelaire's ques-tion *à propos* of the calumniators of Poe, and to ask whether there ought not to be a law to keep curs out of the cemeteries.   If there is one thing of which we can reasonably feel certain in Wagner's case, it is that he was honest in his declaration that he desired no more than an income sufficient to allow him to compose in comfort.   He firmly believed that art should be the property of the community, and not of individuals ; and there was surely nothing unreasonable in the demand, on the part of the greatest musician of modern times, that he should have his ordinary wants supplied in return for the artistic treasures he was willing to bestow upon his countrymen. It throws a strange light upon our social ideals that while the thousands of social drones who derive their ignobly misused leisure from the toil of others are regarded as the bright stars of our community, the artist who asked for the necessaries of life in order that he might give the best that was in him for the delight and happiness of thousands, should be regarded as a sponger and a charlatan. He was an idealist, and he met the common fate of idealists; but to regard Wagner's plain requests for money as an indication of the turpitude of his spirit is to show the need of what Nietzsche called a transvaluation of moral values.

It has to be borne in mind, in this as in other matters connected with Wagner, that he was so differently constituted from other men as to make it absurd to apply the ordinary standards of praise and blame to him without some discrimination. Just as we censure the man of slight criminal tendencies and pity the man whose criminal tendencies are abnormally strong—recognising that the very remoteness of the latter from the mean of human structure makes it unscientific to judge him by the mean of human conduct—so, in the case of Wagner, his abnormality of brain in almost all departments warns us of the danger of a mere black-and-white portraiture of him. One has to recognise, in dealing with some of the peculiarities of his conduct, the exaggerated idealism of temperament, the inability to fall into line with the average psychology of men, that confronts us both in his prose-work and in his music. To recognise the abnormality, however, is not to surrender the privilege of criticism. As far as regards the conduct of his daily life, we have tried to estimate him as a whole in which each part is bound up with and dependent upon all the rest, thus avoiding the unscientific course of merely censuring him for his peculiarities, and the equally unscientific course of lauding these peculiarities, irrespective of how far the realisation of the aims for which Wagner strove may have been actually hindered by them. As for his prose-works, we have seen that the idealism of his own daily conduct is there revealed once more ; and we have tried to correlate this phenomenon with the further one of his stupendous musical power, the two being regarded as merely different phases of the same mental structure. We are finally left with his musical work as revealing what we may call the real Wagner, for it is here he breathes the air that is native to him, he being as unfitted for the logical procedure of philosophy as for the logical ordering of his life according to the standards of objective common-sense. His music shows us not only how great was his gift for dramatic expression, but how peculiar was this gift to himself. The points in which his artistic imagination differed from that of other musicians have already been indicated in the preceding pages, and there is no need to recapitulate them here. I desire to close this study by iterating once more that he was the strangest and the saddest of paradoxes ; an artist who thought life greater than art, a pure son of imagination who essayed to spread wings in the atmosphere of reason, a musician who was blind to much of the beauty of music, a poet who was insensible to nine-tenths of the beauties of poetry, a man with his ideas centred entirely in the drama, yet predestined to work in a medium in which it is impossible to realise the drama, an idealist who thought himself a prophet of real things, a Copernicus—to borrow an expressive phrase from one of our own younger writers—in a world of Ptolemaists. And, crowning paradox of all, the purely musical effects which he was so apt to disparage and mistrust have been the secret of his enormous hold upon the public mind for the last quarter of a century. He, who desired not to be listened to merely as a musician, has made his way to the stars on the wings of his music alone. And with the immortality it has won for him he may well rest content; for music such as his must surely lie close to the secret heart of men so long as the race remains responsive to beauty. Nor need he fear competitors in his own field; for setting aside the mere extent of his musical powers, the peculiarity of them indicates that his was a brain of the rarest and subtlest composition, put together cunningly by nature as no musician's brain has been put together before or since. The muse of Poetry seems to have dipped her wings into the lucid stream of Music, disturbing it with suggestions of a world it had never reflected before, deepening its beauty by closer associations with the actual world of men. This was the brain of Wagner. There is none like him, none; it is almost safe to say that there will be none like him to the end of time.

INDEX

A

ABSOLUTE music, 28, 49, 83, 97, 109, 110, 286
"Actors and Singers," 338
Æschylus, 114 *n.*, 199 *n.*
Alceste, 106, 107 *n.*, 138, 140
Algarotti, 138, 139
Amiel, 336, 359, 375
Antigone, 13, 35
Aphasia and music, 165, 166
"Application of music to the drama," 347, 351
Aristotle, 89, 171 *n.*, 183
Armida, 263
Arréat, Lucien, 168 *n.*
"Art and Climate," 53, 75 *n.*
"Art and Revolution," 53, 55–58, 60, 61, 204, 208, 211
"Art-work of the Future," 53, 58, 61–66, 74, 78, 180, 204, 208
Arteaga, 138, 140–147
"Artists of the Future," 58
Athenæus, 171 *n.*
Authority and reason, 206 *n.*
"Autobiographical Sketch," 53, 175, 382

B

BAKER, THEODOR, 168, 170
Bakunin, 375
Balfour, A. J., 206 *n.*
Balzac, 263 *n.*, 374 *n.*
Baudelaire, 14, 215, 373 *n.*, 390
Beaumarchais, 198 *n.*
Beauquier, Charles, 173, 187

Beethoven, 3, 6, 7, 14, 17, 25, 65, 85, 86, 96, 108, 114 *n.*, 143–149, 153, 155–161, 176, 261, 263, 269, 273 *n.*, 322, 340, 347, 350, 371, 373, 374, 375 *n.*
"Beethoven," 112 *n.*, 119 *n.*, 138 *n.*, 148 *n.*, 182 *n.*, 275 *n.*, 322–338, 367, 372 *n.*
Bellini, 167, 261, 263
Bennett, Joseph, 2
Benvenuto Cellini, 17, 132 *n.*
Berkeley, 344
Berlioz, 12, 17, 85, 103, 130–132, 347
Bitter, 200 *n.*
Bodmer, 274
Bosanquet, 240 *n.*
Boyé, 174 *n.*
Brendel, 154
Bricqueville, E. de, 4 *n.*, 107 *n.*, 195 *n.*
Bridges, R., 184 *n.*
Brown, Dr., 168 *n.*, 171 *n.*
—— John, 138, 188
Byron, 375

C

CACCINI, 195
"Capitulation, A," 1 *n.*, 338
Carlyle, 19 *n.*, 55, 262
Carpenter, W. B., 166 *n.*
Carrière, 328
Cecil, H. M., 206 *n.*
Chamberlain, H. S., 61 *n.* 62 *n.*, 73, 125 *n.*, 215, 241, 242, 282 *n.*, 292 *n.*, 293–295, 315, 368–370, 382 *n.*, 388

395

Index

THE END

Printed by BALLANTYNE, HANSON & Co.
Edinburgh & London